# Reasoning, Necessity, and Logic:
# Developmental Perspectives

# The Jean Piaget Symposium Series
## Available from LEA

SIGEL, I. E., BRODZINSKY, D. M., & GOLINKOFF, R. M. (Eds.) • New Directions in Piagetian Theory and Practice

OVERTON, W. F. (Ed.) • The Relationship Between Social and Cognitive Development

LIBEN, L. S. (Ed.) • Piaget and the Foundations of Knowledge

SCHOLNICK, E. K. (Ed.) • New Trends in Conceptual Representation: Challenges to Piaget's Theory?

NEIMARK, E. D., De LISI, R., & NEWMAN, J. L. (Eds.) • Moderators of Competence

BEARSON, D. J., & ZIMILES, H. (Eds.) • Thought and Emotion: Developmental Perspectives

LIBEN, L. S. (Ed.) • Development and Learning: Conflict or Congruence?

FORMAN, G., & PUFALL, P. B. (Eds.) • Constructivism in the Computer Age

OVERTON, W. F. (Ed.) • Reasoning, Necessity, and Logic: Developmental Perspectives

KEATING, D. P., & ROSEN, H. (Eds.) • Constructivist Perspectives on Developmental Psychopathology and Atypical Development

# Reasoning, Necessity, and Logic: Developmental Perspectives

Edited by
Willis F. Overton
*Temple University*

 LAWRENCE ERLBAUM ASSOCIATES, PUBLISHERS
1990   Hillsdale, New Jersey          Hove and London

Lawrence Erlbaum Associates, Inc., Publishers
365 Broadway
Hillsdale, New Jersey 07642

**Library of Congress Cataloging-in-Publication Data**

Reasoning, necessity, and logic : developmental perspective / edited
   by Willis F. Overton.
       p.   cm.
     ISBN 0-8058-0090-5
     1. Reasoning (Psychology)   2. Logic.   I. Overton, Willis, F.
   BF442.R43   1990
   153.4 '3--dc 20                                                89-37787
                                                                    CIP

Printed in the United States of America
10   9   8   7   6   5   4   3   2   1

*To those whose hard work and thoughtful contributions have added significantly to the success of the Temple University adolescent deductive reasoning research project: David, Anita, Gerry, Bob, Jim, Shawn, Jeff, Rick, Kelly, and Mary.*

# Contents

# List of Contributors

**Jeffrey S. Black**—Temple University, Department of Psychology, Philadelphia, PA 19122, USA

**Martin D. S. Braine**—New York University, Department of Psychology, 4 Washington Place—10 FL., New York, NY 10027

**James P. Byrnes**—University of Maryland, Department of Human Development, College Park, MD 20742, USA

**Denys de Caprona**—The University of Geneva, Fondation Archives Jean Piaget, rue de Saussure, 6, 1211 Geneva 4, Switzerland

**Rachel Joffe Falmagne**—Clark University, Department of Psychology, Worcester, MA 01610, USA

**William M. Gray**—The University of Toledo, Department of Educational Psychology, Toledo, OH 43606, USA

**Barbel Inhelder**—The University of Geneva, Fondation Archives Jean Piaget, rue de Saussure, 6, 1211 Geneva 4, Switzerland

**Daniel P. Keating**—Ontario Institute for Studies in Education, 252 Bloor Street W., Toronto, Ontario, Canada, M5S 1V6

**Benjamin Matalon**—The University of Paris, Laboratory of Social Psychology, 18 rue de la Sorbonne—75220 Paris, France

**David Moshman**—University of Nebraska, Educational Psychology, Lincoln, NE 68588-0440, USA

**Frank B. Murray**—University of Delaware, College of Education, Newark, DE 19716, USA

**Willis F. Overton**—Temple University, Department of Psychology, Philadelphia, PA 19122, USA

**Gilberte Piéraut-Le Bonniec**—Ecole Pratique des Hautes Etudes, Laboratoire de Psycho-Biologie de L'Enfant, C.N.R.S.; L.A. No315, 41. Rue Gay-Lussac, 75005 Paris, France

**Robert B. Ricco**—Vassar College, Department of Psychology, Poughkeepsie, NY 12601, USA

**Ellin Kofsky Scholnick**—University of Maryland, Department of Psychology, College Park, MD 20742, USA

# Preface

The primary aim of this book is to describe and examine contemporary theory and research findings on the topic of the nature, origin, and development of deductive reasoning. The field of cognitive psychology is dedicated to the investigation of a broad array of processes including perception, representation, thinking, language, and memory. Reasoning is a particular type of thinking. It is thinking that involves inference. In deductive reasoning the inference process proceeds from the general to the specific. This distinguishes deductive reasoning from inductive reasoning where the process proceeds from the specific to the general. Deductive is also distinguished from inductive reasoning by the fact that deduction yields absolute certainty or necessity, whereas induction yields probability.

Perhaps the issue that most radically divides investigators in this area concerns the role of systems of logic in human deductive reasoning. Those who approach their investigations from the perspective of philosophical rationalism or interpretationism introduce logic systems as models of the underlying deductive capacity of the reasoner. This capacity is often referred to as logical competence, logical structure, or mental logic. Those who favor the approach of philosophical realism and empiricism, oppose the introduction of models of an internalized mental logic. The empiricist argues that knowledge of antecedents and consequences will prove sufficient to explain the behavior that is called reasoning. This argument is taken up more fully in Chapter 1. In this book virtually all of the authors incorporate some form of mental logic into their understanding of the nature of reasoning. The reader is referred to Evans (1982, 1983) for a presentation of views that favor the empiricist perspective. Critiques of several of the empiricist positions are found in Chapters 1, 6, 7, and 8 of the present volume.

Although the authors of this volume tend to demonstrate a unanimity about the mental logic approach, their perspectives diverge when they explore the specific nature, origin, and development of this competence. In most chapters, Piaget's theory is recognized as the standard contemporary treatment of our understanding of the development of deductive reasoning. The authors use this treatment as context to elaborate, affirm, deny, and modify.

Inhelder and de Caprona (Chap. 2) provide a general metatheoretical frame for understanding reasoning competence in their discussion of the role and meaning of structure in Piaget's theory. They also point to the fact that although Piaget offers the standard treatment of reasoning development, this treatment changed in significant ways in the later phases of Piaget's career. In Chapter 1, I elaborate on some of these changes as they directly relate to the development of deductive reasoning. In particular, emphasis is placed on the distinction between a competence system oriented toward logical understanding, and a procedural system oriented toward successful reasoning performance; as well as a deeper understanding that deductive reasoning emerges out of a meaning system.

Piaget's standard models of deductive competence (i.e., the class logic of the concrete period and the propositional logic of the formal period) are described in some detail in Chapters 11 and 12. Gray makes a particularly important point in Chapter 11 when he notes that formal operational thought is not identical with deductive reasoning. That is, formal operational thought involves both "hypothetical" or inductive reasoning, as well as deductive reasoning. It is important to keep this distinction in mind when attempting to apply the results of formal operational research to an understanding of deductive reasoning. This distinction also leads to the recognition that criticisms of formal operational thinking do not necessarily generalize to deductive reasoning (see Keating, Chap. 13).

Chapters 1–5 all discuss Piaget's later understanding of the nature and development of deductive reasoning. Piéraut-LeBonniec (Chap. 4), and Matalon (Chap. 5) explore the central role assigned to meaning systems as they subsume logic systems. These authors describe several research investigations directly related to the increased importance ascribed to meaning as it relates to deductive reasoning. Related research is also described in Chapter 1. Ricco (Chap. 3), explores, in depth, implications that would arise if a competence model described in truth-functional terms were to be supplanted by a competence model described in terms of entailment (or meaning) relations.

Both Braine (Chap. 7) and Moshman (Chap. 10) favor a modified entailment-like competence model that they call inference schemata. However, each describes the origin and development of deductive reasoning in ways quite divergent from Piaget's understanding. Both Braine and Moshman take a relatively strong nativist position about the central core of competence, and each appears to lean toward a more direct learning approach to acquisitions beyond that core. Piaget, on the other hand, continued to maintain that all acquisitions, both competencies and procedures are constructions, produced out of the assimilation/accommodation equilibration process. Braine roots the nativist component of his perspective in evolutionary theory, whereas Moshman discusses later acquisitions in terms of metalogical understanding and metalogical strategies.

Falmagne (Chap. 6), offers a unique argument for the origin and development of logical competence in her discussion of the role played by language. She argues that although the origins of logical competence might be, as suggested by Piaget, sensorimotor in nature, higher forms of logical competence may be derivable from linguistic structures themselves. She further suggests processes according to which this acquisition may occur, and presents several empirical studies in support of her position.

Scholnick (Chap. 8) returns the focus to the nature of deductive reasoning through an analysis of the positions held by several of the authors of the present volume, as well as several other contemporary investigators (e.g., Case; Johnson-Laird). Scholnick's analysis leads her to suggest that, in addition to propositional factors and semantic factors, a complete understanding of deductive reasoning requires the introduction of presuppositional factors. Presuppositions set a pragmatic frame for deductive reasoning, and Scholnick presents several of her own studies that illustrate this role.

Because deduction yields necessity, throughout this book the development of the concept of necessity is explored as a reflection of the development of a system of logical competence (see especially Chaps. 1, 3, 8, and 10). However, in Chapter 9, Murray directly examines the development of this important concept. Murray presents a number of empirical illustrations arising out of his own work on conservation, and goes on to argue that the Genevan theory of equilibration provides a plausible account of the development of the concept of necessity.

In Chapter 12, Black and I explore the relevance of deductive reasoning to the important applied problem of thought disorders. We review the historical literature that has suggested that thought disorders represent a failure of deductive reasoning, and we examine this issue in the light of our contemporary understanding of the nature and development of deductive reasoning.

Finally, Keating (Chap. 13) presents several criticisms of the literature on formal operational thinking that emerge from a deconstructionist and reconstructionist theoretical perspective. Keating's understanding of this perspective, tends to lean heavily in the direction of philosophical realism. As a consequence, his comments often have the familiar ring of the empiricist confronting the rationalist or interpretationist. However, his general caution that there is a limit to reasoning can well be heeded by both groups. Deductive reasoning is a central and essential type of thinking, as it is a central and essential cognitive process. As such, its nature, origin, and development deserve careful investigation and powerful explanations. This does not mean, however, that deductive reasoning, inductive reasoning, operational thinking, or any cognitive process, stands in isolation from the whole of mental life. It is certainly the case that more synthetic positions are needed to establish the integration of these cognitive processes and social-affective processes, into the fabric of general human functioning.

My thanks to the Board of Directors of the Jean Piaget Society for their continuous support in the initiation and execution of the Jean Piaget Society Annual Symposium that formed the original basis for this book, and for their continuing assistance during the production of the book. I also want to thank Lynn S. Liben who, as Series Editor of the Jean Piaget Society Symposium Series, was most helpful in facilitating this project at each step along the way.

Willis F. Overton
*Temple University*

## REFERENCES

Evans, J. St. B. T. (1982). *The psychology of deductive reasoning.* London: Routledge & Kegan Paul.

Evans, J. St. B. T. (Ed.). (1983). *Thinking and reasoning: Psychological approaches.* London: Routledge & Kegan Paul.

# 1

# Competence and Procedures: Constraints on the Development of Logical Reasoning

Willis F. Overton
*Temple University*

On the night of August 31/September 1, 1983, Korean Air Lines Flight 007, on route from Alaska to South Korea, strayed over Soviet air space and was shot down, killing all 269 people aboard. The plane was equipped with a functioning ground-mapping radar. At one point, if the flight had been on course, then the radar would have shown only water. However, the evidence suggests (Hersh, 1986) that the radar showed the land mass of the Kamchatka Peninsula for at least 25 minutes. At a second point, if the flight had been on course, then the radar would have shown the northern Kurile Islands. But the evidence suggests that the radar showed only the Sea of Okhotsk at this time. On both occasions the crew faced a simple deductive reasoning problem. This problem involved the inference rule: If p (on course) then q (radar shows x); not q (radar shows something other than x); therefore, not p (not on course). Had the crew reasoned deductively, the tragedy might have been avoided.

The example of flight 007 illustrates that deductive reasoning is an important skill in the world of everyday events. Deductive reasoning has clear-cut ecological validity. It is well known, of course, that deductive reasoning is the form of inference used in the testing of scientific hypotheses. In fact, the same rule as just described—known also as *modus tollens*—is the deductive inference rule that guides the general scientific strategy of hypothesis falsification. The example of flight 007 illustrates, however, that the use of deductive reasoning goes far beyond concerns of scientific investigations. In fact, deductive reasoning is important whenever arguments are made from general principles to the evaluation of a specific event. Consider, for example, that you want to know if a particular train will take you to Baltimore. People on the platform have no direct information about this train, but several people tell you with certainty: (a) All trains from this platform

1

go to Washington and (b) All trains to Washington stop at Baltimore. Using your deductive reasoning skills you will, of course, board this train with certainty that it will deliver you to Baltimore.

Deductive reasoning also shows its importance when it is violated. For example, to argue seriously, "God loves the poor"; "I love the poor"; therefore "I am God", is an egregious violation of logical rules. This type of violation suggests the possibility that the reasoner has a formal thought disorder (see Black & Overton, Chap. 12 this volume). On the other hand, as Gregory Bateson (1987) has pointed out, to playfully violate logical rules and argue "Men die"; "Grass dies"; therefore " Men are grass" may be a key to understanding creative thinking.

## A THEORY OF DEDUCTIVE REASONING

As a domain that has day to day commonsense importance, deductive reasoning deserves a theory that will explain its nature, origin, and development. Even if one agrees with some critics who claim that people infrequently use logic, it would seem sensible to have a theory to explain this reasoning when it does occur. In fact, a theory of deductive reasoning might best lead to a related theory about the conditions under which logical reasoning is and is not used. Similarly, one can agree with those who say there is more to the human mind than logic, but argue that it would still be valuable to have a theory of deductive reasoning. This theory could provide a basis for making comparisons with the other processes of mind.

A context is needed to approach a theory of the nature, origin, and development of deductive reasoning and to differentiate this process from (while at the same time integrating it with) other mental processes. Thinking is the process concerned with the construction and manipulation of symbols, and deductive reasoning is a type of thinking. Reasoning is thinking that involves inference, that is, the process whereby one proposition (conclusion) is arrived at and accepted on the basis of other propositions (premises) that were originally accepted. Reasoning is thus distinguished from other types of thinking such as associative thinking, fantasy thinking. productive thinking, and creative thinking that do not directly involve the inference process.

Whereas reasoning is one type of thinking, deductive reasoning is one of several types of reasoning processes. Deductive reasoning is unique because it is the only type of reasoning in which the inference process leads from general propositions to particular propositions, and the premises provide absolutely conclusive (necessary) evidence for the truth of the conclusions. Other types of reasoning, including for example, pragmatic reasoning (based on knowledge of context), statistical reasoning (based on probability), and modal reasoning (based on both possibilities and necessities), involve inductive inferences where the inference process leads from the particular to the general. In inductive reasoning, premises provide probable, not necessary, evidence for conclusions.

### Deductive Reasoning and Logic

The following examples will serve as a base to discuss some important distinctions between deductive and inductive reasoning, and between deductive reasoning and logic:

1. All trains to Washington stop in Baltimore.
   The train on Track 6 goes to Washington.
   Therefore, the train on Track 6 stops in Baltimore.
2. All the trains I have ever seen that go to Washington have stopped in Baltimore.
   Therefore, all trains to Washington stop in Baltimore.

Example 1 is a deductive inference, and example 2 is an inductive inference. It should be noted at the outset that logic and deductive reasoning are not identical. Logic is a discipline of study that is not, in itself, interested in the reasoning processes (i.e., inductive reasoning and deductive reasoning) that produce these examples. The reasoning processes themselves are the concern of cognitive and cognitive developmental psychology. Logicians are interested in the products of the reasoning processes that they term *arguments*. From the perspective of psychology, examples 1 and 2 involve types of inferences—a deductive reasoning inference and an inductive reasoning inference, respectively. However, from the perspective of logic, example 1 is a deductive argument, and example 2 is an inductive argument. Logic identifies and analyzes arguments that are accepted as correct or incorrect. Logical reasoning concerns mental processes that are related to logical arguments.

For the logician, an argument is a sequence of sentences or propositions of which one (the conclusion) is said to follow from the others (premises), and the premises are said to provide evidence for the truth of the conclusion. Deductive arguments have the characteristic of being *valid* (correct) or *invalid* (incorrect). To say that a deductive argument is valid is to say that it is absolutely impossible to find situations in which the argument has true premises and a false conclusion. Thus, the conclusion necessarily or logically follows from the premises in a valid deductive argument. Inductive arguments cannot be valid/invalid because the premises provide only probable evidence for the truth of the conclusion. Regardless of how many trains to Washington that one sees stop in Baltimore, there may be some trains that go straight through.

The sentences that compose deductive arguments are true or false, but the argument itself is valid or invalid. Further, a valid argument may have true premises and a true conclusion (e.g., All parents have children; All fathers are parents; Therefore, All fathers have children); false premises and a false conclusion (e.g., All children have siblings; All fathers are children; Therefore, All fathers have siblings); or false premises and a true conclusion (e.g., All children have siblings; All brothers are children; Therefore, All brothers have siblings. The validity of a deductive argument is relatively independent of the truth of its premises and conclusion. The only relation precluded by a valid deductive argument is true premises and a false conclusion.

The *truth* of a sentence or a proposition in a deductive argument is best understood through the concept *possible worlds*. Roughly, a possible world is any situation that is conceivable or imaginable and can be described by a consistent story (Martin, 1987). This means there are many possible words (e.g., the worlds of novels, films, myths, etc.). The commonsense familiar world—called the *actual world*—is one of these possible worlds. A sentence is true in a given possible world when the sentence correctly describes that possible world. Furthermore, a sentence is logically or necessarily true when it is true in all possible worlds.

The distinction between validity and truth leads to another important distinction that is often not kept clear when people investigate deductive reasoning. Such a differentiation is the relationship between the validity and the *soundness* of a deductive argument. For an argument to be sound it must be valid, but it must also be the case that each of the premises are true in the actual world. Thus, some arguments will be valid but not sound, but all sound arguments will also be valid.

Logic, then, is concerned with identifying valid and invalid arguments. In general, it is concerned with identifying the forms or patterns of valid arguments regardless of their specific content. Logicians begin such a task from simple sentences and the *sentential connectives* that join them together (i.e., "not" called *negation*; "and" called *conjunction*; "or" called *disjunction*; "if . . . then" called the *conditional*; "if and only if" called the *biconditional*), and they demonstrate valid and invalid arguments related to these connectives. The elementary arguments that are established as valid are building blocks for elementary *argument forms* or *rules of inference* that are used to analyze more complex arguments. The simplest of these argument forms are:

1. **Modus Ponens**
   If p, then q
   p _____
   Therefore, q
2. **Modus Tollens**
   If p, then q

Not q

Therefore, not p

3. **Hypothetical Syllogism**

If p, then q

If q, then r

Therefore, If p, then r

Here, any content can be substituted for p,q,r, and the argument remains valid. That is, the argument remains valid in all possible worlds.

The general deductive system that incorporates the connectives and inference rules is called a *propositional* or *sentential* logic. A more powerful system that includes the propositional logic but goes beyond it is variously called *quantificational*, *predicate*, or *first-order* logic. This system has features concerned with the internal structure of propositions and the quantification of propositions (i.e., "all", "some", "none") along with the features described by the propositional logic. The simplest kind of quantified arguments are the *syllogisms*. For example:

All B are A

Some C are B

Therefore, Some C are A

Deductive propositional and predicate logics ultimately are formalizations of the commonsense, correct deductive arguments that people engage in on a day to day basis. The logics are attempts to establish rules according to which such arguments proceed. By establishing the rules of valid deductive arguments, a logic also pinpoints the nature of error or incorrect arguments. When logic is seen in this fashion, it again helps to illustrate the distinction between logic and logical reasoning.

## Logic as a Methodological Tool

Logic as a system of coordinated rules is used in two distinct ways in research on deductive reasoning. First, logical systems offer standards for the construction of experimental tasks. These tasks are designed to assess whether reasoning can and does, in fact, conform to the rules of valid and invalid arguments. For example, in a series of studies we (Overton, Ward, Noveck, Black, & O'Brien, 1987; Reene & Overton, 1989; Ward & Overton, in press) presented children and adolescents with conditional propositions (e.g., 'If a student strikes a teacher, then the student is suspended'). Our aim was to examine whether they could reason according to the modus tollens argument form (i.e., a student who strikes the teacher and is not suspended offers conclusive evidence of the rule being broken) while rejecting two invalid forms. In this function logic serves a methodological role.

It is important to note that in serving a methodological role, logic also constrains the nature and design of research efforts. For example, consider the fact that deductive logic as a system of logical truths and valid arguments is tautological in nature. This means that deductive reasoning adds no new knowledge to a situation. Deductive reasoning involves arriving at necessary consequences of premises already accepted. Investigations in this area, therefore, must be designed carefully to prevent arriving at solutions that go beyond the information given. Thus, research designs that allow solutions based on direct perception, semantic memory, or pragmatic inferences are highly suspect if they purport to account for deductive reasoning (Evans, 1982).

## Logic as a Theoretical Tool

Logic as a rule system can also enter deductive reasoning research as a model of the individual's psychological processes that are employed in task solutions. The model operates as a theoretical explanation for predicted or actual findings. Here we return to the issue of a theory of the nature of deductive reasoning. Although it was a major controversy in the past, a strong consensus has recently developed indicating that virtually all normal adults demonstrate the capacity to reason successfully on complex deductive reasoning tasks (see Bady, 1979; Bucci, 1978; Byrnes & Overton, 1986, 1988; Clement & Falmagne, 1986; Moshman, 1979; Moshman & Franks, 1986; O'Brien & Overton, 1980, 1982; Overton, Byrnes, & O'Brien, 1985; Overton et al. 1987; Ward & Overton, in press). The question becomes how best to explain these findings. A major division in the field of deductive reasoning has developed over the issue of whether rules of logic should or should not be employed as a formal representation of mental processes, (i.e., a model) and hence, as a formal explanation of deductive reasoning.

## Competence and Deductive Reasoning

Those who favor the use of logic systems as models of mental processes and thus favor the use of formal explanation have been called philosophical Rationalists (Evans, 1982), Interpretationists and Instrumentalists (Dennett, 1987), the Mental Logic group (Johnson-Laird, 1983), or Competence theorists (Overton, 1985). This group includes, in fact, most of the investigators presented in this volume. The basic position here is that the rules that have been derived to represent the structure of valid arguments may be taken as relatively adequate representations of normative, idealized, abstract operations of mind in this domain. Thus, the claim is made that the individual in some sense "has" the rules, although it is emphatically denied that such rules are conscious or that they implicate any particular material substrate.

Dennett (1987) characterized the status of competence explanations in terms of a fictional notation system:

> The idea of a notational world, then is the idea of a model—but not the actual, real, true model—of one's internal representations. The theorist wishing to characterize the narrow psychological states of a creature, or in other words, the organismic contribution of that creature . . . *describes* a fictional world; the description exists on paper, the fictional world does not exist, but the inhabitants of the fictional world are treated as the notational referents of the subject's representations. (pp. 154–155)

The fact that it is theoretically fictional in nature does not contradict the necessity that it be psychologically real. Any empirical research program in this domain must direct a part of its efforts to demonstrations of the psychological reality of the competence as it is described.

The rule thus described constitute a competence, and the competence is a significant feature of the explanation for adequate performance on deductive reasoning tasks. As Russell (1987) pointed out, this competence is not

> to be regarded as "mental representations" that the adult thinker uses when he reasons, but are idealizations of the system of thought to which the "normal adult" has access. Sometimes the access is good, sometimes poor. (p. 41)

Within the Rationalist group there are ongoing issues concerning the most adequate description of logical competence and the manner in which competence is acquired. In earlier writings Piaget and his colleagues (-Inhelder & Piaget, 1958; Beth & Piaget, 1966) favored a description of competence in terms of the propositional calculus itself (i.e., a simple propositional logic system that formalizes compound statement in terms of the truth values of their connectives). However, in later writings Piaget (1980, 1986, 1987; Piaget & Garcia, 1986) had moved toward a description of competence—following Anderson and Belnap (1975)—as a natural deductive system (i.e., a formalization that focuses on the validity of arguments rather than logical truth and employs only inference rules rather than axioms). Braine (Chap. 7 in this volume), has consistently represented competence in natural deductive system terms.

Acquisition proposals within the competence theorist group offer a range of possibilities, including suggestions that competence is primarily innate (Macnamara, 1986); that competence is partially innate and the rest directly learned (Braine, Chap. 7 in this volume); that language structures provide the basic forms out of which logical deductive competence is abstracted (Falmagne, Chap. 6 in this volume); and finally Piaget's (1986) position that competence is acquired and transformed according to the assimilation/accommodation equilibration process.

## Procedures and Deductive Reasoning

The group that denies the usefulness of formal explanation has been called philosophical Realists (see, Overton, 1989b; Russell, 1987 for a fuller discussion of Realism). This group has a strong commitment to information processing and computational models as explanatory devices. Furthermore, and most importantly, in contrast to the epistemic models developed by the rationalist, the realist models are pragmatic and procedural in nature. These heuristic explanatory models characteristically imitate real or actual actions in real-time (Breslow, 1981; Russell, 1987) rather than abstract idealizations or fictional notation systems. The justification limiting any explanation to such models derives from Craik's (1943) philosophical realist criteria described in *The Nature of Explanation*:

> By model we thus mean any physical or chemical system which has a similar relation—structure to that of the process it imitates. By "relation-structure" I do not mean some obscure nonphysical entity which attends the model, but the fact that it is a physical working model which works in the same way as the process it parallels. . . . My hypothesis then is that thought models, or parallels reality (p. 61)

There have been a range of specific models employed by realists as a group to account for performance on deductive reasoning tasks. Some simple information processing models (Griggs, 1983; Mandler, 1983) claim that direct real world experience stored in memory as counter examples are sufficient to explain reasoning with conditional or other propositions. For example, presented with the conditional 'If a student strikes a teacher, then the student is suspended,' the individual begins with a memory search. If a counter example or a generalization of a counter example is retrieved (i.e., A student who has struck a teacher and not been suspended), the individual asserts that the rule is false, otherwise he asserts it as true.

Other realists, such as Cheng and Holyoak (1985; Cheng, Holyoak, Nisbett, & Oliver, 1986), also claim that direct real world experiences are sufficient. However, here experiences are represented as inductions from pragmatic activities such as "permissions," "obligations," and "causations." The inductions form generalized knowledge structures called "pragmatic reasoning schemas." When similarly structured material is presented at a later time the schema is elicited, and this provides a richer source of examples from which to draw inferences than if the schema is not elicited (see Braine, Chap. 7 in this volume, for a more detailed analysis of this approach).

Johnson-Laird's (1983) work on mental models represents the most systematically developed realist computational model of deductive reasoning. Johnson-Laird's mental models are, following Craik, presumed actual procedures and representations derived from the real world that the individual employs when processing specific reasoning tasks in real time. Johnson-Laird (1983) wrote that "models contain elements that are merely imitations of reality—there is no working model of how their counterparts in the world operate, but only procedures that mimic their behavior" (p. 10). (see Braine, Chap. 7 in this volume; Macnamara, 1986; Russell, 1987; Scholnick, Chap. 8 in this volume, for more detailed analyses of mental models.)

In examining theories of the nature of deductive reasoning we thus find that this domain is currently being explained by two broad classes of seemingly incompatible theories—*competence* theories and *procedure* theories. Competence theories describe normative abstract idealizations taken to represent operations of mind that are relatively enduring, universal, and applicable to a broad range of phenomena. The competence—also called structures (see Inhelder & de Caprona, Chap. 2 in this volume)—thus described, has been formulated in terms of the rules of deductive logic when the domain of explanation is deductive reasoning. Competence is primarily formal or syntactic in nature. Procedure or process theories describe specific representations and procedures as these are applied in real-time to local problems. Procedures involve specific interpretations and are primarily semantic in nature.

## Critiques of Competence and Procedures

It is important to note, but not surprising, that critiques presented against each class of theory have been argued from the strength of the critic's theory to the weakness of the theory under review. Critiques of competence theories focus on the failure of deductive competence to account for concrete events such as situational effects, content effects, and pragmatic factors that occur in actual chronological time (real-time). (see Keating, Chap. 13 in this volume.) Johnson-Laird's objections are typical. He argued (1983) that, according to competence theories, people should not make mistakes, and semantic content should not influence task solutions:

> The most glaring problem is that people make mistakes. They draw invalid conclusions, which should not occur if deduction is guided by mental logic. . . . The underlying assumption of any formal logic . . . is that deductions are valid in virtue of their form, not their content. If a rule of inference is laid down in the mind, it should apply whatever the content of the proposition. (pp. 25–30)

Johnson-Laird's and similar objections (see Keating, Chap. 13 in this volume) hold only if competence theories are understood as procedures. That is, as discussed by Russell (1987), they hold only if the claim is made that competence operates as an effective procedure in real-time, which should, therefore, inevitably produce the correct answer regardless of content or other situational factors. The significant fact here, of course, is that competence theories need not and do not make such a claim. Competence theories make the epistemic claim that when deductive competence is properly accessed and implemented it will lead to valid solutions. Proper access and implementation are procedural issues. Competence theorists may be criticized for failing to develop a procedural component as part of a general theory of deductive reasoning. However we cannot expect a competence theory to be a procedure theory.

Critiques of procedure theories have focused on the inadequacy of procedures to account for the specifically logical (i.e., necessary and universal) features of deductive reasoning. Recent empirical work (Overton et al., 1987; Pollack, Ward, & Overton, 1988; Reene & Overton, 1989; Ward & Overton, in press) has suggested that the direct memory positions and pragmatic positions are not sufficient to account for logical features that go beyond the effects of local content. Further, Braine (Chap. 7 in this volume) argues that the principal value of the pragmatic approach has been in demonstrating the facilitative effect of local content rather than as a general account of deductive reasoning. Evans (1982), raised the methodological question of whether memory and pragmatic investigations can, in principle, yield general explanations of *deductive reasoning*, because their designs are based on features that go beyond the information given.

Russell's (1987) critique of mental models asserts that a mental model is not an account of "comprehension or logical understanding itself, but rather, a way of conceptualizing the real-time mental life of a rule-follower" (p. 44). Scholnick (Chap. 8 in this volume), in turn, argues that logic enters mental models in implicit and unanalyzed ways through the theory of reference and through the effective procedures Johnson-Laird has described. Braine (Chap. 7 in this volume), maintains that mental models can, at best, account for only a small subset of reasoning problems.

## TOWARD AN INTEGRATED COMPETENCE-PROCEDURES THEORY

The apparent incompatibility between competence and procedure theories can be maintained only to the degree that one type of theory is seen as a substitute for the other. To the extent that they are seen as individuated but interrelated components of a general theory of deductive reasoning, the incompatibility vanishes. The rejection of any position that maintains that competence and procedure theories can substitute for each other forms the foundation for the construction of a general competence-procedure theory of deductive reasoning. This idea is both the thesis of, and the point of development for, the rest of this chapter.

From the integrative competence-procedure position, competence theory is designed to explain the comprehension or understanding of logic. Competence describes general performance specifications, but it is neutral on how the system is to be accessed or implemented (Dennett, 1987). Procedure theory is designed to explain the real-time processing that provides access to and the implementation of competence. Stated differently, competence describes the epistemic (universal) subject, and procedures describe the psychological (individual) subject.

Before exploring in detail a specific competence-procedure theory, a few preliminary metatheoretical issues require discussion. These issues are all related to the basic theme that any integrated approach will emerge out of some commitment to a general functionalist theory of the nature of mind. However, the very nature of functionalism is broad (Overton, 1984), and the most viable candidates for an adequate theory include those that pay serious attention to description of what is variously called organismic "design," "form," or "organization" (see Dennett, 1987; Lycan, 1987).

The idea of procedures emerges directly from a functionalist context, and procedures have been interpreted in several distinct ways. *Machine functionalism* and *psychofunctionalism* are two forms of functionalism that take the Turing machine as their basic model of mind (Garfield, 1988). In both interpretations, procedures are understood as real-time processing mechanisms that are constrained by the categories of this physical computational device. *Representational functionalism* (see Lycan, 1981; Pylyshyn, 1984), on the other hand, eliminates the machine requirement and asserts that whatever procedural scheme happens to be developed it must attend to real-time processing in relation to inputs, outputs, and other internal states in order to be counted as functional.

This variety of functionalist accounts of logical reasoning procedures is illustrated by Johnson-Laird's (1983) frequently expressed commitment to the Turing machine model, and Macnamara's (1986) explicit rejection of such a model. Macnamara (1986), in fact, shunned the very use of the term procedure because of its machine and psychofunctionalist implications:

> A procedure is an electronic device that in the last analysis can be described completely in the language of physics. I do not call the mind's interpretative devices *procedures* but simple *interpreters*. (p. 35)

Because the kinds of procedures that can be used to account for the actual processing of deductive problems are limited only by functional criteria—real-time processing and sensitivity to inputs, outputs and internal states—the number of candidates for designation as procedures is large. For example, it could be the case that people process deductive problems by reasoning in terms of truth tables (Osherson, 1975), by reasoning in terms of Venn diagrams (Revlis, 1975), by reasoning in terms of natural deductive procedures (Braine, Chap. 7 in this volume), by mental models, by pragmatic methods, or by various methods employing direct experience. Further, procedures may reflect individual differences or individual strategies, and, as a consequence, different people may at different times and under different circumstances use different procedures in the actual processing of deductive problems.

The variety of potential specific procedural models has noteworthy implications for the relationship between competence and procedures. A significant—but frequently missed—point is that empirical research designed to examine the viability of particular procedural models is not directly relevant to the notation used in the formalization of competence models. Thus, for example, Braine (Chap. 7 in this volume) suggests that empirical work has generally shown that people do not actually use truth tables in solving deductive problems. This research is valuable in ruling out truth tables as a procedural model. However, the research is irrelevant to the question of whether truth functional rules are an adequate representation of competence. The empirical findings would be relevant only under the assumption that there is or must be an identity between competence and procedures. Yet, identity implies that the one could be a substitute for the other, and this substitution position has been explicitly rejected because it precludes efforts to integrate competence and procedure theories.

The point being made is illustrated concretely in considering Piaget's early competence theory, which was described in truth functional notation. Although there may be good theoretical and empirical reasons for abandoning this notation, the empirical fact that people do not actually reason according to truth tables is not one such reason. Competence provides general constraints on performance: It does not define specific access and implementation procedures.

The same argument holds in the case of research findings that support a particular procedural model. Braine (Chap. 7 in this volume), for example, seems to employ the same notation (i.e., natural deductive system inference rules), both for his competence theory (primary logic) and his procedure theory (secondary logic). This is theoretically acceptable, although it is just as acceptable to have one notation for competence and another for procedures. What would not be acceptable, however, would be to argue that research support found for natural logic reasoning at the procedure level generalizes as support for the competence level.

Having located procedures in a broad spectrum of functional meanings, the relationship between competence and procedure is illustrated by describing it in terms of levels of analysis or levels of explanation. Following Dennett (1987) and Marr (1982), it is possible within what Lycan (1987) called a Homuncular Functionalist theory of mind, to distinguish three levels of the analysis of objects. At the highest or most abstract level analysis proceeds according to Dennett's *design strategy*. At this level, the actual details of the system under consideration are ignored, and operating on the assumption that the system has a certain design (also referred to as a "form," organization," or "structure"), predictions are made that the object will behave as it is designed to behave. Here, one begins with the question of what general function the system serves (e.g., deductive reasoning), and one then describes a design (e.g., a logic system) that serves this function. This description constitutes the competence of the system. At the next, and more particular, level, which Marr (1982) called the *algorithmic* level, analysis proceeds according to one of the specific *functionalist* strategies described earlier. Here, one pays attention to the actual processes and details of the system and tries to specify the processes that access and implement competence (e.g., specific representations, mental models, inference rules, and interpreters). This specification constitutes the procedures of the system. Finally, at the most particular level of analysis, called the *hardware* level, a physical strategy is employed and attempts are made to describe the physical mechanisms (e.g., physiological mechanisms) that implement the design-constrained procedures.

What remains unstated in this metatheoretical description of the relation between competence and procedures is any statement of how such a scheme would incorporate a developmental or change dimension. There are several potential solutions to this problem (e.g., traditional nativist and empiricist accounts of the nature of design, algorithm, and hardware), but the solution proposed by the specific theory to be examined next is one that replicates the levels of analysis at several developmental levels. That is, design, algorithm, and hardware descriptions are repeated at each major epoch of developmental change. The assumption, here, is that the general design strategy operates to describe the completed system, but there may be several qualitative design transformations—along with several algorithm and hardware changes—on the way to the completion of this design.

This metatheoretical, levels of analysis, formulation is helpful in sorting out theoretical tasks, as well as specific empirical methodologies, related to competence-procedures. This formulation also helps in setting the context for considering a specific theory of deductive reasoning development that incorporates an integrated competence-procedure approach. This specific theory should properly be considered Piaget's because it emerges from his later writings. However, because the theory also contains essential features that Piaget did not directly discuss, I maintain the tradition of referring to it as a neo-Piagetian theory.

## A COMPETENCE-PROCEDURE DEVELOPMENT THEORY

For a significant portion of this career, Piaget tended to limit his writings to the design strategy discussed above. He proposed deductive reasoning as a general function of the system and described a design (the propositional calculus) that served this function. The design was variously characterized as the "INRC group," the "structure of formal thought," or "second order operational structures." Whatever its detailed characterization, the design was always understood as the competence of the normal adult with respect to mathematical-logical or deductive reasoning. Further, because Piaget's theory is developmental-transformational in character, he also described designs at each major developmental epoch. These served the general function, but were more restricted, less flexible, and less mobile than the relatively complete adult design. Thus, for infancy and toddlerhood he described a logic of action ("sensorimotor schemes") and representations; for childhood he described a class logic of hierarchies, relations, quantifiers ("concrete operational structures," or "groupings"). Each incomplete design description constitutes the organism's logical competence relative to the normal functioning adult's deductive competence. Each incomplete design is functional in nature in that it arises out of the individual's real-time actions in relation to the commonsense actual world and in relation to the hardware available.

In the latter part of his career, Piaget, aided by his collaborator, Inhelder (see Inhelder & de Caprona, Chap. 2 in this volume), moved to expand his theory of logical reasoning by focusing increased attention on the algorithmic level of analysis and formulating with greater precision his concept of procedures. This in no way devalued the design analysis; it simply increased the scope of the general theory.

In the most contemporary extension of the theory, Piaget (1987a, 1987b) described the individual as having two cognitive systems. The *competence system* functions to understand the world. It is composed of the relatively stable, relatively enduring, and universal designs just described. This is the epistemic subject, and the designs are considered to be complete, as in the highest level of deductive competence, or incomplete, as in concrete operational logic.

The *procedure system* functions to assure success on problems. It is composed of individuated, real-time action systems that may be sequentially ordered but are not enduring in the way that the competence system endures. A procedure is an action means to an end or goal. It is context dependent, and context includes both the available competence and information inputs (e.g., success at baking a cake requires stirring, mixing, and beating, but a recipe and ingredients form the necessary context for these procedures). The procedure system constitutes the psychological subject, and procedures are considered to be sufficient or insufficient, rather than complete or incomplete.

The account of the origin and development of these systems rejects the "Tinfoil Man" (Lycan, 1987) and "mind-as-machine" (Lakoff, 1987) metaphors of machine functionalism. In their place, the theory substitutes a biological metaphor that is closely aligned with Lycan's (1987) Homuncular

Functionalism, Lakoff's (1987) "functional and conceptual embodiment," and Johnson's (1987) "body-in-the-mind" approach. This biological metaphor identifies growth as originating in organized activity and proceeding according to processes that result in the differentiation and hierarchic integration of systems and subsystems.

### Competence and Procedures: Developmental Origins

From the above biological functionalist perspective, the initial state of the organism is conceptualized as an *organized* system of biological activity. This system is itself differentiated into systems and subsystems arranged as an integrated set of hierarchies at the biological level, but it is initially neutral (undifferentiated) with respect to psychological processes and systems. Psychological organization and processes differentiate out of this neutral matrix through physical bodily activity. Thus, the acquisition of both competence and procedure systems initially emerges from the embodied experiences of the organism. Following sufficient development at this sensorimotor level, further differentiations and integrations lead to new systems, which are characterized as "representational" or "conceptual," and this is identified as the *preoperational* level. The process continues, and ultimately leads to a level at which the acquired system can be characterized as a relatively complete logic system and the procedures that access and implement this competence. This level is identified as the level of *formal deductive reasoning*.

Assimilation/accommodation is the familiar embodied dialectical mechanism that Piaget used in this developmental account. Assimilation and accommodation are two sides of the same activity—adaptation (see Gray, Chap. 11 in this volume). Assimilation reflects the postulation that activity always proceeds out of some organization. Thus, it is the conservative component of the dialectic process. Assimilation is the activity component that interprets (even at a bodily level of interpretation) the actual world resistance that it comes up against. Assimilation is an act of *integration* in that the resistance is transformed into the organization of the system. Assimilation, therefore, is the activity that gives meaning to the world. When the infant sucks, what a third person observer would call the mother's breast, a suckable is created by the infant. This suckable is a part of the infant's organized activity and the meaning of the object is just that activity.

Accommodation reflects the fact that every activity leads to a change in the organization of the system. It is the progressive component of the assimilation/accommodation dialectic. Just as affirmations naturally lead to negations in a dialectic model, accommodations are the natural result of assimilations. Accommodations are *differentiations* that occur in the system. Just as a suckable is created when the infant sucks the mother's breast, this suckable is now a novel feature and, hence, a differentiation of the suckable system.

*The Origin of Procedures.*   Beginning from biological "organization" and "activity," early *psychological differentiations* yield classes of motor schemes designed to *interpret* the resistances of the actual world and *implement* actions that succeed in that wold. These schemes become *interpretative/implementation procedures* (Piaget's "presentation" and "procedural" schemes), and they further differentiate, at representational and operational levels, into classes of procedures described earlier (e.g., mental models and Venn diagrams).

Two important consequences that have direct relevance for competence follow from this account of the origin and development of the procedure system. First, given that the initial psychological (sensorimotor) development is procedural in nature, and given that procedures develop in the context of some type of competence, it follows that the root competence that necessarily forms the context for interpretation/implementation/implementation psychological procedures cannot be either psychological or representational. This root competence, then, must be the organized activity, itself. This means that any strictly nativist account for the later acquisition of logical competence is rejected at the start. Although biology (organized activity) is essential, it is essential in the constraints and opportunities it introduces and not through providing an unlearned set of logical rules or elements.

A second implication of this account of the origin and development of the procedural system is that it makes it clear that the original psychologic (sensorimotor) and representational forms of logical competence must i tially differentiate out of the procedure system. Thus, the account of the quisition of competence systems is based on a thoroughg functionalism. It is not, however, an account based on premises of learning or empirical induction.

It is beyond the scope of this paper to present a detailed description of the manner in which sensorimotor procedures yield the operational structures that constitute the incomplete logical competence system of the concrete operational period, and the relatively complete competence system of the formal operational system. Some mention must be made of this process however, because it involves the development of the understanding of "necessity"; a concept that is critical to all deductive reasoning.

*The Origin of Competence and Necessity.*   In essence, the position being described makes the claim that logical necessity is a systemic expression of a logical deductive model. This model represents the relatively complete deductive competence system of the adolescent or young adult. Competence derives from a synthesis of procedural necessities and possibilities, developed first at the sensorimotor level. The infant's early understanding of "the real" (that which is), "the necessary" (that which must be), and "the possible" (that which might be) are constructions (deriving from organized action and the resistance it meets ) that differentiate out of the initially psychologically neutral activity matrix. Necessity is the expression of integrations realized through the activity of assimilation. Possibility is the expression of differentiations realized through the activity of accommodation. To illustrate this, consider further the example of sucking. Newborn sucking (biological assimilation) yields a result. It is when sucking meets a resistance (in the sense of failing to yield a result) that a compensation (accommodation) occurs. This variation of the original assimilation creates a new potential possibility that, when actualized, becomes a new assimilation (sensorimotor). Here then, we have the first sensorimotor differentiation into necessity (assimilation), possibility (potential variations or accommodations), and reality (continued resistances).

This sensorimotor procedural origin of necessity and possibility establishes the base for progressive (higher level conceptual and propositional) coordinations of possibilities—with their flexibility—and necessities—with their self-regulating system character—into increasingly complete competence systems. This means that the understanding of "logical necessity" that becomes evident in children and adolescence is never the direct product of a "hardware" level of explanation (as nativists might suggest), nor is it the product of inductive generalization drawn from direct observations of the world (see Murray, Chap. 9 this volume; Moshman, Chap. 10 this volume). Logical necessity is characteristic of a logical model—from the point of view of logic—or the deductive competence system—from the point of view of psychology. The developmental question is not how either the brain or the world generates feelings of "must" (see Murray, Chap. 9 in this volume). The developmental question is how an action understanding of "must" becomes transformed into a propositional understanding of logical necessity (see Inhelder & de Caprona, Chap. 2; Murray, Chap. 9; Ricco, Chap. 3 in this volume for further discussion of necessity at each level of development).

Having *seen* a thousand trains going to Washington and stopping at Baltimore may yield a *contingent* (i.e., based on empirical knowledge) truth, and a very strong feeling that this train must stop at Baltimore: It does not, however, yield logical necessity. Possessing a system of understanding that generates integrations such as "All A's are B; This is an A; Therefore, this is a B" does yield logical necessity, and this is independent of any particular set of empirical observations concerning A's or B's. If all trains to Washington stop at Baltimore, and, this is a train to Washington, then this train will stop in Baltimore. This statement is a logical necessity, and this has nothing to do with empirical observations of trains. The logical necessity comes from the formal or syntactical organization among the parts of the sentence, or generally, among sets of propositions. It is this organization, beginning in biology as an initial pattern of action, becoming transformed through actions in the world into the sensorimotor "must," and undergoing transformations onto the planes of representations and operations, that comes to constitute the relatively complete deductive competence system of the adult.

In summary, the relatively complete deductive competence system takes the form of a logical deductive model, and the system differentiates out of sensorimotor procedures. As both the competence system and the procedure system advance and become projected onto higher levels of knowing (i.e., the representational or conceptual, followed by the epistemic), deductive competence becomes transformed and increasingly comes to more adequately serve the function of logical comprehension or logical understanding. Interpretative/implementation procedures increasingly serve the function of providing access to, and implementation of, the competence.

## The Nature of Competence: Meaning, Implication, and Relevance

In describing deductive competence as a system of understanding that takes the form of a logical deductive model, it becomes clear that it is important to consider the specific character of the logical model chosen to describe the system. The issue here is that the model chosen has implications for the theory of the development of the system, as well as for the specific nature of the system, itself.

Historically, logic was viewed as a kind of Platonic ideal. That is, logic was considered to be a set of absolute truths, and this set was independent of the experiences and understandings of humans. Given this view, it is not surprising that the logical models that were developed were primarily "extensional" in nature, and dealt with truth as a relationship of correspondence between sentences and the actual or real world. These truth-functional models (e.g., the propositional calculus) were, in fact, used by Piaget as a notational device to describe the deductive competence of the operational periods. However, because Piaget's general theory takes a rationalist or constructivist position, and asserts that all knowledge—including logical knowledge—is ultimately a product of human actions, the use of the realist truth-functional models has been seen recently as something of an embarrassment for the theory. In other words, it seemed somewhat odd for a system that is so radically 'intensional' or constructivist at its root, to be so radically "extensional" in its description of logical competence. Toward the end of his career, Piaget began to deal with this seeming inconsistency in two ways. On the one hand, he initiated some suggestions (Piaget & Garcia, 1986) that might ultimately lead to changes in the notation of the competence model, moving from a propositional calculus towards a natural deductive system. On the other hand, he devoted more attention to describing how the competence system could be better understood as an intensional system that subsumed an extensional system. That is, he developed the groundwork to demonstrate that a *seemingly* extensional system can, in fact, emerge out of an intensional system.

The possible revision of Piaget's theory to a new notation system for the competence model will not be elaborated here, except to mention that these notations are described by Braine (Chap. 7 in this volume) and Ricco (Chap. 3 in this volume). The effort to make the whole logical competence model more coherent by explicitly subsuming the extensional to the intensional, however, requires further comment because it serves to integrate and provide a developmental component for the strong cognitive embodiment position currently being offered by others (e.g., see Lakoff, 1987; Johnson, 1987).

Piaget made several strategic moves in this modification of the competence model:

1. There was a reaffirmation that the competence system is a system of meanings, and these arise out of the embodied experiences of the biological organism. Thus, whatever the specific character of the deductive competence system, it must arise out of the meaning system that the organism constructs through its actions.

2. The concept of *implication* was made central to the nature of the competence system. Implication has always had an important place in the system, but now it became the root concept.

3. It was suggested that an embodied form of implication represents an early sensorimotor acquisition, and provides the base for later developmentally transformed and elaborated forms of implication, which themselves appear to be extensional.

4. The logical concept of *relevance* was introduced as an important bridge between meaning and implication.

5. The traditional operational (truth-functional) logical competence model was suggested as being one specific instance of the advanced extensional forms.

The reaffirmation that all meaning, and, hence, all knowledge, arises out the physical actions of the individual requires little comment. This has always represented the core of Piaget's constructivism, and it is codified in the concept "assimilation," which is understood as the primary cognitive process (see Overton, 1989a). The organism gives meaning to the world through its actions—in particular, the actions defined by assimilation. Thus, logical knowledge must be rooted in, and derived from, early meanings, and not imposed by some independent set of external truths (see Ricco, Chap. 3 in this volume, for a further discussion of this idea that a theory of meaning subsumes a theory of logic).

*Implication* is a relation that holds between premises and conclusion, or between antecedent and consequence, as in the proposition "If p, then q." When the relation of implication holds we can then say that p *implies* q. In fact, when p implies q, the argument is defined as a deductive argument. The issue, then, is to specify exactly what defines this relation between antecedent and consequence (premises and conclusion). The answer is that the relation is defined as implication if and only if, it *could not* be the case that the antecedent (premise) is true and the consequent (conclusion) false. Thus, the implication relation is defined as a logical necessity (*could not be the case* in any possible world). This relation is also referred to as *logical truth*, *entailment*, and *validity* (see Matalon, Chap. 5; Piéraut-LeBonniec, Chap. 4; Ricco, Chap. 3 in this volume for further discussions of entailment).

Implication, then, is a necessary relationship that leads from one state of affairs to another. But we have already seen that from an embodiment position necessity originates out of the organized actions of the individual beginning at the sensorimotor level. Thus, implication at a propositional epistemic level as, for example, in the modus ponens argument ("If p, then q; p; therefore q"), finds its primitive and incomplete origins in the preconceptual sensorimotor level of implication (e.g., If I pull on the blanket, then I will bring the toy on top of the blanket closer). At the preconceptual sensorimotor level, implication is a clearly defined relation between actions, and, thus, an intensional and intuitive sense of "must." At the representational level, the intensional "must" appears in verbal form. At the formal or epistemic level, the *matrix* of meanings that have been intentionally generated produce an understanding of logical necessity that has the appearance of being purely extensional in nature.

Implication was made central to the competence model, in part, to clarify how a seemingly external state of affairs like logical truth and validity can emerge out of the organized activities of the individual. In the earlier system, implication played a critical role in formal thought, but implication had no clear direct roots in the early system of meanings. Instead, implication was understood to be an operation that was built up from the primitive operations "and," "or," and "not" that were acquired in the concrete operational period. Implication then, in the original system, represented an integration of these atomic elements, and this integration developed at the epistemic level, or level of formal reasoning. In the modified system it is still predicted that a full deductive understanding of implication, including its various equivalent transformations (i.e., "not p or q"; "not the case that p and not q"), will not be available until adolescence. However, primitive analogues of implication, including action implication as already described, and causal sequences that mimic implication, and are incorporated in language, will be available at earlier levels.

Although this discussion of implication demonstrates the critical role of meaning (i.e., necessity is an assimilation, and hence, a meaning) it does not capture the full importance of meaning in the system. The introduction of the logical concept of *relevance* both forms an important bridge between meaning and implication, and expands on the definition of implication itself. For any conditional proposition ("If p, then q") there may be some identifiable, meaningful relationship, linkage, or connection between the antecedent (p) and consequent (q) clauses, or there may be none. For example, for the conditional proposition, "If he is a bachelor, then he is unmarried," there is an identifiable relationship that is *definitional* in nature. For the conditional, "If you use your computer on the job, then it is tax deductible," there is an identifiable relationship, and it is *conventional* in nature. However, for the conditional, "If the moon is made of blue cheese, then oceans are full of water," there is no identifiable, meaningful connection between antecedent and consequence. The presence of a meaning relationship between antecedent and consequence is termed relevance in logic.

Relevance is a condition that is used in logic to distinguish genuine implication, or simply implication, from a weaker form of implication termed 'material implication,' (also called the 'material conditional'). Thus, the concepts *implication*, *logical truth*, *entailment*, and *validity* require not only a necessary relationship between antecedent and consequence as discussed earlier, but a relevance relationship as well.

Piaget used the relevance relationship, which he called "meaning implication," or "signifying implication," to further establish the central role of implication in the new competence model. This development, in turn, further demonstrates both that the apparent extensional system develops out of the meaning system, and that primitive forms of implication precede the relatively complete form evident in formal deductive reasoning (see, Inhelder and de Caprona, Chap. 2; Matalon, Chap. 5; Piéraut-LeBonniec, Chap. 4; Ricco, Chap. 3 in this volume, for further discussions of signifying implication and relevance). Piaget accomplished these purposes by arguing that a relevance connection—defined as assimilation—is basic to any action sequence that involves knowing, from the sensorimotor to the formal deductive level.

At the sensorimotor level, the relevance connection occurs between actual actions (e.g., "If I pull on the blanket, then I will bring the toy on top of the blanket closer"). If toy-blanket is not assimilated (given a meaning linkage) to pulling the blanket, then the *action implication* vanishes. At the representational level, the action meanings become incorporated in language (e.g., "If it rains, then the bicycle will get wet"). Here, the *causal implication* occurs only if a relevance relationship is formed such that "wet bicycle" is given a meaning linkage to "rain." Finally, at the epistemic level, the relevances and logical necessities join to form the deductive competence system that operates as a structured whole. This system, representing a developmental transformation of the earlier systems, permits the kind of logical understandings that involve *genuine implication*, entailment, logical truth, and validity that are evident in traditional deductive reasoning problems.

In summary, Piaget's most recent writings offer at least an outline of a theory of the nature, origin, and development of deductive reasoning. The theory begins from an embodiment assumption, and pictures development as a series of differentiations and integrations of knowledge structures. These begin with actual physical actions and at each new major level of integration the structures become transformed into representational and epistemic systems. With respect to offering a comprehensive theory of deductive reasoning, a key feature of Piaget's approach is that, consistent with the thesis of this paper, it recognizes the necessity of both competence and procedural systems. To paraphrase Kant, available understanding (competence) without accessibility and implementation (procedure) is barren; procedure without competence is blind.

## RESEARCH ON DEVELOPMENT AND COMPETENCE-PROCEDURES

For the past several years, my students and I have been investigating problems related to the developmental availability of deductive reasoning competence and real-time procedures that access and implement competence. Conditional ("If . . . then . . .") sentences are central to deductive reasoning because they can express implication. Because of this, reasoning with conditionals has been the focus of our research.

Our general working hypothesis has been that the competence to reason deductively is not systematically available until the adolescent years, and, once available, a variety of real-time procedures may be required to successfully access and implement the competence. The concept of "systemic availability" refers to the fact that deductive understanding involves a network of inference rather than being limited to only one or two specific types of inferences. For example, it may be the case that young children understand some form of the inference "If p, then q; p; therefore q." However deductive systemic availability is in evidence only when this becomes the valid modus ponens inference rather than a promise, a causal, or temporal sequence. Furthermore, this modus ponens inference is, in fact, a modus ponens inference only when it becomes a part of a network of inferences, including the valid modus tollens ("If p, then q; not q; therefore not p"), and the invalid inference forms, denied antecedent ("If p, then q; not p; therefore not q"), and affirmed consequence ("If p, then q; q; therefore p").

In an early series of studies (O'Brien & Overton, 1980, 1982), we examined competence availability, and the manner in which interpretation of the conditional sentence influences accessibility. In everyday usage people may interpret "If . . . then . . . " sentences as causal, temporal, or biconditional ("If and only if") relationships, rather than as a relationship of material implication. When the task is designed to evaluate the understanding of formal implication, the other types of interpretations yield the appearance of poor logical performance. However, the failure may be the product of poor access to the logical competence, rather than the absence of this competence.

These studies employed a contradiction training technique. Participants in grades 3, 4, 7, 12, and college were presented with an incomplete conditional rule: "If a worker is ____ years of age, or older, then that person will receive at least $350 each week." Following the rule presentation, a series of 12 exemplars of ages and salaries were given (e.g., A 20-year-old who makes $50 per week; A 60-year-old who makes $600 per week). The task was to select, for each exemplar, what could be inferred about the missing age in the rule (i.e., "The age in the rule is more than. . . ."; "The age in the rule is . . . at most"; "Nothing at all").

During the early trials there is a tendency to make inference errors, suggesting that participants fail to interpret the rule as a conditional. However, on the sixth trial an exemplar was presented that directly contradicted such faulty interpretations. It was expected that this procedure would facilitate access, via interpretative procedures, to the appropriate logical competence for those individuals who had this competence available. The results of these studies demonstrated the availability of competence at grade 12 and at the college level. That is, at these age levels the contradiction training successfully facilitated performance, and this enhanced performance generalized to other deductive reasoning tasks. The studies did not, however, show any evidence of the availability of competence at ages earlier than the 12th grade, and this became an issue for later investigations.

The issue of the availability of competence, and the role of interpretative procedures in accessing this competence, was also explored in an elderly population (Overton & Franco, 1984). A group of college participants and a group of elderly (mean age = 69.4 years) were evaluated with the contradiction training paradigm. These findings again demonstrated that, at both ages, interpretative procedures are influential in accessing available competence. For both groups performance was facilitated by the contradiction training, and this generalized to another deductive task. Furthermore, the study yielded some initial evidence suggesting that deductive competence remains largely available during the late adult years.

The manner in which the conditional sentence is interpreted is a basic issue for procedural models of deduction. However, there are other classes of variables, both organismic and environmental, that also implicate real-time procedures. One class is cognitive style. In an effort to analyze the role of cognitive style in accessing and implementing available deductive competence, an investigation was conducted with participants from grades 8, 10, and 12 (Overton, Byrnes, & O'Brien, 1985). The contradiction training paradigm was again employed, but in this study the participants were also tested for Reflective-Impulsive cognitive style (by means of the Matching Familiar Figures test). As in the earlier research, it was found that the availability of deductive competence was in evidence at grade 12, but not earlier. At this grade, contradiction training enhanced performance and generalized to another deductive task. A reflective cognitive style was found to enhance performance at all age levels. However, for the generalization deductive task, the benefits of a reflective style were limited primarily to those individuals who had demonstrated the availability of competence. Thus, it appears that once deductive competence is available, and interpretative procedures access this competence, a reflective cognitive style operates as a procedural support to further facilitate implementation of the competence.

The fact that the contradiction training paradigm did not yield evidence of deductive competence prior to grade 12 precluded any exploration of the role of interpretative procedures during childhood and early adolescence in these early studies. This led to a more direct exploration of the understanding of "If . . . then . . ." sentences, and precursors to such understandings. In order to claim a formal deductive understanding of "If p, then q" as an implication, it must be shown that it is recognized that: (a) particular instances of the antecedent (p) and consequence (q) clause of the sentence are permissible, (b) other instances are not permissible, and (c) others are indeterminate. Specifically, given "If p, then q," it is the case that "p and q" is permitted, "p and not q" is not permitted, and "not p and q" and "not p and not q" are indeterminate. For example, with the sentence "If it has rained, then the grass is wet," finding an instance of "rain and wet" supports the truth of the sentence; finding "rain and not wet" falsifies the sentence; and finding "not rain and wet" or "not rain and not wet" yield uncertainty about the truth of the sentence.

An obvious precursor to a formal deductive understanding of implication is the understanding of the certainty and uncertainty of conclusions. Unless it is recognized that it is *certain* that "p and not q" falsify the sentence, and unless this knowledge is coordinated with the certainty and uncertainty of the other instances, a formal deductive competence cannot be claimed. In an initial study (Byrnes & Overton, 1986), we examined the ability of children at grades 1, 3, and 5 to draw certain and uncertain conclusions. It was expected, following Piaget's work on necessity (1987a, 1987b), that concepts of certainty and uncertainty would first develop in nonformal concrete and causal contexts, and only later in formal deductive contexts. At each grade, the children's conclusions were evaluated in all three contexts (i.e., concrete = a task requiring conclusions about whether objects would fit into openings in a box; causal = a task requiring conclusions about pictured causal sequences; formal deductive = conditional syllogisms).

Our predictions were supported, and we found that an understanding of, and discrimination between, certain and uncertain conclusions is mastered in concrete and causal context by grade 5. However, this understanding is just beginning to emerge at grade 5 for formal deductions. This is consistent with Piaget's position that formal competence begins to become available around 10–12 years. If this is the case, it appears that the next several years may be a period of consolidation for the formal competence, which only then demonstrates systemic availability.

In the next study (Byrnes and Overton, 1988), we focused more specifically on the understanding of "If p, then q" as a formal implication. Participants at grades 3, 5, 8 and college level were evaluated with several procedures designed to elicit: (a) understanding of the coordination between permitted and nonpermitted instances of formal implication, and (b) understanding of the distinction between the conditional and other propositional types, particularly the biconditional ("If and only if"). The findings demonstrated that a significant increase in the understanding of formal implication occurs between grade 3 and 5, and again between grade 8 and college level.

The results of this study again support the position that formal deductive competence begins to emerge in an incomplete form around 10–12 years of age and then goes through a consolidation process. Another important finding of this study was that the primary improvement that occurs between grade 8 and the college level is in the ability to distinguish the conditional from the biconditional. Because both the conditional and biconditional are formal deductive relationships, it can be speculated that the period beginning at approximately grade 8 marks the time during which novel interpretative procedures are acquired to adequately interpret and implement the deductive competence. That is, it may be the case, as with means-ends relationships generally, that the emergence of a novel competence initially uses old procedures, and, subsequently, new procedures are acquired to meet the demands of the new competence.

When the findings of these latter two studies are considered together, a pattern begins to emerge. This pattern suggests that the period between approximately 10–14 years is the time of achievement and consolidation of formal competence, and the period between approximately 14–18 years is the time during which novel procedures, adequate to the novel competence, are developed. This schema would also account for why the contradiction training paradigm, employed in our earlier research, was unable to detect the availability of competence prior to grade 12. This paradigm was designed to introduce a formal contradiction that would lead the person from one formal interpretation of the conditional (the biconditional) to another formal interpretation (the conditional). However, distinguishing among such formal interpretations is exactly the interpretative procedural skill that may develop only in the later adolescent years. Thus, the contradiction training paradigm may be evaluating a later developing procedural skill.

Once this skill is operating (i.e., by grade 12) it can access competence, but not before.

Following from the difficulty in detecting deductive competence in early adolescence, we began another series of studies designed to again focus on the issue of developmental availability. After examining several deductive tasks, pilot work led us to a modification of the Wason (1983) selection task. This task presents the participant with a conditional rule (e.g., "If a person is driving a motor vehicle, then the person must be over 16 years of age"). Four cards are also presented. The participant is told that each card has information on one side about whether a person is driving and on the other side about the age of the person. The problem is to select those cards, and only those cards, that would necessarily have to be turned over to determine if the rule is being broken (i.e., false).

The four card surfaces in view correspond to: (a) the affirmation of the antecedent (p) of the rule (i.e., a person driving); (b) the denial of the antecedent (not p) (i.e., A person not driving); (c) the affirmation of the consequent (q) (i.e., A person 18 years of age); and (d) the denial of the consequent (not q) (i.e., A person 14 years of age). The correct deductive choices for the falsification of the rule consist of selection of the p card and the not q card. The reason for this is that it is these cards, and only these cards, that could possible yield the "p and not q" instance that is required for deductive certainty. That is, the card "A person driving" (p) might yield "A person 14 years of age" (not q) on the other side, thus giving a necessary falsification of the rule. Similarly, the card "A person 14 years of age" might yield "A person driving" on the other side, again showing the necessary falsification instance.

The selection task is clearly a deductive reasoning task, and one that requires coordination among the permissible and impermissible instances that define implication. Although it focuses on the certainty of the modus tollens inference, it involves the recognition and coordination of the other inference forms, as well. Thus, from a formal perspective, the selection task is well suited for evaluating the systemic availability of deductive competence. Because the rules can be varied in terms of semantic content, the selection task also presents the opportunity to explore procedures that access and implement competence.

Our first set of studies using the selection task (Overton et al., 1987) examined the development of deductive availability and the role of semantic content in accessing and implementing this competence. In Experiment 1, participants at grades 8, 10, and 12 were tested on several familiar content, and several abstract content, selection problems. In Experiment 2, participants at grades 4, 8, and 12 were tested on the familiar problems used in Experiment 1. In Experiment 3, participants in grades 4, 6, and 8 were tested on new familiar content problems, familiar content problems with conditional clauses reversed, a meaningful but unfamiliar problem, and an abstract problem.

The findings of these studies were strongly supportive of the developmental competence-procedure model that has been described. First, at all levels, participants performed poorly when abstract problem content (e.g., "If there is a vowel on one side of the card, then there is an even number on the other side") was used. This is consistent with Wason's (1983) suggestion that abstract content presents the individual with an overload of information that cannot adequately be represented as coherent whole. That is, abstract content fails to engage an adequate representational procedure, and, thus, does not generally access competence, even when deductive competence is available.

An improvement in performance found for familiar, and, to a lesser extent, meaningful but nonfamiliar semantic content, is understood by considering schemata (see Mandler, 1983) as a basic procedure for representational integration. According to this explanation, familiar content produces the greatest facilitation because it most readily evokes world-knowledge schemata. These schemata operate as frames or integrating devices, and, thus, permit ready access to and implementation of available competence. Meaningful but nonfamiliar material is indirectly related to world-knowledge schemata: Hence, it is less adequately integrated and less facilitative. Abstract content fails to invoke any integrating mechanism. This explanation is also consistent with the lack of any transfer effects from familiar content to abstract content investigated in Experiment 1.

Although the nature of semantic content is an important factor with respect to the access and implementation of competence, the findings supported the position that semantic content cannot, in itself, explain performance. Poor performance in grades 4 and 6 on even highly familiar problems, variable adequacy across conditions at grade 8, and the consistently adequate performance at grades 10 and 12 all suggest the developmental view that formal deductive competence becomes available in adolescence. This position was given further tentative support by findings of a developmental improvement between grades 8 and 12 on even the abstract problems (Experiment 1), and a logically systematic responding at grade 8 to problems that had their clauses reversed from the usual semantic order (Experiment 3).

Following from this set of selection task studies, we continued to examine the procedural role of familiarity in relationship to the developmental availability of deductive competence. In the next investigation (Ward & Overton, in press), however, familiarity was defined in terms of the *relevance* relationship between antecedent and consequence clauses of the conditional rule (see the earlier discussion of logical relevance). Based on ratings obtained from children at grade 5, a group of high relevant (e.g., "If a person is driving a motor vehicle, then the person is over 16 years of age") and a group of low relevant (e.g., "If a person is driving a motor vehicle, then the person is a school teacher") conditional rules were formulated and placed into a selection task context. Participants at grades 6, 9, and 12 were tested on these selection task problems.

It was predicted that a high propositional relevance would operate as a facilitative procedure only after deductive competence became available in adolescence. This prediction was supported. At grade 6, logical solutions were infrequent regardless of the relevance of the rule content. At grades 9 and 12, low relevant content continued to result in poor performance. However, performance improved significantly between grades 9 and 12 when the content of the conditional rule involved a high degree of relevance between antecedent and consequent clause. Such results further suggest that prior to adolescence deductive competence is not systemically available, and familiarity of semantic content can be considered facilitative, but it cannot explain deductive reasoning, itself.

The most interesting developmental finding of this study is that the performance found at each age level for the high relevant groups very closely match the performance levels found for the familiar content problems in Experiments 1 and 2 of the earlier investigation. This consistency occurred despite the fact that the several studies involved different experimenters, different methods, and different problem content. There are a number of ways to measure deductive success. However, consistency of completely correct deductive solutions across varying content is the most meaningful theoretical measure of deductive competence. Using the criterion of a minimum of 60% of the problems solved with a correct deductive solutions, the following emerges as the percent of individuals at each grade level who evidence available deductive competence: *Grade 4* = 14% (Experiment 2); *Grade 6* = 24% (present study); *Grade 8* = 42% (Experiment 2)–48% (Experiment 1); *Grade 9* = 44% (present study); *Grade 10*–68% (Experiment 1); *Grade 12* = 75% (Experiment 2)–80% (present study)–86% (Experiment 1). Similar results are found when scoring is done simply in terms of number of correct solutions across all problem.

This consistent, but indirect, evidence for developmental changes in the availability of deductive competence across the several studies, and the similarity of scores at each age level across the several studies, led us to undertake a longitudinal investigation to further examine the development of deductive competence (Reene & Overton, 1989). Participants at grades 6 and 8 were tested on the high relevant selection problems from the Ward and Overton (in press) study. They were then retested a year later at grades 7 and 9. Grades 6 and 7 did not differ in performance, whereas grade 9 showed a significant improvement over grade 8. Using the consistency of solution criterion described above, the percent of individuals at each grade level who evidenced available deductive competence was: *Grade 6* = 17%; *Grade 7* = 38%; *Grade 8* = 38%; *Grade 9* = 60%. These longitudinal findings are highly consistent with the earlier cross-sectional research. Testing is currently being conducted on the third year of this project.

In addition to scoring the selection task according to number of correct solutions and according to consistency of correct solutions, it is possible to examine error response patterns. For example, selection of the p card and the q card yields the p, q error pattern. This pattern, which represents a matching of the selection cards to the antecedent and consequence clauses of the rule, has generally been interpreted as a failure of logical understanding. In the described studies, as would be expected, this pattern decreases directly in relation to increasing age. Another error pattern, which presents greater developmental interest, is the p,q, not q pattern. Wason and Johnson-Laird (1972) suggested that this pattern represents partial insight into the correct logical solution. Here, the individual selects the correct p card and the correct not q card, but contaminates the solution by continuing to choose the matching q card.

In a recent study (Pollack, Ward, & Overton, 1988), we explored the hypothesis that the p,q, not q error pattern may mark a developmental transition in the progression toward a systemic available deductive competence. In reviewing the error data from the Overton et al. (1987) study, we found that in two of the three experiments there was an inverted U-shaped relationship between grade (4, 8, and 12) and selection of the p,q, not q pattern. Grade 8 constituted the maximum point of the curve. This finding, along with Wason & Johnson-Laird's interpretative suggestion, led to the further exploration of this pattern for individuals at grades 4, 5, 6, 8, 9, 12, and college level. The high relevant selection task problems from the Ward and Overton (in press) study were used in this investigation. The results supported the conclusion that there is a curvilinear relationship between grade and the p,q, not q pattern. Grade 8 constituted the maximum point of the curve, whereas Grades 4 and college level constituted the minimum points. When these findings are considered in the light of the Byrnes and Overton (1986, 1988) investigations, additional weight is added to the suggestion that at approximately 14 years of age (grade 8) a transition occurs. This transition may mark the end of the consolidation of formal competence and the beginning of the development of novel procedures designed to access this competence.

As a final note, it should be mentioned that this general research project has had a continuing interest in the availability and accessibility of deductive competence during the late adult years. Our general working hypothesis has been that, under normal processes of aging, deductive competence remains available during the late adult years, but access and implementation may become limited. Earlier, it was noted that the Franco and Overton (1984) investigation, using the contradiction training paradigm, offered some tentative support for the availability of competence in the late adult years. In a more recent investigation, we (Overton, Yaure, & Ward, 1986) conducted two studies designed to further examine this issue. In both studies, college level participants and elderly adults (mean age = 69.3 years, Study 1; 71.3 years, Study 2) were tested on selection task problems.

In Study 1, the problems were composed of the familiar content problems of Experiments 1 and 2 of the Overton et al. (1987) investigation. The results of this study again yielded tentative support for the conclusion that deductive competence remains available during the late adult years as no differences were found in the performance of the young and elderly groups. In Study 2, the test problems were designed to be particularly age appropriate for the elderly population (e.g., problems concerning medications and prescriptions, pensions and age, identification cards, and free bus passes). However, the findings of this study showed that elderly performed significantly more poorly than the young group. These findings have led us to begin to explore questions of whether the degree of agreement/disagreement with the presented rule, or, the degree of emotional involvement in the issue portrayed by the rule, may interfere with the interpretation and implementation of available deductive competence.

## CONCLUSIONS

The basic thesis of this chapter has been that an adequate theory of the nature, origin, and development of deductive reasoning requires both competence and procedural models. Competence models offer explanations for understandings of logic at different levels of development. Procedure models offer explanations for how competence is accessed and implemented in real-time at various levels of development. A developmental account of the differentiations and integrations of these systems through several levels of knowing, as presented in Piaget's later writings, offers research scientists a rich conceptual framework for generating a coherent body of empirical hypotheses. The research program described in these last several pages is a continuing effort designed to explore, examine, and elaborate the empirical implications of this framework.

## ACKNOWLEDGMENTS

I would like to acknowledge the helpful criticisms of earlier drafts of this paper by Nora Newcombe, Rick Pollack, Kelly Reene, and Mary Winn.

## REFERENCES

Anderson, A. R., & Belnap, N. D., Jr. (1975). *Entailment: The logic of relevance and necessity*. Princeton, NJ: Princeton University Press.

Bady, R. J. (1979). Students' understanding of hypothesis testing. *Journal of Research in Science Teaching, 16*, 61–65.

Bateson, G. (1987). Men are grass: Metaphor and the world of mental process. In W. I. Thompson (Ed.), *Gaia, a way of knowing* (pp. 1–15). Great Barrington, MA: Lindisfarne Press.

Beth, E. W., & Piaget, J. (1966). *Mathematical epistemology and psychology*. Dordrecht: Reidel.

Breslow, L. (1981). Reevaluation of the literature on the development of transitive inferences. *Psychological Bulletin, 89*, 325–351.

Bucci, W. (1978). The interpretation of universal affirmation propositions. *Cognition, 6*, 55–77.

Byrnes, J. P., & Overton, W. F. (1986). Reasoning about certainty and uncertainty in concrete, causal, and propositional contexts. *Developmental Psychology, 22*, 793–799.

Byrnes, J. P., & Overton, W. F. (1988). Reasoning about logical connectives: A developmental analysis. *Journal of Experimental Child Psychology, 46*, 194–218.

Cheng, P. W., & Holyoak, K. J. (1985). Pragmatic reasoning schemas. *Cognitive Psychology, 17*, 391–416.

Cheng, P. W., Holyoak, K. J., Nisbett, R. E., & Oliver, L. M. (1986). Pragmatic versus syntactic approaches to training deductive reasoning. *Cognitive Psychology, 18*, 293–328.

Clement, C. A., & Falmagne, R. J. (1986) Logical reasoning, world knowledge, and mental imagery: Interconnections in cognitive processes. *Memory & Cognition, 14*, 200–307.

Craik, K. (1943). *The nature of explanation* Cambridge, England: Cambridge University Press.

Dennett, D. (1987). *The intentional stance*. Cambridge, MA: MIT Press.

Evans, J. St. B. T. (1982). *The psychology of deductive reasoning*. London: Routledge & Kegan Paul.

Garfield, J. L. (1988). *Belief in psychology*. Cambridge, MA: MIT Press.

Griggs, R. A. (1983). The role of problem content in the selection task and in the THROG problem. In J. St. B. T. Evans (Ed.), *Thinking and reasoning: Psychological approaches* (pp. 16–47). London: Routledge & Kegan Paul.

Hersh, S. M. (1986). The target is destroyed. *The Atlantic, 258*, 46–69.

Inhelder, B., & Piaget, J. (1958). *The growth of logical thinking from childhood to adolescence*. New York: Wiley.

Johnson, M. (1987). *The body in the mind*. Chicago: University of Chicago Press.

Johnson-Laird, P. N. (1983). *Mental models*. Cambridge, MA: Harvard University Press.

Lakoff, G. (1987). *Women, fire, and dangerous things. What categories reveal about the mind*. Chicago: University of Chicago Press.

Lycan, W. (1981). Toward a homuncular theory of believing. *Cognition and Brain Theory, 4*, 139–160.

Lycan, W. (1987). *Consciousness*. Cambridge, MA: MIT Press.

Macnamara, J. (1986). *A border dispute: The place of logic in psychology*. Cambridge, MA: MIT Press.

Mandler, J. M. (1983). Structural invariants in development. In L. S. Liben (Ed.), *Piaget and the foundations of knowledge* (pp. 97–124). Hillsdale, NJ: Lawrence Erlbaum Associates.

Marr, D. (1982). *Vision*. Cambridge, MA: MIT Press.

Martin, J. N. (1987). *Elements of formal semantics*. New York: Academic Press.

Moshman, D. (1979). Development of formal hypothesis-testing ability. *Developmental Psychology, 15*, 104–112.

Moshman, D., & Franks, B. A. (1986). Development of the concept of inferential validity. *Child Development, 57*, 153–165.

O'Brien, D., & Overton, W. F. (1980). Conditional reasoning following contradictory evidence: A developmental analysis. *Journal of Experimental Child Psychology, 30*, 44–60.

O'Brien, D., & Overton, W. F. (1982). Conditional reasoning and the competence-performance issue: A developmental analysis of a training task. *Journal of Experimental Child Psychology, 34*, 274–290.

Osherson, D. (1975). Logic and models of logical thinking. In R. J. Falmagne (Ed.), *Reasoning: Representation and process* (pp. 81–91). Hillsdale, NJ: Lawrence Erlbaum Associates.

Overton, W. F. (1984). World views and their influence on psychological theory and research: Kuhn-Lakatos-Laudan. In H. W. Reese (Ed.), *Advances in child behavior and development* (Vol. 18, pp. 191–226). New York: Academic Press.

Overton, W. F. (1985). Scientific methodologies and the competence-moderator-performance issue. In E. Neimark, R. DeLisi, & J. Newman (Eds.), *Moderators of competence* (pp. 15–41). Hillsdale, NJ: Lawrence Erlbaum Associates.

Overton, W. F. (1989a). Review of Piaget, J. "Possibility and necessity. Volumes 1 & 2." *Contemporary Psychology, 34*, 629–631.

Overton, W. F. (1989b). The structure of developmental theory. In P. van Geert & L. P. Mos (Eds.), *Annals of theoretical psychology* (Vol. 6). New York: Plenum.

Overton, W. F., Byrnes, J. P., & O'Brien, D. P. (1985). Developmental and individual differences in conditional reasoning: The role of contradiction training and cognitive style. *Developmental Psychology, 21*, 692–701.

Overton, W. F., & Franco, R., (1984). *Deductive reasoning in young and elderly adults: A competence-moderator-performance approach.* Paper presented at the biennial meeting of the Southeastern Conference on Human Development, Athens, GA.

Overton, W. F., Ward, S. L., Noveck, I. A., Black, J., & O'Brien, D. P. (1987). Form and content in the development of deductive reasoning. *Developmental Psychology, 23*, 22–30.

Overton, W. F., Yaure, R., & Ward, S. L. (1986). *Deductive reasoning in young and elderly adults.* Paper presented at the biennial meeting of the Southeastern Conference on Human Development, Nashville, TN.

Piaget, J. (1980). *Recent studies in genetic epistemology.* Geneva: Cahiers Foundation Archives Jean Piaget No. 1.

Piaget, J. (1986). Essay on necessity. *Human Development, 29*, 301–314.

Piaget, J. (1987a). *Possibility and necessity. Volume 1. The role of possibility in cognitive development.* Minneapolis, MN: University of Minnesota Press.

Piaget, J. (1987b). *Possibility and necessity. Volume 2. The role of necessity in cognitive development.* Minneapolis, MN: University of Minnesota Press.

Piaget, J., & Garcia, R. (1986). *Vers une logique de signification.* Geneva: Editions Murionde.

Pollack, R. D., Ward, S. L., & Overton, W. F. (1988). *Early adolescence: A transitional time in logical reasoning.* Paper presented at the biennal meeting of the Society for Research in Adolescence, Alexandria, VA.

Pylyshyn, Z. (1984). *Computation and cognition: Toward a foundation for cognitive science.* Cambridge, MA: MIT Press.

Reene, K. J., & Overton, W. F. (1989). *Longitudinal investigation of adolescent deductive reasoning.* Paper presented at the biennial meeting of the Society for Research in Child Development, Kansas City, MO.

Revlis, R. (1975). Syllogistic reasoning: Logical decisions from a complex data base. In R. J. Falmagne (Ed.), *Reasoning: Representation and process* (pp. 93–133). Hillsdale, NJ: Lawrence Erlbaum Associates.

Russell, J. (1987). Rule-following, mental models, and the developmental view. In M. Chapman & R. A. Dixon (Eds.), *Meaning and the growth of understanding* (pp. 23–48). New York: Springer-Verlag.

Ward, S. L., & Overton, W. F. (in press). Semantic familiarity, relevance, and the development of deductive reasoning. *Developmental Psychology.*

Wason, P. C. (1983). Realism and rationality in the selection task. In J. St. B. T. Evans (Ed.), *Thinking and reasoning: Psychological approaches* (pp. 44–75). London: Routledge & Kegan Paul.

Wason, P. C., & Johnson-Laird, P. N. (1972). *Psychology of reasoning: Structure and content.* Cambridge, MA: Harvard University Press.

# 2

# The Role and Meaning
# of Structures
# in Genetic Epistemology

Bärbel Inhelder
Denys de Caprona
*University of Geneva*

What is the importance of the concept of structures in Piaget's genetic psychology and epistemology? What kind of structural analyses did he carry out, and how did such analyses contribute to the development of his theory?

Piaget was a many-sided thinker, and the impressive results he achieved in his diverse enterprises preclude any direct, straight-forward answers. As psychologists who have been closely associated with Piaget's work (one of us for many years), we shall try to elucidate the problem of structures and structuralism from various angles by looking at different periods of Piaget's work, and also by referring to some of our own work and to what we see as possible future developments.

The following important point should be retained: Piaget did not regard structuralism as a doctrine and certainly not as a philosophical theory; he valued it as a method and shared this view with a number of other proponents of structuralism, including Lévi-Strauss. In his short work entitled *Structuralism* (1970), Piaget made his standpoint abundantly clear: He emphasized the very real contributions structuralist methodology made to several scientific disciplines, and he also pointed out that it cannot be an exclusive method. Discussing his own search for structures in genetic psychology and epistemology, and taking into account certain developments in mathematics, Piaget argued for a synthesis of static structural descriptions and a more dynamic genetic approach. When he described structures as totalities that include their own transformational rules bearing on relations rather than on elements, he clearly emphasized the non-associationist nature of structures. When Piaget spoke of their self-regulatory aspects, he referred to the possibility of developmentally determining the processes by which structures gradually become self-regulated.

At other times and in other works, Piaget expressed different opinions about the role of structures. In the 1940s, when Piaget was beginning to exhibit cognitive structures in the child's thinking, his main concern was epistemological, in the sense that he meant to characterize the cognitive core common to all individual subjects at the same developmental level. For this task it is essential to identify the shared features of various forms of knowledge, that is, the structures of the epistemic subject.

In this connection a number of misunderstandings can be avoided. It has often been said, for example, that the structures Piaget proposed were devoid of content, that they were immutable, and that the resulting view of intellectual development was an abstract, predetermined hierarchy of structures. However, in fact, Piaget was proposing an orderly growth of systems of thinking that gradually become independent of the incidental aspects of knowledge: their compass increases, they become more flexible, and better adapted to the psychological reality of the child and the adolescent, as well as to objects of knowledge.

The basic tenets of Piaget's structuralism, thus, become comprehensible as does its development in the later, as yet not widely known, studies that were carried out in the 1970s, as we shall see below. What is striking throughout Piaget's endeavor is his epistemological way of asking questions about cognitive development and of using structures as a means of understanding what may be called the epistemic subject. Before Piaget, nobody had studied space, time, and causality as related systems. Structural analysis clearly was the most appropriate tool for investigating the organization and relationships of these systems; epistemologically, their relatedness makes it possible to envisage the sensorimotor, as well as the conceptual construction of a general view of reality by all human beings, along scientific and rationalist lines. In this way, space, time, and causality were considered to be adaptive schemes whose development, in Piaget's view, paralleled that of scientific, mainly logical-mathematical, thinking.

It may well be asked how far this view of the development of knowledge is specific to our societies and whether in other cultural contexts cognitive growth would be different. For understanding Piaget's conception of structures as a method of analyzing cognitive progress, it is sufficient to realize that they serve the purpose of reconstituting the genesis of knowledge, which is never observable directly.

Another point to remember is that the kinds of structures Piaget posited are very different from those hypothesized e.g., by Gestalt theory. Piaget's structures are never static nor fixed, but they should be viewed as a series of achievements in the course of a constructive process that can be traced back through actions and operations that form its constitutive links.

In other words, Piaget's structuralism is instrumental; it is a form of analysis that uses structures as flexible instruments in the study of thought and introduces an open-ended conception of psychological reality. Structures are neither static nor devoid of content: They provide the means for *structuring* content—be it concrete or symbolic—thus determining the characteristics of the new structures so created. Structures serve as models of analysis to account for both scientific norms (in such fields as number, measurement in geometry, physical quantities, etc.) and for normative facts that characterize the achievement of certain cognitive constructions in child thought. In this view, discontinuities become relativized if considered in the light of antecedent structures. Longitudinal studies have shown that an incomplete network of relations will undergo sudden change: The system seems to close. Faced with a counterargument, the child repeats his conservation answer and adds "It's got to be like that, it couldn't be different," thus expressing a feeling of necessity. All at once the solution has become obvious and necessary. To the extent that a discontinuity exists, it only manifests itself after the event, liberating the subject from his earlier constructive activity and its accompanying errors whereas ensuring the conservation of what was acquired. This latter aspect is important, for, once constituted, a structure is preserved, and it can only be destroyed by certain pathological processes.

Structural discontinuity, thus, does not appear as an absolute principle, but it expresses one aspect of a many-sided process in the development of structures. The content of structures has to be similarly relativized. Structures may be freed from specific contents, but the structuring process always deals with specific contents. (Moreover, it should not be forgotten that contents can be highly abstract objects of thought: They are not limited to concrete, reality-laden physical entities.)

The importance of this more relative view of structures and their contents is particularly clear with reference to the problem of "décalages." Initially (Piaget & Inhelder, 1974), the so-called horizontal décalages had been interpreted as due to a gradual application of the same structure to ever-more complex contents. Until Piaget and Garcia (1974) published their volume *Understanding causality*, content was supposedly to offer specific resistances to the full development of a structure. With the studies on causality, however, objects were seen to play a positive role in the subject's structuralizations: As Piaget used to say, they not only hit one another, but sometimes, when he tries to construct causal relationships, they also strike the subject literally and figuratively.

The flexible conception of structures is also reflected in the way Piaget developed his theory. The origins of Piaget's structuralism were already apparent in his early and youthful philosophical novel, *Recherche* (Piaget, 1918). His major interest then was in the relationship of parts to the whole, in the organic relations necessary for a whole to be preserved through time: Furthermore, although structures continued to play an important part in his later work, their impact changed when he elaborated his epistemological and psychological theories.

At the time he wrote *Recherche*, Piaget was primarily working as a biologist concerned with classificatory systems. His lasting interest in classification, and his many experimental studies on the subject, certainly stem from his initial work on taxonomy; but, as has long been obvious, classificatory systems are instrumental—they are descriptive tools. Another example of Piaget's instrumental and methodological use of structures is the following: When he developed models that might account for structural levels in cognitive growth, he was greatly stimulated by the works of the French group of mathematicians called *Bourbaki*, and he used Bourbakian structures as a means of obtaining a clearer picture of psychological development, particularly as regards arithmetical and geometrical constructions. In the case of spatial concepts (Piaget & Inhelder, 1956), psychological development seemed to reflect the formal filiation of structures, but to the reverse of historical order, seeing that Euclidian and projective structures were historically developed well before topology. Psychologically, primitive topological relations (separations, envelopment, connectivity, etc.) are a necessary basis for the construction of metrical relationships.

Another example of the importance of the structuralist approach to psychological development is provided by the work, *The Growth of Logical Thinking From Childhood to Adolescence* (Inhelder & Piaget, 1958), a joint study by Inhelder and Piaget; because the example involves the type of collaboration that gave rise to the book, I will have to speak in my own name. Although Piaget was engaged in the formalization of logical constructions, I directed a series of studies on the development of experimental strategies methods with subjects from 5 to 15 years old. To give an example: I studied the isolation of variables in an experiment during the course of which the subjects were asked to evaluate the flexibility of rods of different materials (steel, brass, etc.), of different lengths, diameters, and cross-sections (round, square, etc.). I found that, other things being equal, the separation of variables was possible only if it was mediated by operations involving a combinatorial system and systematic proofs. Specifically, the subject needs to understand that, in order to establish a given relationship, he must compare selectively certain pairs of rods rather than others. Then he must proceed to a combinatorial operation to establish a system of implications between a factor and its outcome. In general, my results gave evidence for the existence of a new stage in the construction of methods of experimental verification in adolescents. It was only when we compared our findings that we saw the striking convergence between the empirical results and the formal analysis. The operations that appeared in adolescents, but had not been observed in children, were found to fit Piaget's formal framework, which showed the importance of the dual structure of lattices and of the group of four transformations (the Klein group). It became clear, furthermore, that the operational structures of adolescent thinking clarify, retroactively, the concrete operations of the earlier developmental period. Concrete operations are characterized either by reversibility through inversion or by reversibility through reciprocity. The formal operations of adolescents integrate them into one system.

The concrete operations, themselves, led to further analyses at later dates and to a refinement of their structures on the basis of the psychological reality of development. To account for conservation principles, we had to assume the existence of a set of organized operations that would produce the notion of invariance. A new series of experiments led to reinterpretations that allowed a better assessment of the relevant operations. For example, it was not until much later (Inhelder, Blanchet, Sinclair, & Piaget, 1975) that an important operation, *commutability*, allowed us to consider conservation as fundamentally dependent on compensatory changes in spatial position. Our observations in the older experiments on conservation showed that when children try to establish relationships between height and width, for example, they come to realize that it is possible to displace some parts of the object from one dimension to the other, and, thus, they equalize the differences. The new observations supported the idea that conservation rests on commutability (i.e., the understanding that the whole is conserved when parts taken away at one place are added at another place).

Another example of the heuristic fertility of structural analysis is to be found in the studies on *Learning and Cognitive Structures* (Inhelder, Sinclair, & Bovet, 1974). When investigating the logic of classes and relations, Piaget sought to show the similarities and differences of these two apparently separate systems, and, in particular, came to conceive of the construction of number as a synthesis between the two subsystems. The studies on learning explored the possibility that operatory progress obtained in several learning sessions in one type of problem would influence the solution of a different type of problem. Certain transfers proved indeed possible (e.g., between class inclusion and conservation of quantities). This approach also led to a clarification of the links between the so-called infralogical operations, based on the way continuous objects (such as space or physical quantities) are dealt with, and logical operations based on the treatment of discrete objects.

The above examples illustrate what may be called a reconstitutive method, whereby structural analysis leads to a reinterpretation of earlier data in the light of new findings and to a new, integrative understanding of what previously appeared to be separate systems. This is in accord with the idea Piaget frequently emphasized from the outset (i.e., that there is no absolute beginning and no absolute end in cognitive development), and this is equally true of the elaboration of his own theory. All cognitive constructions stem from earlier achievements that can be shown to possess both more general and weaker structures (as was most clearly demonstrated with respect to the development of geometrical concepts).

Many examples of Piaget's search for very general, but weaker structures that are the source of later operatory structures are to be found in his work in the late 1960s and 1970s. An interpretation of the pre-operatory period in terms of lack of decentration ("egocentrism") was felt to be insufficient. A study of the mathematical concept of *functions* (Piaget, Grize, Szeminska, & Vinh-Bang, 1968) led him to show that pre-operatory thought, although irreversible, does establish cognitive links of a certain type, such as one way mappings, and, therefore, prepares the operatory structures proper.

The following will serve as an example: Given a string X–Y–Z passing around peg P and hanging down. End X is tied to a spring S. Peg P and spring S are fixed on a vertical board. At the other end, Z, different weights can be attached. A child at semi-operatory level may understand that the change in length of S depends on W, but will not admit that the length of string XYZ remains the same (i.e., is conserved). Later, at the stage of concrete operations, the child will argue that, as YZ lengthens, YX shortens and vice versa, and that the total length is conserved. (See Fig. 2.1.)

The studies (Piaget 1980c) of *correspondences* (i.e., the ability to make one-to-one comparisons) and of *morphisms* and *categories* (Piaget, Henriques & Ascher, in prep.) (i.e., the ability to establish relations prior to the mastery of transformations) were intended to go even further towards explaining the growth of basic, yet flexible and general, structures in young children.

In the last years of Piaget's research at the International Center for Genetic Epistemology, the reconstitutive method led to the study of implication and meaning, two concepts central to the definition of basic logical links on which operatory logic is based. His interest (Piaget, 1980b) in *dialectics*, for example, was related specifically to a process-oriented study of logical implications. The concepts of "meaning" and "meaning implication" were among the most important ones, and they were central in defining a "protologic" of development. In their book, *Toward a Logic of Meanings* (in prep.), Piaget and Garcia endeavoured to describe a logic of meanings free of extensional logic. Such a logic does not supersede operatory logic but is part of it. Their work is based on the idea that the logic of meanings is more primitive than, yet constitutive of, the logic of statements (See also Matalon, Chap. 5; Piéraut-LeBonniec, Chap. 4; Ricco, Chap. 3 in this volume). This is yet another instance of Piaget's interest in early, deeprooted preliminary constituents of logical thinking. Piaget and Garcia conclude that all knowledge contains an inferential dimension in the form of implications between meanings that, at the outset, introduce a relational dimension linking non-isolated schemes. This quest for logical preliminaries yielded surprising results that seemed to contradict earlier findings and hy-

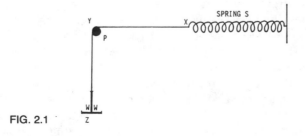

FIG. 2.1

potheses of genetic psychology. Propositional logic had previously been described as the ultimate stage of intellectual development, whereas the new research on meaning showed an early appearance of the sixteen operations of propositional logic. These operations, however, are not yet part of structured wholes; they appear initially only in the form of pairs of actions and operations linked by early forms of implication.

All these examples illustrate what has been called the reconstitutive method, that is, a quest for the preliminaries to, and conditions for, a future development of logical thinking. As in the case of the logic of meanings, the studies on *possibility* and *necessity* (Piaget, 1987a, 1987b) yielded results that seemingly contradicted earlier findings. Previously it was thought that the understanding of necessity and possibility occurred at the end of cognitive development, in the sense that necessity was considered as indicating the closing of structures, because necessary relations were regarded to be possible only in closed structures; similarly the creation of a full range of possibilities through hypothetical thinking was thought to occur only when cognitive structures were liberated from content, and, thus, opened the way to free combinations between the operations of highly evolved structures. The new approach brought to light the early appearance in the child of the understanding of certain forms of possibility and necessity (see also Murray, Chap. 9; Ricco, Chap. 3 in this volume), which were thought of as depending on what Piaget called "necessitating" processes and on processes involving the creation of new possibilities. Whereas the former view looked for what was possible and necessary in the cognitive structures once they were constituted, the reconstitutive approach identified processes that lie at the very origin of operatory structures.

All this illustrates Piaget's efforts to develop models that would be closer to the way of thinking of children and of human beings in general. He was aiming at an understanding of natural logic, of the logic of the acting, speaking and reasoning subject. In so doing, he was constantly driven to refine his interpretation of cognitive development. A number of his co-workers have pursued the path indicated by this overall cognitive theory—each one along his or her own particular line, and Piaget's flexible approach to the understanding of cognitive development has taught us not to turn the theory into a rigid, closed system.

At the core of his theory is a constructive view of development. Studies carried out in the 1970s corroborate this long-held view and provide better insight into the processes that underlie cognitive constructions. The resulting perspective of development is that of a series of reconstructions and reconstructive processes that take place at every developmental level. The stage of formal operations can, thus, be seen as reconstructing the concrete stage. This latter reconstruction was described by Piaget in terms of algebraic structures, and the Klein group was shown to permit operations that hitherto had belonged to separate classes and relations to be integrated into a single comprehensive structure. Development, thus, becomes a sequence of hierarchically ordered systems. To speak of formal thinking as more evolved merely amounts to acknowledging that, in development, sub-systems gradually become ordered under "systèmes d'ensemble" or structured wholes (see Black and Overton, Chap. 12; Murray, Chap. 9 in this volume).

This perspective of development does not, however, imply a steady, linear course. Once again, it is necessary to return to the investigations carried out in the 1970s. When Piaget tackled the problem of *dialectics* (Piaget, 1980b), *contradiction* (Piaget, 1980a), and elaborated some aspects of his *equilibration model* (Piaget, 1985), he became aware of the cognitive conflicts that occur in the course of construction.

Similar phenomena were noted in other studies of learning (Inhelder, Sinclair, & Bovet, 1974) in which young children were presented with a variety of situations that required simultaneous use of different cognitive subsystems. Only through interaction of the subsystems could conflicts be resolved, and only then could they give rise to a new construction. In epistemology and psychology, constructive processes play a major part. There is no denying that the physical and social environment contributes to the acquisition of knowledge, but the aspect of development under consideration here is the process of construction and how it evolves in the development of cognition. The same considerations should apply equally to future, as yet unexplored, directions in genetic psychology.

The consequences of such a dynamic conception of structuralism, especially with respect to formal thinking, need to be pointed out. It is not the aim here to deal with all the functional aspects of Piaget's theory; yet, without reference to them, its structural aspect cannot be understood (see Inhelder & de Caprona, 1987). This theory provides a hierarchically organized sequence of forms of knowledge; such a static description must be complemented by a description that accounts for developmental dynamics. This latter aspect was developed by Piaget in his equilibration model, which defines a series of regulatory mechanisms that explain how cognitive structures gradually become self-regulatory. The structures can be conceived of as representing privileged moments in the constructive process whenever regulations form completely compensatory systems.

We shall not enumerate the many implications of such a model which, in the 1970s, provided the basis for most of Piaget's psychological and epistemological studies on *reflective abstraction* (Piaget, 1977), on *cognitive awareness* (Piaget, 1976), on *contradiction* (1980a), etc. What is relevant is Piaget's purpose. His aim was to bring to light very general mechanisms of development, which would be partly independent of structural organizations and would yield a theory of how the various forms of knowledge are constructed. This study proved to be of broad scope. In their book entitled *Psychogenesis and the History of Science*, Piaget and Garcia (1989) set out to establish a common mechanism in the history of physics and mathematics, especially geometry, and in the development of corresponding notions in the child. The important point is that the analysis was carried out at the level of the mechanisms themselves and not at the level of correspondences between structures, which obviously differed with respect to organization and complexity, not to mention the differences in the reflective conscious elaboration of structures of the scientist and the child.

As far as formal thinking is concerned, this approach entails certain consequences, especially with respect to stage theory. Time and again, it has been asked whether Piaget's description of the formal stage was accurate, and whether further trends of development, beyond formal operations, could be identified. Such questions may—but need not—lead to epistemological fallacies. As far as the description of the formal operational stage is concerned, there is undoubtedly room for new formalizations and the identification of structures that provide a better account of what goes on in the adolescent's mind. This possibility of improvement is inherent in structualism as a methodology. As to the question of whether the formal is the ultimate stage in development, this is not really what is at stake in Piaget's theory, as a too literal reading might suggest. Stage theory, as such, was not a major concern of Piaget's when he set out to study the functional mechanisms of development. Although it seems necessary to describe formal structures that integrate the previously separate structures of concrete operations, what is important is the description of the mechanisms through which this integration takes place. These mechanisms are general ones and do not preclude further development of cognitive structures or cognitive styles beyond formal operations.

The implications of the equilibration model clearly indicate the limits of structural analysis. As a static description of developmental levels, it certainly cannot fully account for the dynamics of development. Its very limitations compel us to consider additional and complementary types of analyses.

The structures Piaget demonstrated in the so-called "classical" theory of cognitive development provide an overall architecture of knowledge. Once again, the first author will speak in her own name. I was first interested in the way such a development occurs through dynamic constructive processes that ensure the transition from one structural level to another; the studies on learning I undertook with my colleagues set out to answer these kinds of questions. Subsequently, I felt the need to refine this process-oriented analysis of construction by going further in the direction of some hitherto less well-known aspects of psychological functioning. Given the architecture of knowledge Piaget provided, and which defines the epistemic subject, I tried to study psychological processes more amenable to direct observation in particular problem-solving situations.

To be sure, it took a while before the full implications of such a functional, dynamic version of constructivism for psychology were realized. My first interest was in studying the dynamics of development, itself. At a time when cognitive science and the problem-solving theories were not sufficiently developed, and their impact on psychology was not yet perceived, our research stayed at the macrogenetic level (in the hope of contributing to an understanding of the mechanisms of development). In the studies on learning, the specific purpose was to investigate some of the mechanisms responsible for the transition from one structural level to the next. The aim was to capture some of the dynamics that would account for the macrogenetic structural sequences that Piaget had described in the "classical" part of his work. Thus, the specific conditions of equilibrium or disequilibrium between systems or subsystems were studied; situations were analyzed that exhibited conflicts between several subsystems, each one of which had its own pace of development. For Piaget, the structural aspect of knowledge that determines the hierarchical order of its successive forms did not account for its dynamics, and he himself sought to complement his structural theory by developing an equilibration model.

Subsequently, it became important to transcend the macrogenetic levels of analysis and refine our understanding of functional mechanisms through the study of various aspects of the acquisition of knowledge to which insufficient attention had been paid, in particular on what I considered its "procedural aspects."

With my collaborators, I studied problem-solving procedures and their representations with children between the ages of 4 and 11. In one of the studies (Karmiloff-Smith & Inhelder, 1975), the children were asked to balance blocks of which some could be seen to be weighted asymmetrically, others were so weighted but invisibly. The results showed how children invented different procedures, corresponding to different representations and action-theories. At certain levels and in certain situations, children think that blocks will only balance when the support is "in the middle" whereas at other levels children take into account the fact that the blocks are weighted on one side.

We may hypothesize that the microgenesis of procedures observed during a problem-solving episode becomes a basis for the macrogenetic evolutions over a longer time-span. During the short time-span, a problem is assimilated to existing schemes, which must be accommodated and coordinated in order to produce a solution. Microgenetic development is both a product of macrogenesis and a source of potential macrogenetic progress (Inhelder & de Caprona, 1987).

This procedural aspect of knowledge acquisition became the central point of a new interest in problem-solving situations, shared by other psychologists. This concern with procedures may be compared with the earlier analyses in terms of structures. In a paper entitled *Procedures and Structures*, which appeared in 1980 in a volume of essays in honor of Jerome S. Bruner, Piaget and one of us (Inhelder & Piaget, 1980) tried to distinguish and to relate what belonged to structural analysis and what belonged to procedural analysis. Once again, what is important, here, is the very process of structuration. Inhelder and Piaget (1980) wrote:

> The essential difference that distinguishes procedures and structures is the following: although both procedures and structures are based on transformations, pro-

cedures carry out, or make use of, transformations, in order to attain a great variety of specific goals. Procedures are thus fundamentally temporal processes. Structures, however, link transformations one to another and extract connections to form atemporal systems. The only goal involved is the very general goal of understanding the nature of the system, common to all structures (p. 22).

In the same text, it is point out that relationships between procedures and structures exist:

Without a doubt, making structures is a certain type of goal-oriented activity, and it therefore entails the use of various procedures. However, once a structure has been discovered or elaborated, it loses its teleonomic dimension. Reciprocally, using a procedure to obtain a particular physical result may lead to the discovery of a structure. Once established, the structure becomes atemporally stable. It is also worth noting that when the subject uses some of the operations of a structure when carrying out a procedure, he uses the operation locally or momentarily, and this *is* a temporal procedure, or part of one. However, if the operation is reinserted into the corresponding structure, its structural character is once more established (p. 22).

Piaget and one of us, thus, tried to lay the foundations for distinct but complementary analyses of knowledge. This complementarity also holds for nontransformational procedures and structures. For example, correspondences and morphisms typically represent operations that are nontransformational in that they simply establish static relations between elements, as when a subject establishes one-to-one correspondences between the elements of two sets. These operations may appear in procedural contexts or belong to an atemporal structural organization. The adjective, "atemporal," here, means that once instituted, the structures are liberated from an actual, successive, context-bound enactment of operations; they, thereby, ensure a permanence of knowledge in ever-varying environmental conditions. Indeed, their major role is to ensure stability of our knowledge of the world. Lack of such stability would deprive knowledge of all consistency and would make it depend on the variations of a changing environment. Structural analysis, furthermore, enables us to be aware of the upper and lower limits of knowledge at a given period in development, that is, it gives us the background against which procedural knowledge can best be studied.

## ACKNOWLEDGMENTS

The authors thank M. Simmel, H. Sinclair, and M. Sinclair for critical reading of the manuscript.

# REFERENCES

Inhelder, B., Blanchet, A., Sinclair, H., & Piaget, J. (1975). Relations entre les conservations d'ensembles d'éléments discrets et celles de quantités continues [The relationships between the conservation of discrete elements and the conservation of continuous quantities]. *Année psychologique, 75*, 23–60.

Inhelder, B., & de Caprona, D. (1987). Introduction. In B. Inhelder, D. de Caprona, & A. Cornu-Wells (Eds.), *Piaget today* (pp. 1–14). Hillsdale NJ: Lawrence Erlbaum Associates.

Inhelder, B., & Piaget, J. (1958). *The growth of logical thinking from childhood to adolescence: An essay on the construction of formal operational structures.* London: Routledge & Kegan Paul. (First French ed. 1955)

Inhelder, B., & Piaget, J. (1980). Procedures and structures. In D. R. Olson (Ed.), *The social foundations of language and thought* (pp. 19–27). New York: Norton. (First French ed. 1979)

Inhelder, B., Sinclair, H., & Bovet, M. (1974). *Learning and the development of cognition.* Cambridge MA: Harvard University Press. (First French ed. 1974)

Karmiloff-Smith, A., & Inhelder, B. (1975). If you want to get ahead, get a theory. *Cognition, 3*, 195–212.

Piaget, J. (1918). *Recherche.* Lausanne: Ed. La Concorde.

Piaget, J. (1970). *Structuralism.* New York: Basic Books. (First French ed. 1968)

Piaget, J. (1976). *The grasp of consciousness, action and concept in the young child.* Cambridge MA: Harvard University Press. (First French ed. 1974)

Piaget, J. (1977a). *Recherches sur l'abstraction réfléchissante* [Experiments in reflective abstraction]. Paris: Presses Universitaires de France.

Piaget, J. (1977b). *The development of thought: Equilibration of cognitive structures.* New York: Viking Press. (First French ed. 1975)

Piaget, J. (1980a). *Experiments in contradiction.* Chicago: University of Chicago Press. (First French ed. 1974)

Piaget, J. (1980b). *Les formes élémentaires de la dialectique* [The elementary forms of dialectics]. Paris: Gallimard.

Piaget, J. (1980c). *Recherches sur les correspondances* [Experiments in correspondences]. Paris: Presses Universitaires de France.

Piaget, J. (1985). *The equilibration of cognitive structures: The central problem of intellectual development.* Chicago: University of Chicago Press. (First French ed. 1975)

Piaget, J. (1987a). *Possibility and necessity. Vol. 1: The role of possibility in cognitive development.* Minneapolis: University of Minnesota Press. (First French ed. 1981)

Piaget, J. (1987b). *Possibility and necessity. Vol. 2: The role of necessity in cognitive development.* Minneapolis: University of Minnesota Press. (First French ed. 1983)

Piaget, J., & Garcia, R. (1974). *Understanding causality.* New York: Norton. (First French ed. 1971)

Piaget, J., & Garcia, R. (1989). *Psychogenesis and the history of science.* New York: Columbia University Press. (First French ed. 1983)

Piaget, J., & Garcia, R. (in preparation). *Toward a logic of meanings.* Hillsdale, NJ: Lawrence Erlbaum Associates. (First French ed. 1987)

Piaget, J., Grize, J. B., Szeminska, A., & Vinh-Bang. (1977). *Epistemology and psychology of functions.* Dordrecht: D. Reidel. (First French ed. 1968)

Piaget, J., Henriques, G., & Ascher, E. (in preparation). *To compare and transform.* Hillsdale NJ: Lawrence Erlbaum Associates. (French ed. in press)

Piaget, J., & Inhelder, B. (1956). *The child conception of space.* London: Routledge & Kegan Paul. (First French ed. 1948)

Piaget, J., & Inhelder, B. (1974). *The child's conception of quantities: Conservation and atomism.* London: Routledge & Kegan Paul. (First French ed. 1942)

# 3

# Necessity and the Logic of Entailment

Robert B. Ricco
*Vassar College*

In ordinary discourse, when we say of two statements or terms, A and B, that A "entails" B, or, equivalently, that A "implies" B, we generally mean that to say A is to say B (among other things). We assert, in other words, that B is in some sense *implicit* in A, and that A, in its meaning, contains the meaning of B. An entailment between *terms* is typically represented as the relation of subject to predicate in an analytic proposition, for example, "All bachelors are unmarried males." Being a bachelor entails being an unmarried male because the meaning of the predicate term, "unmarried male" (B), comprises a part of the meaning of the subject term, "bachelor" (A). Entailment relations between terms are definitional and state a relation of class inclusion. To be a bachelor means, in part, to be unmarried and male. The class of bachelors is contained within the larger class of unmarried males, which also includes other individuals not properly referred to as bachelors, for example, children, the Pope, and so on.

Given that A entails B, we fully expect there to be a valid and necessary means of showing that B as consequent, or conclusion, "follows from" A as antecedent, or premise, and may be "inferred," "deduced," or "derived" from A. We experience the *logical necessity* of this inference as resulting from the *implicitness* of B in A. Thus, we can substitute for the term, "bachelor," a conjunction of the various elements of meaning that comprise its definition. Such a conjunction would certainly contain "unmarried" and "male." It might also include some stipulation that would exclude males below a certain age, of certain religious beliefs, and so on. Because each conjunct must be true when the full conjunction is true, our knowledge that someone is a bachelor allows us to infer that he must be unmarried and male.

Entailment relations can obtain among *statements* or *propositions* as well as terms. For example, consider the statement, "It is raining and I am outside without benefit of protective covering" (A), and, "I am wet" (B). It is certainly meaningful to speak of A as entailing B. By substituting for parts of A on the basis of semantic equivalence, it should be possible to demonstrate that A contains an assertion that I am in physical contact with water, or, equivalently, that I am wet. Because B is implicit in A, B can be arrived at on the basis of A and is, thus, logically necessary, given A.

Inherent in natural language and our intuitions about clear thinking and valid reasoning, an intimate relation exists between *entailment and implicitness*, on the one hand, and *inference and logical necessity* on the other hand. An inference is clearly valid and logically necessary when it is based on an entailment relation (i.e., an implicitness of the inferred in that from which it is inferred). Conversely, we most readily speak of A as entailing B, and, therefore, of B as implicit in A, when B can be shown to be derivable or inferable from A.

In his later writings on necessity, Piaget (1986, 1987A; see also Inhelder & de Caprona, Chap. 2 in this volume) formulated the position that entailment, as the implicitness of one meaning in another, is the foundation of all valid inference. Inference based on entailment, in turn, provides the clearest justification and most valid basis for judgments of necessity. Piaget referred to inference based on entailment as *signifying implication* (Piaget, 1980, 1986, 1987, p. 137; see also Matalon, Chap. 5; Piéraut-LeBonniec, Chap. 4 in this volume). For example, "*If* someone is a bachelor, *then* he is an unmarried male," is a signifying implication based on the entailment relation between "bachelor" and "unmarried male." Signifying implication is present at all levels of cognitive development. Not only propositions, terms, and concepts can enter into entailments that support signifying implications; actions can entail other actions as well.

Piaget contrasted the preeminence of signifying implication as a basis for judgments of necessity with alternative bases, both logical and physical. In truth-functional or extensional logic, in order for a statement, B, to be entailed by a statement, A, and, therefore, to be validly inferable from A, it is required, merely, that the truth of A guarantee the truth of B (i.e., it must be impossible for B to be false when A is true). This necessary relation between the truth-values of A and B *does not* insure the implicitness of B in A. For example, the statement, "The world is round" (A), validly entails the statement, "Either I am tall or I am not tall" (B), in truth-functional logic, because B can never be false, and, thus, can never be false when A is true. Further, using the axioms and/or inference rules of most truth-functional logics, a valid derivation of B and A can be constructed. Yet, it is quite obvious that the meaning of B is in no way implicit in A.

In truth-functional logic, therefore, judgments of necessity that accompany valid inference or deduction are not based on any clear notion of the implicitness of conclusion in premises. This renders the status of necessity problematic in truth-functional logic; because it allows for cases where a statement is validly derived from premises that do not contain the meaning of that statement.[1]

Signifying implication also provides a more secure foundation for necessity than do physical bases (i.e., cause-effect relations). Logical necessity, the necessity with which conclusion stands to premises in a valid inference, is of a higher order than physical necessity, because the latter can be enriched by the former (Piaget, 1986; Piéraut-Le Bonniec, Chap. 4 in this volume). The physical necessity with which effect stands to cause is, in itself, close to a mere regularity of occurrence, a purely contingent state of affairs. Judgments of physical necessity are given meaningful grounds and become additionally compelling when a model or theory is provided for the causal relation (Overton, 1984, 1985; Piaget, 1986; Piéraut-Le Bonniec, Chap. 4 in this volume). The relation between such a model and the causal relations it explains is an entailment and signifying implication, and, thus, involves logical necessity (Piaget, 1986). Given the validity of the model, the causal relation *must* obtain.

This understanding of signifying implication as providing the strongest grounds and clearest justification for judgments of necessity was critical for Piaget, because signifying implication, inference based on entailment, is implicit in the very nature of cognitive structures. A cognitive structure may be defined as a system of signifying implications obtaining among a set of cognitive transformations (Piaget, 1986). In terms of the structure of which it is a part, each transformation entails the possibility of certain other transformations to which it is *necessarily* related. These necessary relations among transformations can be represented as signifying implications. For example, in the sensorimotor logic, schemes constitute the transformations of the logic, and reciprocal assimilations among schemes represent signifying implications integrating the schemes into a logic, and, thus, a structure (Piaget, 1986). When a scheme, y, is assimilated to a scheme, x, an entail-

---

[1]Piaget (1986, 1987) also rejected modal logic as the structural or formal basis for a developmental theory of necessity. In modal logic, necessity is rendered as a logical connective, or operator, and defined in terms of possibility (i.e., the necessity of A is logically equivalent to the impossibility of not A) (Lewis & Langford, 1932). Piaget found fault with the treatment of necessity in modal logic on two grounds. first, like truth-functional logic, modal logic fails to adequately ground judgments of necessity in meaningful inference (i.e., the implicitness of conclusion in premises). Second, although modal logic as a competence model could provide a structural, a priori account of the role of necessity in mature human thought, it does not seem suitable to providing a structural, developmental account of the possibility of change in the nature of human judgments of necessity.

ment of y by x obtains, and this entailment supports the necessary inference or signifying implication: if x, then y.

Construing signifying implication as the basis of cognitive structures provides a formal account of the a priori basis of necessity (Piaget, 1986, 1987). Structures underlie the child's organization of experience. The extent of the role of necessity in that organization will be a direct function of the necessary relations (i.e., signifying implications) comprising the particular structures available to the child at a given phase of development. This explains why valid judgments of necessity are both present at all levels of development and increasingly more complex and general with development (Piaget, 1986; see also Inhelder & de Caprona, Chap. 2 in this volume). With the progressive integration or closure of structures, their signifying implications become more numerous and richer (Piaget, 1986, 1987, p. 139). Corresponding to this structural development, the child's judgments of necessity develop from stimulus- or data-bound and local in scope to deductive and universal (Piaget, 1987).

However, Piaget (1980, 1986) realized that establishing signifying implication as the most natural and valid format for judgments of necessity was to some extent incompatible with his employment of a truth-functional logic as the structural competence model of formal thought. As mentioned, truth-functional logics do not adequately tie the entailment of B by A, and the valid inference of B from A, to the implicitness of B in A. For this reason, such logics fail to characterize inference, and, thus, logical necessity, in terms of signifying implication. In Piaget's (1980, 1986, 1987, p. 138) last writings, he made reference to the formulation by Anderson and Belnap (1962, 1975) of a logic of entailment, intended to insure that valid entailment and inference in formal logic require some sense of implicitness. In these references, Piaget further indicated his intentions to modify or revise the formal operational logic in terms of this logic of entailment.

Although Piaget apparently did not have time to pursue these plans, it is evident that the relation of entailment and signifying implication to judgments of necessity was becoming a central construct in Piaget's genetic epistemology. Further, it is clear that Piaget saw a logic of entailment as a formalization, at the propositional or formal operational level, of the notion of signifying implication (Piaget, 1980). In light of this development, a discussion of both the failure of truth-functional logic to support judgments of necessity and the importance of a logic of entailment in correcting this inadequacy would be helpful in appreciating Piaget's last and possibly most significant contributions to a logic of necessity. This chapter will center around such a discussion, focusing on the status of necessity in truth-functional logic and the logic of entailment.

In addition, the final section of this chapter will discuss the employment of a logic of entailment to augment the formal operational competence model. It will be argued that the truth-functional basis of formal operational logic fails to adequately distinguish between issues of necessity and contingency in hypothetico-deductive thought. It is suggested that the power and scope of the formal operational logic as a hypothetico-deductive logic could be increased by incorporating non-truth-functional elements, such as signifying implication as represented within a logic of entailment. Before proceeding with these discussions, the importance of signifying implication as the basis of cognitive structures will be elaborated upon.

## SIGNIFYING IMPLICATION AS THE A PRIORI BASIS FOR JUDGMENTS OF NECESSITY

If, as Kant argued, judgments of necessity are a priori (i.e., they originate in mind and not in a reality independent of mind), then it must be possible to establish a basis for such judgments in specific properties of mind. Piaget (1986, 1987) suggests that relations of signifying implication among transformations form the basis of cognitive structures and constitute the specific properties of mind underlying judgments of necessity. Thus, within an intact structure (a system evidencing some degree of closure and self-regulation), a given transformation carries within it the possibility of other transformations to which it is specifically related. These entailments among transformations support signifying implications expressing the necessary relations defining a given cognitive structure. Signifying implications within structures become manifest in necessary relations among meanings constructed by the child (Piaget, 1987; see also Inhelder & de Caprona, Chap. 2 in this volume).

Within the sensorimotor logic, the logic of schemes, signifying implication takes the form of reciprocal assimilation among schemes (Piaget, Grize, Szeminska, & Vinh-Bang, 1977, p. 174; Piaget, 1986). Through reciprocal assimilation the "consideration or use" (Piaget, 1986, p. 308) of one scheme comes to entail that of another. To use Piaget's example, the child may have a scheme, x, for the placement of an object upon a support, and a second scheme, y, for the acquisition of an object by pulling it toward the self. Scheme x comes to *entail* scheme y, and y is assimilated to x, when the child recognizes that the success of y can be dependent upon the spatial relation between the object and support implicit in x. In this was, x and y come to share an element of meaning. The coordination of schemes x and y may be expressed as a signifying implication, and the child's actions engender this as a tacit inference: given x, it is *necessary* that y.

Reciprocal assimilations or coordinations among schemes determine the unique necessary relations comprising the structure of sensorimotor logic. In a *grouping*, logical equivalences among transformations of classes and relations determine the necessary relations that define the structure. Each transformation in a grouping is logically equivalent to, and may be defined in terms of, certain combinations of other transformations. These logical equivalences are entailments and the basis of signifying implications (Inhelder & Piaget, 1964, pp. 280–295; Piaget, 1986). In grouping I, the logical addition of classes in a hierarchy, the generation of a class, B, by the additive combination of its subclasses, (A + A' = B), is logically equivalent to the combination of two other transformations decomposing B into its subclasses, (B − A' = A) + (B − A = A'). It is this logical equivalence that supports the signifying implication defining the crucial grouping property of reversibility: *If* a class, B, (e.g., flowers) results from the composition of a class, A, (roses) with its complement, A' (other flowers), *then* A may be obtained by the subtraction of A' from B (Piaget, 1953). Signifying implications among transformations with classes enable the child to consider a class from within a hierarchy, (i.e., as simultaneously subordinate and superordinate to other classes). This involves multiple simultaneous relations of necessity that can be generalized across a variety of contexts and content (Piaget, 1987).

The signifying implications that obtain within a given structure attest to its degree of closure or integration (Piaget, 1986, Piaget, 1987, p. 4). Piaget (1986) suggested that the logico-mathematical competence models can be compared and arranged along a continuum in terms of the richness of signifying implications they engender. Richer signifying implications integrate more complex properties, afford the construction of more elaborate and adequate explanations, and entail "more consequences and tighter mutual connections" (Piaget, 1987, p. 139).

The INRC group structure of the formal operational competence model consists of richer signifying implications, and, thus, a greater integrity and closure, than the semilattice groupings of the concrete operational model (Inhelder & Piaget, 1958; Piaget, 1986). One indication of this is the greater recursiveness of the former structure. Recursiveness refers to a structure's capacity to define a given transformation in terms of other transformations. In the additive combination of classes, relations of logical equivalence among transformations are confined to immediate vertical relations within the hierarchical structure of the logic (Piaget, 1986). The INRC group, however, is not so restricted (Piaget, 1986). Each of the four transformations comprising the group is definable in terms of each of the other transformations (e.g., N = RC, N = IN, R = CN, R = IR, C = RN, C = IR, I = NRC (Inhelder & Piaget, 1958).

Because signifying implications are relations of logical necessity, the richness of signifying implications constituting a given logico-mathematical structure is an index of the scope and complexity of the necessary relations the child can construct on the basis of that structure (Piaget, 1986, 1987). The coordination of sensorimotor schemes affords the construction of isolated, and, thus, local, or context-bound, necessities. Signifying implications among concrete and formal operations, on the other hand, afford the construction of multiple and simultaneous necessary relations, allowing more general and complex judgments of necessity (Piaget, 1986, 1987, p. 140).

Signifying implication, therefore, provides both an a priori basis for judgments of necessity, and an account of the conditions under which such judgments will obtain at each phase of development. On this basis, signifying implication assumes a central role in Piaget's genetic epistemology considered as a logic of necessity.

In the introductory discussion, it was argued that signifying implication provides the strongest grounds on which to assert a necessary relation. The clear justification for judgments of necessity provided by signifying implication may be contrasted with the precarious basis provided for such judgments by mathematical, truth-functional logics. These logics are a common source of competence models for structural theories. The problematic status of necessity in mathematical logic must be a concern for any structural theory of necessity employing logical competence models that are truth-functional.

The formal operational logic is a truth-functional logic. As discussed, the signifying implications defining the lattice and group structure of the formal operational logic are richer than those defining the grouping structure of the concrete operational logic, and, in this regard, the formal operational logic supports an a priori, structural account of the developing role of necessity in the child's thought (Piaget, 1986). However, the individual formal operations are truth-functional operations and must represent necessity as a function of truth, not meaning. This has been a problematic treatment of necessity in formal logic, and the formal operational competence model is not immune to these difficulties.

## NECESSITY IN TRUTH-FUNCTIONAL AND ENTAILMENT LOGIC

To reason deductively, or inferentially, is to proceed from one state of affairs, represented as a set of premises, to a second state of affairs as conclusion, the truth of which follows necessarily from the truth of the premises. Such derivation, or inference, seems valid and compelling, and its conclusion necessary, to the extent that it proceeds strictly on the basis of the information contained in the premises, and, thus, to the extent that the conclusion can be shown to be implicit in the premises. Where the semantic relation of conclusion to premises is unclear or where the derivation is made dependent upon information not contained in the premises, we feel compelled to provide some special justification for asserting the validity of the derivation and the necessity of the conclusion. Because such justification cannot appeal simply and directly to the relation of conclusion to premises, it is an indirect and less adequate means of supporting claims of validity and necessity.

The ancient Greeks established the importance of implicitness to inference and logical necessity in their formulation of a science of reasoning, the formal discipline of logic. This importance was maintained throughout the greater part of this discipline's history (Anderson & Belnap, 1975). Syllogistic inference, the heart of Aristotelian logic, is readily translated into relations of class inclusion. Relations of inclusion are necessarily relations of implicitness. Valid syllogistic inference, therefore, is constrained to conditions of inclusive relations among meanings (Kneale & Kneale, 1962).

However, the supplanting of traditional Aristotelian logic by mathematical, or formal, logic in the nineteenth and twentieth centuries (e.g., Boole, Frege, Russell, Whitehead), whereas preserving and, indeed, giving precise formulation to the close connection between entailment and inference, engendered a relaxation of the criterion of implicitness for valid entailment and inference (Anderson & Belnap, 1975). As noted previously, the requirement that the conclusion be implicit in the premises became a requirement, merely, that the truth of the premises guarantee the truth of the conclusion. At the heart of this relaxation is the assumption that relations between meanings can be reduced to relations between truth values. This reduction of meaning to truth, and the accompanying relaxation of the criterion of implicitness, led to the generation of powerful abstract calculi whose utility lay in their seemingly complete independence from content.

With the contemporary consideration of formal logics not merely as powerful tools of analysis but as possible competence models of human thought, the reduction of meaning to truth and the relaxation of the criterion of implicitness become problematic in their underemphasis of the role of content in human reasoning. Cognition does not consist of a manipulation of abstract forms given arbitrary empirical interpretations. Form and content are interdependent in human thought (Overton, Ward, Novec, Black, & O'Brien, 1987; Piéraut-Le Bonniec, Chap. 4 in this volume).

Previous discussions of logics as competence models have not stressed the importance of an interdependence of form and content to the role of necessity in both formal logic and human thought. The emphasis on form and truth over content, or meaning, in formal logic provides inadequate support for judgments of necessity. The problematic role of necessity in formal logic, in turn, threatens competence models based on formal logic. Because a suitable competence model must give an account of the possibility of valid judgments of necessity, it must provide within itself a secure foundation for such judgments.

## Truth-Functional Paradoxes

In what sense is meaning reduced to truth in formal logic? How does such a reduction affect the nature of entailment and inference? In order to address these questions, some basic structural properties of formal logic will be discussed.

The chief characteristics of classic mathematical logic, in both its propositional and quantificational variants, are that it is truth-functional, extensional, and two-valued (Kneale & Kneale, 1962; Leblanc & Wisdom, 1976). On this basis, classical logic shall be referred to as truth-functional logic. Only the propositional variant of truth-functional logic will be discussed. However, unless otherwise indicated, the properties attributed to propositional logic can be shown to hold for quantificational logic as well.

Expressions in truth-functional logic are built through the use of certain logical connectives, such as conjunction ("and"), disjunction ("or"), negation ("it is not the case that. . . ."), implication ("if. . . . then. . . ."), etc. The typical symbols for these connectives are, respectively: &, V, $-$, $\supset$. Logical connectives compose complex expressions from basic or atomic statements that contain no connective. For example, "The train was late *and* I missed my appointment." "*If* the sun is out, *then* the clothes will dry." Each connective engenders a specific truth function by which it generates, for each expression it composes, a truth value on the basis of the truth values of the expression's atomic components (Leblance & Wisdom, 1976). Thus, the connective for conjunction requires that both conjuncts be true in order for the conjunction to be true. In all other cases, the conjunction is false. A disjunction is true if at least one disjunct is true, and it is false otherwise. An implication is false when the antecedent ("the sun is out") is true and the consequent ("the clothes will dry") is false, and it is true otherwise.

From the above, the truth-functional character of mathematical logic should now be clear. The truth value of a complex expression is *fully* determined by the truth values of its basic or atomic components, and the truth functions of the logical connectives out of which it has been composed (Leblanc & Wisdom, 1976). Thus, *all* expressions in truth-functional logic have a truth value (i.e., they are either true or false). Further, it is only the truth values of atomic components, not their *meanings*, that are brought into relation by logical connectives in generating a truth value for a complex expression.

The meaning of an expression in truth-functional logic *is* its truth value. In effect, truth-functional logic employs only two meanings, true and false. Although the truth of an atomic statement depends on the specific claims it makes concerning some state of affairs in the world, it is not the content of those claims, but the simple fact of their correctness or incorrectness that is of concern to mathematical logic. Truth is, thus, construed in terms of reference or correspondence. In this sense, truth-functional logic is extensional, because nonlogical terms are assumed to be meaningful in so far as they designate or refer to something (Leblanc & Wisdom, 1973). Again, however, it is the appropriateness of their reference, not the content, that is important.

Issues of meaning, or content, in truth-functional logic (i.e., semantic issues), are strictly issues of truth (Kahane, 1973; Leblance & Wisdom, 1976). Thus, semantic aspects of such properties as *validity* and *consistency* in truth-functional logic are defined entirely in terms of truth. An argument is valid if and only if the conclusion cannot be false when the premises are true. Two expressions are consistent if and only if there is at least one truth-value assignment to their atomic components on which both expressions are true. The meaning of an expression independent of its truth value is irrelevant to questions of validity and consistency in truth-functional logic.

Necessity in truth-functional logic has a semantic and a syntactic aspect (See Scholnick, Chap. 8 in this volume). Because meaning is equated with truth, necessity, as a *semantic* property, is defined in terms of truth. Thus, an expression in truth-functional logic is necessary if it must be true (i.e., if it is true under all possible truth-value assignments to its atomic components). This is to say that *necessary truths* are true by virtue of their structure alone, the particular combination of logical connectives they engender. For example, "*If the world is round, then* either I am tall *or* I'm not," $p \supset (q \lor - q)$, is true whether or not the world is round or I am tall, because one of the disjuncts must obtain. Necessary truths are often called *logical truths* or *tautologies* (Kahane, 1973).

The syntactic aspect of necessity concerns the process of inference or derivation. As a *syntactic* property, necessity characterizes the relation of premises to conclusion in a valid derivation (i.e., a derivation employing the axioms and/or inference rules of the logic in an appropriate manner). Under such a derivation, the conclusion follows necessarily from the premises. Axioms and inference rules allow one to substitute an expression for another expression with which it is logically equivalent. A finite set of necessary truths are selected as axioms because they allow a wide range of substitutions (Kahane, 1973). Inference rules generally correspond to the logical connectives of the logic. For each connective there is an inference rule that allows that connective to be introduced or eliminated from an expression (Leblanc & Wisdom, 1976). For example, the inference rules for conjunction allow a conjunction to be asserted on a set of premises from which each conjunct has been validly derived. Conversely, each conjunct can be asserted individually on a set of premises from which the conjunction has been derived (Leblanc & Wisdom, 1976).

The semantic and syntactic aspects of necessity are *interdependent*. If a conclusion can be validly derived from a set of premises (syntactic necessity), then given the premises, the conclusion *must* obtain, i.e., if the premises are true, the conclusion must be true (semantic necessity). It is *entailment as a metalinguistic property* in truth-functional logic that most clearly captures this intimate relation between the dual aspects of necessity. Entailment conjoins semantic and syntactic necessity, because it expresses the necessary relation between the truth values of the premises and conclusion of a valid argument. In truth-functional logic, the property of entailment is typically defined as follows:

> A set of statements $\{A_1 \, \& \, A_2 \, \& . \, . \, . \, . \, A_n\}$, call it S, *entails* a statement B, if and only if there is no truth-value assignment to the members of S and to B such that B is false when the conjunction of statements comprising S is true. (Beth, 1955; Leblanc & Wisdom, 1976, p. 34)

This may also be expressed as an *implication* meeting the requirements of a *logical truth*:

> S *entails* B if and only if $(A_1 \, \& \, A \, \& . \, . \, . \, . \, A_n) \supset B$ is *necessarily* true. (Beth, 1955; Leblanc & Wisdom, 1976, p. 34)

As noted previously, an implication in truth-functional logic is false only when its antecedent is true and its consequent false. On this basis, the two definitions may be seen to be equivalent. An entailment is, thus, a *logical* or *necessary implication*, an implication that is necessarily true (i.e., true by virtue of its form). A merely contingent implication can never constitute an entailment.

A valid derivation can always be put in the form of an entailment or logical implication, with the premises as antecedent and conclusion as consequent. Thus, the premises of a valid derivation entail, or logically imply, the conclusion, and if a set of statements, S, entails a statement, B, then B is derivable from S.

The semantic relation expressed by entailment, and, thus, by the relation of premises to conclusion in a valid argument, must be stated as a relation between truth values and not meanings in mathematical logic. But does this amount to a relaxation of the criterion of implicitness? Is truth-functional entailment really so different from an intuitive sense of entailment as an inclusion of meanings? After all, if two properties or meanings are related such that one is assumed by, or contained in, the other, then the truth conditions of the propositions denoting them should be necessarily related. That is, the truth of one proposition should guarantee the truth of the other.

Although the truth-functional definition of entailment does, indeed, insure that a relation of implicitness between properties or meanings will be a valid entailment in formal logic, it also allows for numerous cases where a statement can validly entail another statement despite a lack of any clear sense of implicitness. Truth-functional entailment is equivalent to logical implication (i.e., an implication that is necessarily true). The consequent can never be false when the antecedent is true. One condition that can insure that an implication is necessarily true and, thus, constitutes a valid entailment, is the sharing by antecedent and consequent of one or more statements, for example, (p & q)⊃q, or (p & q)⊃(q V r). This condition suggests some degree of implicitness of consequent in antecedent.

However, another way of insuring that an implication is a necessary truth concerns the logical structure of the antecedent independent of the consequent, or of the consequent independent of the antecedent. If the antecedent is a necessarily false expression, then it can never be true when the consequent is false. Therefore, the implication can never be false and will constitute a logical implication and valid entailment. The most infamous case meeting this condition is (p & −p)⊃q. For example, "*If* the world is round *and* it isn't round, *then* I am tall." The antecedent is a contradiction and necessarily false. The implication must be true regardless of the content of the consequent and its relation to the antecedent.

Conversely, if the consequent of an implication is a necessarily true expression, then the consequent can never be false when the antecedent is true. The implication will be necessarily true, and, therefore, it will be a logical implication and valid entailment. The most straightforward case, here, is p   (q V −q). For example, "*If* the world is round, *then* either I am tall *or* I'm not." In a two-valued logic, the consequent, (q V −q), is necessarily true. The implication must be true regardless of the content of the antecedent. Both the above expressions, (p & −p)⊃q and p⊃(q V −q), are logical implications and, thus, valid entailments. Yet in each expression, no aspect of the consequent is implicit in the antecedent. In both cases, q, the only statement in the consequent, does not appear in the antecedent. Thus, the definition of entailment in terms of truth is clearly a relaxation of the criterion of implicitness. Requiring merely that the truth of A guarantee the truth of B does not insure that B will be implicit in A.

Because truth-functional logic preserves the vital connection between entailment and valid inference, if A entails B, then B is inferable from A. This means that for valid entailments like those just discussed, where there is no sense of implicitness, a valid derivation of consequent from antecedent is possible, and indeed is guaranteed, in truth-functional logic, despite the irrelevance of antecedent as premise to consequent as conclusion. Thus, q is derivable from (p & −p), and (q V −q) is derivable from p.[2] This, in turn, means that the mechanisms of deduction for truth-functional logic (i.e., the axioms and/or inference rules), allow a valid derivation to become dependent on information that is introduced in the course of the derivation and is

---

[2]A derivation of (q V −q) from p is presented in Table 3.1 below. Each step in the derivation is numbered on the far left. Justifications for each step appear on the right. These primarily consist of inference rules. The most important inference rule employed is the so-called Deduction Theorem, more formally referred to as, ⊃I, the interim rule for introducing an implication into a derivation. This rule states that if a statement, B, is derivable from a set of premises, S, plus a statement, A, then (A⊃B) may be asserted upon the set, S, alone. A is referred to as the hypothesis of the deduction.

not contained in the premises. This is clear from the above examples. In each case, the statement, q, comprising the consequent/conclusion, is not contained in the antecedent/premise.

In what sense is the role of necessity in truth-functional logic made problematic by the reduction of meaning to truth and a relaxation of the criterion of implicitness? Consider, first, the semantic aspect of necessity. Recall that a statement is necessary in truth-functional logic if it must be true. As seen above for entailments or logical implications, the truth of a statement can be insured by aspects of form that are wholly independent of meaningful (non-truth-functional) relations among individual atomic components of the statement. This allows for the formulation of expressions that cannot be false and are, thus, logically necessary, but which express entailments between statements that are wholly irrelevant to one another. The status of such expressions as "necessary truths" seems paradoxical. The truth-functional or extensional characterization of necessity can be contrasted with a definition of necessity in terms of meaning rather than truth. Under this more intuitive sense of semantic necessity, a statement is necessary if a *reason* can be provided for it, for example, if it is implicit in another state of affairs whose truth can be known or assumed (Piaget, 1986).

Consider now the syntactic aspect of necessity (i.e., the logical necessity with which a conclusion stands to the premises of a valid derivation). Syntactic necessity in truth-functional logic is not clearly supported by the meaningful relation of conclusion to premises. Thus, a direct appeal to the implicitness of conclusion in premises cannot always be made in justifying a judgment of syntactic necessity. What remains as justification is merely the plausibility of the mechanisms of deduction (i.e., the particular axioms and inference rules employed in truth-functional logic for proceeding in step-by-

---

The first step in the derivation is to state the antecedent, p, of the logical implication or entailment at issue, as the sole premise of the derivation. In the second step, q is asserted as the hypothesis of an application of $\supset$I. q is asserted on the premise, p. In step 3, q is simply reiterated or restated. As a result of this reiteration, q may be said to have been derived from p plus q. On the basis of $\supset$I, therefore, (q $\supset$ q) may be asserted on the premise, p, alone. This is done in step 4. Finally, step 5 substitutes (q V − q) for (q $\supset$ q) on the basis of a logical equivalence between the two expressions. Both are true under the same truth-value assignments to their atomic components.

TABLE 3.1
Derivation of (q V − q) from p

| Step | | Justification |
|---|---|---|
| 1 | p | premise |
| 2 | q | hypothesis |
| 3 | q | from 2 by reiteration |
| 4 | q $\supset$ q | from 2,3 by  I |
| 5 | q V − q | from 4 by logical equivalence |

step fashion from premises to conclusion). But equivalent truth-functional logics can differ in the axioms and inference rules they employ. There does not seem to be an absolute, objective basis for the selection of axioms and inference rules in logic (Kahane, 1973, pp. 326–343). The justification of judgments of necessity on the basis of plausible mechanisms of deduction is necessarily less compelling than justification based on such mechanisms *plus* implicitness.

There are additional difficulties for necessity in truth-functional logic that can be briefly mentioned. If the consequent of an implication is a tautology, and the antecedent is a contingent statement, then a contingency can entail and imply a necessary truth, and a necessary truth can be derived from a contingency. Likewise, if the antecedent of an implication is a necessarily false statement, such as (p & – p) above, and the consequent is a tautology, then a falsehood entails a necessary truth, and necessary truth can be derived from a falsehood. The entailment of logical necessity by contingency and by necessarily false statements would seem to establish a rather precarious basis for necessity.

## Anderson and Belnap's Entailment Logic

Several attempts have been made to amend truth-functional logic so as to avert the paradoxical entailments and inferences that are problematic for the role of necessity in formal logic (e.g., Ackermann, 1956; Nelson, 1930). One of the more ambitious and successful formulations is Anderson and Belnap's (1975) Full Calculus (E) of Entailment.

In Anderson and Belnap's E calculus, entailment is a logical connective, and not *merely* a metalinguistic property as in truth-functional logic. The entailment connective (denoted ' → ') may be read, "That. . . .entails that. . . . ." However, because all entailments can be expressed as necessary implications, the entailment connective may also be read, "If. . . . then. . . .", providing it is not confused with truth-functional implication (i.e., logical implication). The entailment connective is *not* a truth-functional connective. Expressions composed through the entailment connective do not have a truth value, properly speaking. Entailments in the E calculus are *valid* or *invalid*, but not true or false. Further, the validity of an entailment is not a function of the truth values of its component statements, but is dependent on certain relations between the meanings of these components, namely, relations of *implicitness*. Because the entailment connective is not truth-functional, expressions involving this connective cannot be restated in purely truth-functional terms (i.e., employing only truth-functional connectives). The E calculus also includes the truth-functional connectives for negation ( – ), conjunction (&), and disjunction (V) (Anderson & Belnap, 1975).

The notion of a valid entailment in E (i.e., an entailment with implicitness), was most explicitly presented by Anderson and Belnap in regard to first-degree entailments. These are expressions involving a *single entailment connective*, all other connectives in the expression being truth-functional. Anderson and Belnap (1975) defined a valid entailment as one that involves the *sharing* of a statement or proposition between antecedent and consequent. For entailments featuring fairly simple antecedents and consequents, this may be formally defined as follows:

An *entailment* $A \rightarrow B$ is *valid* if and only if it can be rendered in the form:

$$(A_1 \& A_2 \& \ldots . A_n) \rightarrow (B_1 \vee B_2 \vee \ldots . B_m),$$

where each of A and B is an *atomic statement*, and such that some $A_i$ is the same as some $B_j$. (Anderson & Belnap, 1975)

The validity of entailments featuring more complex antecedents and consequents (i.e., where $A_i$ and $B_j$ are not atomic statements) is established by determining if they can be construed as a series of valid entailments in the above sense.

The following is an example of a valid entailment: "That politicians are corrupt *and* the world is round *entails* that the world is round *or* dreams are wish fulfillments," $(p \& q) \rightarrow (q \vee r)$. This entailment is valid because the antecedent is a conjunction, the consequent is a disjunction, and the statement, q ("the world is round"), is shared by antecedent and consequent. If the two cases of paradoxical, truth-functional entailment are recalled from the previous discussion, it can be readily seen that they are not valid entailments under the above definition. Thus, $(p \& -p) \rightarrow q$ and $p \rightarrow (q \vee -q)$ are invalid because they do not involve the sharing of a statement (Anderson & Belnap, 1962, 1975; Belnap, 1960).

Valid entailment in Anderson and Belnap's E calculus, (i.e., entailment that meets the above definition), has been referred to in the logic literature as *entailment with relevance*, and this terminology shall be used, henceforth, in this chapter. All valid entailments in E are necessary truths in truth-functional logic when the entailment connective is replaced with truth-functional implication. However, not all truth-functional entailments are valid entailments in E (Anderson & Belnap, 1975). Thus, the impossibility of the consequent being true when the antecedent is false is a necessary but not sufficient condition of valid entailment in E. Another necessary condition is the implicitness of consequent in antecedent, defined as the sharing of a statement. This latter condition is necessarily independent of the truth values of antecedent and consequent. On this basis, it is evident that Anderson and Belnap's logic of entailment is not a full reduction of meaning to truth.

Entailment in Anderson and Belnap's E calculus is not only a logical connective. It is also a *metalinguistic* property, as in truth-functional logic (i.e., entailment expresses the relation of premises to conclusion in a valid derivation). When applied to the relation of premises to conclusion, the notion of entailment with relevance cannot be given the straightforward, explicit formulation possible for defining a valid first-degree entailment. Nonetheless, the relevance of premises to conclusion in the sense of statement sharing, and, thus, the valid entailment of conclusion by premises, is insured by careful construction of axioms and inference rules; substitutions made in the course of a derivation are *constrained* by the premises, and proceed strictly on the basis of the premises (Anderson & Belnap, 1962, 1975). In this way, valid derivations cannot become dependent on contingent information introduced during the course of the derivation and not contained in the premises. This insures that the notion of relevance as statement sharing is implicit in the relation of premises to conclusion.

The employment, in entailment logic, of a criterion of implicitness in both the semantic properties of the logic (i.e., the definition of valid entailment), and the syntactic properties (i.e., the mechanisms of deduction), insures a basis in meaningful inference for logical necessity. Inferences and, thus, judgments of necessity within such a logic, are justified on the basis of the implicitness of the inferred in that from which it is inferred. The truthfunctional threat to necessity posed by the possibility of valid inference in the face of a complete irrelevance of premises to conclusion is averted.

Further, necessity is defined in terms of a semantic relation, not in terms of truth. This is to say, a valid entailment, an entailment with relevance, is necessary not because it cannot be false, but because it involves a semantic relation between expressions (i.e., the sharing of a statement). In this way, necessity can never be attributed to an expression that involves a semantic anomaly (i.e., one that asserts a relation between statements that have nothing in common). As discussed, such anomalies are possible for relations of logical implication and truth-functional entailment.

Entailment supports valid inference in logic. "That A entails that B," insures that B follows *necessarily* from A and can be derived from A. This inference is captured by implication, "If A, then B." Thus, entailment can be expressed as an implication. The rendering of truth-functional entailment as *logical* implication has been discussed at length. Logical implication is defined as a necessary relation between truth values (i.e., the consequent can never be false when the antecedent is true). The form of implication appropriate to entailment with relevance, entailment in Anderson and Belnap's logic, is *signifying* implication (i.e., implication based not on a consistency of truth values, but on an implicitness of consequent in antecedent, an implicitness of inferred in that from which it is inferred). Entailment with relevance is, thus, consistent with Piaget's attempts to provide, in signifying implication, a valid basis for judgments of necessity. Entailment with relevance as a basis for valid inference maintains an emphasis on the interdependence of form and content, and a claim that judgments of logical necessity are, in part, judgments of relevance and of the extent to which reasons can be provided for the connectedness of experience.

## THE FORMAL OPERATIONAL LOGIC

In an earlier section of this chapter, it was argued that cognitive structures are composed of signifying implications among cognitive transformations. As noted previously, the signifying implications defining the group/lattice structure of the formal operational competence model are richer than those defining concrete operational and preoperational competence models. As such, the formal operational logic is part of a plausible, a priori account of the child's developing competence in constructing necessary relations. However, the individual formal operations, as truth-functional operations, must reduce necessary relations among meanings to necessary relations among truth values. This is a questionable treatment of necessity, both in logic and in a competence model of human thought.

Truth-functional logic provides an inadequate, paradoxical basis for judgments of logical necessity. This inadequacy is tied to the domination of content by form, leading to an irrelevance of premises to conclusion in valid inference. How might this general inadequacy of truth-functional logic lead to problems for the formal operational logic? It will be suggested in this section that the reduction of meaning to truth in the formal operational logic prevents the logic from adequately representing the subtle relationship between contingency and necessity in hypothetico-deductive thought.

Inhelder and Piaget (1958) offer the formal operational logic as a competence model of hypothetico-deductive thought. Such thought involves the formulation of competing hypotheses about conditional or causal relations among variables, the systematic testing of hypotheses, and the evaluation of hypotheses on the basis of specific empirical outcomes (Inhelder & Piaget, 1958). An hypothesis is represented in the formal operational logic as a contingent implication (e.g., "If John mows the neighbor's lawn, then he will earn spending money for the week"). This hypothesis asserts that John's mowing the lawn is a sufficient cause of his receiving spending money. Implication as a contingent expression differs from logical implication in that the latter can never be false. Logical implication is a necessary truth (i.e., true by virtue of its form), and, therefore, true under all possible truth-value assignments to its atomic components. The truth of a contingent implication, however, is always relative to a particular truth-value assignment. Hypotheses must be represented, at least in part, as contingent expressions in logic, because they are falsifiable. Indeed, one of the hallmarks of formal operational thought is an appreciation of precisely what empirical outcome will falsify a given hypothesis.

The truth-functional basis of formal operational logic is adequate for

representing the aspects of hypothetico-deductive thought with which Inhelder and Piaget (1958) were concerned in *The Growth of Logical Thinking From Childhood to Adolescence*. For example, in hypothesis formation,
Inhelder and Piaget focused on the child's ability to construct the set of all
*logically possible* combinations of variables, not simply the set of meaningful combinations. Further, in order to systematically test hypotheses
through the employment of a falsification strategy, the child need only be
concerned with the simple fact of the relative occurrence or non-occurrence
of cause and effect. This is easily represented in terms of necessary relations
among truth values. Thus, in order to evaluate the truth or falsehood of the
above hypothesis, one would simply need to determine for each week under
consideration, whether it is true that John mows the lawn and false that he
receives spending money. What, if any, meaningful relation obtains between
mowing a lawn and earning spending money is irrelevant to the truth status
of the hypothesis. Finally, truth functions are adequate for distinguishing
between types of causal relation. In order to verify that a cause is merely
sufficient to an effect, and not necessary and sufficient, the child need only
determine that the effect can occur without the cause. In truth-functional
terms, the cause would be sufficient if the antecedent of the hypothesis
could be false when the consequent were true.

Implication as contingent and truth-functional, however, does not represent the full logical form of an hypothesis. In conjunction with his later
work on necessity, Piaget (1986) gave increasing emphasis to a dimension of
hypothetico-deductive thought not addressed in *The Growth of Logical
Thinking from Childhood to Adolescence*, and not readily represented in
the formal operational logic. This concerns the meaningful connection between cause and effect (i.e., the reasons or explanations in terms of which
the causal relation makes sense). Hypotheses asserting causal relations are
derived from theories and models, either tacitly or explicitly (Lakoff, 1987;
Overton, 1984, 1985). As partly defined from within the theory or model,
the antecedent of an hypothesis will share elements of meaning with the
consequent. This sharing constitutes an entailment and provides a necessary
basis for the causal relation. Given the applicability of the model, the causal
relation must obtain.

Consider again the hypothesis, "If John mows the neighbor's lawn, then
he will earn spending money for the week." This is readily seen to be a contingent implication. It is an assertion whose truth depends on the occurrence of certain events. The contingency of this expression is further
underscored by the fact that the concept of "mowing the lawn" does not, in
and of itself, contain any sense of "earning spending money." As discussed,
for the purposes of hypothesis testing, any semantic relation between antecedent and consequent is irrelevant. However, in making sense of this hypothesis, we undoubtedly apply certain tacit cognitive models of human
society (Lakoff, 1987) in terms of which this causal relation would be rea-

sonable and expected. For example, John's being paid for mowing the lawn would make sense from within an idealized cognitive model of employment, wherein the performance of work entitles one to financial compensation. A more specific employment model, articulating a proportional relationship between amount of work done and amount of payment due, could help make sense of the particular amount of money earned by John. Thus, the employment model might maintain that if a person performs work as a job or service, they *must* be financially compensated in proportion to the amount of work. As embedded within such a cognitive model, "mowing the lawn" is partly defined as a service rendered for modest payment. As so defined, the antecedent shares elements of meaning with the consequent, and, thereby, entails the consequent. On the basis of this sharing, the consequent follows necessarily from the truth of the antecedent, and may be derived from an analysis of the meaning of the antecedent. Given the applicability of the employment model to the case of John, and given that John mows the lawn, it follows necessarily that he will receive spending money. On the basis of its embeddedness in a cognitive model, the hypothesis has the form of a signifying implication, an inference based on a semantic relation. As a signifying implication the hypothesis asserts a necessary relation, not a contingent relation.

The sharing of meaning between antecedent and consequent, the entailment of consequent by antecedent, the necessity of the consequent given the truth of the antecedent, as well as the derivability of the consequent from the antecedent, are all relations foreign to contingent implication and definitive of signifying implication. Falsifiability and truth-functional representation are properties foreign to signifying implication, and definitive of contingent implication. Thus, the logical form of an hypothesis involves both contingent and signifying implication. The necessity of an hypothesis concerns the meaningful basis provided by a model, or theory, for the co-regularity of occurrence asserted by the hypothesis. The contingency of the hypothesis concerns the applicability of the model. For example, it may be that John is mowing the lawn as a favor to his neighbor, in which case the employment model would be inappropriate. Falsification of the hypothesis, however, does not falsify the model, because models are not logically dependent on hypotheses. (See O'Brien, Costa, & Overton, 1986; Overton, 1985).

Due to its truth-functional basis, the formal operational logic cannot represent signifying implication. Signifying implication, inference based on an implicitness of the inferred in that from which it is inferred, must be rendered as logical implication in truth-functional logic. Logical implication states a necessary relation between the truth values of premises and conclusion. However, as discussed in the previous section, the impossibility of the conclusion being false when the premises are true is necessary but not sufficient to insure meaningful inference.

Much debate has centered around Piaget's dissatisfaction with the extensional and truth-functional basis of the formal operational logic, and his intention to move toward a "logic of meanings" (e.g., Beilin, 1985; Piéraut-Le Bonniec, Chap. 4; Scholnick, Chap. 8 in this volume). On the occasions where Piaget has suggested modifications in the operatory logics, he has consistently referred to Anderson and Belnap's logic of entailment (Piaget, 1980, 1986, 1987, p. 138). This strongly suggests that Piaget intended the logic of entailment to constitute a model for his proposed logic of meanings.

The present analysis has suggested that the representation of signifying implication, and not merely the structural embodiment of it, is critical to a logical competence model of hypothetico-deductive thought. A logic capable of representing signifying implication cannot be a truth-functional logic, although it can include truth-functional connectives and operators. A subsumption of the current formal operational logic within a logic of entailment, possibly a version of Anderson and Belnap's E calculus, could yield a competence model that would provide a more properly semantic, less truth-based account of the child's judgments of necessity at the propositional level. The formal operational logic as a logic of entailment would feature both signifying and contingent implication, increasing its scope as a model of hypothetico-deductive thought.

There are several affinities between the logic of entailment presented in this chapter and the formal operational logic. These affinities make an integration of the logics feasible. For example, as previously discussed, Anderson and Belnap's logic of entailment is inclusive of truth-functional logic in a manner analogous to the inclusion of propositional logic within quantificational logic. Further, the lattice properties critical to the formal operational logic may be shown to hold for the logic of entailment, as well (Dunn, 1975). Also, entailment with relevance incorporates logical implication as a necessary but not sufficient condition of valid entailment and inference. Finally, entailment with relevance is irreducibly a relation between propositions (i.e., a second order operation). Although attempts to integrate the two logics would encounter numerous difficulties, the above points of compatibility suggest eventual success for such a project. In any event, the expansion of Piaget's operational logic along non-truth-functional lines seems a promising means of increasing the interdependence of form and content within the logic, without sacrificing core properties of the logic. Whereas the outcome of such a project might well lead, as Piaget has suggested, to a "decanted version" (Piaget, 1980, p. 7) of the operational logic, it must also constitute "an extension of earlier work" (Piaget, 1980, p. 5).

## REFERENCES

Ackerman, W. (1956). Begrundung einer strenger Implikation. *Journal of Symbolic Logic, 21*, 113–128.

Anderson, A. R., & Belnap, N. D., Jr. (1962). The pure calculus of entailment. *The Journal of Symbolic Logic, 27*, 19–52.

Anderson, A. R., & Belnap, N. D., Jr. (1975). *Entailment: The logic of relevance and necessity, Vol. 1.* Princeton, NJ: Princeton University Press.

Beilin, H. (1985). Dispensable and indispensable elements in Piaget's theory: On the core of Piaget's research program. In J. Montangero (Ed.), *Genetic epistemology: Yesterday and today* (pp. 107–125). New York: Graduate School and University Center, CUNY.

Belnap, N. D., Jr. (1960). Entailment and relevance. *The Journal of Symbolic Logic, 25*, 144–146.

Beth, E. W. (1955). *Semantic entailment and formal derivability.* Amsterdam: Noord-Hollandsche.

Dunn, J. M. (1975). Intensional algebras. In A. R. Anderson & N. D. Belnap (Eds.), *Entailment: The logic of relevance and necessity, Vol. 1.* Princeton, NJ: Princeton University Press.

Inhelder, B., & Piaget, J. (1958). *The growth of logical thinking from childhood to adolescence.* New York: Basic Books.

Inhelder, B., & Piaget, J. (1964). *The early growth of logic in the child.* New York: Norton.

Kahane, H. (1973). *Logic and philosophy.* Belmont, CA: Wadsworth.

Kneale, W., & Kneale, M. (1962). *The development of logic.* Oxford: Clarendon Press.

Lakoff, G. (1987). *Women, fire, and dangerous things.* Chicago: University of Chicago Press.

Leblanc, H., & Wisdom, W. A. (1976). *Deductive logic.* Boston: Allyn & Bacon.

Lewis, C. I., & Langford, C. H. (1932). *Symbolic logic.* New York: Century Press.

Nelson, E. J. (1930). Intensional relations. *Mind, 39*, 440–453.

O'Brien, D., Costa, G., & Overton, W. F. (1986). Evaluations of causal and conditional hypotheses. *Quarterly Journal of Experimental Psychology, 38A*, 493–512.

Overton, W. F. (1984). World views and their influence on psychological theories and research: Kuhn-Lakatos-Laudan. In H. W. Reese (Ed.), *Advances in Child Development and Behavior, 18*, 194–226. New York: Academic Press.

Overton, W. F. (1985). Scientific methodologies and the competence-Moderator-performance issue. In E. Neimark, R. DeLisi & J. Newman (Eds.), *Moderators of Competence* (pp. 15–41). Hillsdale, NJ: Lawrence Erlbaum Associates.

Overton, W. F., Ward, S. L., Noveck, I. A., Black, J., & O'Brien, D. P. (1987). Form and content in the development of deductive reasoning. *Developmental Psychology, 23*, 22–30.

Piaget, J. (1953). *Logic and psychology.* Manchester, UK: Manchester University Press.

Piaget, J. (1980). Recent studies in genetic epistemology. *Cahiers Foundation Archives Jean Piaget, No. 1.*

Piaget, J. (1986). Essay on necessity. *Human Development, 29*, 301–314.

Piaget, J. (1987). *Possibility and necessity (Vol. 2): The role of necessity in cognitive development.* Minneapolis: University of Minnesota Press.

Piaget, J., Grize, J. B., Szeminska, A., & Vinh-Bang. (1977). *Epistemology and the psychology of functions.* Dordrecht: Reidel.

# 4

# The Logic of Meaning
# and Meaningful Implication

G. Piéraut-Le Bonniec
*Laboratoire de Psycho-Biologie de l'Enfant*

The general focus of this chapter will concern the nature of the relationship between antecedent and consequent clauses of "if . . . then" propositions and the manner in which this relationship influences logical reasoning in a problem-solving context. Specifically, an argument will be developed to show the differential outcomes of considering the "if . . . then" relation as based only on correlated events (i.e., *material implication*), and considering the "if . . . then" relation as based on the manner in which one clause is meaningfully related to the other (i.e., *genuine implication*). Following the development of this argument, we will show examples of the manner in which genuine implication can be employed as a model for problem solving.

It is well known that the logical structures of thought, the development of which Piaget described, were not based on the intension or meaning of classes, but on the logic of classes taken from the point of view of class extension. Mathematics is based precisely on this extensional logic, and Whitehead and Russell's *Principia Mathematica* is the classic reference for this form of logic. However, the last studies of the Centre International d'Epistémologie Génétique de Genève (see Piaget & Garcia, 1987) were conducted in an effort to go beyond extensional theory and to examine the complementary aspect of meaning and reason, when reason is understood as the implicit organization of meaning (see also, Inhelder & de Caprona, Chap. 2 in this volume). This change of perspective offers the potential of eliminating some of the obstacles that have confronted investigators in the areas of formal logic and formal logical reasoning.

Indeed, long ago, logicians, themselves, found difficulty with what some writers have called the "paradoxes of material implication" (Copi, 1965, p. 28), and psychologists have long recognized that formal logic cannot pro-

TABLE 4.1
Truth Table for *Material Implication* ($\supset$) of Proposition: "If water is made
up of hydrogen and oxygen, then Christmas day is December 25th."

| p | q | $p \supset q$ |
|---|---|---|
| Water is made up of hydrogen and oxygen, | Christmas day is December 25th. | |
| true (or 1) | true (or 1) | true (or 1) |
| true (or 1) | false (or 0) | false (or 0) |
| false (or 0) | true (or 1) | true (or 1) |
| false (or 0) | false (or 0) | true (or 1) |

*Note.* "$\supset$" is read "If p, then q."

vide a complete and adequate model of thinking. In particular, a major problem that all investigators face, for a variety of different reasons (Piéraut-Le Bonniec, 1980), is the issue of how to understand the nature of implication.

Given two propositions, $p$ and $q$, each of these propositions can either be true or false, supposing that decision criteria are available. Taken together, there are four possible combinations: a) $p$ is true and $q$ is true, b) $p$ is true and $q$ is false, c) $p$ is false and $q$ is true, d) $p$ is false and $q$ is false. The relation, "if $p$ then $q$" ($p \supset q$), holds if we do not have $p$ true and $q$ false (or $p$ and not$-q$), as can be seen in Tab. 4.1.

Let us now assign a meaning to $p$ and to $q$; take, for example:

$p$ = "this animal is a dog."
$q$ = "this animal is a mammal."

The implication, "if this animal is a dog, then this animal is a mammal," holds, because there are no examples of dogs that are not mammals ( = all bitches have nipple). This is what I term "meaningful implication," in that people are willing to acknowledge that there is a meaningful relation between the fact of being a dog and the fact of being a mammal.

Now let us assign another meaning to $p$ and $q$:

$p$ = "water is made up of hydrogen and oxygen."
$q$ = "Christmas day is December 25th."

The implication, "if water is made up of hydrogen and oxygen, then Christmas day is December 25th," also holds valid, because it is true that Christmas day is always on December 25th. The fact that this relation, termed "material implication," holds may appear of little value in daily life. However, it is useful, here, to distinguish between the meaning and the truth value of a proposition. Many people would agree to the validity of the following implication: "If X is unemployed, then X is lazy." This relation is not meaningless. However, the validity of an implication of this type can, nevertheless, be challenged, because it would not be difficult to demonstrate that certain unemployed people are not lazy. This is why mathematicians and logicians prefer to reduce propositions to their truth values and eliminate meaning when attempting to prove their theorems.

However, many logicians have attempted to construct logical systems in which meaningless implications could not be possible, and these attempts have taken one of two directions. The first consists in trying to soften the opposition between true and false, either by introducing intermediate values between 0 and 1, like Lukaciewicz' $1/2$ value (Lukaciewicz, 1953, 1970) or by introducing modal operators (e.g., logical necessity and logical possibility), as Lewis and Langford did (1932). The other direction—and the one of interest here—is to try to reintroduce into extensional logic part of comprehension in the form of a relation called *pertinence relation*. This is what Anderson and Belnap (1962) attempted to do by introducing constraints on meaning, but they did so with formal, logical proofs in mind. They adopted a notation, which, when applied to a given statement (itself formalized in terms of $p$s and $q$s, etc.), prohibited the introduction of irrelevant premises in the course of sequential proof. Hence, Anderson and Belnap tried to formalize the notion of relevance or pertinence that would be applicable to any statement (see Ricco, Chap. 3 in this volume).

Unfortunately, none of the proposed logical systems has been able to provide a satisfactory solution to the problems they were designed to solve, and they, too, including Anderson and Belnap's, present their own paradoxical problems. However, these attempts do hold some limited interest to the non-logicians; and mathematicians, for whom extensional logic was constructed, find such system satisfactory, if it is used appropriately and not to deduce the date of Christmas from the chemical composition of water.

Psychologists approach this problem differently. The logician's model of reasoning cannot be considered a general model of thought processes any more than a treatise of virtue can be considered a general description of human behavior. In fact, a large body of literature has developed (e.g., Piaget, 1962; Johnson-Laird, Legrenzi, & Legrenzi, 1972; Wason, 1966, 1968, 1983; Wason & Johnson-Laird, 1968, 1972) indicating that people do not spontaneously employ formal logical rules in testing the validity of implication when the relation between $p$ and $q$ is totally arbitrary; when the terms, themselves, are abstract; or when implication is reduced to its complementary aspect (i.e., implication reduced to a consideration of *only* the possible combinations of truth values apart from the meaning of the propositions) (see Matalon 1962, Chap. 5 in this volume.)

Recent investigators in this area (e.g., Griggs, 1983; Overton, Ward, Noveck, Black, & O'Brien, 1987) have focused on the issue of whether performance would be enhanced on the conditional reasoning (implication) task, referred to as the "selection task" or the "four card task," if the content of $p$ and $q$ were less arbitrary, less abstract, and had greater familiarity to the subjects. In general, it has been shown that after subjects develop the necessary logical competence, their knowledge about problem content and experience with counter examples enhances performance. However, the series of studies by Overton and his colleagues (Overton, et al., 1987) demonstrates that this matter is not as cut and dried as it might initially seem. That is, for several conditional statements whose content should have been thoroughly familiar (i.e., "If a student has more than 10 absences in a school year, then the student must repeat the school year"; "If a student is in school, then the student is not playing a radio"), the performance of all subjects, including teenagers (13–18 years), was exceedingly poor. Does this mean that such adolescents fail to reach the stage of formal logic? Given the other data of these studies (see also Byrnes & Overton, 1986; Overton, Byrnes, & O'Brien, 1985), this possibility is difficult to accept, and it seems more likely that the problem must be posed in a different manner. Thus, I would like to look at the work that has been carried out by the Centre International d'Epistémologie Génétique over the last few years, in the hope of shedding some light on this matter.

Piaget noted (1987) that the most fruitful endeavour undertaken by logicians to relate formal logic to natural logic was that of Anderson and Belnap, who introduced the *entailment operator*. The use of such an operator is not pertinent unless the two propositions, $p$ and $q$, have something in common. The distinction that logicians make between material implication and the entailment operator would correspond to the difference between formal implication and what Piaget called *signifying implication* (cf. Piaget, 1986; see also Matalon, Chap. 5; Ricco, Chap. 3 in this volume). *Formal implication* exists in situations where $p$ and $q$ are simply correlated. An example would be Matalon's method (1962) where red and green lights go on and off according to an arbitrary rule chosen by the experimenter: "If the red light is on, then the green one is on." There is *signifying implication* in a situation where the meaning of proposition $p$ is "included" in the meaning of $q$.

Piaget believes that a precursor to such signifying implication appears early in child development. Thus, it is very early in life that the babies understand that if an attractive toy is on a support, they can get it by pulling the support toward them. The baby's behavior presupposes that she/he has understood the reason for the relation between the toy and the support; the test of the baby's understanding of the necessity of the relation is that she/he does not grab the support if the toy is placed beyond it. Operating on the level of a logic of action, the baby would, thus, be guided by a signifying implication.

Piaget emphasized the fact that the real world does not present meaningful regularities that the child simply abstracts. The child, through exploration into the reasons for a given state of affairs, invests things with meaning. In this way, she/he constructs larger and larger models that per-

mit him/her to eliminate progressively what Piaget (1976) called "false necessities" (i.e., constraints that the subject believes to be warranted but are
subsequently recognized as unwarranted when the view of the situation is
broadened). These false necessities are progressively replaced by necessities
whose reasons the subject understands as a result of the building up of a
system of meanings.

This new approach implied new cognitive concepts. Unfortunately, except for his "Essai sur la nécessité" (1977, translated into English in *Human Development*, 1986), in which Piaget introduced the notions of
*signifying implication* and *reason*, the only material on this subject are a
few unpublished papers and our recall of discussions at the Center. As a
consequence, there is little available evidence to support the view that any of
us correctly understood Piaget's thinking. For this reason, I wish to emphasize that, although the ideas to be presented are fully dependent on the person we affectionately called "the Boss," I cannot be sure that they are
faithful, and I will assume the entire responsibility for what might appear
inconsistent or uninteresting.

First, I would like to clarify what I mean, here, by *reason*. The reason for
which statement A is true must not be confused with the proof that a formal demonstration of the statement's validity would provide. *Reason* is
what allows us to understand the meaning of A: it is what explains A (cf.
Halbwachs, 1981).

Consider an example in which two sets having an identical number of
items are arranged differently. In set 1, the items are in close proximity, and
in set 2, they are far apart. We know that very young children think that the
two sets are not equal in number (they often think that the set that takes up
the least amount of space is also the smallest in number). It is not until a
child is capable of making a one-to-one correspondence, using his/her fin-
gers, that she/he will be able to understand that the two sets have the same
number of items. This is not a formal demonstration, but it is an explanation. The fact that each item of set 1 corresponds to an item in set 2 is the
*reason* that the two collections have the same number of items. Statement
A, "to each element of one set corresponds exactly one element of the other
set," is immanent from the meaning of statement B, "two sets are equal."
A *meaningful implication* will join the two propositions, because statement
A is correctly understood as the *reason* for B:

$$A \underline{\qquad R \qquad} B,$$

which yields "*p* implies *q*," in *meaning*:

$$p > q.$$

This relation is transitive if the meaning of a third statement, C, is included in the meaning of A and B. For example, let C be the statement, "the

order in which the items of the two groups taken two by two is of no importance." This gives: "A is the reason for B, and this is the reason for C,"

$$(A \xrightarrow{\quad R' \quad} B) \xrightarrow{\quad R'' \quad} C,$$

or, $p$ implies $q$, and this implication implies $r$,

$$(p > q) > r.$$

The second implication, in a way, is a consequence of the preceding one, and Piaget called this a *proactive implication*.

The subject might also want to know the reason for the first signifying implication. In this case, she/he would then make up a statement whose meaning would include the meanings of A and B. For example, here, D = "A number (N) has necessarily one and only one successor that is that number plus 1." This is the reason that, if for each item of a set an item corresponds in the other set, these two sets are equal:

$$D \xrightarrow{\quad R \quad} (A \xrightarrow{\quad R' \quad} B) \xrightarrow{\quad R'' \quad} C$$

or

$$s > (p > q) > r.$$

This implication is called *retroactive*; it depends on the questions the subject is capable of asking as she/he works on understanding a problem. It should be noted that Piaget mentioned that this distinction between proactive and retroactive implication was earlier presented in Pierce's work (predictive and retrodictive implications). Thus, referring to Johnson-Laird (1983), generating reasons can be said to build models that relate previously formulated meanings.

Given the foregoing description of the nature and relationship of "meaning," "reasons," and types of "signifying" implication, a major issue still exists. This involves the question of whether these cognitive concepts can, in fact, adequately account for behavior. In the following, I will attempt to demonstrate, through the presentation of some empirical data, that these concepts can, indeed, adequately account for problem-solving behavior. This demonstration, however, is further complicated by the developmental assumption, also to be examined, that the capacity to employ correctly implication is linked to the following fact: In a given situation, the subject does or does not possess an available model, and, this, in turn, presupposes an organization of meanings in terms of *reason*.

Data from two empirical problem-solving studies will be presented. The first is a developmental study that I conducted in Geneva at the International Center of Genetic Epistemology (Piéraut-Le Bonniec & Rappe du Cher, 1982). The second is a study on adult reasoning conducted by J. B. Grize and myself (1983).

In these studies, subjects were presented with a problem and asked to reason the solution. The focus of inquiry is on whether and at what age level subjects generate meaningful implications (i.e., meaningful hypotheses about problem solutions); the manner in which subjects employ evidence situations [i.e., Cases 1 ($p$ and $q$), 2 ($p$ and not-$q$), 3 (not-$p$ and $q$), and 4 (not-$p$ and not-$q$)] to test (i.e., verify or falsify) the hypotheses and the way subjects understand implication when presented with contradictions.

In order to grasp properly this research, it is best briefly to contrast it with the traditional conditional reason problem, such as the Wason "selection task" or "four card problem" mentioned earlier. In the Wason task, subjects are presented with explicit hypotheses in the form of a conditional statement ("If . . . then . . . "). In the research presented, here, the subject must generate his own meaningful implication or hypothesis. The presence or absence, and the nature, of this hypothesis is abstracted from the subject's protocol by the investigator. In the Wason task, following the presentation of the hypothesis, subjects are given explicit evidence situations and asked to test the hypothesis. In the research presented, here, the evidence situations are organized by the subjects, themselves, and the organization and testing is abstracted from the subject's problem-solving protocol.

## EXPERIMENT 1: THE LENGTH OF THE PERIMETER OF A SQUARE

A square is a geometric figure. In other words, a square is a shape that is the result of properties that mathematicians have decided to give it. Squares are not found in nature, but man may sometimes recognize shapes in the real world that resemble a square corresponding to this definition (i.e., an area bounded by four equal sides that meet at right angles). Any number that defines the length of the perimeter (P) of a square is equal to four times N, where N is the length of any given side ($P = 4 \times N$ and $N = P/4$). An additional constraint can be introduced by stipulating that this number, N, be whole. Thus, the number that defines the perimeter cannot be odd. But there are constraints on even numbers as well. For example, 20 works, as it is made up of 4x5, but 18 does not ($18/4 = 4.5$), if we accept the whole number constraint.

It is in just such a situation that we have given children a reasoning problem, as the elements that made up the perimeter of the squares that we used could not be cut into smaller pieces. thus, the length of each rod served as a single unit. Each square was defined by the number of rods per side. Thus, its perimeter was defined by a whole number of rods. Furthermore, these rods were solid and rigid and could not be joined together in any way, except at right angles or as a straight continuation of each other. Thus, only squares or rectangles could be formed, but ovals could not.

The subjects were shown the three models of squares presented in Fig.

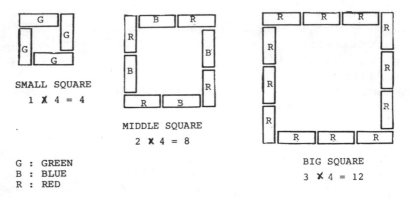

SMALL SQUARE
1 ✗ 4 = 4

MIDDLE SQUARE
2 ✗ 4 = 8

BIG SQUARE
3 ✗ 4 = 12

G : GREEN
B : BLUE
R : RED

FIG. 4.1   The three models of squares.

4.1. Their attention was drawn each time to the number of elements making up each side and to the total number of rods that were used to form the square. There were two experimenters. From a box containing a large number of rods, the subject and one of the experimenters (E1) each took 4 yellow ones, 12 green ones, and 2 blue ones, giving each one 18 identical elements (we checked that the subject knew how to count satisfactorily to 18).

The second experimenter (E2) then asked the subject a few simple questions: (a) "With what you have in front of you, could you make a small square with one rod on each side?"; (b) "With what he has in front of him, could Eddy (E1) make a big green square with three rods on each side?"; Then came the critical question, (c) "Do you think that with what Eddy has in front of him, he can make a *very* big square with all his rods in such way that *there won't be any left over*?"

The subjects were expected to respond to the critical question by saying that this situation was impossible, because if they made a square with 4 rods per side, there would be two left over, and if they made one with five rods per side, there would be two rods missing. If a subject answered the critical question, the experimenter (E1) pretended to take some rods out of the box that was hidden behind a screen. Then, he said to the subject: "Now I have enough rods to make a square bigger than all the ones we made before. How many rods do you think I have taken?" The subject was expected to answer: "At least two, or six, or ten, etc."

Finally, the child was asked what would happen if the experimenter took lots of rods, for example, 500 and 999, etc. "How do you know whether Eddy can make a *very, very* big square with all his rods in such way that *there would not be any left over*?"

The subjects were divided into three age categories: age 5:0 to 7:5 years (N = 13), age 7:6 to 9:11 years (N = 14), age 10:0 to 13:0 years (N = 14).

Five reasoning levels were obtained in response to the crucial question.

## Level 0

The problem was not understood at all. There were two types of stereotyped responses: "It can be done, because there are a lot"; or, "it cannot be done, because there aren't many," or "there aren't enough." When asked to try to make a square with their rods, the subjects put them end to end and then tried to close the figure. At this level, *square* only means *closed shape*, with a rough relationship between the size of this shape and the quantity of rods needed to form it.

## Level 1

On the critical question, the subjects stated that they did not know, and that they would have to try. Then, they realized that it was not possible to make a square with 18 rods. They explained quite well that either there would be some rods left over or there would not be enough. However, they could not say why. At this level, one of the fundamental properties of a square (i.e., that it has four equal sides) has been established, and this constraint is felt very strongly. However, the notion that the perimeter is equal to the sum of the lengths of the four sides has not been established, and the subjects do not ask questions concerning this. A square cannot be made with 18 rods because of the two "disturbing" rods that remain or are missing.

## Level 2

The subjects do not use the rods, and, instead, they consider imaginary squares. They reason with numbers by adding the number of rods needed for the sides (e.g., 4 + 4 + 4 + 4, etc.). They come to the conclusion that it is not possible to make a square with 18 rods, but they cannot explain why. If asked if they can make a square with 19 rods, they start counting again, 4 + 4 + 4 + 4, or 5 + 5 + 5 + 5, etc. At this level, the notion that the perimeter is equal to the sum of the lengths of the four sides of a square has been established. However the children do not relate the fact that a square has four equal sides to the properties of the numbers that can be whole number measurements of the perimeter.

## Level 3

The child reasons by using the numerical property of evens and odds. A square can be made if we have an even number of rods. For example, Luc (11;2) said: "Four on each side? No, there are too many . . . no, not enough . . . ah, yes you can since it's an even number." And for the question about 22 rods he answered: "Yes you can since it's an even number." This child did not find it necessary to check his answer with the rods themselves.

At this level, one of the geometric properties of a square has been related

TABLE 4.2
Truth Table for *Meaningful Implication* ( > ) of Proposition: "If a number is
the length of the perimeter of a square, then this number is even."

| | p | q | p > q |
|---|---|---|---|
| | A number, N, is the length of the perimeter of a square. | This number, N, is even. | |
| *Evidence Situation* | | | |
| Case 1 | true | true | true |
| Case 2 | true | false | false |
| Case 3 | false | true | true |
| Case 4 | false | false | true |

*Note.* " >" is read "If *p*, then *q*."

to one of the properties of those whole numbers that can be the length of its perimeter. A square is a shape whose elements are paired; this appears in the way in which subjects often make a square. When asked to "try," they first make *two* sides that meet at right angles, and then the *two* other sides and finally they put the *two* pieces together. Thus, there is some symmetry in a square and this means that only even numbers can measure its perimeter. In terms of reasons, this can be expressed in the following manner:

A = The existence of some symmetry in a shape
B = The number that measures this shape is even.
    A ——R—— B (A is the reason for B):
    (A ——R—— B) is the reason for C.
C = A square has a perimeter whose length is an even number.
    (A ——R—— B) ——R'—— C.

Into the meaning of *square* is entered the meaning: "its perimeter is an even number." This yields the *meaningful implication*: "If a number is the length of the perimeter of a square, this number is even." The truth table for this conditional statement is provided in Table 4.2.

As can be seen in Table 4.2, there are four possible evidence situations that would support (i.e., True $p > q$) or falsify (False $p > q$) this implication. These evidence situations correspond to cases where 1) $p$ and $q$ is found to be in evidence, 2) $p$ and not-$q$ is found, 3) not-$p$ and $q$ is found, and 4) not-$p$ and not-$q$ is found. Case 1 (N is the length of the perimeter of a square, and N is an even number ) would verify or support this implication for numbers 16, 20, 24, etc. Case 2 would falsify the implication if it were found in the experimental situation, but it is not, because the elements cannot be cut. This case is, therefore, not informative for the subjects. Case 3 (N is not the length of the perimeter of a square, and N is an even number) is found in the experimental situation: the number, 18, is an example of this situation, but it does not falsify the implication. Thus, it is no longer informative for the subjects.

Similar considerations hold for Case 4. It is the converse implication, "if a number N is even, then this number is the length of the perimeter of a square," which is informative. At this level of reasoning, subjects come to understand that the two propositions, "N is an even number" and "N is the length of the perimeter of a square," are not equivalent. The recognition of this nonequivalence of propositions means that the subject also understands that the implication ($p > q$) and its converse ($q > p$) are not equivalent. This appears in the reasoning protocol of Stephane (age 8:11):

E2: "And if you had 25 rods?"

S:  "You can't."

E2: "Explain."

S:  "No, you can't, because there'll be one left: You need an even number."

E2: "Well, how about 22? Does that work?"

S:  "No, it doesn't make a square, because you can have 5 on each side, and there would still be some left over."

E2: "But it's an even number."

S:  "Maybe you need 26?"

E2: "Why could it work with 26?"

S:  "Because 12 plus . . . because if you put 6 on each side, that makes 24—no, you can't."

E2: "But it's an even number."

S:  "Yeah."

E2: "So your idea doesn't work. How do you know if a number works?"

S:  "I don't know . . . I count them, and if it doesn't work, it doesn't work."

The subject has understood that evidence Case 2 (N is an even number, and N is not the length of the perimeter of a square) falsifies the implication that had served as his guide until then. This difficulty made some subjects reconsider their reasoning, for example, Sebastien and Cyril.

Sebastien (10:4):

E2: "Do you think he can make a square with all his pieces?"

S:  "Yeah."

E2: "Why?"

S:    "Well, because it's even."

E2:  "How many rods will the square he makes have on each side?"

S:    "5. No, because that'll make 20, and he has 18, altogether. I don't think he can do it."

E2:  "Why?"

S:    "Because you can't, because 18 can't be divided by 4."

E2:  "Before you said that you had to have an even number. Does it work with 22?"

S:    "No!"

E2:  "Why?"

S:    "Because there would be two too many."

E2:  "With 26, how do you know if you can make a square?"

S:    "I'd use a two times-table."

E2:  "And with a two times-table, do you think you would know if you could make a square with 26 rods?"

S:    "I don't know."

E2:  "Isn't there a better table?"

S:    "Oh yes, if you can divide by 4, you know that you can make a square. Yeah, sure, 26 can't be divided by four."

Cyril (10:10):
"You have to have an even number . . . but you have to try it out to see. I can do it with multiples of 4 . . . and multiples of 4 are always even numbers."

## Level 4

The child uses divisibility by 4. He has understood that we were working with a general rule that was good for any number, no matter how high it was. All he had to do was check to see if it was a multiple of 4, for example, Robert (9:10):

E2:  "With 44, what must you do to know?"

S:    "44 . . . 44 . . . you need 4 times something, but it's not sure that it'll work . . . ah, you can do 4 times 11."

E2:  "And can division help?"

S:    "Yeah, you see if you have O."

François (12:0):

E2:  "For example, with 950, what would you do to know if you could make a square using all the rods and with no rods left over?"

S:    "I divide by 4."

At this level, the square is seen as having double symmetry. It has four equal elements. In terms of reasons we have:

A = A shape is bounded by 4 equal sides.
B = Its perimeter is equal to four times the length of any side:

$$A \xrightarrow{\quad R \quad} B.$$

C = The length of the perimeter of a square is a multiple of 4.

$$(A \xrightarrow{\quad R \quad} B) \xrightarrow{\quad R' \quad} C.$$

Into the meaning of *square* is entered the meaning, "its perimeter is a multiple of 4." This yields the meaningful implication: "If a number is the length of the perimeter of a square, then this number is a multiple of 4."

This last implication will be termed "direct signifying implication," in that it is directly generated by considering a specific property of the squares. Consider, now, the converse implication that is one that answers the original question asked of the subjects ("Can he make a square with 18 rods in such way that there won't be any left over?"). The converse is: "If a number is a multiple of 4, then this number is the length of the perimeter of a square."

As shown in Table 4.3, Case 1 supports the validity of the implication in direct and converse implication. Cases 2 and 3 are more complex. For case 2, the direct implication (N is the length of the perimeter of a square and N is not a multiple of 4) is impossible in the experimental situation, and the subjects at this level know the reasons why. The converse implication (N is a multiple of 4 and N is not the length of the perimeter of a square) does not arise in the experimental situation for two reasons. First, the rods can only be assembled at right angles, and it was decided that only squares would be made. Second, other experimental situations could exist, where other geometric figures were allowed, such as diamonds or rectangles (16 could be the perimeter of a rectangle whose sides have the length of 3 and 5: 3 + 3 + 5 + 5). For case 3, the direct implication (N is not the length of the perimeter of a square and N is a multiple of 4) equals the converse implication of case 2. The converse implication (N is not a multiple of 4, and N is the length of the perimeter of a square) does not arise in the experimental situation, because the rods cannot be divided. But in a situation where the rods could be cut up, 18 would be an acceptable number, as it is the product of 4.5 multiplied by 4.

It would be interesting to see how a fifth level would be structured in relation to a generalization of the model (i.e., in relation to the subject's understanding of other geometric forms and other number properties).

The distribution of the levels of reasoning as a function of age is presented in Table 4.4. As it can be seen, in this specific situation, level 4 (recognizing the nonequivalence of $p > q$ and $q > p$) does not appear in a significant proportion of the subjects until the 10–12 age group.

TABLE 4.3
Truth Tables for direct Signifying Implication and Converse Implication
of Proposition: "If a number is the length of the perimeter of a
square, then this number is a multiple of 4."

| | Direct signifying implication | | |
|---|---|---|---|
| | *p* | *q* | *p > q* |
| | A number, N, is the length of the perimeter of a square. | This number, N, is a multiple of 4. | |
| Evidence Situation | | | |
| Case 1 | true | true | true |
| Case 2 | true | false | false |
| Case 3 | false | true | true |
| Case 4 | false | false | true |
| | Converse implication | | |
| | *p'* | *q'* | *p > q* |
| | A number, N, is a multiple of 4. | This number is the length of the perimeter of a square. | |
| Evidence Situation | | | |
| Case 1 | true | true | true |
| Case 2 | true | false | false |
| Case 3 | false | true | true |
| Case 4 | false | false | true |

What do these results mean? The notion whose development we have studied concerns the link between a geometric property and a numerical one. It is the establishment of these two properties and their intersection that permits the child to give the reasons why a number can or cannot be the length of the perimeter of a square. Reasons, in turn, lead to the generation of implications that are tested by various cases of evidence. The point of interest, then, was to see what information the children took out of the situa-

TABLE 4.4
Levels of Reasoning as a Function of Age

| | Levels | | | | |
|---|---|---|---|---|---|
| Ages | 0 | 1 | 2 | 3 | 4 |
| 5:0 – 7:5   (N = 13) | .61 | .30 | .07 | | |
| 7:6 – 9:11  (N = 14) | | .35 | .35 | .14 | .14 |
| 10:0 – 12:11 (N = 14) | | | .07 | .28 | .64 |

tion and what questions they asked. From the foregoing study, it can be seen that the development of an implicative model of a field depends on the construction of meaning and reasons, and the ability to test adequately implication involves the development of skills in detecting reasons an implication might be invalid (case 2) and reasons for which $p$ or $q$ could be true or false.

## EXPERIMENT 2: ADULT REASONING
## IN ARGUMENT SITUATIONS

This study briefly demonstrates how adult subjects manifest their comprehension of an implication in argument situations. J. B. Grize and I (1983) studied how contradiction is used in arguments. One of the best ways to demolish an adversary is to prove that what he has said is contradictory, or that his actions contradict what she/he says. We initiated this study by analyzing various types of articles in the press. The articles chosen were political and scientific texts as well as several novels. The primary criterion for selection was that the author had to deny explicitly a contradiction and to explain what it consisted of. The texts chosen were then presented to subjects who were asked if the author was right, and if he wasn't, to explain in what way they thought he was wrong. As we often chose controversial texts, subjects often invested strongly in the discussion.

The following is one of the texts selected from a novel and used in the study (Martin du Gard, R., *Les Thibault*):

> Everytime Antoine thought of Jacques' ideas, he found himself up against a fundamental contradiction: how could his brother who *hated violence* with the passion of all his intelligence and being—and he had proven this when he did not hesitate to sacrifice his life to preach brotherhood and to sabotage the war—how could he have, for years, *militated in favor of social revolution*, which is the *worst kind of violence* there is. (Our translation. Martin du Gard, R., 1955, Volume II, p. 838)

It must be understood that, in the novel, Jacques died by dropping anti-military tracts over the French and German lines at the beginning of the first World War.

Before making his remarks about his brother's conduct, Antoine found the following implication valid: "If one hates violence, then one does not militate in favor of social revolution" (see Table 4.5). If this implication is valid then case 2 is not expected: $p$ ("one hates violence") is true and $q$ ("one *does not* militate in favor of social revolution") is false, therefore "one hates violence and *does* militate in favor of social revolution." If this case should occur, it would concern a crazy person! Half of the subjects to whom this text was presented agreed with the author, did not question the

TABLE 4.5
Truth Table for Signifying Implication of Proposition: "If one hates
violence, then one does not militate in favor of social revolution."

| | p | q | p > q |
|---|---|---|---|
| | One hates violence. | One does not militate in favor of social revolution. | |
| Evidence Situation | | | |
| Case 1 | true | true | true |
| Case 2 | true | false | false |
| Case 3 | false | true | true |
| Case 4 | false | false | true |

implication and gave reasons for it. However, the other half tried to show
that this was not contradictory and, thus, show that Jacques' conduct was
coherent. Some subjects began by saying: "There are people who like violence, but who aren't in favor of social revolution." This is evidence case 3.
But they do realize that this does not solve the problem and that the real solution lies in falsification (case 2). Then, the subjects argued that there is
somebody, Jacques for example, who is right in hating violence and militat-
ing in favor of social revolution. Furthermore, they sought reasons to justify
case 2. Among the most frequently mentioned reasons was the idea that
there are different types of violence, and some of these, although they might
not be good, would at least be acceptable (e.g., the violence necessary to
bring about a social revolution), which would be a way to prevent foreign
wars. The solutions chosen by the subjects to defend the coherence of Jacques' conduct were, in fact, of little concern to us, here. An important concern regards how the subjects correctly manipulated the implications when
in a situation where they could organize and/or transform meanings as they
searched for the reasons that permitted them to do so.


## CONCLUSION

The research presented in this chapter is suggestive in nature and does not
attain the more definitive status of research whose experimental conditions
permit statistical treatment of the data. However, the goal of this work was
to demonstrate that an individual's reasoning cannot be dissociated from
the individual's knowledge of the topic under consideration. Moreover, one
must always ask what any experimental setting means for the subject. Consider the following classic examples that involve the Wason selection task.
The experimental situation gives the subject a hypothesis or implication and
asks the subject to test this implication by selecting, from a group of four

cards, the card or cards containing evidence that would prove the implication to be true or false.

In some of the research using this experimental method (e.g., Wason, 1966, 1968; Wason & Johnson-Laird, 1972), one of the implications that the subject is put to work on is: "If a card has a vowel on one side, then it has an odd number on the other side." Unless the subject has been trained in this type of play activity, he must be quite surprised when given such an implication. What kind of meaning or reason could possibly justify such an implication, and what kind could falsify it? Given such a meaningless situation, the subject tends to select the cards in a random fashion and, thus, performs poorly according to the arbitrary criterion established by the experimenter.

As a second example, consider the modification of the Wason selection task established by Cox and Griggs (1982) and used by Overton et al. (1987). The subject is presented the following implication: "If a person is drinking beer, then the person must be over 21." Here, again, the general nature of the task is to select, from cards containing evidence, the card or cards that prove the implication true of false (the four response alternative are the following: card 1: a person is drinking beer, $p$; card 2: a person is drinking coke, $-p$; card 3: a person is 22 years old, $q$; card 4: a person is 14 years old, $-q$). In this task, subjects perform outstandingly well. But the problem is to establish what question they are answering when they select cards 1 and 4. The experimenter asks: What card or cards would prove the implication to be *true* or *false*; for example, when arriving in a foreign country, one might wonder whether it is *true* that, in this country, people under 21 do not drink beer, or are forbidden to do so. But, this is not a usual situation; perhaps, the subject thinks that in this country there *is* a law that forbids people under 21 from drinking beer, and the subject is responding to the question: "Is the law being correctly *observed* or not?" The subjects imagine they are policemen who must make a round of the bars to make sure that the people drinking beer are at least 21 and that those who appear younger do not drink beer. This situation, which is much easier to construct, requires selecting the same cards, and this may be why subjects score exceptionally high.

Next, take the example of the following implication, described earlier in this chapter, that was also used by Overton et al. (1987), with groups of adolescents: "If a student has more than 10 absences in a school year, the student must repeat the school year." This problem puts the students in a very difficult position, and, as mentioned earlier, they perform poorly on it. In fact, subjects have no reason to question if it is *true* that such a decision was made by the school authorities. Moreover, they have no reason to question the application of this decision. Anyone under 21 might disobey the law and drink beer, but students are not at all free to refuse to be kept from passing into the next grade if their teachers have decided they must be kept back.

The rule can neither be questioned nor transgressed; confused, the subjects turned their cards over at random.

I think that, in fact, by the time a child reaches his/her teens, she/he is able to reason according to rules for which formal logic *might be* considered to be an *abstract model*. But this would be true *only under the condition* that the reasoning is to be applied to fields in which the subjects have knowledge and experience and in situations that make sense to them. For a subject to be able to test his/her hypothesis in the form of a conditional statement, she/he must be able to ask the right questions and find the reasons that shed light on the problem situation.

If we accept that intelligence is the most highly developed adaptation to life that nature ever invented, I believe that reasoning must be studied in situations that mean something to the subject. This is a psychological topic; but learning to use implication as the logician does is a pedagogic problem. My hope is that the introduction of the notions, *reasons* and *signifying implication*, presented here, lead to new, more rigorous research that will increase our understanding of the human mind.

## REFERENCES

Anderson, A. R., & Belnap, N. D. (1962). The pure calculus of entailment. *The Journal of Symbolic Logic, 27*, 19–52.

Byrnes, J. P., & Overton, W. F. (1986). Reasoning about certainty and uncertainty in concrete, causal, and propositional contexts. *Developmental Psychology, 22*, 793–799.

Copi, I. M. (1965). *Symbolic logic* (2nd ed.). New York: Macmillan.

Cox, J. R., & Griggs, R. A. (1982). The effects of experience on performance in Wason's selection task. *Memory and Cognition, 10*, 496–502.

Griggs, R. A. (1983). The role of problem content in the selection task and in the THROG problem. In J.ST.B.T. Evans (Ed.), *Thinking and reasoning: Psychological approaches* (pp. 16–47). London: Routledge & Kegan Paul.

Grize, J. B., & Piéraut-le Bonniec, G. (1983). *La Contradiction: Essai sur les opérations de la pensée* [Using contradiction in argument situations]. Paris: Presses Universitaires de France.

Halbwachs, F. (1981). Significations et raisons dans la pensée scientifique [Meaning and reason in the scientific thought]. *Archives de Psychologie, 49*, 199–229.

Johnson-Laird, P. N. (1983). *Mental models: Toward a cognitive science of language, inference, and consciousness* Cambridge: Cambridge University Press.

Johnson-Laird, P. N., Legrenzi, P., & Legrenzi, M. (1972). Reasoning and a sense of reality. *British Journal of Psychology, 63*, 395–400.

Lewis, C. I., & Langford, C. H. (1932). *Symbolic logic.* New York: Century. (2nd ed., 1959).

Lukaciewicz, J. (1953). A system of modal logic. *Journal of Computing Systems, 1*, 111–149.

Lukaciewicz, J. (1970). *Selected works.* L. Borkowski (Ed.). Amsterdam: North-Holland.

Martin du Gard, R. (1940). *Les Thibault, Epilogue.* Paris: Gallimard. (1955, *Oeuvres complétes*, volume II, pp. 759–1011).

Matalon, B. (1962). Etude génétique de l'implication [Genesis of implication study]. In J. Piaget (Ed.), *Etudes d'Epistémologie Génétique*, XVI. Paris: Presses Universitaires de France.

Overton, W. F., Byrnes, J. P., & O'Brien, D. P. (1985). Developmental and individual differences in conditional reasoning: The role of contradiction training and cognitive style. *Developmental Psychology, 21,* 692–701.

Overton, W. F., Ward, S. L., Novec, I. A, Black, J., & O'Brien, D. P. (1987). Form and content in the development of deductive reasoning. *Developmental Psychology, 23,* 22–30.

Piaget, J. (1976). Le possible, l'impossible et le nécessaire [Possibility, impossibility and necessity]. *Archives de Psychologie, 44,* 281–299.

Piaget, J. (1977). Essai sur la nécessité [Essay on necessity]. *Archives de Psychologie, 45,* 235–251.

Piaget, J. (1979a). *Introduction* (24th Genetic Epistemology Symposium). Geneva: International Center of Genetic Epistemology. Unpublished manuscript.

Piaget, J. (1979b). *La Raison: Introduction* [The Reason: Introduction]. Geneva: International Center of Genetic Epistemology. Unpublished manuscript.

Piaget, J. (1980a). *la raison en tant qu'objet de la compréhension* [The reason as an aspect of meaning understanding]. Geneva: International center of Genetic Epistemology. Unpublished manuscript.

Piaget, J. (1980b). *Documents préparatoires au Symposium* [Introductive papers to the 25th symposium]. Geneva: International Center of Genetic Epistemology. Unpublished manuscript.

Piaget, J. (1986). Essay on necessity. *Human Development, 29*(6), 301–314.

Piaget, J., & Garcia, R., (1987) *Vers une logique des significations* [To a logic of meaning]. Geneva: Murionde.

Piéraut-Le Bonniec, G. (1980). *The development of modal reasoning.* New York: Academic Press.

Piéraut-Le Bonniec, G., & Rappe du Cher, E. (1982). Le périmètre du carré: Exemple de construction d'une coordination de significations [The perimeter of the square: a meaning network to be built up]. *Archives de Psychologie, 50,* 285–301.

Wason, P. C. (1966). Reasoning. In B. Foss (Ed.), *New horizons in psychology* (pp. 135–151). Harmondsworth, England: Penguin Books.

Wason, P. C. (1968). Reasoning about a rule. *Quarterly Journal of Experimental Psychology, 20,* 273–281.

Wason, P. C. (1983). Realism and rationality in the selection task. In J. St. B. T. Evans (Ed.), *Thinking and reasoning: Psychological approaches* (pp. 44–75). London: Routledge & Kegan Paul.

Wason, P. C., & Johnson-Laird, P. N. (1968). *Thinking and reasoning.* Harmondsworth: Penguin Books.

Wason, P. C., & Johnson-Laird, P. N. (1972). *The psychology of reasoning: Structure and content.* Cambridge, MA: Harvard University Press.

# 5

# A Genetic Study
# of Implication[1]

Benjamin Matalon
*Centre International d'Epistemologie Genetique*
Translated by James P. Byrnes

The "fit" between natural thought and the various early systems of formal logic proposed by logicians is often poor, but this fact is rarely contested by contemporary philosophers and scientists. Improving the fit between the early models and natural thought, however, is not the goal of contemporary logicians. Most works of logic merely mention in passing that certain concrete interpretations can be given to the logical symbols of standard theorems that produce phrases that the entire world would agree are absurd.

In general, implication is considered to be the source of this discordance, because of paradoxical theorems in which it plays a central role: This is why we have devoted this work to a psychological study of implication. We hope to clarify the relations, which certainly exist, between natural implication and the implication of logicians.

Although we have decided to begin the study of "natural logic" by way of the implication operator, this does not mean we do not admit that other logical operators also pose problems. Perhaps negation, or similarly conjunction, pose fundamental problems, which we hope to be able to study in the future. However, because these operators can only be studied through the cognitive manipulations in which they take part, we will be necessarily grappling with problems of deduction, and it is in the particular case of implication that the problems of deduction can be studied most directly.

The "paradoxes" of implication that are usually cited amount to two types:

---

[1]This article originally appeared as Matalon, B. (1962). Etude genetique de l'implication. In E. W. Beth, J. B. Grize, R. Martin, B. Matalon, A. Naess, & J. Piaget (Eds.), *Implication, formalisation et logique naturelle.* (Vol. XVI of *Etudes D'Epistemologie Genetique*, pp. 69–93). Paris: Presses Universitaires de France. Reprinted by permission.

1. A false proposition implies any other proposition.
2. Two true propositions imply each other.[2]

This latter theorem serves as a point of departure for making our problem precise. In order to appreciate when the paradoxes are exactly found, we can pose to ourselves the following question: *Given two propositions, what relation(s) must exist between them for it to seem acceptable to relate them through "if . . . then", or through another equivalent relation?*

We could also define implication as a relation which gives rise to *modus ponens*,[3] and pose the problem: *What relation(s) must exist between two propositions for the subject to accept that the truth of one follows from the truth of the other?*

These are two *a priori* distinct problems that correspond to the *introduction* and *elimination* of implication, respectively. It is not implied here that the same response could be given to both questions.

In this work, we largely limit ourselves to the second of these problems, that which bears on the elimination of implication; that is, we will consider the possible inferences that can be derived from a statement that has the structure of an index or indication. We will, however, devote a few pages to a preliminary study bearing on certain aspects of the introduction of implication.

In a previous study,[4] we showed that, in cases when the relation between the antecedent and consequent is easily perceived, a modus ponens inference between antecedent and consequent is solved relatively easily by young children. However, our previous goal was not the study of implication, itself, and the task materials used were not perfectly adequate for this purpose. Thus, we take up the problem again and make our hypotheses more precise.

We can suppose that "natural" implication ($\rightarrow$) is a relation that, when "complete" (we come back to this point later), gives rise to the same inferences as material implication; thus:

---

[2]Translator's note: Using the truth table method of proving theorems, it is possible to show that both "$-p \rightarrow (p \rightarrow q)$" and "$p \rightarrow (q \rightarrow p)$" are tautologies (i.e., statements that are always true). Matalon translates these expressions here. The paradoxes are apparent when one introduces meaningful content, such as "that the earth is not round implies that if the earth is round then Reagan is President," for the symbols of the first expression.

[3]Translator's note: There are four standard syllogism arguments constructed around a statement of implication, each of which consists of a major premise, a minor premise, and a conclusion. These are: *modus ponens* (i.e., If p then q; p is true; therefore, q is true); *denial of antecedent* (i.e., If p then q; not-p is true; q is indeterminate); *affirmation of consequent* (i.e., If p then q; q is true; p is indeterminate); and *modus tollens* (i.e., If p then q; not-q is true; therefore, p is not true).

[4]Matalon, B. (1963). Etude de raisonnement à récurrence sur un modele physique. In P. Greco et al. *La Formation des raisonnements recurrentiels* (Vol. XVII, *Etudes d'Epistemologie Genetique*). Paris: PUF.

| p → | p → q | p → q | p → q |
|---|---|---|---|
| p | not-q | not-p | q |
| q | not-p | indeterminate | indeterminate |

However, additionally, there exists a supplementary, concrete relation between p and q, which renders the modus ponens (or eventually *modus tollens*) evident, or observable.[5] If this hypothesis is true, the genetic study must permit us to find a stage where implication is "incomplete," that is, when only a part of the theoretically possible inferences are effectively realized. These inferences are made possible by this supplementary observable relation, whereas the others are only possible through recourse to the structure of implication, properly speaking.

From this perspective, material implication[6] would give rise (if it exists) to late-developing inferences, and it would always be complete. In effect, material implication comes down to its combinatorial aspect, which is evident if one defines it through its truth table. The subject has nothing else at his disposal, for making inferences, than the list of possible and impossible cases. Given that this would be an entirely formal analysis, one would expect such reasoning to be late developing.

## EXPERIMENT: MATERIAL IMPLICATION

### Method

These considerations have led us to construct the following experiment: We propose two situations to our subjects (9–11 years of age): In the first, the

---

[5]In every study, it is only necessary to consider implication as "complete" if one is assured that it is, indeed, transitive, that is, when "p → q" and "q → r", the subject is capable of accepting "p → r," or if starting from two implications and p, one can deduce r without necessarily passing through q. We have studied this problem in the course of the study on reasoning about recurrence, mentioned earlier. We do not return to this here.

[6]Translator's note: Logicians reserve the term "material implication" for the truth table interpretation of the symbolic expression "p ⊃ q." Every "if-then" statement can be expressed as material implication simply by determining the truth values of their conjunctions, "p and q," "not-p and q," "not-p and not-q," and "p and not-q". If the first three conjunctions turn out to be true and the last to be false, the expression is a case of material implication. Thus, material implication is true of every "if-then" statement. However, this conception only captures a part of the meaning of the "if-then" statements that we normally use. The rest of the meaning comes from the *relation* of "p" to "q." This might be causality, or the fact that "q" is the logical consequence of "p," etc. Regardless, it is possible to construct "if-then" statements that do express material implication, but are meaningless precisely because they lack the connection. For example, "if acid is vinegar, then some men have beards" is a case of material implication, but one that is meaningless (Copi, 1955).

relation between the antecedent and consequent is "intelligible" or clear;[7] in the other, in contrast, the relation between antecedent and consequent is equally possible given a truth table, but appears to be arbitrary or contingent. For convenience of vocabulary, we call the relation in the second situation, henceforth, "material implication," because it comes very close to this logical relation. (It is, nevertheless, evident that the relation studied here is still quite different from the relation that bears this name in classical logic.)

We posed the following three groups of questions:

1. Those that ask subjects to recognize the possible and impossible cases when presented to them.
2. Those that ask subjects to enumerate the possible and impossible cases on their own.
3. Those that require the four inferences listed earlier (modus ponens, however, also initially plays the role of defining the relation).

Given our hypotheses, we can predict the order of success on these groups of questions. In the case when the situation is a concretization of material implication, complete success on these problems should be solved in the order 1, 2, 3. In effect, in order to solve all four inferences, subjects have to take the ensemble of the possible and impossible cases (i.e., question group 2) into consideration, and it can be expected that complete success occurs developmentally later.

In contrast, in the case of "natural" implication, the modus ponens should appear the earliest, following success on question group 1. Modus tollens that require hypothetico-deductive reasoning, but not a combinatory structure, come next. Finally, success on question group 2, and recognition of the indeterminate inferences requiring a combinatory structure, should appear last. Such an approach does not permit us to make precise hypotheses regarding the nature of the supplementary relation that is added to (and substitutes for), material implication. Our experiment will show, all the more, that the task material we have chosen does indeed play such a role.

## Material and Instructions

The goal of the experiment was to study the behavior of our subjects given problems that require inferences of the type modus ponens or modus tollens, when the relations given (which can be expressed in the form of implications), seem to be arbitrary (although they are possible). In order to correctly respond to some of the questions posed, the subjects have to utilize the combinatorial aspect of implication.

---

[7]Translator's note: By "intelligible," Matalon means that the relation between antecedent and consequent reflects an observable property of an apparatus. In this way, "if p then q" is not really an inference, but a simple "reading off" of properties of an apparatus.

The material consists of two small electrical lights, one red and one green, hidden behind a screen having two opaque windows that can be opened and closed, each corresponding to a light. A barrier placed between the lights does not permit one light to be seen when the window corresponding to the other is open.

A switch placed behind the apparatus allows the experimenter to illuminate, at will, only one of the two lights, both of them, or to switch them both off.

Each subject is shown that there is a light behind each window that can be illuminated or turned off. Then he is told these two lights cannot be turned on and off at random. In order to communicate the relation between the lights, we employed three different verbal formulations, each for a different group of subjects:

Rule 1. If the red light is turned on, then the green one is turned on.

Rule 2. One never has only the red light turned on.

Rule 3. To turn on the red light, the green light must be turned on.

These three statements communicate the same relation: *the illuminated red light implies that the green light is turned on*.

After having the subject repeat the rule and assuring ourselves that he understood, the following questions were posed to him:

QA: What are the possible and impossible combinations of lights?

Obviously, this question could not be posed in this form, although we did not try to find a unique formulation that would be comprehended by all of our subjects. It was generally necessary to give long explanations whereas avoiding giving examples. In particular, we found some success in using the following explanation: "If both doors are opened at once and we fidget with the buttons in every possible way, what would we see?" The subject often responded to this question using one of the combinations (generally, "both turned on"), and it was then possible to enumerate others through questions like: "Could it be otherwise?" Question A corresponds to the subject's ability to generate all the possible combinations on his own (i.e., questions group 2).

QB: Recognition of the possible and impossible combinations.

These latter questions are simpler and were more easily comprehended. They were the following:

B1. With this apparatus, could the red light be turned on and the green light turned on?

B2. The red turned on and the green turned off?
B3. The red turned off and the green turned on?
B4. The red turned off and the green turned off?[8]

QA' If the enumeration of the possible and impossible cases had been incorrect, we repeated question A.

QC: Inferences.

The following questions were then posed successively:

C1. The red light is turned on (the corresponding window is opened).
    What about the green?
C2. The red light is turned off. . . .
C3. The green light is turned on. . . .
C4. The green light is turned off. . . .

C1 and C4 correspond, respectively, to modus ponens and modus tollens, and C2 and C3 are indeterminate.[9]

When the subject had given his response, he was asked to justify it. The problem was repeated by the experimenter as often as it seemed necessary, but without giving supplementary explanations.

## Subjects

The experiment was conducted with 30 subjects, aged 9.3 to 11.6, the median age being 10.2.

We used Genevan primary school students. Each subject was the right age for his class.[10]

Each rule was given to a group of 10 subjects, with the assignment of subjects into the three groups made at random. The median ages of each of the three groups were: (a) Rule 1: 10.0; (b) Rule 2: 10.4; (c) Rule 3: 9.8.

---

[8]Translator's note: Letting "p" = "The red light is on" and "q" = the green light is on," B1 = "p and q"; B2 = "p and not-q"; B3 = "not-p and q"; and B4 = "not-p and not-q".

[9]Translator's note: Actually, C1–C4 correspond to the second premise of each of the four inferences, with the rule being the first premise.

[10]Due to the small number of subjects at our disposal, we have not adopted the usual approach of genetic studies, where groups of different ages are constituted and their behaviors are compared. We prefer, here, to treat our subjects as constituting a single group (independent of age), and, through a hierarchical analysis, demonstrate successions of behaviors. This procedure permitted us to avoid any problems arising from the fact that certain behaviors appeared at very different ages according to the subject. In researching the hierarchical scale in the total group studied, we rely uniquely on the constancy of the order of appearance of behaviors without attaching an age to this appearance. This method seems justifiable to us, because we were primarily interested in the relations between behaviors involved, and only secondarily in the ages at which the behaviors appeared.

TABLE 5.1
Experiment 1: Number of correct responses to each question

| Questions | Groups | | | Total |
|---|---|---|---|---|
| | Rule 1 | Rule 2 | Rule 3 | |
| B1 (R + G +) | 9 | 9 | 10 | 28 |
| B2 (R + G −) | 5 | 7 | 4 | 16 |
| B3 (R − G +) | 9 | 5 | 9 | 23 |
| B4 (R − G −) | 8 | 8 | 9 | 25 |
| $A_0$ (enumeration) | 2 | 0 | 3 | 5 |
| C1 (R + G ?)[a] | 10 | 8 | 9 | 27 |
| C2 (R − G ?)[b] | 2 | 2 | 2 | 6 |
| C3 (G + R ?)[c] | 2 | 1 | 2 | 5 |
| C4 (G − R ?)[d] | 4 | 7 | 4 | 15 |

[a]Modus Ponens, correct response is "Yes"
[b]Denial of Antecedent, correct response is "Can't tell"
[c]Affirmation of Consequent, correct response is "Can't tell"
[d]Modus Tollens, correct response is "No"

## Results

We began by examining the correct responses, correctly justified, and by deducting the relation between the behaviors in which we were interested. Then, we completed our initial results with a more clinical analysis.

Because question A (the enumeration of the possible and impossible cases) was difficult to pose, we have only taken account, in certain cases, of the result of the repetition of this question (i.e., question A'). It is possible that the experimenter's enumeration found in question B could have facilitated performance on A', but it is improbable that a subject who is incapable of responding correctly and who lacks the necessary structures could completely memorize such a list.

### Frequency and hierarchy of success

Table 5.1 indicates the number of correct responses to each question (N = 10 per each group).

From this table, the questions can be regrouped into three categories of increasing difficulty:

Category A. The recognition of possible combinations and modus ponens.

Category B. The recognition of impossible combinations and modus tollens.

Category C. The enumeration of possible and impossible combinations and the indeterminate inferences.

Among the questions of even one category, there exists a significant association, and, in each group, the three categories form a Guttman scale, if the fact of responding correctly to more than half of the questions of this category is taken as the criterion for success in a category.

Four stages can, thus, be defined: complete failure, success at category A only, success at categories A and B, and, complete success.

The clinical analysis helps us to better comprehend this order.

### Clinical analysis

Almost all the subjects are capable of correctly responding to the question requiring a modus ponens (C1) and to those which bear on the recognition of the possible cases (B1, B3, B4). These responses are given with a sentiment of very striking obviousness, certainly for the modus ponens:

> A. E. (aged 10.0): *The red light is turned on. What about the green? -* Turned on too. - *How do you know this?* - When the red light is on, the green light is on.

A. E.'s justification of his response, like most of his comrades', amounts to repeating the problem. These children were manifestly embarrassed when asked to give a supplementary justification, because such a conclusion seems evident to them.

The recognition of possible cases presents a few more difficulties, although almost all of the subjects arrived at these correctly. These difficulties arise, more often, from the transformation of the relation into a symmetrical relation. As soon as the subject has comprehended that the two lights do not play the same role, the recognition of possible cases becomes easy:

> R. B. (aged 10.4): *Can the red be turned off and the green turned on? - No. - Why not? -* It is necessary for the red to be be turned on, too. - *Is that what you remember that I just now told you about the lights? -* Yes, when the red is turned on, the green is turned on. - *And when the red is turned off, can the green be turned on? -* Yes, why not? - *And can the red be turned off and the green turned off? -* Yes, also.

The questions of category B (modus tollens and the recognition of the impossible combination) are more difficult and presuppose acquisition of modus ponens. It can be assumed that modus tollens relies on hypothetico-deductive reasoning. In effect, in order to correctly make an inference of this type, it is necessary to be capable of posing an hypothesis ("The red light is turned on") that one nullifies, subsequently, in relation to its consequence with the given reality. For example:

R. C. (10.2):  The red light is turned off. - *How do you know?* - You
have said that when the red is turned on, the green is
turned on. - *But now, are you sure that the red is, indeed, turned off?* - Yes, if the red had been turned on,
the green would have been turned on with it.

In reasoning of this type, the appearance of recourse to the combinatory
structure is not observed; only the ability to reason about hypotheses intervenes. This is confirmed by the fact that some subjects who had correctly
carried out the modus tollens were not necessarily capable of spontaneously
enumerating the ensemble of possible and impossible cases, whereas they all
responded correctly to a question requiring a modus ponens and recognized
the different possible and impossible cases when these were presented.

In the interpretation of these results, it is necessary, nevertheless, to take
account of the difficulty of posing the problem requiring spontaneous enumeration (question A); it is possible that, notwithstanding our efforts, certain subjects did not comprehend what we expected them to do, but were,
nevertheless, competent enough to enumerate the possibilities. However, the
fact that this question forms a coherent scale with the two other categories
shows that the problems arising from this factor of poor comprehension
were probably not important.

In some subjects, some apparently correct modus tollens were, in reality,
due to the interpretation of the problem as a symmetrical relation;[11] that is,
that the two lights are turned on or switched off together. This transformation of the asymmetrical implication relation is obviously difficult to reveal
by examining only the responses to question C4. In order to eliminate such
pseudo-successes, we took account not only of the response and its justification, but also responses to the other questions.

The subjects of the group corresponding to rule 2 ("One never has only
the red light turned on") seemed to handle modus tollens more easily than
others. This problem requires no other supplementary hypothesis: The correct response is merely a translation; all that it is necessary to do, additionally, is to imagine the two lights on simultaneously.

---

[11]Translator's note: Matalon suggests that children transform the implication relation into
a biconditional equivalence relation. A biconditional equivalence relation ("q, if and only if
p") is symmetrical, in that, given "p," one can deduce "q," and vice versa. An implication relation, on the other hand, is asymmetrical, in that, if "p" is true (e.g., "it is a dog"), then "q"
may be deduced (e.g., "it is a mammal"), but one may not deduce "p," given the truth of
"q." The correct inference is "one cannot know whether p is true if q is true;; (e.g., "if it is a
mammal, it may or may not be a dog"). The symmetry of the biconditional comes from the
fact that the only cases that can be true in this relation are "p and q" and "not-p and not-q"
(i.e., both true together, both false together). Even adults are sometimes found to incorrectly
consider "if-then" as a biconditional: However, they can be corrected with minimal feedback.
(See Byrnes & Overton, 1986 and Overton, Byrnes, & O'Brien, 1985).

> N. A. (aged 10.8): The red is turned off. - *Why?* - You just said that the green is turned off. Then the red would be turned on all by itself, and that could not be.

As compared to the other two rules, rule 2 requires one less step in the reasoning. The subjects in the other two groups, after having posed the hypothesis, "the red is turned on," have to deduce (by modus ponens) "the green is turned on;" those of the rule 2 group could be limited to confronting the rule expressed, itself, in terms of a combination (both lights on) with a particular combination (red turned on, green turned off).

The questions of category C (indeterminate inferences and spontaneous enumeration of possible and impossible combinations) require cognition of the complete combinatory structure, in addition to the simpler hypothetico-deductive reasoning that we examined in the preceding paragraph.

In effect, to establish that a situation is indeterminate means to say that the two responses are equally possible, whereas knowing that only one corresponds to the reality. It is, therefore, indispensable for the subject to first abstract sufficiently from the material, and, second, that he master the entire set of possibilities in order to establish that they are all compatible with the problem. Here is an example of a failure, tied to a "hitching on" to one of the possible responses (rule 1):

> H. L. (aged 9.10): *The red light is turned off. - What about the green? -* It is turned off also. *- How do you know? -* Because you have said that when the red is turned on, the green is also turned on. Now, I see that the red is turned off, then the green is too. *- Could it be that the green could still be on? -* No, since it is turned off! *- Now, I am changing everything. [indicating to the subject that it is a new trial]. The red is again turned off, what about the green? -* It is turned on. *- How do you know? -* The green can be turned on by itself, it is not like the red. *- Just now, you said that it was off. -* That has changed.

This example shows us well the difficulty tied to the notion of indetermination: The subject is capable of correctly justifying each of his responses, but not of coordinating them in such a way as to draw the conclusion that both are possible, and, therefore, that one could not know which is the correct one.

The next level is attained when the subject can handle the complete combinatory structure and is found, therefore, capable of taking both inferences into consideration simultaneously.

P. E. (aged 11.3): One cannot know! - *Why not?* - Maybe you have turned on the green. - *Do you know whether I have turned it on?* - No, it is possible to turn off the red and turn off the green.

The response "one cannot know," is very difficult to obtain from children.[12] In effect, all their attitudes, and certainly their school attitudes, lead them to admit that a problem only has one solution: This is certainly an obstacle that has to be taken into account in the appreciation of the preceding results, but it is not the only obstacle, nor the most important. To respond, "One cannot know" (and not simply, "I do not know"), supposes that one is capable of posing several hypotheses, of establishing that there are no other possibilities, and demonstrating that these hypotheses lead to two different conclusions. It is normal that this would be a late-developing behavior. Additionally, for thought which is still very tied to the concrete, it is difficult to dissociate a reality and the judgment about this reality. However, although the subject knows well that the light is either turned on or turned off, that these two states are exclusive, and, therefore, that only one of these responses is "true," he is being asked for a response on another level, a level that, in fact, bears on his knowledge of possibilities and not on the state of the material.

One way for the subject to escape the indetermination is for him to transform the implication into a symmetrical relation: By admitting that both lights are always simultaneously turned on or turned off, it becomes possible to respond without difficulty to all the questions. It is not possible to ascertain from our results whether this symmetrization is a reaction to the difficulties tied to the manipulation of indetermination or a more profound tendency.[13] We will return to this problem in the general conclusions.

Taken together, these results confirm our hypothesis. Among the numerous deductions that one can carry out starting from a statement of an implication, certain ones appear much earlier than others: These are those deductions that most directly translate the statement of the relation.[14] To the extent that the inference demanded requires a greater number of cognitive transformations of the initial statement, the difficulty augments, and the reasoning has to become more and more formal. It would be possible to

---

[12]Translator's note: This finding has been corroborated by a number of recent studies. Byrnes and Overton (1986), for example, found that children below the age of 10-11 do not comprehend the indeterminate inferences even using very familiar rule content and multiple trials of explicit feedback.

[13]Translator's note: It appears to be a "more profound tendency," in that recent studies (e.g., Byrnes & Overton, 1986) indicate a structural change and not simply a response bias.

[14]Translator's note: This is analogous to the "matching bias" found in the adult cognitive literature, where only the cases stated in the rule (i.e., "p" and "q") are considered in inferences (see Evans, 1982).

characterize an inference by its "distance" from the initial statement, a distance that is measured by the number of operations necessary.

## EXPERIMENT 2. NATURAL IMPLICATION

In the experiment that we have just discussed, the implication relation between antecedent and consequent proposed to the subject was absolutely arbitrary. The material utilized, which probably helped the subjects to concretize the questions to a certain extent, did not give them any information capable of guiding them: There was no reason, in the eyes of our subjects, for the two lights to be related in the manner that we indicated, or similarly, that they be related in any way at all. In order to respond correctly, our subjects had used nothing other than the most abstract characteristics of the problem.

In contrast to the former task, we sought to construct a more natural situation, where the relation that interests us would truly seem like an inherent property of the material and which would additionally be a familiar and evident property.

### Material and problems

In front of the subject is placed a "village" of plastic material constituted by a large, circular town square surrounded by five houses, a post office, a church, and a school.

The square is completely enclosed, except for a spot where a road bordered by barriers and trees comes to an end. One house is placed at the beginning of this road. At the extremity of the road, opposite to the village, a "man" (*bonhomme*) is placed. It is explained to the subject that the man lives far from the village and that the only way for him to enter the town is by way of the road, because all around are fields through which he is not allowed to walk. As the man is moved up to the town, it is pointed out that, in doing so, he passes in front of the house at the beginning of the road.

The implication on which the questions are going to bear is the following: "If the man has been to the post office, then he has passed in front of the house."

We then posed the following questions:

Q1a. The man went to the post office. Did he pass in front of the house? (modus ponens)

Q1b. The man did not go to the post office. Did he pass in front of the house? (denial of antecedent)

Q1c. The man passed in front of the house. Did he go to the post office? (affirmation of consequent)

TABLE 5.2
Experiment 2: Number of subjects giving correct responses

| Questions | Age | | | |
|---|---|---|---|---|
| | 6 years | 7 years | 8 years | Total |
| 1a | 15 | 20 | 10 | 45 |
| 1b | 1 | 4 | 2 | 7 |
| 1c | 6 | 5 | 3 | 14 |
| 1d | 14 | 16 | 10 | 40 |
| 2a | 15 | 18 | 10 | 43 |
| 2b | 13 | 17 | 10 | 40 |
| 2c | 12 | 10 | 9 | 31 |
| 2d | 10 | 8 | 0 | 18 |

Q1d. The man did not pass in front of the house. Did he go to the post office? (modus tollens)

Q2a. Is it possible that one day the man passed in front of the house and went to the post office? (p & q)

Q2b. Is it possible that he did not pass in front of the house and went to the post office? (p & not-q)

Q2c. Is it possible that he passed in front of the house and did not go to the post office? (not-p & q)

Q2d. Is it possible that he did not pass in front of the house and did not go to the post office? (not-p & not-q)

After each response we tried to obtain a justification.

The experiment was carried out on 45 subjects from ages 6.4 to 8.7 of primary schools in Geneva. There were 15 six-year-olds, 20 seven-year-olds and 10 eight-year-olds. Their median age was 7.2.

**Results**

Table 5.2 gives the number of correct responses to each question for the three groups considered.

Question 1a, which corresponds to modus ponens, was solved by all the subjects. We took it, moreover, as an indication of comprehension of the problem, providing supplementary indications for the subject when it seemed that the had not comprehended it. In effect, some began by saying that, perhaps, the man had taken another route or had walked across the fields. In any case, it was not difficult to make children of this age comprehend that there truly were no other routes. Subjects easily admitted that people who had been to the post office had necessarily passed in front of the house. The problem amounts to our determining exactly what it is that subjects can infer when placed in front of material that they know "obeys" modus ponens.

The two indeterminate questions (1b and 1c) were solved by few of the subjects, without perceptible change between six and eight years of age. This result confirms the hypothesis that we made in the previous section: Recognizing the indetermination of such questions activates a form of reasoning of a combinatory nature, or one which comes close. The concrete character of the questions posed helped the subjects significantly more for the determinate inferences than for the indeterminate ones.

The responses that we considered as correct did not exactly correspond to those that the older subjects gave in experiment 1: We were content when the subject established the possibility of several responses without him necessarily being able to integrate this in the affirmation that "one cannot know."

> J. P. (aged 7.5): *The man has not been to the post office. Has he passed in front of the house?* - He has been to the school. - *Has he passed in front of the house?* - Yes, in order to go to the school. - *Are you sure that he has been to the school?* - Perhaps he stayed at the house. - *Has he passed in front of the house?* - Ah, no then! - *Can one know whether he has passed in front of the house?* - By looking at it. - *And without looking at it?* . . . .

The incorrect responses correspond, in almost all cases, to a symmetrization of the implication that transforms it into equivalence. However, it seems that this transformation is not carried out in the same fashion when the statements are given in the affirmative or negative form. This might explain the fact that at all ages fewer correct responses are found to question 1b (*the man has not been to the post office*) than to question 1c (*the man has passed in front of the house*). In order to comprehend this difference, it is necessary to remark that the negations of these two propositions, "he went to the post office" and "he has passed in front of the house," are not made in the same fashion.

In effect, "he has passed in front of the house" is only opposed by "he has not passed in front of the house"; the "universe of discourse" corresponding to the proposition is dichotomized in a very simple way, and the different concrete eventualities that could correspond to "he has not passed in front of the house" are not, most of the time, distinguished. In contrast, "he has not been to the post office" corresponds to "he has been to the church, or he has been to the school, or he is staying at the house." The universe in question is more complex than in the previous case, and it is composed of three terms that are not communicated to the subject in the same way: In giving the problem, one has drawn the subject's attention to the village, beyond the post office, school and the church, without explicitly stating the possibility that the man may not come to the village at all.

When one affirms to the subject that "the man passed in front of the house," it suffices, in order to recognize the indetermination of the response, to take into consideration the church and the school.

> A. R. (aged 8.0): *The man passed in front of the house. Has he been to the post office?* - He has been to the school. - *Are you sure that he has been to the school?* - Perhaps he has been to the school, perhaps to the post office.

In contrast, in the other case, the indetermination can only be recognized by taking into consideration the totality of possibilities, in particular, those that are of a different nature than others and that are not often envisioned.

> E. D. (aged 7.10): *The man has not been to the post office. Has he passed in front of the house?.* - Yes. - *How do you know?* - He has been to the church. - *You are sure he has been to the church?* - To the school. - *Has he passed in front of the house?* - Yes, there is no other route. - *The other day, a small boy told me that he is staying at it [the house].* - Then he has not passed in front of the house. - *If one knows only that he has not been to the post office, does one know whether he has passed in front of the house?* - No, he is staying at the house.

In this case, the usual difficulty of simultaneously considering both possibilities was reinforced by the fact that the different eventualities were not perceived as being of the same nature.

Question 1d, the modus tollens, was very frequently solved by all the eight-year-old subjects. This result is all the more striking, because we considered all responses, justified only by a symmetrization of the relation as errors.

The correct responses were given with a sentiment of obviousness almost as great as for modus tollens. It is, contrary to what had gone on in the previous experiment with the lights, interesting to note that the correct response does not require hypothetico-deductive reasoning: It is a simple reading of the properties of the material.[15]

> J. D. (aged 7.3): *The man has not passed in front of the house. Has he been to the post office? -* Ah, no! *- Why? -* He could not take another route.

The difference can be seen between the modus tollens required, here, and that required in the previous experiment: If the subjects had reasoned in the same way in both cases, they would have said (in front of the village): "If he had been to the post office, he would have passed in front of the house. . . ." No subject evidently proceeded in this indirect, hypothetical manner. All those who responded correctly were content, as in the above example, to make an appeal to the properties evident in the material that they had in front of their eyes.

The responses to questions 2a–2d (recognition of possible and impossible combinations) express the evidence of the relations that intervene: With very few exceptions, all the subjects admitted that it was possible that the man passed in front of the house and went to the post office (2a), and, also, that it was impossible that he went to the post office without having passed in front of the house (2b). Moreover, those subjects who had, nevertheless, totally permitted this latter eventuality [i.e., p & not-q is possible], did so by modifying the given data: Their responses were always of the type: "he took another route." The failures to this question, therefore, express more the difficulty for the experimenter to communicate a relatively abstract problem about concrete material in a stable fashion than a limitation on the level of reasoning, itself.

The possibility of combination 2c (passing in front of the house without going to the post office) was sometimes denied; It is a matter again of the symmetrization of the relation:

> A. L. (aged 7.6): *Is it possible that he passed in front of the house and did not go to the post office? -* No, he did not take another route.

The last combination (the man did not pass in front of the house and did not go to the post office) shows a very curious genetic evolution: The num-

---

[15]Translator's note: this problem confronts any study that attempts to assess propositional reasoning in young children. Often, to make the task easier, a concrete apparatus is used as the referent for an "if-then" statement. However, although the questions corresponding to modus ponens, etc., are really about the *rule* and what can be deduced from it, the subjects do not consider the rule but the apparatus, itself, when answering questions. Consulting the apparatus, however,, is not propositional reasoning. Hence, using this methodology leads to false positive assessments. This seems to partially account for the high rate of success in young children found in Kuhn (1977) and Rumain, Connell, and Braine (1983).

ber of correct responses decreased from six to eight years of age, becoming zero in the latter group.

This fact is difficult to interpret using only our results. It seems that it is tied to an abstraction increasing in relation to the material. The youngest subjects had admitted easily enough that the man could sometimes not proceed, even if they were found to be incapable of correctly using this fact in their inferences. The older children, in contrast, had reasoned about a "universe of discourse" already affording a certain degree of abstraction that they had constituted by considering only the cases directly tied to the village, that is, those to which the instructions had drawn their attention. The combination proposed would not be judged, then, on the basis of its intrinsic likelihood, which is how the youngest subjects judged, but in reference to this universe that encompasses only the cases tied directly to the movement of the man. This hypothesis, relative to an abstract "universe of discourse" emerging from the subject's view of the givens, comes close to the hypothesis we made concerning responses to the indeterminate questions. It remains, nevertheless, to be verified, notably by further studying what happens after the age of eight.

A study that we carried out on some 10- and 11-year-olds has shown that even if the number of children who accept the possibility of the man staying at the house increases, there, nonetheless, exist certain reservations at this age. Certain subjects expressed these reservations by saying that, according to instructions, the man went to the village. In contrast, if it was explained that there are several persons at the house when the man visits, the majority of subjects, similar at eight years, admitted without difficulty that it was possible that certain of them remained at the house, and, therefore, did not go to the post office. Although these results are still insufficient, we can propose an hypothesis: Beginning at seven to eight years, subjects constitute, starting from the material, a relatively abstract schema that includes only some of the possibilities that they reason about: Interestingly enough, this schema begins by being, at certain points, less effective than the direct consideration of concrete properties of the material.

### Interpretation of the Findings

We asked some of our subjects, at the end of the experiment, to tell us how they would explain the problem to one of their comrades in order that their comrades would always respond correctly. In the three "lights" groups, the responses either amounted to the repetition of the problem instructions, sometimes distorted in the sense of the symmetrization, or to an enumeration of questions with their responses.

In contrast, several subjects of the "village" group had affirmed that it suffices to say that the man could not proceed in any other way than in front of the house in order to go to the village. This result suggests that the better expression for the relation between the house and the post office would not be "If the man had been to the post office he had passed in front of the house," but rather, "it is necessary to pass in front of the house in order to go to the post office." This formulation is more general than the first, because it states a permanent property of the village, and of the route, and not only of the movements of the man. Moreover, the first formulation, the usual "if-then" of logical analyses, appears to be a consequence of the second, although in what concerns the man, the first would be equivalent to the second.

The reason why modus tollens in the case of the village was so easily solved by subjects is: There is not reason to pose by hypothesis what one seeks to nullify; one only has to establish that a necessary condition is not fulfilled.

Usually the relation of implication is interpreted as the expression of causality or of a logical consequence. We have, here, an example in which these interpretations are not applied; it would be, rather, a relation of condition: "*P implies q*" could be translated by "*q is the (necessary) condition for p.*" The symmetrization of the relation would, then, correspond to a confusion between necessary condition and sufficient condition.[16]

## EXPERIMENT 3. A STUDY ON AN ASPECT OF THE INTRODUCTION OF IMPLICATION

So far, we have limited our study to the problem of determining how subjects interpret the relation (that we as adults interpret as implication) when this relation was presented to them. As we have already remarked, this approach leaves open the complementary problem: Under what conditions would a subject admit that a relation of implication exists between two given propositions? It is this problem that we attempt to address, next, in an exploratory study.

In current language (this is the case to which we are limited), the introduction or acceptance of a relation that we judge to be capable of being formalized as an implication depends on at least two groups of factors. On the one hand, semantic factors (the "sense," or meaning, of the relation and the propositions that it joins) and, on the other hand, more formal factors like

---

[16]Translator's note: It is possible to couch logical relations such as the biconditional and implication in terms of *conditionship* (Wartofsky, 1968). The truth conditions of implication imply that "p" is a sufficient condition for "q," but it is not a necessary condition. For example, in the statement, "if it rains then the grass gets wet," "rain" is sufficient to cause "wet grass," but it is not the only cause. In contrast, the biconditional expresses necessary and sufficient conditions between "p" and "q": For example, "The grass gets wet if and *only if* it rains."

the truth value of the initial propositions.[17] In order to demonstrate this latter factor, we have asked some subjects to judge the admissibility of statements of the form, "if p . . . then q . . . ," where "p" and "q" were chosen from sufficiently different domains in meaning, in such a way that there would be no semantic justification for an implication relation between them. In these conditions, where the truth is very artificial, we can ask: Are there any combinations of truth values of p and q where placing them into a relation by "if-then" seems to be more acceptable? Moreover, in analyzing subjects' rejections of these combinations, we can hope to obtain, by contrast, some idea of certain valid conditions of admissibility among them.

We tested 20 adults, the majority of whom were students in psychology; none had received formal training in logic.

The first question was: "What do you think of sentence 1: "If elephants are pink, then 2 + 2 = 4?"

After having had them make their reservations and objections explicit, we asked them to judge, in the same manner:

2. If elephants are grey, then 2 + 2 = 4.
3. If elephants are pink, then 2 + 2 = 5.
4. If elephants are grey, then 2 + 2 = 5.

If we interpret the "if-then" of these phrases as a material implication, all these propositions are admissible, and only the last is false.

The reactions to sentence 1 were those that one would expect—All the subjects responded with vigor, and their arguments can be said to amount to two principal types: "It is absurd" or "It is false."

The arguments of the first type ("it is absurd") were justified by subjects by the fact that the two propositions have no relation to each other, that the color of elephants has nothing to do with numbers, etc.

The rejection, because of the falsity of the phrase, could have two meanings, according to whether what they had judged false was the antecedent ("elephants are pink") or the entire sentence; it is false to deduce "2 + 2 = 4" from the color of elephants.

After the initial shock caused by this phrase, the others seemed less unacceptable. It is possible that the strong initial reaction could be attributed to surprise. However, some subjects to which we presented the same four sentences in writing, asking them to judge each one after having read them all, also indicated a particular aversion to sentence 1. It presented, therefore, a more markedly unacceptable character than the others, which is confirmed by a detailed analysis of the responses.

Along more general lines, the order of admissibility of the four sentences

---

[17]Translator's note: Overton, Ward, Noveck, Black, and O'Brien (1987) discuss this issue in the consideration of both form and content.

was the following: (3) false → false, (2) true →true, (4) true → false, and (1) false → true.

Sentence 3 was relatively better accepted than the others, because everything is false, and that if, in every way, one is found outside of reality, anything can become acceptable.

Sentence 2 was somewhat less acceptable, because one is found in the domain of truth where certain attitudes of coherence circulate that the phrase seems to violate. However, this very requirement of coherence led some subjects to admit the possibility of a relation between terms pertaining to different domains. As one of them said: "Everything holds. Why could not one find one day a relation between arithmetic and the color of elephants?"

Sentence 4 was rejected more for being false than for being inadmissible. It is well known that, although elephants are grey, 2 + 2 does not make 5. It would seem that the fact of being able to reject the sentence proposed avoids having to be preoccupied with judging its coherence or its meaning. If it is rejected, because it is false (from the point of view of admissibility), it would be less scandalous than the others.

Last, we discovered that sentence 1 was unanimously rejected as false and absurd at the same time.

From such results we can draw some conclusions:

1. The first conclusion, evident from the start, is that the subjects do not judge these sentences in a formal manner, but base their judgments on their content. They look for, before anything else, a link between the two basic propositions.
2. The notions of true and false, applied to propositions, so composed, mean something different to subjects than the corresponding logical notions. Even if sentence 4 is, indeed, judged false, in accord with the formal criteria, none of the other propositions is judged true, except for sentence 2, and even then, under the condition that it turn out to be true at some later date. We see that truth and falsity do not play symmetrical roles: Truth has to be demonstrated whereas falsity, it seems, could be established in a more immediate fashion. It is necessary, however, to guard against generalizing this conclusion too far: It could be due to the unusual character of the propositions utilized in this experiment, which make the judgments of falsity particularly easy.
3. The subjects were scarcely able to distinguish between inadmissibility and falsity, these two notions probably being poorly differentiated by them. Rather than two judgments being situated on different planes, it would seem to be, rather, a matter of two forms of rejection of a proposition for subjects.
4. The acceptance of the implication between p and q is linked to the

recognition of "something in common" between p and q; at an upper limit this could simply be truth or falsity. In effect, the most inadmissible propositions were sentence 1 and sentence 4 (true-false and false-true).

5. Implication is frequently seen as a justification of the consequent by the antecedent. Certain subjects rejected sentence 1 and sentence 2, because "one does not have to go to see the color of elephants in order to know that 2 + 2 = 4." It seems that one of the functions of p → q would be to permit being indirectly assured of the truth of q through the intermediary of establishing the truth of p. The latter proposition would play, then, the role of an index of q, when the latter could not be directly verified.

Moreover, some nonsystematized attempts have shown us that, because "2 + 2 = 4" is generally considered to be *a priori* truth, it is, in general, difficult to admit propositions of the form, "if p, then 2 + 2 = 4," unless p is truly related, such as another simple arithmetic statement. In effect, if q is universally recognized as true in an evident fashion, a phrase of the form, "if p then q," is useless, affords no information, and would, therefore, be rejected.

## CONCLUSIONS

These genetic studies show that formal implication reduced to its combinatory aspect[18] is the result of an evolution and only appears at the formal level. At lower levels, implication is only handled in a partial fashion; that is, only a part of the possible consequences of the statement are effectively drawn by the subject.

At lower levels, which correspond to the concrete stage and to the onset of the formal, the relation between combinations of truth values does not figure prominently: In order for implication to be manipulable in the form of inferences, it must express a concrete relation corresponding to some accepted properties of the material on which reasoning must bear. These inferences appear all the more earlier in children the less they require manipulations of the relation, such as it is communicated to them (i.e., fewer cognitive transformations of the rule) or such as it is drawn by them from the material. Moreover, the genetic evolution, that is, the order according to which the different inferences become possible in the course of

---

[18]Translator's note: "Reduced to it's combinatory aspect" means the ability to generate the possible combinations of the antecedent and consequent in an "if-then" statement using truth values or affirmed and negated versions of these components (e.g., "p and q," "not-p and q," etc). Thus, in the "lights" experiment, this ability amounts to the enumeration of possibilities. This is a formal, computational analysis of a sentence and the variables it describes.

development, depends on the meaning of the relation that is expressed by the implication.

At the higher level, that is, after twelve years of age, the subjects are capable of constructing the entire set of possible and impossible cases that correspond to the concrete relation, which reflects the nature of this level of thought. Therefore, these older subjects handle the given relation as the implication relation of logicians. At this level, there is no fundamental difference between the formal laws of inference regarding implication and the corresponding inferences actually carried out in natural thought. The divergence between natural thought and formal systems certainly appears in the conditions of the *introduction* of implication (i.e., what conditions have to exist between p and q in order for it to be acceptable to relate them through "if p then q"): Only the relations between truth values of propositions are required by classical formal logic, and these do not suffice for subjects. Our study shows that even adults will not agree to relate two propositions by "if . . . then . . . ," or any other equivalent expression, on the basis of only truth values, nor will they agree to pass the truth of one to the other.

Thus, the meaning of implication intervenes in two principal ways in natural thought: In the course of development, it performs a function of concrete support to reasoning; the importance of this function diminishes to the extent that thought approaches the formal level. Adult reasoning seems to be possible once the implication is accepted. That does not mean to say that such reasoning functions effectively. Reasoning about symbols, such as p or q, is always more difficult than reasoning that bears on concrete givens. Nevertheless, it seems that, in contrast to children, the adult is capable of purely formal reasoning.[19] However, even the adult needs an interpretation of the relation in order to accept it.

Regarding the meanings that can be attributed to implication, they could be of several types. Usually one thinks first of causality or logical consequence: "P → q" corresponds then to "p entails q." In this case, the modus ponens is evident and precocious, because, in fact, it is nothing more than

---

[19]Translator's note: A distinction must be made between "purely formal reasoning," as it is used, here, and "formal operational thought." In his *Etudes* and other works, Piaget argued that the manipulation of mathematical symbols ("x," "y," etc.), as in algebra, or of logical symbols ("p," "q," etc.), as in logical proofs, represents "purely formal reasoning," because it does not matter what the symbols stand for in these endeavors. The reasoning required in the studies presented, here, however, consists of the cognitive manipulation of *interpreted* propositions (i.e., propositions that have meaning). Piaget's and Matalon's works do not imply, therefore, that formal operations consists of first converting phrases into "p" and "q" and performing logician's proofs on them, or that free-floating formalisms get "filled in" with content when reasoning begins. Instead, it is more the case that meaningful propositions are transformed and coordinated in formal operational thought. In time, with expertise, a formal operational subject can also cognitively manipulate the "meaningless" symbols of algebra or logic.

the most immediate translation of the relation of entailment or causality.[20] But other interpretations, we have seen, are possible: In particular, when q is a *condition* of p ("for p it is necessary that q," "q, if p"). In this case, the movement of thought goes from q to p. What is important and characterizes the relation, is no longer the conjunction p and q, but the *impossibility of p without q*. The modus tollens, then, appears very soon; the other inferences require an abstraction in relation to the concrete given.

These two relations that we have mentioned (consequence and condition) are situated at the semantic level: They are interpretations of the formal relation. A third type of relation, which has been suggested to us by the experiment on the introduction of implication, takes its importance at the pragmatic level. This is the relation of index: "P is an index of q." Its principle characteristic is its use in knowing q when one could not directly attain it. This pragmatic aspect of implication could explain the aversion of natural thought to admitting certain formally correct propositions. For example, it is evident that a proposition of the form, "p → q," when p is false, could not be used in order to know q. It would, therefore, be rejected.

To the extent that the relations become less interpretable, as in the case of the "lights" material, the combinatorial aspect becomes more important. But it remains, nonetheless, necessary that the two propositions placed in relation could be conceived as pertaining to the same "domain"; the relation between the red and green lights could appear to be completely arbitrary, but is was, nonetheless, admitted by all the subjects that a relation between them was possible. This notion of "domain" remains to be made precise. But it is difficult to foresee an even partial formalization of natural thought that does not take it into consideration. It is probably a matter of a limitation of the type that intervenes in the groupings: Certain operations are only possible by degrees (little by little).

Nothing allows us to affirm that the three possible interpretations of im-

---

[20]Translator's note: It should be pointed out that an implication statement expressing entailment is different than one expressing causality (Copi, 1955). If an entailment relation exists between p and q, then q is said to "follow from" or be "deducible from" p. To be specific, if p is true, then q *has to be* true (i.e., the case "p and not-q" is impossible). In technical terms, entailment is a property of the metalanguage or metalogic of a system and deriving "q" from "p" depends on formal axioms and proof procedures. Thus, entailment is usually not intended for interpreted propositions. To illustrate with content, however, we can see that only tautologous statements, such as "if p, then p," or definitional statements, such as "if John is a bachelor, then John is an unmarried man," can express entailment the way logicians define it, because there is no semantic content that can be sued in the expression, "if p then q," such that the case "p and not-q" will *always* be impossible. This fact is especially true of causal content, because causal hypotheses are often empirically derived and are often falsified in the future (and always falsifiable). If entailment is taken as a belief-state, however, such that the speaker *believes* that "p and not-q" could never happen, then causal content and other contents could be couched in terms of entailment. Perhaps Matalon is referring to this kind of "entailment" (See Ricco, chap. 3 in this volume, for a detailed discussion of entailment).

plication that we have established (relations of consequence, condition, and index) are the only possible ones. Other studies of the same type would be necessary or eventually, analyses of existing texts in order to find some other interpretations, if such alternative interpretations exist.

## ACKNOWLEDGMENTS

This study has been conducted in collaboration with J. B. Grize, who initially supported a psychological study of implication. I thank him heartily for his help.

## REFERENCES

Byrnes, J. P., & Overton, W. F. (1986). Reasoning about certainty and uncertainty in concrete, causal and propositional contexts. *Developmental Psychology*, *22*, 793–799.

Copi, I. M. (1955). *Introduction to logic*. New York: Macmillan.

Evans, J. St. B. T. (1982). *The psychology of deductive reasoning*. London: Routledge & Kegan Paul.

Kuhn, D. (1977). Conditional reasoning in children. *Developmental Psychology*, *13*, 342–353.

Matalon, B. (1963). Etude du raisonnement àpar récurrence sur un modele physique. In P. Greco, B. Inhelder, B. Matalon, & J. Piaget (Eds.), *La formation des raisonnements recurrentiels* (Vol XVII *Etudes d'Epistemologie Genetique*, pp. 283–316). Paris: Presses Universitaires de France.

Overton, W. F., Byrnes, J. P., & O'Brien, D. P. (1985). Developmental and individual differences in conditional reasoning: The role of contradiction training and cognitive style. *Developmental Psychology*, *21*, 692–701.

Overton, W. F., Ward, S. L., Noveck, I. A., Black, J., & O'Brien, D. P. (1987). Form and content in the development of deductive reasoning. *Developmental Psychology*, *23*, 22–30.

Piaget, J. (1962). Introduction. In E. W. Beth, J. B. Grize, R. Martin, B. Matalon, A. Naess, & J. Piaget (Eds.), *Implication, Formalisation et Logique Naturelle*. (Vol XVI of *Etudes D'Epistemologie Genetique*, pp. 1–7). Paris: Presses Universitaires de France.

Rumain, B., Connell, J., & Braine, M. D. S. (1983). Conversational comprehension processes are responsible for reasoning fallacies in children as well as adults: If is not the biconditional. *Developmental Psychology*, *19*, 471–481.

Wartofsky, M. W. (1968). *Conceptual foundations of scientific thought: An introduction to the philosophy of science*. New York: Macmillan.

# 6
# Language and the Acquisition of Logical Knowledge

Rachel Joffe Falmagne
*Clark University*

A comprehensive account of logical development will have to address two kinds of questions, each on a different scale of time and generality. At the most general level, such an account will have to articulate the course of logical development in the context of cognitive development as a whole; it will also have to describe the control processes that regulate, coordinate, and integrate the various acquisitions that proceed concurrently. At the more specific level, an account of logical development must specify the processes underlying microdevelopmental changes, that is, the course of those specific acquisitions that proceed within the context of more general trends and reorganizations. In doing so, it must specify the interplay between the individual's intrinsic mechanisms for acquiring and constructing logical knowledge, and the relevant empirical experience.

It is primarily this second kind of question that this chapter will address. Specifically, the focus of this essay will be on the process of acquisition of principles of deductive inference and of elements of propositional logic at a formal level; the proposal will be developed that knowledge of these principles is derived, in part, from linguistic sources, in partial analogy to the process of syntax acquisition. Yet, these questions must be framed and formulated in the context of the more general developmental concerns; thus, in the last section of this article, I return to the broader epistemological issues concerning logical development, in order to place the discussion in its proper theoretical perspective.

Before going on, it will be useful to pause for a moment and articulate one basic presupposition of this discussion, namely the assumption that people do have deductive principles as part of their cognitive repertoire, and that those principles are represented mentally in some kind of abstract code. There exist some theoretical controversies surrounding this issue in the cognitive literature. On the one hand, some positions maintain, on a variety of conceptual and epistemological grounds, that standard logic, as a whole and complete system, does characterize the laws of thought. Piaget (1953, 1970) and Inhelder and Piaget (1958), in particular, have argued that the standard propositional calculus is the end product of logical development at the formal operational stage. Cohen (1981) has made a similar claim, although on different epistemological grounds and from a non-genetic point of view. At the other pole, some investigators (e.g., Johnson-Laird, 1983; Cheng & Holyoak, 1985) reject the notion that there is *any* formal system of rules that would underlie deductive inference. Finally, other accounts (e.g., Braine, 1978, chap. 7 in this volume; Braine, Reiser, & Rumain, 1984; Gentzen, 1969; Rips, 1983) maintain that the propositional calculus is not a psychologically viable model, and they propose various alternative systems of formal deductive schemata that presumably capture people's logical competence in a psychologically realistic way.

Several issues are often conflated in this area of debate in the literature and, more generally, in debates about human rationality. These issues should be distinguished in the interest of clarity. First, the global issue about human rationality (e.g., Cohen, 1981) is distinct from the question of whether people have a set of formal deductive principles as part of their cognitive repertoire. It is important to realize that, even if the propositional calculus is not a realistic model of human logical cognition, it remains theoretically plausible that people's deductive competence includes *some* formal, abstract schemata. Thus, one can make that assumption without necessarily committing oneself to the propositional calculus as a cognitive model, and this is what I will do here. These schemata are formal in the sense that, once a schema is accessed, it is the logical form of the statement that drives the deductive process. Note that it is not suggested that those schemata are used in all instances in which they are relevant (for a fuller discussion of those points, see Falmagne, Singer & Clement, 1989).

Second, the fact that people make deductive errors or the observation that reasoning often relies on content rather than on logical form, is not, in itself, sufficient grounds for rejecting the assumption of formal schemata (as, e.g., Johnson-Laird, 1983, pp. 39–40, appears to do). Curiously, although this obvious point has become a truism in the study of syntactic aspects of language (i.e., grammatical errors do not mean that we do not have grammar), it is ignored or glossed over in many current discussions of logical cognition. (However, see Cohen, 1981 and Falmagne, 1975, on issues regarding the assessment of competence; Overton, 1985 on related issues; and Feldman & Toulmin, 1976 on issues regarding the assessment of mental structures.)

Finally, assuming that people do have knowledge of formal logical principles as part of their cognitive repertoire need not imply that those formal principles constitute a complete logic, in the logician's sense of completeness. They may simply constitute a fragment of such a logic, a fragment sufficient for human functional purposes. These principles presumably include simple inference schemata, such as modus ponens, which seems to be a direct deductive counterpart of the meaning of "if", simple disjunctive syllogisms, etc., as well as some more complex inferences (e.g., modus tollens or inference schemata such as those proposed by Braine, 1978; Gentzen, 1969; and Rips, 1983).

It seems useful to point out, here, that this is a more liberal notion of logical knowledge than the Piagetian concept of formal operations, but that it shares with it the notion that people do have a formal representation of logical relations and principles. The following discussion focuses on the process through which those principles are acquired, and also briefly examines further developments that occur after they have been acquired.

In the next section, I discuss general plausibility arguments, largely of a conceptual kind, for invoking language as a putative source of logical knowledge. The second section examines, in a speculative way, the cognitive processes underlying the acquisition of deductive schemata through that route, and places that discussion within more general concerns regarding logical development. Illustrative data supporting the feasibility of this proposal are then summarized in the third section as an empirical anchor for those speculations. Finally, epistemological considerations concerning the acquisition process and the role of language in this proposal are discussed in the fourth section.

## LANGUAGE AS A SOURCE OF LOGICAL KNOWLEDGE: GENERAL ARGUMENTS

The hypothesis is proposed that knowledge of principles of deductive inference is derived, in part, from linguistic sources, in partial analogy to the process of acquisition of syntax. I will argue that logical knowledge is derived both from an apprehension of the structure of language itself, and from the correspondences between linguistically expressed propositions and empirical states of affairs; this second, empirical source of knowledge, of course, ensures that the resulting logical system remains semantically sound and internally consistent (although not necessarily complete). Specifically, the hypothesis is that one of the processes underlying the development of deductive competence is a process of abstraction of logical forms from contentful linguistic input.

This is not to say that logical knowledge can only be gained through language or that logical cognition is contingent upon the availability of language to the individual; nor is it suggested that logical development as a whole is functionally dependent on language development. Rather, I will argue that language, as a symbolic system, is one of the sources from which logical knowledge is acquired, and I will support that proposal through a mixture of conceptual, linguistic, and empirical arguments. I will also try to show how the above process articulates with other capacities; in particular, the last section of this article will address the relations between the linguistic and nonlinguistic routes to logical knowledge.

Although some logical structuring may already be present in early senso-rimotor activities (Langer, 1980; Piaget, 1936; Sugarman, 1983), it seems plausible that, once language acquisition has begun, and particularly in the later stages of language development, language, itself, becomes a vehicle for acquiring logical structures, particularly the deductive structures of propositional reasoning.

At least two lines of evidence support this possibility (even if we leave aside philosophical arguments stressing the relations between language and logic). The first concerns the role of logic in linguistic theory and the existence of some parallels between logic and syntax regarding their relation to language. The second, associated line of evidence is a psychological plausibility argument.

First, from a linguistic point of view, there are important analogies between logic and syntax. Both are formal systems of rules that underlie natural language. The relations between syntactic structures and logical structures have been discussed extensively in the linguistic literature (although the exact nature of that relation is a matter of current debate, e.g., Davidson & Harman, 1975; Hornstein, 1984; Sommers, 1982). Also, both logic and syntax, as formal systems, interface with semantics in roughly similar ways to produce the meaning of a sentence (e.g., Lycan, 1984; May, 1985). There are limitations to this analogy, because logical rules are constrained to be consistent with states of affairs in the world in a way that syntax is not (i.e., logical rules ensure that, given factually true premises, only factually true conclusions will be derived)—but these do not affect the force of the present argument.

Second, turning to the psychological consequences of that observation, given the parallels and overlaps between logic and syntax, the fact that children do acquire the syntax of their language makes it plausible to assume that they are equipped for acquiring logical principles as well via linguistic input. The field of language acquisition, especially the work derived from Chomsky's theory, has provided evidence that the child acquires an extraordinarily complex and abstract system of syntactic rules in the process of acquiring language. Whether or not one endorses the assumptions made in that field about the nature of the learning process and about the nature of the learning organism (e.g., see Sinclair, 1976, p. 201, and Piaget, 1980, pp. 57–61, for a critique of Chomsky's nondevelopmental characterization of the learning organism), there is no question that *what* is being learned is an abstract and complex system of formal rules. The child is capable of acquiring such a system on the basis of linguistic input and of semantic and referential information. Logical principles could, therefore, plausibly be acquired through that route as well.

Here, we must distinguish between early syntactic and advanced syntactic development. A number of investigators have argued that early syntactic categories and relations are rooted in action schemata (e.g., Sinclair, 1973), in event schemata (Nelson, 1985, 1986), or on representations of prototypical scenes (Slobin, 1985), although this point of view is not uncontroversial. In contrast, it is widely believed, in keeping with current linguistic theory, that advanced syntactic development involves rules of a largely formal kind, although the acquisition process has been described as relying, in a crucial way, on the child's semantic and pragmatic understanding (Gleitman & Wanner, 1982; Pinker, 1984; Tavakolian, 1981). The focus of this article is on deductive logical principles that are of a propositional kind, and, therefore, it is primarily the functional analogies between logic and the more advanced, formal phase of syntactic knowledge that the argument in this section has stressed. It must be noted, however that the particulars of the process of acquisition of logical principles from linguistic sources may change with the child's level of linguistic competence, as do the particulars of the process of syntax acquisition.[1] In the final section of this article, I will return to broader developmental issues concerning the functional relations between language and thought.

The theoretical notions outlined above are not formulated within a Piagetian framework, and it is, therefore, important to situate the present position with regard to Piaget's theory, which is the major existing theoretical proposal regarding logical development. I will limit myself to the specific statements of that theory that are the pivotal point of dialogue for the present argument.

According to Piaget, language does play a functional role in the development of logical structures, but that role is subsidiary, and the genetic roots of logical structures are strictly nonlinguistic (e.g., Piaget, 1963/1969). The specific function of language differs for concrete versus formal operations. Regarding the former, the role of language as a symbol system is merely to provide mobility and generality to concrete operations. Regarding formal operations and the attainment of propositional logic, which are closest to our present concerns, the role of language becomes more central, and language may even be necessary to the achievement of a fully elaborated system of thought. Yet, it is necessary as mode of expression and regulation and as a means of "symbolic condensation" (Piaget, 1964/1967); i.e., it serves a supportive rather than a constitutive function. It is not a source of logical knowledge; in particular, in relation to the specific focus of this chapter, it is not the source of knowledge of principles of deductive inference.

---

[1]I wish to thank Nancy Budwig for interesting discussions of those issues.

However, as argued above, it does seem plausible that, once the child becomes a linguistic being, the linguistic domain, itself, provides an avenue for logical acquisitions. In fact, it is interesting to note that a great deal of Piaget's argument against this possibility rests on his description of formal operations as "structures d'ensemble," characterized by the lattice of possible combinations and the group of four transformations (see, e.g., Piaget, 1963/1969, 1964/1967). Single logical operations and deductive principles are not considered formal unless this entire structure is in place. A liberalized version of Piaget's theory, in which this structural requirement would be lifted, may actually allow for a conception of the role of language compatible with the present conception.

The argument developed to this point is a plausibility argument for the linguistic route to logical knowledge. In the next section, more specific speculations about the acquisition process are discussed. Before proceeding to those speculations, however, a brief word of caution will be useful. A considerable body of work conducted within the Piagetian framework has examined the effectiveness of linguistic training for acquiring certain cognitive constructs, such as conservation and concepts of classification and seriation (e.g., Inhelder & Sinclair, 1969; Inhelder, Sinclair, & Bovet, 1974; Morf, Smedslund, Vinh-Bang, & Wohlwill, 1959). This work has predominantly provided negative evidence about the effectiveness of linguistic training for those acquisitions (although, Beilin, 1976 and others have challenged that conclusion). These results have been interpreted as indicating that language has a subsidiary status with respect to the formation of logical structures. However the logical structures tapped by that work are different from those of concern here. Conservation is a largely empirical phenomenon, despite the cognitive operations that it involves. Furthermore, concepts of class inclusion and seriation pertain to the logic of classes and relations. In contrast, the focus of the present discussion is on general deductive principles and logical structures of a propositional kind (that is, on principles that have a more direct structural and functional relation to language). Thus, the existing results originating from the Piagetian research on language and "logic" do not have a direct, substantive bearing on the present issues.

## THE PROCESS OF ACQUISITION
## OF DEDUCTIVE SCHEMATA

How are deductive schemata acquired or constructed so that they come to be known at a formal level (i.e., so that the child comes to have a formal representation of a deductive schema)? It is hypothesized that this happens in part through a process of abstraction of logical forms from specific, meaningful instances embodying that form. Thus, the child would abstract structural concepts corresponding to inference schemata from the linguistic input and from appropriate feedback either from the adults or from real world events about which inferences are correct and which are not. (Feedback is essential to this account, of course).

There is, however, a potential conceptual and metatheoretical problem in this account. After all, how can the child identify the logical structure of the argument, unless the child already understands the argument? Furthermore, one might argue that understanding the argument presupposes apprehending its logical form. This is a typical bootstrapping problem that is faced by any account of induction: How can one induce something that one does not already know?

As will be discussed later in this section, the acquisition process is not assumed to be strictly inductive; important, nonempiricist ingredients are assumed to play a crucial role in interaction with inductive procedures. However, inductive processes are sufficiently central to the hypothesized acquisition process to require that the bootstrapping issue be addressed.

In the present account, bootstrapping is provided by the conjunction of two important facts. The first is related to the role of logic in linguistic theory. Work in linguistic semantics makes it clear that the semantic representation of a sentence does include its logical form (see, e.g., Lycan, 1984; May, 1985, for extensive treatments of that question). Thus, the very process of understanding language involves mentally representing logical structures. Clearly, the foregoing statement does not presuppose that the child or the adult will apprehend the logical structure of a sentence whose logical structure he/she does not know. Rather, the point it that the logical structure of a sentence or set of sentences is embedded in the structure of contentful and semantic relations characterizing that sentence, and, therefore, is implicitly available at that contentful level for further acquisition at a formal level.

The second fact that converges to enable the necessary bootstrapping is that, at the early phase of acquisition, before the logical form is known at a formal level, the meaning of a sentence, as well as the relations between sentences, are understood by means of semantic relations and event and action schemata that are available to the child. These schemata consist of information organized around different classes of events, specifying both invariant and optional aspects of those events, and prototypical relations between events or event components. It is widely accepted that such knowledge structures are implicated in memory and language comprehension (Bobrow & Norman, 1975; Bower, Black, & Turner, 1979; Bransford & Johnson, 1972; Rumelhart, 1980; Rumelhart & Ortony, 1977; Schank, 1981; Schank & Abelson, 1977). In the study of early language development, some investigators have argued that knowledge structures of that kind form the basis from which early semantic and, most crucially for the present argument, syntactic knowledge is derived (Nelson, 1985, 1986; Slobin, 1973, 1985). Likewise, on the present account, at the initial phase of acquisition, it is possible to understand a deductive argument on the basis of the thematic and pragmatic structure by using elementary semantic relations, event schemata and schema-related procedures.

Thus, at this initial phase, the functional representation of the sentence or of the argument is meaningful, or content-specific, and it is this functional representation that underlies understanding of the sentence or of the argument. Put another way, the argument can be understood in a rudimentary way at that contentful level without having an *explicit mental representation* of its logical form.

At a somewhat more advanced, intermediate phase of understanding, the child is able not only to understand the argument, but also to carry out spontaneous correct deductions when the material is meaningful and familiar to him/her, although unable to carry out the same logical inference with unfamiliar or abstract material. In those cases, the functional representation of the sentence still is a schema-based, contentful representation. Yet, at this intermediate stage, the child does have some content-specific deductive procedures that manipulate contentful representations. Thus, the deductive process is carried out in this contentful mode. As an example, many conditional "if-then" statements refer to events that have causal structure (e.g., "If you push your doll, it is going to fall"). Prior to apprehending the general properties of conditional statements (i.e., those formal properties that are common to causal statements, to some temporal statements, and to statements expressing threats and promises), the child understands the causal relation between events marked by "if-then"; the statement is understood at that thematic, causal level (see, e.g., Bowerman, 1986),[2] and so are the subsequent events (i.e., the doll falling when it is, indeed, pushed). The formal properties of conditional statements are implicit in that causal structure, as they are in other relevant thematic structures (e.g., temporal structures, such as "If it is six o'clock, then mother arrives home"; and pragmatic structures of threats and promises, such as "If you do your homework, then you'll get to go to the movies"). When the doll does fall as a result of being pushed, when the mother does arrive home at six o'clock, or when the reward is given after the child completes the homework, each of those thematically specific inferential structures is presumably understood or carried out in its specific thematic mode (causal, temporal, or pragmatic), not unlike the process hypothesized by Cheng and Holyoak (1985).[3]

However, and most importantly, each of these inferential events contains, embedded within it, the abstract structure of a modus ponens inference (if

---

[2]I am indebted to Nancy Budwig for bringing this article to my attention initially.

[3]However, Cheng and Holyoak assume that thematic deductive schemata of that kind are the end product of development, whereas the present account assumes the further emergence of a more abstract formal representation.

p, then q; p; therefore, q). This is the crucial fact that will enable subsequent development of a formal understanding, namely the fact that the logical structure of the argument is *implicit* in its thematic structure although it is not apprehended and is not explicitly represented.

In early phases of understanding, the logical structure has not been disembedded from its contentful realizations. This disembedding is presumed to occur through a process of abstraction as the child encounters the same logical form embedded in different contentful realizations but marked lexically by the connective "if-then." As described previously, while the child either conducts or understands each of those specific inferences on the basis of their contentful mental representation, the common logical form is implicit in the representation and processing of these arguments, although it is not functionally directing them. When the child subsequently realizes that the same mental procedure is involved in inferences carried out in those various thematic modes, in response to (at the time) context-specific meanings of "if-then," a formal mental representation of the logical form of the inference emerges. Thus, disembedding occurs through a process similar to the Piagetian reflective abstraction from the child's own mental procedures.

The acquisition process just outlined is assumed to apply both to those simple, almost lexical inferences such as modus ponens, which have been argued (e.g., Braine, 1978) to constitute the very meaning of "if-then," and to those more complex inferences such as modus tollens ("If p, then q; not q; therefore, not p"), and so on. Thus, in the example given earlier in this section, the abstraction process led the child to acquire the formal structure of a modus ponens inference and, correspondingly, the conditional structure of "if-then" as part of the lexical entry of that connective. In the next section, acquisition of more elaborate conditional inferences will be illustrated empirically and discussed.

Earlier in this chapter, I suggested some parallels between logic and syntax as formal systems structuring language, and I speculated that there may be parallels in their acquisition process as well. In that context, it is interesting to note that investigators in the area of syntax acquisition have had to invoke, as we had to do here, a "semantic bootstrapping" process to be able to account for the acquisition of syntactic rules (Gleitman & Wanner, 1982; Pinker, 1984; Grimshaw, 1981); in other words, the child must have *some* semantic, pragmatic, and referential understanding of the sentence before being able to generate hypotheses about the syntactic structure of the sentence. Thus, in the initial phases of acquisition of syntax, the child learns to structure his/her linguistic environment syntactically by exploiting the interconnections between syntactic, semantic, and contextual aspects of language. (The relative role of formal and semantic/contextual ingredients in that acquisition is different for those different investigators, but a detailed discussion of those issues is beyond the scope of this paper.) In a similar fashion, I have proposed that the child structures the linguistic environment logically, in terms of the logical form of deductive arguments, by exploiting the interconnections between logical structure, event structure, and semantic relations.

A few comments about the nature of the acquisition process are in order. First, this acquisition is not assumed to be strictly inductive, in contrast to what an empiricist account would maintain. I will return to this point in the final section, when discussing epistemological considerations. In particular, concurrent acquisitions of the kind that I have described clearly do not proceed independently from one another; in addition to "direct" learning and abstraction of logical principles, we must assume the operation of autonomous rational constructions and regulations. For instance, it is unlikely that a person who has acquired three of the four deductive principles of conditional inference is dependent on environmental input for acquisition of the fourth principle. Indeed, one of the experiments to be described in a later section provides interesting evidence to that effect. Conversely, if an inference schema were contradictory with respect to a previously acquired schema, cross-consistency checks, and elimination or synthesis, would presumably occur.

Second, and importantly, the data provided by the child's linguistic and nonlinguistic environment only afford information about the *correctness* (or incorrectness) of inferences. In order to infer that a given inferential form is *valid*, a cognitive leap from recognition of correctness to ascription of validity is necessary (clearly, again, a nonempiricist ingredient in the acquisition process).

Third, we must obviously assume that what can be acquired at a certain point may be subject to structural constraints imposed by the level of cognitive functioning of the child, as a number of theorists have argued. In particular, on the present account, we must assume that those logical acquisitions that are linguistically based and those acquisitions that are not will converge, as will be discussed in the final section of this article. Nevertheless, the development of specific logical competencies within those constraints and within those regulations needs to be understood, and the foregoing speculations are an attempt to do so.

The discussion to this point has focused on the process of acquisition of deductive principles at a formal level. What happens next, once those principles are acquired? I have argued, elsewhere (Falmagne, 1980, 1989), that two levels of mental representation must be distinguished in logical cognition: The long-term memory representation of logical knowledge (including deductive schemata) and the functional representation of the sentence or problem in working memory (the representation on which the deductive process operates). When the formal structure of the problem is recognized (i.e., when a mapping occurs between the problem and some logical form available in long-term memory), then the functional representation is formal, and deduction happens in that mode. However, when the formal structure of the problem is not recognized (although that logical form may be available in long-term memory), the functional representation is contentful, and deduction occurs in that mode (Clement & Falmagne, 1986; Falmagne, Singer, & Clement, 1989; see also, Hoch & Tschirgi, 1985; Overton, Ward, Noveck, Black, & O'Brien, 1987).

Therefore, development beyond acquisition of a formal deductive principle (presumably the case in adults) involves an enrichment of the cues and processes that point to that schema in its various instantiations, so that deduction can be carried out with explicit reliance on logical form in an increasingly broader range of situations. (Notions related to these, although only partly so, have been discussed by Braine & Rumain, 1983, as "comprehension factors in reasoning," and by Overton, 1985.) The development of deductive reasoning in adolescence and adulthood may largely involve this greater and greater effectiveness in the "translation" process that accesses deductive schemata, in ever more complex linguistic embodiments. It may, furthermore, continue to involve the formal structuring described in this section.

## SOME EMPIRICAL ILLUSTRATIVE DATA

This section will briefly examine findings from three studies conducted by my research group that support the assumption that formal deductive schemata can be acquired through a process of abstraction from linguistic instances. The first two studies focus on a deductive principle that is sometimes used correctly by children in suitable meaningful contexts; the results will suggest that, in the course of the experimental manipulation, a formal representation of the principle emerged, at least for some children. The third study focuses on a (indeterminate) deductive principle, which is not mastered at all, at any level, initially; the results suggest that an entirely novel acquisition may have occurred in that case.

It is important to stress very clearly the status of these studies with respect to the present theoretical argument. They are conceived of as "feasibility" studies at the psychological level. Their aim was to assess whether children have the necessary cognitive capacity that would make the hypothesized acquisition process viable. The experiments are not thought to mimic the real life experience; they are intended to illustrate the feasibility of acquiring a formal principle through abstraction from contentful instances.

The first two experiments (Falmagne, Thompson, & Bennett, 1979; Thompson, 1977) focused on one pattern of conditional inference, modus tollens, respectively in third and fifth graders, and in fourth graders (with ages ranging from 7:11 to 11:2 years, overall). This pattern is not well mastered by children in that age group, as documented by a range of results in the literature (see Braine & Rumain, 1983 for a review; and see Byrnes & Overton, 1986) and by the error rate in our control groups. Children at those grade levels received a number of different "word problems" of the modus tollens form (e.g., "If it is Friday, then Bob has math; Bob doesn't have math today; Is it Friday?", with the three response choices "yes," "no," "can't tell") mixed with other problems. Children received feedback after each response about what the correct response was, but no explanation and no direct instruction was given. A transfer session without feedback then assessed whether children had abstracted the logical form of a modus tollens inference. The transfer session included several types of problems of the same logical form (modus tollens) as those encountered during training, but differing from them in surface structure (in a manner to be described shortly), so as to distinguish abstraction of a general concept specifically based on the *logical form* of the argument from learning of a narrow concept based on surface structure cues. The two experiments used the same general procedure and design, with some differences not relevant to the present discussion.

The results, comparing performance on the transfer task in the experimental groups described above to that of controls who only received the transfer task, or to controls who received irrelevant, nonconditional training, indicated that training was effective. Furthermore, importantly, in both studies, the effect extended to all new variations included in the transfer task.

Thus, transfer occurred when the conditional statement in the first premise was expressed with the consequent clause *preceding* the antecedent clause (e.g., "Mary has gym today if it is Tuesday") in contrast to the training problems in which the consequent clause was second, which rules out possible irrelevant concepts based on clause order. Transfer extended to problems using the connective "when-then," logically equivalent to "if-then" (with one qualification not relevant here), which indicated that the concept abstracted was not connective-specific. Transfer also extended to problems in which the second premise (the "not q" clause) lexically negated the "q" clause in the first premise, rather than negating it propositionally (e.g., "The book is red" is negated lexically by "The book is blue," and propositionally by "The book is not red"), which demonstrated that the concept attained relied on negation at the level of logical form rather than on surface structure negation. Thus, the concept acquired appears genuinely to rely on the logical form of the inference rather than on surface structure cues.

Finally, and most crucially, transfer extended to nonsense problems that had the logical form of a modus tollens inference but used nonsense content words (e.g. "If Paul fibbles, then he thabbles."). In fact, the improvement was largest for those problems, whose error rate in the experimental group became equivalent to the error rate of meaningful problems, whereas the error rate was close to chance for the controls. Because the children had not received nonsense problems during training, this finding strongly suggests that children abstracted the structure of a modus tollens inference at a formal level and were able to recognize it in problems devoid of referential meaning (i.e., that children constructed a formal representation of the principle).

Although children generally do poorly with the modus tollens inference, they occasionally seem to be able to use specific content-bound procedures that lead them to the correct answer; this appears to occur particularly when the material is immediately familiar (Kuhn, 1977; Overton, Ward, Noveck, Black, & O'Brien, 1987). As a consequence, the present findings probably do not point to a novel acquisition, although this might be true of some of the younger children. Rather, these findings, particularly those regarding nonsense problems, presumably indicate that training resulted in a new level of abstraction of children's mental representation of that schema. More specifically, they suggest that a formal representation of the schema became available. Note that this is, in itself, of interest, as our theoretical focus is the emergence of a formal representation of deductive principles.

However, in terms of the general acquisition process discussed earlier, it is important to determine whether entirely novel inferences can be acquired through that process. Sarah Bennett Lau examined this question in her dissertation (Bennett Lau, 1983). The particular inference of interest was the indeterminate conditional inference, affirming the consequent ("If p then q; q; no conclusion can be drawn about p") (For instance, "If the boy is wearing his red shirt, then he is looking in the mirror; the boy is looking in the mirror; Is he wearing his red shirt?"). One hundred children, 10- through 11-years-old, (fifth graders) served as subjects.

It has been well documented that people, and particularly children, have difficulty recognizing the indeterminate character of affirming the consequent arguments (AC) and of the other indeterminate conditional argument, denying the antecedent (DA). (See Braine & Rumain, 1983; Kodroff & Roberge, 1975; O'Brien & Overton, 1980, 1982; Taplin, Staudenmayer, & Taddonio, 1974.) A number of accounts of that difficulty have been proposed, some of which invoke lexical ambiguity or conversational conventions (e.g., Rumain, Connell, & Braine, 1983; Wason & Johnson-Laird, 1972). This is not the place to review that specific issue in detail. However, for the sake of the present discussion, the important point to note is that children do show the usual difficulties, even in tasks in which the information is conveyed entirely nonverbally via the properties of a visual display (Champaud, 1985; Champaud & Jakubowicz, 1979). This indicates that the difficulty cannot be explained by linguistic, conversational factors exclusively.[4] Thus, the overall converging evidence is that this is simply not a deductive schema that people of that age have in their mental repertoire.

---

[4]The only attempts to override this difficulty that have proven successful have involved explicitly stating countermanding implicative statements that make explicit the asymmetry of the conditional relation (Overton, Byrnes, & O'Brien, 1985; Hoch & Tschirgi, 1985; Rumain, Connell, & Braine, 1983). That this method has been successful is interesting but ambiguous regarding our present concerns: It can be argued that a different deductive schema is involved in that case, a schema involving three, rather than two, premises. The authors interpret their results as indicating that the lexical entry for "if-then" is the conditional but that conversational conventions are responsible for the usual biconditional results. However, as stated in the text, children's "conditional" difficulties remain in tasks that are entirely nonverbal.

The main purpose of this experiment was to examine whether an entirely novel schema could be abstracted from thematic instances, as the acquisition hypothesis maintains. A second focus was to examine whether acquisition of a novel schema would lead to reorganization of existing schemata. Specifically, because treating affirming the consequent as indeterminate entails recognizing the asymmetry of the conditional relation, we asked whether this acquisition would lead to insight into the "companion" inference, denying the antecedent. This is an important question in the context of global concerns about reorganizations and regulations in the course of concurrent acquisitions.

The general design and procedure were similar to those of the previous studies, with the transfer task, again, including nonsense problems, problems with reversed clauses and problems with alternative connectives. In addition, this study also varied the connective used in training, to assess whether expressions including modal terms (e.g., "If Jack wears his plaid pants, then he *has to* wear this green shirt") or nonpropositional connectives ("*Whenever* Jack wears his plaid pants, then he has to wear his green shirt") would be more effective than the standard "if-then" formulations as vehicles for acquiring the structure of the indeterminate affirming the consequent argument. Aside from these three experimental groups, one control group received *nonconditional* indeterminate arguments during training, and a second control group only underwent the transfer task.

As in the previous experiments, training (with feedback but without explanations) was effective: All three experimental groups performed better than either control group on the transfer task. Importantly, the fact that the experimental groups were superior to the control group trained with *nonconditional* indeterminate problems shows that the relevant ingredient in training was the specific structure of *conditional* indeterminate arguments, rather than general exposure to indeterminate arguments. As was the case in the previous studies, transfer effects extended across all the new variations of affirming the consequent inferences in the transfer task. Thus, training in this study, also, led to abstraction of the logical form of the inference: The structural concept acquired was abstract enough to span variations in surface structure and several lexical variations in the expression of conditional relations, indicating that the concept was not connective-specific, and the concept was abstract enough to enable recognition of the relevant logical form when nonsense content was used. Of further importance, given the variety of results in the literature mentioned earlier, this result is likely to point to a novel acquisition.

Regarding the second question, concerning spontaneous reorganizations, learning of one indeterminate inference (affirming the consequent) did, indeed, have repercussions on children's understanding of the other, companion inference (denying the antecedent); performance with denying the antecedent improved despite the fact that children had never encountered that inference during training. Although this difference just missed significance, it, nevertheless, constitutes an extremely important suggestion that acquisition of this structural concept of an affirming the consequent inference may have led the child to reconceptualize her/his understanding of the conditional relation as an asymmetrical relation.

What do those results mean? In the context of the argument developed to this point, they mean that children are cognitively equipped for abstracting logical forms on the basis of linguistic experience with that logical form embedded in contentful material, and feedback. In other words, children appear to be cognitively equipped for carrying out the abstraction process that has been hypothesized to underlie the acquisition of logical knowledge via the linguistic route. In the case of modus tollens, this abstraction was presumably carried out from an initial fragmentary, thematically restricted understanding of the inference. In this case, children reached a higher level of abstraction in their mental representation of the principle. In contrast, in the case of the indeterminate inference, what took place may have been the abstraction of an entirely new schema.

Two points need to be stressed before concluding this section. First, as indicated previously, these studies should be thought of as feasibility studies. They do not purport to argue that a major, long-term developmental change was produced by our experimental manipulation. Rather, they attempt to demonstrate *in vitro*, so to speak, that abstraction of logical forms can occur on the basis of linguistic experience coupled with feedback.

The second point is extremely important. In these studies, all the relevant problems used in *training* had the same surface form, aside from having the same logical form (e.g., the "if" clause always preceded the "then" clause), and the second premise always used explicit, propositional negation rather than lexical negation. So, the children *could* have abstracted that narrow concept tied to surface structure, and that would have been a correct concept to abstract, given their experience. However, this was not the case, since learning transferred to the entire range of surface variations that had never been encountered. Thus, children made the cognitive leap of abstracting the deeper, *logical* form of the inference, rather than its surface form. The significance of this observation is discussed in the next section.

## EPISTEMOLOGICAL CONSIDERATIONS

In these concluding comments, I will address two epistemological issues, one concerning the nature of the acquisition process, the other concerning the functional role of language in logical development.

The acquisition process outlined in this discussion is not assumed to be strictly inductive, in contrast to what an empiricist epistemology would hold. One of the ways in which it is not regards autoregulations, which are assumed to occur in the course of concurrent acquisitions. As an illustration, Bennet Lau's (1983) results suggest that acquisition of one indeterminate conditional inference led children to reconceptualize their understanding of the conditional relation as asymmetrical and to "invent" the other indeterminate inference.

The observation made in the preceding section, that children in our studies appeared to make the cognitive leap of abstracting the logical form of the inferences rather than its surface form, points to another nonempiricist feature of the acquisition process. This observation is of particular interest in light of the previous discussion concerning the parallels between logic and syntax and the possible (although partial) parallels between logic acquisition and syntax acquisition. It is widely believed (e.g., Baker & McCarthy, 1981; Chomsky, 1980a,b; Lust, 1981; Pinker, 1984) that, in the process of acquiring syntax, the range of hypotheses that the child will entertain for specific syntactic rules is constrained in a principled way. What we may be observing, here, is a similar phenomenon, that is, in searching for formal regularities in the structure of deductive arguments, the child bypasses a set of logically irrelevant hypotheses.

Returning to the nature of the acquisition process, a strictly rationalist account, that is, that logic would be, in some wholesale sense, "innate," seems as unappealing intellectually as a strictly empiricist assumption, and, furthermore, utterly vague, unless such an account specified the nature of the initial state of knowledge in the infant and the conditions required for the actualization of the final state. Both empirical and philosophical considerations suggest that the acquisition of logical knowledge is both constrained and made possible by fundamental properties of the mind—minimally by fundamental cognitive ways of processing experience.

There are two components in the above statement: capacity and constraint. Regarding the former, one basic cognitive function implicated in the acquisition process described is the human capacity for abstraction. That capacity operates in the early stages of development in the emergence of the symbolic function, and it operates at later stages of development in the formal structuring that underlies syntactic development, for example. It provides the mechanism for qualitative discontinuities in the development of thought and of language. The acquisition process described in this chapter, leading to the formal representation of deductive schemata, relies on this abstraction capacity in a fundamental way. A second basic cognitive function is implicated in the cognitive leap that the child must make in order to ascribe *validity* to a given inference form on the basis of observations regarding the *correctness* of specific inferences instantiating that form, as was remarked previously.

Secondly, it seems natural to posit that the domain of possibilities entertained in the course of the inductive process involved in acquisition of logical principles is constrained in a principled way. On the other hand, what constraints should be invoked is far from being clear at this point.[5] In the case of syntax acquisition, Chomsky (e.g., 1980a) postulates the existence of innate linguistic universals as constraints for the child's syntactic hypotheses. But note that there are two parts to that claim. One is that there must be constraints on grammar. The other is that those are language-specific, rather than being general cognitive constraints. Whereas the first claim seems compelling, both on conceptual and on empirical grounds, the second is not, even in the case of syntax. In the case of logic, such a claim would be even more implausible, of course, because logic cannot possibly be an autonomous formal system functionally separate from other capacities.

Reinforcing the previous point about logic, constraints from nonlinguistic cognitive structures need to be invoked in the present account, because the linguistic and nonlinguistic sources of logical knowledge must merge into a coherent logical system. As will be elaborated shortly, this merging is made possible by the fact that language, itself, is structured in a way that makes it semantically sound.

Turning now to the functional role of language in logical development, it is worth reiterating that the present account is not intended to account for all of logical development. It is not suggested that logical knowledge is only gained through that route. Rather, the argument is that language is one of the sources from which logical knowledge is gained. The functional relationships between language and thought do change in the course of development, as both Piaget (e.g., 1964/1967) and Vygotsky (1962, 1978; See also Wertsch, 1985, pp. 77–129) have argued on different grounds. In that context, it is natural to assume that the functional relations between language and, specifically, logical structuring, change in a similar manner, and that, in the course of that development, the epistemological force of language increases and perhaps is radically transformed as an instrument of logical knowledge. This would mean that, although the origins of logic might be sensorimotor, as argued by Piaget, Inhelder, Sinclair, and others, higher forms of logic might be derivable from linguistic structures themselves. In particular, deductive propositional inference obviously bears a close epistemological relation to language, and, therefore, is a plausible candidate for such an acquisition route.

Naturally, if logical knowledge can be derived from linguistic as well as nonlinguistic sources, those two acquisitions must merge into the same coherent logical system. This is, of course, made possible by the fact that language, itself, is structured so as to be semantically consistent. Thus, logical principles derived from language are guaranteed to lead to empirically sound deductions, as are logical principles derived from nonlinguistic routes. This statement, of course, presupposes at least a moderate realist po-

---

[5]Although, there have been isolated proposals on specific points (Osherson, 1977) regarding constraints on the naturalness of logical connectives.

sition on the foundations of logic, but moderate realism on that matter seems eminently sensible.

In relation to the preceding remarks on the nature of the acquisition process, the fact that the linguistic and nonlinguistic routes to logical knowledge must merge into a coherent logical system suggests many points of dialectical exchange between the present theory and Piaget's theory, although the epistemological force of language is distinctively greater in this proposal than it is in Piagetian conceptions of development.

## ACKNOWLEDGMENTS

The research reported in this article was supported, in part, by Grant SED 80-21459 from the National Science Foundation.

I wish to thank Nancy Budwig, Michael Bamberg, and Willis Overton for their helpful comments and suggestions on the manuscript, and Rochel Gelman, Sylvia Scribner, Beatrice de Gelder, and Sarah Bennett Lau for useful discussions on an earlier version.

## REFERENCES

Baker, C.L., & McCarthy, J. J. (Eds.). (1981). *The logical problem of language acquisition*. Cambridge, MA: MIT Press.

Beilin, H. (1976). Constructing cognitive operations linguistically. In H. Reese (Ed.), *Advances in child development and behavior* (Vol. 2, pp. 67-106), New York: Academic Press.

Bennett Lau, S. (1983). *The learning of indeterminate arguments by children in the context of a syllogistic reasoning task*. Unpublished doctoral dissertation, Clark University.

Bobrow, D. G., & Norman, D. A. (1975). Some principles of memory schemata. In D. G. Bobrow & A. M. Collins (Eds.), *Representation and understanding: Studies in cognitive science*. New York: Academic Press.

Bower, G. H., Black J. B., & Turner, T. J. (1979). Scripts in text comprehension and memory. *Cognitive Psychology, 11*, 177-220.

Bowerman, M. (1986). First steps in acquiring conditionals. In E. Traugott, A. ter Meulen, J. S. Reilly, & C. A. Ferguson (Eds.), *On conditionals*. Cambridge: Cambridge University Press.

Braine, M. D. S. (1978). On the relation between the natural logic of reasoning and standard logic. *Psychological Review, 85*, 1-21.

Braine, M. D. S., Reiser, B. J., & Rumain, B. (1984). Some empirical justifications for a theory of natural propositional logic. In G. H. Bower (Ed.), *The psychology of learning and motivation: Advances in research and theory* (Vol. 18, pp. 313-371). New York: Academic Press.

Braine, M. D. S., & Rumain, B. (1983). Logical reasoning. In J. H. Flavell & E. M. Markman (Eds.), *Carmichael's handbook of child psychology. Vol. III. Cognitive development* (pp. 263-340). New York: Wiley.

Bransford, J. D., & Johnson, M. K. (1972). Contextual prerequisites for understanding: Some investigations of comprehension and recall. *Journal of Verbal Learning and Verbal Behavior, 11*, 717-726.

Byrnes, J. P., & Overton, W. F. (1986). Reasoning about certainty and uncertainty in concrete, causal, and propositional contexts. *Developmental Psychology, 22* 793-799.

Champaud, C. (1985). Acceptation et refus de l'indetermination chez des enfants de six a huit ans (Acceptance and rejection of indeterminacy in six to eight years olds). *Archives de Psychologie, 53*, 205, 273–292.

Champaud, C., & Jakubowicz, C. (1979). Situation hypothetique et conditions de production des enonces avec SI: Etude genetique (Hypothetical situations and conditions for production of "if" statements: A genetic study). *Bulletin de Psychologie, 32*(341), 773–790.

Cheng, P. W., & Holyoak, K. J. (1985). Pragmatic reasoning schemas. *Cognitive Psychology, 17*, 391–416.

Chomsky, N. (1980a). On cognitive structures and their development. In M. Piattelli-Palmarini (Ed.), *Language and learning: The debate between Jean Piaget and Noam Chomsky* (pp. 35–52). Cambridge, MA: Harvard University Press.

Chomsky, N. (1980b). *Rules and representations*. New York: Columbia University Press.

Clement, C. A., & Falmagne, R. J. (1986). Logical reasoning, world knowledge, and mental imagery: Interconnections in cognitive processes. *Memory & Cognition, 14*, 299–307.

Cohen, L. J. (1981). Can human irrationality be experimentally demonstrated? *Behavioral and Brain Sciences, 4*(3), 317–370.

Davidson, D., & Harman, G. (1975). *The logic of grammar*. Encino, CA: Dickenson Publishing.

Falmagne, R. J. (1975). Overview: Reasoning, representation, process, and related issues. In R. J. Falmagne (Ed.), *Reasoning: Representation and process* (pp. 247–264). Hillsdale, NJ: Lawrence Erlbaum Associates.

Falmagne, R. J. (1980). The development of logical competence: A psycholinguistic perspective. In R. Kluwe & H. Spada (Eds.), *Developmental models of thinking* (pp. 171–197). New York: Academic Press.

Falmagne, R. J. (1989). *Formal and nonformal aspects of deduction*. Paper presented at the Annual Meeting of the Society for Philosophy and Psychology, Tucson, AZ.

Falmagne, R. J., Singer, J., & Clement, C. (1989). *Imagery and deductive processes in conditional reasoning*. Manuscript under review.

Falmagne, R. J., Thompson, D., & Bennett, J. (1979). *Patterns of deductive inference in children: Investigation of a possible acquisition process*. Unpublished manuscript, Clark University.

Feldman, C. F., & Toulmin, S. (1976). Logic and the theory of mind. In J. K. Cole (Ed.), *Nebraska Symposium on Motivation*. Lincoln, NE: University of Nebraska Press.

Gentzen, G. (1969). Investigations into logical deduction. In M. E. Szabo (Ed. & trans.), *The collected papers of Gerhard Gentzen*. Amsterdam: North-Holland. (Original work published 1935).

Gleitmen, L., & Wanner, E. (1982). Language acquisition: The state of the state of the art. In E. Wanner & L. Gleitman (Eds.), *Language acquisition: The state of the art* (pp. 3–48). Cambridge: Cambridge University Press.

Grimshaw, J. (1981). Form, function, and the language acquisition device. In. C. L. Baker & J. J. McCarthy (Eds.), *The Logical problem of language acquisition* (pp. 165–182). Cambridge, MA: MIT Press.

Hoch, S. J., & Tschirgi, J. E. (1985). Logical knowledge and cue redundancy in deductive reasoning. *Memory & Cognition, 13*, 453–462.

Hornstein, N. (1984). *Logic as grammar*. Cambridge, MA: MIT Press.

Inhelder, B., & Piaget, J. (1958). *The growth of logical thinking from childhood to adolescence*. New York: Basic Books.

Inhelder, B., & Sinclair, H. (1960). Learning cognitive structures. In P. H. Mussen, J. Langer, & M. Covington (Eds.), *Trends and issues in developmental psychology*. New York: Holt, Rinehart, & Winston.

Inhelder, B., Sinclair, H., & Bovet, M. (1974). *Learning and the development of cognition*. Cambridge, MA: Harvard University Press.

Johnson-Laird, P. N. (1983). *Mental models*. Cambridge, MA: Harvard University Press.

Kodroff, J. K., & Roberge, J. J. (1975) Developmental analysis of the conditional reasoning abilities of primary-grade children. *Developmental Psychology*, *11*, 21-28.

Kuhn, D. (1977). Conditional reasoning in children. *Developmental Psychology*, *13*, 342-353.

Langer, J. (1980). *The origins of logic*. New York: Academic Press.

Lust, B. (1981). Constraints on anaphora in child language: A prediction for an universal. In S. L. Tavakolian (Ed.), *Language acquisition and linguistic theory*. Cambridge, MA: MIT Press.

Lycan, W. G. (1984). *Logical form in natural language*. Cambridge, MA: Bradford Books.

May, R. (1985). *Logical form: Its structure and derivation*. Cambridge, MA: MIT Press.

Morf, A., Smedslund, J., Vinh-Bang, & Wohlwill, J. (1959). *L'apprentissage des structures logiques*. Cahiers d'epistemologie genetique IX. Paris: Presses Universitaires de France.

Nelson, K. (Ed.). (1985). *Making sense: The acquisition of shared meaning*. New York: Academic Press.

Nelson, K. (1986). *Event knowledge: Structure and function in development*. Hillsdale, NJ: Lawrence Erlbaum Associates.

O'Brien, D., & Overton, W. F. (1980). Conditional reasoning following contradictory evidence: A developmental analysis. *Journal of Experimental Child Psychology*, *30*, 44-60.

O'Brien, D., & Overton, W. F. (1982). Conditional reasoning and the competence-performance issue: A developmental analysis of a training task. *Journal of Experimental Child Psychology*, *34*, 274-290.

Osherson, D. (1977). Natural connectives: A Chomskyan approach. *Journal of Mathematical Psychology*, *16*, 1-29.

Overton, W. F. (1985). Scientific methodologies and the competence-moderator-performance issue. In E. Neimark, R. DeLisi, & J. Newman (Eds.), *Moderators of competence* (pp. 15-41). Hillsdale, NJ: Lawrence Erlbaum Associates.

Overton, W. F., Byrnes, J. P., & O'Brien, D. P. (1985). Developmental and individual differences in conditional reasoning: The role of contradiction training and cognitive style. *Developmental Psychology*, *21*, 692-701.

Overton, W. F., Ward, S. L., Noveck, I. A., Black, J., & O'Brien, D. P. (1987). Form and content in the development of deductive reasoning. *Developmental Psychology*, *23*, 22-30.

Piaget, J. (1936). *La naissance de l'intelligence chez l'enfant*. Neuchatel: Delachaux et Niestle.

Piaget, J. (1953). *Logic and psychology*. Manchester: Manchester University Press. Also in H. E. Gruber & J. J. Voneche (Eds.) (1977). *The essential Piaget* (pp. 445-481). NY: Basic Books.

Piaget, J. (1967). *Six psychological studies*. New York: Random House. (Original work published 1964).

Piaget, J. (1969). Language et operations intellectuelles. In *Problemes de Psycholinguistique*. Paris: Presses Universitaires de France. (Language and intellectual operations, In H. Furth (Ed.), (1969), *Piaget and knowledge* (pp. 121-132). New York: Prentice-Hall). (Original work published 1963).

Piaget, J. (1970). Piaget's theory. In P. H. Mussen (Ed.), *Carmichael's manual of child psychology*. New York: Wiley.

Piaget, J. (1980). Introductory remarks. In M. Piattelli-Palmarini (Eds.), *Langauge and learning: The debate between Jean Piaget and Noam Chomsky* (pp. 57-61). Cambridge, MA: Harvard University Press.

Pinker, S. (1984). *Language learnability and language development*. Cambridge, MA: Harvard University Press.

Rips, L. (1983). Cognitive processes in propositional reasoning. *Psychological Review*, *90*(1), 38-71.

Rumain, B., Connell, J., & Braine, M. D. S. (1983). Conversational comprehension processes are responsible for reasoning fallacies in children as well as adults: *If* is not the biconditional. *Developmental Psychology*, *19*, 471–481.

Rumelhart, D. (1980). Schemata: The building blocks of cognition. In R. J. Spiro, B. C. Bruce, & W. F. Brewer (Eds.), *Theoretical issues in reading comprehension* (pp. 33–58). Hillsdale, NJ: Lawrence Erlbaum Associates.

Rumelhart, D. E., & Ortony, A. (1977). The representation of knowledge in memory. In R. C. Anderson, R. J. Spiro, & W. E. Montague (Eds.), *Schooling and the acquisition of knowledge*. Hillsdale, NJ: Lawrence Erlbaum Associates.

Schank, R. C. (1981). Language and memory. In D. A. Norman (Ed.), *Perspectives on cognitive science*. Hillsdale, NJ: Lawrence Erlbaum Associates.

Schank, R. C., & Abelson, R. P. (1977). *Scripts, plans, goals, and understanding*. Hillsdale, NJ: Lawrence Erlbaum Associates.

Sinclair, H. (1973). Language acquisition and cognitive development. In T. Moore (Ed.), *Cognitive development and the acquisition of language* (pp. 9–25). New York: Academic Press.

Sinclair, H. (1976). Developmental psycholinguistics. In B. Inhelder & H. H. Chipman (Eds.), *Piaget and his school* (pp. 189–218). New York: Springer-Verlag.

Slobin, D. I. (1973). Cognitive prerequisites for the development of grammar. In C. A. Ferguson & D. I. Slobin (Eds.), *Studies of child language development*. New York: Holt, Rinehart, & Winston.

Slobin, D. I. (1985). Crosslinguistic evidence for the language making capacity. In D. I. Slobin (Ed.), *The crosslinguistic study of language acquisition: Vol. 2. Theoretical issues*. Hillsdale, NJ: Lawrence Erlbaum Associates.

Sommers, F. T. (1982). *The logic of natural language*. New York: Oxford University Press.

Sugarman, S. (1983). *Children's early representational thought*. Cambridge: Cambridge University Press.

Taplin, J. E., Staudenmayer, H., & Taddonio, J. L. (1974). Developmental changes in conditional reasoning: Linguistic or logical? *Journal of Experimental Child Psychology*, *17*, 360–373.

Tavakolian, S. L. (1981). *Language acquisition and linguistic theory*. Cambridge, MA: MIT Press.

Thompson, D. (1977). *The effectiveness of two types of training for the acquisition of a deductible rule of inference in children*. Unpublished master's thesis, Clark University.

Vygotsky, L. S. (1962). *Thought and language*. Cambridge, MA: MIT Press.

Vygotsky, L. S. (1978). Tool and symbol in child development. In M. Cole, V. John-Steiner, S. Scribner, & E. Souberman (Eds.), *Mind in society*. Cambridge, MA: Harvard University Press.

Wason, P. C., & Johnson-Laird, P. N. (1972). *Psychology of reasoning: Structure and content*. London: Batsford.

Wertsch, J. V. (1985). *Vygotsky and the social formation of mind*. Cambridge, MA: Harvard University Press.

# 7

# The "Natural Logic" Approach to Reasoning

Martin D. S. Braine
*New York University*

This chapter aims to provide an overview of the ideas and rationale of the "natural logic" approach to reasoning (e.g., Braine, 1978; Braine, Reiser, & Rumain, 1984; Braine & O'Brien, 1989). It also discusses consequences of these ideas for development. I begin with some rather commonsensical ideas about the probable evolutionary function of logical reasoning. These suggest that it would be useful to distinguish between primary (primitive) and secondary (educated) logical skills. I then describe what the natural-logic approach claims are the primary skills that evolved along with language and culture. Then, I discuss the interface of these skills with pragmatic factors in comprehension and reasoning, and with other, less directly "logical" modes of reasoning, especially the use of mental models. Finally, I discuss the developmental origins of these skills in children.

## PRIMARY AND SECONDARY
## LOGICAL REASONING SKILLS

To many people, logical reasoning seems to present an odd and difficult, but erudite, mixture of the obvious and the counterintuitive; it is without any apparent social point (except, perhaps, as an intellectual game), the average person is not very good at it, and it has little practical everyday use. From this perspective, it is rather implausible to claim that there is a natural logic that is universal among people. Therefore, I want to begin by looking at logical reasoning skills from the point of view of human bio-cultural evolution, considering what practical purpose they might have served and might still serve.

What functions could logical reasoning skills have performed for hunter-

gatherers or other kinds of preliterate human adaptations? Moreover, because much that such skills did for our ancestors they probably still do for
us, what lessons about the nature of logical reasoning might those functions
have for us as cognitive scientists? What should it lead us to expect about
subjects' performance on logical reasoning tasks?

One might think that this evolutionary perspective would be hopelessly speculative. However, I believe that there are some plausible things to be said, and
that these provide a very commonsensical way of thinking about logical reasoning. Moreover, they lead to a conception of what untutored logical skills should
be expected to be like that conforms well with the evidence.

What I propose is the following. Logical reasoning provides some elementary information integration processes serving primarily two purposes. The
first purpose is to facilitate verbal interaction by providing a set of inferences
that are made automatically in processing discourse. The other purpose is to integrate information received from different sources or at different times.

Let us consider discourse processing first. In recent years, partly as a result of
trying to build computationally realizable models of text comprehension, we
have become more and more aware of the very many inferences that people appear to make automatically in understanding discourse, whether written or spoken. Current work has been slowly making an inventory of the various kinds.
Although not all of these inferences properly qualify as "logical," many do, as
illustrated in the following brief story which is one of several that Lea, Fisch,
O'Brien, Noveck, and I are using in a current study of logical inferences that are
automatically made in comprehending text. The stories are presented on a
screen one sentence at a time, and each sentence disappears after it has been
read. The subject has to judge whether the final sentence makes sense in the
context of the story. One example is:

> The floor lamp was not working.
> "The problem must be in either the fuse, the wire connection, or the
> bulb," Susan thought.
> She checked the fuse, and the fuse was alright.
> She thought that the wire connection was no good, but her father said
> that wasn't so, because he had tested the connection.

One possible final sentence reads:

> So she concluded that the problem must be in the bulb, and went out
> to buy a new one.

The alternative final sentence reads:

> So she concluded that there was nothing she could do to make the
> lamp work.

Note that to judge the sensibleness of the final sentence, one must have made certain inferences while reading the text—inferences of a sort traditionally called "logical." Specifically, one must have inferred that the wire connection was okay while reading the fourth sentence—a very elementary inference but one that is, nevertheless, logical in nature. Also, given the three alternatives stated in the second sentence, one must appreciate that the third and fourth sentences eliminate two of them, so the remaining one must be the source of the trouble—another traditionally logical inference. If these inferences were not made while reading the first four sentences, there would be no basis for preferring one final sentence over the other.

Our stories are read rather than spoken, and, of course, our preliterate ancestors could not read. But the need for automatic inferences is even greater for oral texts than for written ones, because written texts are usually durable and can be reread, whereas oral texts disappear as they are spoken, so inferences have to be made immediately.

The other primitive purpose of logical reasoning skills—integrating information coming from different sources or at different times—is what Aristotle called "practical reasoning." For example, you know that one of two alternatives must hold; later on you learn that one does not hold; so you conclude that the other does. For another example, let us imagine a scenario that might be appropriate for a hunter-gatherer context: Somebody tells you, "If I leave two crossed sticks on the beach, then our hunt was successful, and you should join us at Saber-tooth Lake"; that evening you go to the beach and find two crossed sticks, and you conclude, by the very elementary inference known to logicians as modus ponens, that the hunt was successful. One could think of many such examples; even in preliterate cultural environments human beings would need some information integration processes like these.

In sum, for purposes of discourse comprehension and practical reasoning, even in preliterate human societies, some basic information integration processes of a kind we now call logical would be needed. However, although our ancestors would need these sorts of information integration abilities, their living conditions would not demand a number of other abilities that we often think of as part of logical reasoning. Let us now survey those that they would not need.

First, possession of the kinds of inferences illustrated would enable our ancestors to carry out some short chains of direct reasoning, but, beyond that, their logical reasoning ability may well have been quite limited. Thus, there seems to be no reason to expect them to have developed much facility in executing long, complex chains of reasoning, or with argument strategies that involve deliberate use of the reductio ad absurdum. Complex chains of reasoning tend to make considerable demands on memory, and, in the absence of written language, what our ancestors could do would be limited by the capacity of working memory, as we are now in processing spoken discourse. (Our ancestors may well have had potential for such skills, but there is no reason to expect that their life circumstances would have led them to develop them.)

Second, there is no particular reason to expect them to have had much skill in compartmentalizing information. One of the games we often play with subjects in the psychological laboratory is to give them a set of premises and test their knowledge of what follows from the premises. One of the conventions of this game is that the subject is supposed to set aside background knowledge and consider what follows just from the premises. However, in the practical reasoning I have attributed to our preliterates, they always reason from *all* the information available. Artificially setting aside part of what you know is an academic game, and there is no reason to assume that our ancestor's life conditions would lead them to acquire much skill at that game.

More generally, there is no reason to expect that our preliterate ancestors would have had much skill at a kind of language comprehension that I have, elsewhere, called "analytic" (Braine & Rumain, 1983). It is useful to draw a distinction, which several people have in fact drawn (e.g., Donaldson, 1976), between "ordinary" comprehension and "analytic" or "literal" comprehension. Ordinary comprehension involves grasping what a speaker has in mind: It uses all cues available—what the speaker said, what speaker and listener know, both in general and specifically about the situation that is the subject of the conversation, and the information's plausibility. Analytic comprehension, on the other hand, is concerned with what a sentence means; that is often not the same as what the speaker meant by the sentence. One uses analytic comprehension, for instance, in trying to understand tax regulations: If the government's words do not commit you to paying a tax, you do not pay it. Lawyers often use it (e.g., in seeking loopholes in a law). We also use analytic comprehension in philosophy and linguistics when discussing issues in linguistic semantics. Analytic comprehension is a rather academic task and not an easy skill. Everyone, including our putative illiterate ancestors, can be expected to possess, or to have possessed, a good deal of skill at ordinary comprehension. That is, we all have a lot of practice and skill at guessing what people mean by what they say (and a good deal is now known about the pragmatic principles involved). No doubt it is because listeners have this skill that speakers can be, and very often are, careless in how they express ideas in words, relying on the likelihood that the listener's skills in guessing will make up for their own imprecisions in speaking. Be that as it may, the universal information integration processes of a logical nature that I have been talking about use the output of ordinary comprehension processes. In contrast, analytic comprehension presupposes literacy: One needs a representation of a sentence in a durable form, which stays around to be contemplated and discussed, in order to work out what the *sentence* is committed to.

Now note that the important logical concept of "following from" depends in large part on analytic comprehension. When we ask what follows from a sentence, we often mean what follows *just* from the sentence, in abstraction from what the speaker plausibly meant in the situation, and in abstraction from knowledge other than that of the language in which the sentence was communicated. Thus, there is no reason to expect that our ancestors would be practiced in this notion of "following from" (i.e., in what philosophers and logicians call "entailment").

In general, there would be no point to anyone's acquiring skill at analytic comprehension until there were laws, and lawyers or judges, and written texts with meaning to be discussed and entailments to be worked out. These things would be expected to be products of a complex, literate culture with a class of people with academic, or quasi-academic, legal, or theological goals that lead them to worry about what sentences mean, rather than what people mean by sentences. Note that what I have just said means that it must be possible to have information integration processes—that is, make inferences of a logical sort—without mastering compartmentalization, or having much skill at analytic comprehension or at understanding and working out entailments.

The preceding arguments indicate that in discussing logical reasoning, one should distinguish between what I shall call "primary" and "secondary" logical reasoning skills. The primary skills are the information integration processes of a logical sort that we share with the rest of humanity, literate or illiterate. These are logical inferences carried out in comprehension of discourse and in practical reasoning; making them demands only ordinary speech comprehension, which may involve all the usual pragmatic processes, and no compartmentalization of information into "premises" and other knowledge is required. There is every reason to think that these primary skills will turn out to be universal (e.g., all languages seem to have much the same set of logical or quasi-logical notions expressed by words or particles like English *if, or, and,* other conjunctions, *not, all, any, some,* etc., and the same primitive inferences seem to be associated with them as in English). It has been argued elsewhere (Braine, Reiser, & Rumain, 1984) that these primary skills form a "natural logic"—kinds of inferences that are performed essentially errorlessly, and often automatically, and that have a form that has traditionally been called "logical."

The secondary logical reasoning skills are quasi-academic. They are those, as I have discussed, that depend on literacy and a concern with language, *qua* language—they require a degree of compartmentalization of information and analytic comprehension. Notions like "following from" and entailment depend on them. I call the secondary skills "quasi-academic" to imply that they depend on literacy and schooling. However, there is very little direct teaching of them in school: Children are taught to read, and words and sentences and their meanings are discussed, to some extent, in classes (e.g., English classes). But what teaching there is of these secondary skills is highly informal, so it should be no surprise that most children and adults have not acquired very much of them.

It follows from the above that, in discussing any particular logical reasoning skill—for example, its universality, its developmental origin—it is very important to distinguish whether one is discussing a primary skill or a secondary one. Very different theoretical issues may be involved. For instance, findings that children or adults are poor at certain logical tasks have significance for the natural logic approach only when primary skills suffice to solve the tasks: Only the primary skills are claimed to be universal. The term "natural logic," as I use it, refers only to the primary skills.

## THE NATURE OF THE PRIMARY SKILLS

But what are these primary skills like? I and my colleagues believe that they consist of a set of inference forms coupled with a simple reasoning program for applying them to information available. The inferences of the set are very easy indeed and made essentially without error by adults (Braine et al., 1984). We believe that they are often made more or less automatically, and that they are understood early by children (Braine & Rumain, 1983). A specific proposal about the set of primitive inference forms and the associated reasoning program for applying them has been worked out for propositional reasoning (i.e., for inferences that depend on the meanings of *if*, *and*, *or*, and negation). A set of inference forms (schemas) was presented in Braine et al. (1984, Table 1), along with a specification for a model reasoning program of adult subjects (Braine et al., 1984, Table 3). The program was derived from data on subjects' propositional reasoning and models how they make inferences from information given. The "direct reasoning routine" of that program appeared to be universal among the subjects, and we propose that it is part of the primary skills. (The program also contains a nonroutine part that does not belong to the primary skills; it represents the logical reasoning strategies that subjects have learned that go beyond the primary skills.)

Table 7.1 lists and illustrates the inference schemas, and Table 7.2 presents the direct reasoning routine of the reasoning program: Both are revised from the presentation in Braine et al. (1984.)[1] Table 7.1 is composed

---

[1]The revisions have two sources. First, Braine et al. (1984) sought to model the reasoning of our adult subjects and included two schemas that play no role in the direct reasoning routine; these are omitted form Table 7.1, as they are probably not part of the primary skills. Second, there were errors: It came to my attention that we had overlooked a way in which the reasoning routine could get into an infinite loop. Correcting that error led to renumbering the schemas to make it easy to treat Schemas 1–3 as a group in the reasoning routine. It also became clear that Schema 6 should be treated as an equivalence.

of four subgroups of schemas: Schemas 1–3, 4–5, 6–12, and 13–14. The first three schemas make inferences that are intuitively rather obvious and trivial, and two of them could easily lead to infinite loops in which they continuously reapply. The routine therefore uses them only when they would be immediately useful—when their use would lead to direct verification or falsification of a conclusion, or enable another inference to be made. Schemas 4 and 5 define contradictions, and the routine uses them only in the Evaluation Procedure to bring about the response of False. Schemas 6–12 are the core group for making inferences; they are used without restriction whenever they are applicable (see Step 3 of the reasoning routine). Schemas 13 and 14 have to do with suppositional reasoning, and they have very restricted roles in the universal reasoning routine—Schema 13 is involved only at Step 2, and Schema 14 only in the falsification step of the Evaluation Procedure. (For the other uses of Schemas 13 and 14, in the suppositional reasoning of adult subjects, see the discussion of indirect reasoning strategies in Braine et al., 1984.)

Table 7.3 gives some examples of how the direct reasoning routine uses the schemas to find answers to some simple deductive reasoning problems presented to subjects in the form of puzzles. The middle column outlines the series of inferences made by the routine in response to each of the problems on the left. Step 3 is the part of the routine where almost all the inferences are made. This operates by applying to the information available whichever of the core inference schemas (i.e., Schemas 6–12) can be applied; the information inferred is added to the stock of information, and whatever core schemas can be applied are again applied, and so on. The nature of the schemas is such that it is rare that the process can be repeated more than a very few times. Thus, in Problem 1 of Table 7.3, Schema 6 of Table 7.1 (which cancels a double negative) is the only schema that applies to the given propositions; it is applied on the first cycle of the routine and adds the information that there is a fox in the box, as shown in the middle column; Schema 7 of Table 7.1 is now the only schema that applies, and it leads to the conclusion that there is no pear in the box. After each inference is made, when there is a conclusion to be evaluated, the routine tests it for identity or contradiction with the propositions in the growing stock of information. Thus, on Problem 1, a match is found on the second cycle of the routine between the conclusion and the inference just made. On Problem 2, a response of "False" is triggered by the incompatibility of the finding that there is not a banana and not a cow (the third inference shown in the middle column) with the conclusion to be evaluated, that there is one or the other. On Problem 3, there is no conclusion to be evaluated, but the routine operates to make inferences in the same way as in the previous problems; it makes the three inferences shown, and then it stops, as it can make no further inferences.

There are several kinds of evidence for the system proposed. A first kind

TABLE 7.1
Inference Schemas of Natural Propositional Logic

| # | Schema | Example |
|---|--------|---------|
| 1. | $p_1; p_2; \ldots p_n$ <br> $p_1 \text{ AND } p_2 \text{ AND} \ldots \text{ AND } p_n$ | E.g., There is a cat; There is an apple/∴ There is a cat and an apple |
| 2. | $p_1 \text{ AND} \ldots \text{ AND } p_i \text{ AND} \ldots \text{ AND } p_n$ <br> $p_i$ | E.g., There is a chicken and a horse/∴ There is a chicken. |
| 3. | $p \text{ AND } (q_1 \text{ OR} \ldots \text{ OR } q_n) \equiv (p \text{ AND } p_1) \text{ OR} \ldots \text{ OR } (p \text{ AND } q_n)$ | E.g., There is a grape, and there is a lemon or an egg/∴ There is a grape and a lemon, or there is a grape and an egg. |
| 4. | $p; F(p)$ <br> INCOMPATIBLE | E.g., There is an orange; There is not an orange/INCOMPATIBLE. |
| 5. | $p_1 \text{ OR} \ldots \text{ OR } p_n; F(p_1) \text{ AND} \ldots \text{ AND } F(p_n)$ <br> INCOMPATIBLE | E.g., There is a dog or a tiger; There is not a dog and there is not a tiger/INCOMPATIBLE. |
| 6. | $F[F(p)] \equiv p$ | E.g., It is false that there is not a banana/∴ There is a banana. |
| 7. | $\text{IF } p_1 \text{ OR} \ldots \text{ OR } p_n \text{ THEN } q; p_i$ <br> $q$ | E.g., If there is either a cow or a goat, then there is a pear; There is a cow/∴ There is a pear. |
| 8. | $p_1 \text{ OR} \ldots \text{ OR } p_n; F(p_i)$ <br> $p_1 \text{ OR} \ldots \text{ OR } p_{i-1} \text{ OR } p_{i+1} \text{ OR} \ldots \text{ OR } p_n$ | E.g., There is a strawberry or a blackberry; There is not a strawberry/∴ There is a blackberry. |
| 9. | $F(p_1 \text{ AND} \ldots \text{ AND } p_n); p_i$ <br> $F(p_1 \text{ AND} \ldots \text{ AND } p_{i-1} \text{ AND } p_{i+1} \text{ AND} \ldots \text{ AND } p_n)$ | E.g., It is false that there is both a plum and a pineapple; There is a plum/∴ There is not a pineapple. |

10.  $p_1$ OR...OR $p_n$; IF $p_1$ THEN q; ...; IF $p_n$ THEN q

$$q$$

E.g., There is a fox or a wolf; If there is a fox, then there is a nut; If there is a wolf, then there is a nut /∴ There is a nut.

11.  $p_1$ OR...OR $p_n$; IF $p_1$ THEN $q_1$; ...; IF $p_n$ THEN $q_n$

$$q_1 \text{ OR...OR } q_n$$

E.g., There is a duck or a goose; If there is a duck, then there is a plum; If there is a goose, then there is a cherry /∴ There is a plum or a cherry.

12.  IF p THEN q; p

$$q$$

E.g., If there is a grapefruit, then there is an elephant; There is a grapefruit /∴ There is an elephant.

13.  Given a chain of reasoning of the form

Suppose p
- - - -
q

One can conclude: IF p THEN q

14.  Given a chain of reasoning of the form

Suppose p
- - - -
INCOMPATIBLE

One can conclude: F(p)

*Note.* The order of conjuncts and disjuncts and of the propositions in numerators is immaterial. Where there are subscripts, *i* indicates anyone of the subscripted propositions. F(. . .) indicates that " . . ." is false. [F( ) is commonly realized as negation when the negated proposition is realized as a single clause or sentence in surface structure.] "INCOMPATIBLE" stops a chain of reasoning, except as provided for in Schema 14 and the Evaluation Procedure of the reasoning program (Table 7.2). Schemas 3 and 6 are formulated as equivalences to indicate that propositions of the indicated forms can be substituted for each other when they occur within longer propositions. (Directionality of Schema 6 is controlled by the reasoning program.) Schema 13 says that if *q* can be derived with the aid of the supposition *p*, one can conclude IF *p* THEN *q*. Schema 14 says that a supposition leading to an incompatibility is false. These two schemas have limited use in the universal reasoning program: Schema 13 figures only in Step 2, and Schema 14 only in Part (b)of the Evaluation Procedure. See Braine and O'Brien (1989) for a restriction on Schema 13 relevant to counterfactual conditionals.

The schemas are illustrated (right hand column) with proposition content (toy objects in a closed box) from the kinds of problems cited in Table 7.3.

TABLE 7.2
Direct Reasoning Routine: A Specification
for a Universal Reasoning Program

---

The program, as stated, applies to problem situations where there is a conclusion given whose truth is to be evaluated. When there is no specific conclusion to be evaluated (i.e., when subjects are just making inferences from the information they have), Steps 1 and 2 and the Evaluation procedure are inapplicable: The routine comprises Step 3 only. The routine terminates when the conclusion is evaluated, or when no new propositions are generated at Step 3.

STEP 1. Evaluate the given conclusion against the premises, using the evaluation procedure. If the evaluation is indeterminate, then:

STEP 2. If the given conclusion is an *if-then* statement, add the antecedent to the premise set and treat the consequent as the conclusion to be tested; use the evaluation procedure to test the new conclusion against the augmented premise set. If the evaluation is indeterminate (or if Step 2 did not apply), then:

STEP 3. For each of Schemas 6 through 12 (schema 6 in the left-to-right direction only), apply it if its conditions of application are satisfied or if its conditions of application can be satisfied by first applying one or a combination of Schemas 1, 2, and 3. (In the case of Schema 8, apply it if its conditions of application can be satisfied by previously applying Schema 6 in the right-to-left direction.) Add the propositions deduced to the premise set. When there is a conclusion to be evaluated, use the evaluation procedure to test the conclusion against the augmented premise set; if the outcome of the evaluation is indeterminate, repeat Step 3. When there is no conclusion to be evaluated, just repeat Step 3. (In executing Step 3, no schema is applied whose only effect would be to duplicate a proposition already in the premise set.)

EVALUATION PROCEDURE. To test a given conclusion against a premise set: (a) if the conclusion is in the premise set or can be inferred by applying one or a combination of Schemas 1, 2, and 3, respond "True"; (b) if the conclusion, or an inference from it by Schema 2, is incompatible (by Schemas 4 or 5) with a proposition in the premise set or with a proposition that can be inferred from the premise set by applying one or a combination of Schemas 1, 2, and 3, respond "False."

---

*Note.* The "premise set" at any point comprises the original premises together with any propositions that have been added at Steps 2 or 3. The conditions of application of a schema are satisfied when the premise set contains propositions of the form specified in the numerator of the schema; to apply the schema is to deduce the corresponding proposition of the form specified in the denominator of the schema. The equivalences (Schemas 3 and 6) are applicable when all or part of a proposition in the premise set matches the form specified on one of the sides of the equivalence; application consists in generating the proposition in which the matching material is replaced by the corresponding content with the form specified on the other side of the equivalence.

is evidence for the primitiveness of the inference forms: They are extremely easy for adults and available early to children. Adults make very few errors on problems like those of Table 7.3, and they perform essentially errorlessly on maximally simple problems, i.e., problems that can be solved with one of the inference forms of the set, without any other complexity (Braine et

TABLE 7.3
Illustrations of how the direct reasoning routine solves problems.

| Problem | Solution steps | Relevant schema |
|---|---|---|
| 1. If Fox or Cat, then not Pear<br>False that not Fox | | |
| ? Not Pear ? | Fox<br>Not Pear<br>True | (6)[a]<br>(7) |
| 2. Not both Plum and Banana<br>Plum<br>Not Cow | | |
| ? Banana or Cow ? | Not Banana<br>Not Banana and not Cow<br>False | (9)<br>(1)<br>(5) |
| 3. Goat or Elephant<br>Not Goat<br>If Elephant, then Lemon<br>Not both Lemon and Pineapple | | |
| ? What follows ? | Elephant<br>Lemon<br>Not pineapple<br>That's all. | (8)<br>(12)<br>(9) |

Note. Subjects reason about what is in a closed box that can contain toy animals and fruit. The table presents propositions in schematic form: If Fox or Cat, then not Pear = If there is either a fox or a cat in the box, then there is not a pear; Fox = There is a fox in the box, etc.

Under "Problem," the premises are given above the line, and below it, between question marks, is the conclusion to be evaluated. The column "Solution steps" records the sequence of inferences drawn, in order, culminating in the response to the problem. The column "Relevant schema" indicates the inference schema in Table 7.1 that determined the form of the inference made at each solution step.
[a]I.e., Schema 6 in Table 7.1.

al., 1984); the simplicity does not depend on use of any particular kind of content. The literature has dwelt so much on the logical errors made by subjects that it is easy to miss the fact that there exists a set of very simple inference forms. For most of these inference forms—not all have been investigated—there is also evidence that they are available to children by around school-entering age or earlier (see Braine & Rumain, 1983, for a review).

A second kind of evidence, which supports the reasoning program as well as the schemas, is that the system predicts the difficulty of problems with the same kind of content—which problems subjects will be able to solve, and their relative difficulty (Braine et al., 1984). Relative difficulty is accounted for as a function of the number and kind of the inferential steps used to solve them in this system.

The system predicts well not only how difficult problems will be, but, for problems soluble by the direct reasoning routine, the actual sequence of inferences subjects will make. Thus, in problems like those of Table 7.3, subjects may be asked not just to solve each problem, but to write down the sequence of inferences they make in the course of solving it. Thus, the sequence predicted by the program (e.g., the middle column of Table 7.3) can be compared with that written down by subjects. The concordance is good, both for problems where a conclusion to be evaluated is provided and for those where subjects make inferences without any conclusion being given (Braine, 1987; Braine, Noveck, Samuels, Fisch, Lea, & O'Brien, 1989); this fact provides strong evidence that the system captures subjects' actual line of reasoning over a broad class of problems. There is also evidence that the system accounts well for propositional inferences made in comprehending written text (Lea, O'Brien, Fisch, Noveck, & Braine, 1989).

Although a specific model has so far been worked out only for propositional reasoning, we certainly expect that the full natural system goes well beyond this. Extension to reasoning about properties and relations is briefly discussed in Braine and Rumain (1983).

## NATURAL LOGIC AND PRAGMATICS

This conception of the primary skills in no way excludes pragmatics. The inference schemas act on semantic representations. Therefore, *all* pragmatic factors that enter into sentence interpretation affect reasoning, because they affect comprehension and, thus, help constitute the information from which inferences are made. I must stress the point that inference schemas act on semantic representations. Johnson-Laird (1986b) says that a "mental logic" theory would predict that subjects could reason without having understood the meanings of premises. That is simply not true for the primary logical skills. Thus, premises with nonsense content (e.g., *If Seb glatched then Juff kiviled*) should be difficult to make inferences from; that is, because of the difficulty of arriving at a semantic representation for such content, the primary skills may not be engaged. Reasoning from such content is by no means impossible, but it requires additional skills (e.g. metalinguistic skills) over and above the primary ones.

Let us review how pragmatic factors affect interpretation in a manner relevant to reasoning. There are two kinds of pragmatic factors: One is the social frame of discourse; the other is knowledge of subject matter. The social frame of discourse affects comprehension through the "cooperative principle" (Grice, 1975, 1978); that is, speakers try to be as informative, truthful, relevant, and clear as they can, and listeners assume that speakers are trying to be these things. The cooperative principle allows listeners to make many inferences that are not logically necessary ("conversational implicatures"); it is a potent source of error on logical reasoning tasks, because in writing logical reasoning problems experimenters usually are not as informative, truthful, relevant, and clear as they would be in a conversation (see Braine & Rumain, 1983, pp. 267–269, for detailed discussion and examples). "Invited inference" (Geis & Zwicky, 1971) can be viewed as a special case of the operation of the cooperative principle: According to Geis and Zwicky, logical particles often invite certain nonnecessary inferences. For example, a conditional, *If p then q*, invites the inference *if not p then not q* (e.g., *If you mow the lawn, I'll give you five dollars* invites the inference *If you don't mow the lawn, I will not give you five dollars*); the statement form, *Some F are G*, invites the listener to infer that some F are not G. In general, people make these invited inferences unless the discourse content or context gives them some reason to believe them inappropriate (Fillenbaum, 1977; Geis & Zwicky, 1971; O'Brien & Overton, 1982; Rumain, Connell, & Braine, 1983). In practical reasoning, unless people have reason to doubt the candor of their sources, the information from which they reason includes all conversational implicatures and invited inferences of the verbal statements that provided the information.

The other kind of pragmatic factor is subject-matter knowledge. The general principle is that, in practical reasoning, reasoners' knowledge of the subject matter reasoned about influences comprehension and is part of the information from which they reason. Comprehension and reasoning can be affected in at least two ways. First, a statement is more likely to be given an interpretation that is plausible, given the reasoner's general knowledge of the world and specific knowledge of the situation, than one that is implausible. This fact is a consequence of the "plausibility strategy" of sentence interpretation (Bever, 1970), which is well known as a source of errors in comprehension. Second, knowledge of subject matter can be organized according to type (e.g., permissions, obligations, cause-and-effect) (Cheng & Holyoak, 1985; Cheng, Holyoak, Nisbett, & Oliver, 1986), and the knowledge can take a rule-like form that Cheng and Holyoak call a "pragmatic reasoning schema." A pragmatic schema defines relationships that hold for a class of contents. For instance, the "permission" schema specifies rules of the form, "If Action $x$ is to be done, then Condition $y$ must be satisfied"— the condition gives permission for the action, as in the rule, *If printed matter is to go first class, it must carry a 25 cent stamp*. The effect of a pragmatic schema is to enrich the data base for reasoning by defining relationships typical of the content that are richer than would be gotten from natural logic alone. Thus, if an *if*-statement elicits the permission schema, then the contrapositive[2] ("If the condition is not satisfied, then the action cannot be done") becomes more accessible to the reasoner than if the permission schema is not elicited (Cheng & Holyoak, 1985). Pragmatic schemas may nicely explain some of the effects of content in facilitating reasoning, for example, why Wason's (1968) selection task is easier to solve with "permission" content than with more abstract content (Cheng & Holyoak, 1985).

Just how important pragmatic schemas are in reasoning is not now clear. The proposed cause-and-effect schemas have yet to be described precisely, and the "obligation" schema seems to be isomorphic to the "permission" schema. Thus, only one schema (permission/obligation) has so far been specified in detail. In any case, it should be noted that because pragmatic schemas are content-specific (by definition), they cannot account for the fact that the inferences defined in Tables 7.1 and 7.2 are so easy and automatic for subjects, even with highly arbitrary content that falls outside the scope of any imaginable pragmatic schemas (Braine et al., 1984; Braine et al., 1989). Thus, pragmatic schemas make theoretical sense only if they are taken as presupposing a foundation of natural logic, to which they add content-specific supplements.

In general, these pragmatic factors never contradict natural logic or block the operation of the primary logical skills; they always enrich, by adding to the information base or to the inferences made. To make this point convincing, let us consider a range of examples. Consider, first, conversational implicatures and invited inferences. These are always contextually plausible inferences that are logically consistent with the certain information that is available; that is, they supplement natural logic. There are also many inferences that are the joint product of discourse convention and factual knowledge; for instance, a sentence of the form, *p and q*, will be taken to imply *q because p* when the content lends itself to that interpretation (e.g., *He went out in the rain and got wet*). Note that *q because p* is perfectly consistent with *p and q*; it is just informationally richer. That is, this kind of inference supplements natural logic and enriches the information base for reasoning. Enthymemes provide another type of example in which general knowledge enriches the data base for reasoning. For instance, Harris (1975) gave five-year-olds statements like *A mib is a man* and found that they correctly answered questions like *Does a mib eat food? Does a mib have wings?* The children are obviously using their knowledge that men eat food and do not have wings as part of their starting information for logical reasoning. Smith (1979) used a similar inference task with a similar result. Finally, we have just seen that pragmatic reasoning schemas act to supplement natural logic inferences. In particular, the permission schema facili-

---

[2]Given an *if*–statement, *If p then q*, the contrapositive is the statement of the form, *If not q then not p*.

tates solution of the selection task by making the contrapositive of the conditional rule readily accessible to the reasoner. In all these cases, inferences are made that are either not guaranteed or not readily accessible in natural logic. These inferences are additional to those generated by natural logic alone. But inferences that the natural logic system generates are never made wrong by the pragmatically-based inferences.

## NATURAL LOGIC AND MENTAL MODELS

Although the natural logic direct reasoning routine is satisfactory for making the short chains of logical inferences required for understanding discourse and for the kind of practical reasoning discussed earlier, it nevertheless represents a very low level of logical reasoning skill in that there are enormously many valid deductions it will fail to make. Its deficiencies help explain why people are rather poor at solving many logical reasoning problems in experiments and elementary logic courses. Both inside the lab and out of it, people are constantly faced with reasoning problems to which their logical reasoning program is not adequate or not pertinent. So the natural-logic approach does not deny the existence of other methods of reasoning.

Prominent among other methods of reasoning is the strategy of constructing a mental model of the information available and attempting to reason from that (Johnson-Laird, 1983). We think it very likely that subjects often use mental models in reasoning. It is almost certain that a complete account of deductive reasoning will need a subtheory of mental models as well as the approach outlined here, together with other components, for example, Cheng and Holyoak's (1985) pragmatic schemas, as discussed above.

However, Johnson-Laird (1983, 1986a) has claimed that all reasoning can be explained with mental models—no mental logic need to be posited. Propositional reasoning (i.e., the kind of reasoning that Tables 7.1–7.3 are about) provides a possible obstacle to this claim. His only published account of this kind of reasoning (Johnson-Laird, 1986a, pp. 21–27) consists of an algorithm that uses truth tables to compute the semantic informativeness of propositions, and it works by progressively substituting True and False for propositions in premises. The model is illustrated with a problem that has premises of the form:

p and not-q, or r
q

The algorithm makes successive recodings of the first premise as follows:

1. p and not-True, or r
2. p and False, or r
3. False or r
4. r

Although Johnson-Laird (personal communication, 1987) says that no claim to psychological reality for this model was intended that is not clear in his description, so it is fair to point out that there are several problems with the model. First, the algorithm makes extensive use of truth tables, both in the informativeness computations and in the reasoning itself (e.g., in the example problem, the steps from Line 1 to Line 2 and from Line 2 to Line 3 depend on truth tables); but there has been general agreement for some years that ordinary reasoning does not use truth tables (e.g., Braine, 1978; Falmagne, 1980; Fillenbaum, 1977; O'Brien, 1987; Osherson, 1975). Second, the algorithm uses principles very like the inference schemas it seeks to supplant (e.g., the step from Line 3 to Line 4 depends on a principle hard to distinguish from Schema 8 of Table 7.1). Third, the algorithm is not a convincing example of "reasoning without logic" (because it has truth tables and much other logic built into it). Fourth, the algorithm's only "mental models" are the truth tables, and these are not mental models in any ordinary sense of that term in the psychological literature; thus, it is questionable that the model could claim to be a "mental model" theory. Finally, there is no reason to believe that subjects actually go through anything like the reasoning steps performed by the algorithm.[3]

Johnson-Laird's most plausible use of mental models is in his conception of reasoning with categorical syllogisms (e.g., Johnson-Laird & Steedman, 1978; Johnson-Laird & Bara, 1984). Mental models may well play a more crucial role in subjects' methods of solving many of these syllogisms than in problems like those of Table 7.3. For a more general critique of Johnson-Laird's claim that reasoning without logic is possible, see Macnamara (1986, pp. 45–48).

## SPECULATIONS ON HOW CHILDREN ACQUIRE THE PRIMARY INFERENCE SCHEMAS

Assuming that there is a mental logic that is universal, a critical question inevitably arises: What are the developmental origins of the logic? I do not feel ready to propose a fully worked-out answer to this question, but I do

---

[3]Well since this was written, I have seen an unpublished paper (Johnson-Laird & Byrne, 1988) that clearly disavows the model criticized and proposes a new mental-model theory of propositional reasoning. However, it seems to me to be open to objections of the same sort as I raise above against the model discussed, although detailed comment would be inappropriate because the theory may not be in its final form.

wish to discuss some possible answers and associated issues, and make some speculative suggestions.

To my knowledge, the only empirical work on the acquisition of logical reasoning schemas has been done by Falmagne (1980, this volume). Falmagne (1980) wrote that schemas, at least in part, are learned:

> From a concept-learning process whereby the child encounters instances of a given pattern of inference . . . , is given feedback either by other speakers or reality . . . and abstracts the logical structure common to those instances. (p. 182)

One set of her experiments focused on the acquisition of the inference form known as modus tollens; this is the inference, from premises of the form *If p then q* and *not q*, to the conclusion *not p*. The experiments indicate that children of 8–11 years can acquire this form from examples in which feedback is given. The other set of experiments, with children of 10–11 years, shows that children can learn to give "Can't tell" responses on indeterminate problems of the type that often elicit the fallacy called "asserting the consequent." (Given premises of the form *If p then q* and *q*, the fallacy of asserting the consequent is to conclude *p*.) In both cases, Falmagne argued that the subjects abstracted the form of the inference (or noninference, in the case of the indeterminate problem). I have no quarrel with that conclusion, but I do claim that these reasoning forms belong in the category of secondary reasoning skills. On this sort of conditional reasoning problem, it is only modus ponens that is primary.

Modus ponens is the inference in which the premises have the form, *If p then q* and *p*, and the conclusion is *q* (Table 7.1, Schema 12). The evidence is that children make inferences of this form by at least five to six years of age, as early as it seems practicable to test them. Intuitively, if one is unable to make inferences of this form, one does not understand the meaning of *if*. In general, there appear to be some inferences that are so closely tied to the meanings of words that, if the inference is not understood, one is inclined to say that the word is not understood. Modus ponens stands in that relation to *if*. An inference schema that seems to stand in the same relation to *or* is Schema 8 of Table 7.1, which dictates that, given two alternatives, if one turns out to be false, then the other must be true. (If not, the choices were not really alternatives in the first place.) In so far as the primary inferences are tied to the meanings of words like *if*, *or*, etc., a theory of the acquisition of the primary inferences is tantamount to a theory of the learning of the meanings of the words.

Let us now ask: Can Falmagne's proposal for the secondary inferences be generalized to the primary ones? To simplify matters, I consider only *if* and modus ponens. One can readily envisage early learning trials of the following sort:

A parent says "If you open the window, it'll let the wind in." Parent opens the window. "See."

Or:

Parent says, "If you look in the box, you'll find your toy." Child looks in the box with parent's help. Either the toy appears, or there is evident consternation on the parent's part indicating that he or she expected to find it.

Or:

Parent says, "If you wave your glass around, you'll spill your juice. . . . See, I told you so."

These are all practical demonstrations of modus ponens.

Thus, applied to the primary inferences, Falmagne's proposal would amount to the claim that modus ponens is learned through a series of learning trials of this sort. It certainly seems plausible that trials like these will turn out to be necessary for acquiring, at least, *if* and the *if*-modus ponens connection. Testing that hypothesis will be an important piece of research, although a methodologically difficult one. Thus, in general, it seems that the study of the developmental origins of natural logic must lead to a research program of discovering the relevant kinds of learning trials that the environment provides and of verifying that acquisition of the connectives does, indeed, depend on these trials (or of discovering on which experiences the acquisition depends).

However, after we have discovered what the critical learning experiences are for acquiring the connectives, we will still face some profound questions. What are children actually learning from such experiences? They must be learning the words for the connectives in their native language and presumably associations between connectives and inference forms. However, what about the inference forms themselves? It seems unlikely that inference forms, words, and their associations are all learned together, from scratch, so-to-speak; the reasons will become apparent as we consider Macnamara's (1986) thesis.

Macnamara (1986) argued that the mental logic is not learned. He agreed with Fodor (1975) that there must be a language of thought whose relation to the mind is rather analogous to the relation of the machine language to a computer. Fodor argued not only that there is a language of thought but that its logical power must be as great as that of natural languages; moreover, in learning a natural language, the child is essentially learning a translation—a compiler—into the language of thought. Macnamara argued that many basic logical notions must be available to the language-learning child—to begin with, the notions of truth and falsity. The notion of truth is implicit in the child's making of assertions: Assertion presupposes a judgement of truth. With truth, there necessarily goes a notion of falsity; with both of these, there must be some knowledge of the principle of contradiction. For the system of Table 7.1, that would mean that children do not have to learn Schemas 4 and 6, nor Schema 14, as used in the universal reasoning program (these define relations between truth and falsity). Macnamara then proposed, essentially, that children learn the English connectives (*and* and *or*, at least—he does not discuss *if*) by mapping them onto the corresponding connectives of the language of thought, which are assumed to be truth-functional. In effect, for the system of Table 7.1, that would mean that none of the schemas have to be learned. In general form, the Fodor–Macnamara argument is a powerful one: Learning something involves representing it, and that requires a pre-existing system of representation with sufficient resources. Thus, to acquire a mental logic, there must be a pre-existing system in which its constants can be expressed.

I think this argument excludes the possibility that connectives and inference schemas could be learned completely from scratch. Elsewhere (Braine, 1988), I argue that the distinction between predicates and arguments is implicit in all talk about concepts and relations; it is like a Kantian category of thought that has to be taken as present at the outset of language acquisition. Reference, truth, and falsity may well have similar status. However, Macnamara's arguments do not specify the nature of the "language of thought." Obviously, the mere requirement of representability in a "language of thought" greatly underdetermines the form of a mental logic. Macnamara would no doubt agree that there are issues about the acquisition of connectives and schemas that are not touched by his arguments and that there is much more to be said on the subject. Thus, I shall speculate a little. I consider, first, *if*, and then *and* and *or*.

## If

In discussing *if*, I intend primarily to account for the acquisition of modus ponens along with a conditional connective. I shall not be concerned with differences among conditional connectives (e.g., the difference between *when* and *if* in English). If we compare the two (e.g., *When Daddy gets home we'll have dinner* vs. *If Daddy gets home we'll have dinner*), we see that *if* marks uncertainty about the actuality of the antecedent event. Children learn *when* a little before *if* but grasp the difference in usage fairly early (Bowerman, 1986). My proposal is concerned with what these have in common, and it will need further development to account for the difference, which is not universal among languages (cf. Bowerman, 1986).

It seems to me that the toddler has much knowledge about contingencies that is probably relevant to learning a conditional connective and the inferences associated with it.[4] Sensitivity to contingencies is biologically very primitive: Decades of work on learning and conditioning have amply demonstrated that not only human infants but all vertebrate and many invertebrate species learn contingencies readily (e.g., Brogden, 1951; Mackintosh, 1975). Moreover, given a series of contingency learning problems, one after another, as in some learning sets, many mammalian species show improvement; in macaque monkeys and in all hominoid species, including toddler-age human children, the improvement characteristically soon reaches a level of one-trial learning of new arbitrary contingencies (Harlow, 1949, 1958). To learn a new arbitrary contingency in one trial presumably implies a *concept* of a contingency. (Otherwise, how would the subject know how to encode one trial's worth of information?) I conclude, therefore, that at the time they encounter *if* children have a concept of a contingency relation. They may well have concepts of various kinds of contingency relations also, for example, they appear to know a good deal about causal contingencies and means-end relations (e.g., Piaget, 1952, 1954; Langer, 1986).

Let us consider how knowledge of contingencies could be related to the acquisition of modus ponens. Suppose there is a contingency between two events, $E_1$ and $E_2$—that $E_1$ is followed by $E_2$. We may represent the contingency by:

5. $E_1 \rightarrow E_2$

Now, it is true by definition that when $E_1$ occurs, $E_2$ follows. We can represent this fact as:

6. $\dfrac{E_1 \rightarrow E_2;\ E_1}{E_2}$

This expression has the same general form as modus ponens. However, in Formulae 5 and 6, $E_1$, $E_2$, and $E_1 \rightarrow E_2$ are not representations within a child. But suppose, now, that a child has noted the contingency. Because the child has (ex hypothesi) a *concept* of a contingency, it can represent the arrow, and the events themselves can be represented by clauses or sentences. Moreover, to have a concept of a contingency is presumably to know that whenever two events are related as in Formula 5, then Formula 6 will hold for them (i.e., it is to always expect $E_2$ given $E_1$, when $E_1 \rightarrow E_2$). Thus, modus ponens is bound to hold for *if* once the child has associated *if* with the notion of a contingency.

It might be said that the foregoing argument merely fleshes out Macnamara's thesis as applied to *if/when*—the child merely has to map them on to an already existing notion in the language of thought. In one sense, this is

---

[4]I am indebted to Hartvig Dahl for setting me off on this line of thought.

true. However, the fleshing-out adds considerably in that it traces a logical notion, the conditional, to one that is not usually considered logical, a contingency.

## And and or.

For these connectives, I accept Macnamara's idea that children learn *and* and *or* by mapping them on to connectives in the language of thought. However, I question that the connectives in the langauge of thought are conjunction and disjunction of propositions. Here, I would like to revive an earlier proposal (Braine, 1978)—that the root meanings of *and* and *or* have to do with two kinds of lists, more specifically, with two ways in which items can be iterated in lists: joint iteration (*and*) and iteration of alternatives (*or*). In joint iteration all the items from the list are to be selected, in iteration of alternatives at least one. In support of this proposal, it has often been noted that both *and* and *or* have usages that are not derivable from their propositional usages. For instance, although *George and Mary have long hair* can be regarded as short for the conjunction *George has long hair and Mary has long hair, George and Mary are a married couple* obviously cannot be derived from the conjunction *George is a married couple and Mary is a married couple*. Similarly, *tea or coffee* in *What do you want—tea or coffee?* cannot be derived from a disjunction of propositions. The last two examples are readily interpreted as examples of the two kinds of iteration—the first, where all items are to be selected; the second, where at least one is to be. (In the second type, it is normally expected, for good pragmatic reasons, that only one item will be selected, but that is not part of the definition of the list type.)

Data on children's earliest usage of *and* seem to favor the idea that *and* represents iteration, but are not decisive. The earliest conjunctions usually join phrases rather than clauses, but sentences joined by *and* also appear quite early (de Villiers, Tager-Flusberg, & Hakuta, 1977; Lust & Mervis, 1980). In the most favored interpretation, the phrasal usages are not derived from conjoined sentences (e.g., Ardery, 1980; Hakuta, de Villiers, & Tager-Flusberg, 1982), but the matter is in dispute (Lust & Mervis, 1980). Early data on the interpretation of *or* are also consistent with my proposal (e.g. Johansson & Sjolin, 1975).

The idea that the relevant connectives in the language of thought have to do with list organization (ways of iterating items on a list or ways of selecting items) is supported by the observation that language fails to observe certain analogies that hold in logic between relations among propositions and sets. In logic, the following analogy is standard:

Conjunction: Intersection:: Disjunction: Union

However, languages treat conjunction as more similar to union than to intersection: In most (perhaps, all) languages the word that is used to represent a conjunction of propositions (*and* in English, *et* in French, *ve* in Hebrew, *he* in Mandarin, etc.) is also the most usual way to indicate the union of sets and is used to iterate the members of a class. Intersection is typically expressed by relative clauses or other modifiers on a noun. The similarity between conjunction and union would come from the fact that propositions, and facts and events represented by propositions, can be iterated just like other entities. Thus, propositional *and* and *or* or are the special case where the iterated entities are propositions, or facts and events represented by propositions. Note that if the underlying connectives in the language of thought are two kinds of iteration of items on lists, then the various uses of *and* and *or* in English (conjunction and union, in the case of *and*) fall out automatically as a function of the nature of the list content.

Now let us consider how we might get from these ideas to the relevant schemas of Table 7.1. The proposal would be that the schemas are the special cases, in which the list contents are propositions, of more general inference patterns concerning lists. Thus, in their broad versions, Schemas 1 and 2 would concern concatenation of items into lists and extractability of items from lists, Schema 3 is concerned with relations between the two kinds of lists, Schema 8 would eliminate an item form a disjunctive list, and so on.

## SUMMARY AND CONCLUSIONS

I began by arguing that some logical reasoning competence must be universal in the human species, present even in preliterate societies. It would have the adaptive function of providing information integration processes needed in understanding discourse and in practical reasoning (i.e., integrating information arriving from different sources or at different times). It probably evolved along with language and culture. These primary logical reasoning skills (i.e., the universal competence) must be distinguished from secondary reasoning skills, which depend heavily on literacy and a concern with language qua language, and which are often acquired (although in very unequal measure) by educated people in literate societies.

The natural logic theory proposes that the universal primary skills consist of a set of inference forms and a simple program for using them to generate short chains of inferences. I illustrated how this process operates and sketched the nature of the evidence for the system proposed. Perhaps the most notable supporting fact is that the inferences of the set are made essentially errorlessly by adults on problems without other sources of complexity and are available early to children. The existence of this set of very easy inferences has been passed over in the literature, possibly because of a preoccupation with logical error. Errors are overwhelmingly due to processing limitations and to poor secondary skills, not to lack of the primary skills.

In practical reasoning and in discourse comprehension, natural logic and pragmatics work together and enrich each other. Thus, through conversational implicature, invited inference, specific subject-matter knowledge, and pragmatic reasoning schemas, pragmatic factors act to expand the set of accessible propositions from which inferences are made. The natural logic approach is thus not in conflict with pragmatic approaches to reasoning, except in so far as these claim to provide a complete theory by themselves. Similarly, our approach does not deny that subjects use mental models; it only denies that this is their only method of reasoning.

How children acquire the primary inference forms is a fundamental developmental question. Falmagne (1980) proposed that inference forms are abstracted from observing a variety of instances. I argue that this proposal would lead to a plausible conception of the kinds of experiences that are relevant for the acquisition of connectives and of their relation to inference—one that is well worth investigating. However, even if learning depends on the kinds of experiences that Falmagne's theory would lead one to expect, a profound and difficult question arises about the cognitive prerequisites of learning—what cognitive structures and what pre-existing notions must young children have in order for them to learn from the experiences? I speculate that *if* and its relation to modus ponens depend on knowledge of contingencies, and that *and* and *or* and the related schemas are associated with unlearned basic ways of organizing and processing items in lists.

## ACKNOWLEDGMENTS

Preparation of this article was supported by a grant, BNS 8409252, from the National Science Foundation (Martin Braine, Principal Investigator). The article owes a great debt to numerous conversations, discussions, and arguments with David O'Brien over the last several years. I am also indebted to other collaborators in prior work, notably Barbara Rumain and Brian Reiser, and to Bill Overton for comment and stimulus at the last round of revision.

## REFERENCES

Ardery, G. (1980). On coordination in child language. *Journal of Child Language, 7*, 305–320.

Bever, T. G. (1970). The cognitive basis for linguistic structures. In J. R. Hayes (Ed.), *Cognition and the development of language* (pp. 279–362). New York: Wiley.

Bowerman, M. (1986). First steps in acquiring conditionals. In E. Traugott, C. A. Ferguson, J. S. Reilly, S. A. ter Meulen (Eds.), *On conditionals*. Cambridge, UK: Cambridge University Press.

Braine, M. D. S. (1978). On the relation between the natural logic of reasoning and standard logic. *Psychological Review, 85*, 1–21.

Braine, M. D. S. (January, 1987). Some reasons for believing that there is a natural logic. Paper presented at the 12th Annual Interdisciplinary Conference, Jackson Hole, WY.

Braine, M. D. S. (1988). Modeling the acquisition of linguistic structure. In Y. Levy, I. M. Schlesinger, & M. D. S. Braine (Eds.), *Categories and processes in language acquisition* (pp. 217–259). Hillsdale, NJ: Lawrence Erlbaum Associates.

Braine, M. D. S., Noveck, I. A., Samuels, M. A. C., Fisch, S. M., Lea, R. B., & O'Brien, D. P. (1989). Direct evidence for a mental logic. Unpublished manuscript.

Braine, M. D. S., & O'Brien, D. P. (1989). A theory of *if*: A lexical entry, reasoning program, and pragmatic principles. Unpublished manuscript.

Braine, M. D. S., Reiser, B. J., & Rumain, B. (1984). Some empirical justification for a theory of natural propositional logic. In G. H. Bower (Ed.), *The psychology of learning and motivation: Advances in research and thinking* (Vol. 18, pp. 313–371). New York: Academic Press.

Braine, M. D. S., & Rumain, B. (1983). Logical reasoning. In J. H. Flavell & E. M. Markman (Eds.), *Handbook of child psychology*. Vol. III. *Cognitive development* (pp. 263–340). New York: Wiley.

Brogden, W. J. (1951). Animal studies of learning. In S. S. Stevens (Ed.), *Handbook of experimental psychology* (pp. 568–612). New York: Wiley.

Cheng, P. W., & Holyoak, K. J. (1985). Pragmatic reasoning schemas. *Cognitive Psychology, 17*, 391–416.

Cheng, P. W., Holyoak, K. J., Nisbett, R. E., & Oliver, L. M. (1986). Pragmatic versus syntactic approaches to training deductive reasoning. *Cognitive Psychology, 18*, 293–328.

de Villiers, J., Tager-Flusberg, J., & Hakuta, K. (1977). Deciding among theories of the development of coordination in child speech. *Papers & Reports on Child Language Development, 13*, 118–125.

Donaldson, M. (1976). Development of conceptualization. In V. Hamilton & M. D. Vernon (Eds.), *The development of cognitive processes*. New York: Academic Press.

Falmagne, R. J. (1980). The development of logical competence: A psycholinguistic perspective. In R. Kluwe & H. Spada (Eds.), *Developmental models of thinking* (pp. 171–197). New York: Academic Press.

Fillenbaum, S. (1977). Mind your *p*'s and *q*'s: The role of content and context in some uses of *and*, *or*, and *if*. In G. Bower (Ed.), *The psychology of learning and motivation* (Vol. 11, pp. 41–100). New York: Academic Press.

Fodor, J. A. (1975). *The language of thought*. Cambridge, MA: Harvard University Press.

Geis, M., & Zwicky, A. M. (1971). On invited inferences. *Linguistic Inquiry, 2*, 561–566.

Grice, H. P. (1975). Logic and conversation. In P. Cole and J. L. Morgan (Eds.), *Syntax and semantics, III: Speech acts*. New York: Academic Press.

Grice, H. P. (1978). Further notes on logic and conversation. In P. Cole (Ed.), *Syntax and semantics, IX: Pragmatics*. New York: Academic Press.

Hakuta, K., De Villiers, J., & Tager-Flusberg, H. (1982). Sentence coordination in Japanese and English. *Journal of Child Language, 9*, 193–207.

Harlow, H. F. (1949). The formation of learning sets. *Psychological Review, 45*, 51–65.

Harlow, H. F. (1958). The evolution of learning. In A. Roe & G. G. Simpson (Eds.), *Behavior and evolution*. New Haven, CT: Yale University Press.

Harris, P. (1975). Inferences and semantic development. *Journal of Child Language, 2*, 143–152.

Johansson, B. S., & Sjolin, B. (1975). Preschool children's understanding of the coordinates "and" and "or." *Journal of Experimental Child Psychology. 19*, 233–240.

Johnson-Laird, P. N. (1983). *Mental models*. Cambridge, MA: Harvard University Press.

Johnson-Laird, P. N. (1968a). Reasoning without logic. In T. Myers, K. Brown, & B.

McGonigle (Eds.), *Reasoning and discourse processes* (pp. 13-50). London: Academic Press.

Johnson-Laird, P. N. (June, 1986b). The development of reasoning. Paper presented at the Stirling Conference on Human Development.

Johnson-Laird, P. N., & Bara, B. (1984). Syllogistic inference. *Cognition, 16,* 1-61.

Johnson-Laird, P. N., & Byrne, R. M. J. (1988). *Reasoning by rule or model: The case of propositional inference.* Unpublished manuscript.

Johnson-Laird, P. N., & Steedman, M. J. (1978). The psychology of syllogisms. *Cognitive Psychology, 10,* 46-99.

Langer, J. (1986). *The origins of logic: One to two years.* New York: Academic Press.

Lea, R. B., O'Brien, D. P., Fisch, S. M., Noveck, I. A., & Braine, M. D. S. (1989). *Predicting propositional-logic inferences in text comprehension.* Unpublished manuscript.

Lust, B., & Mervis, C. (1980). Development of coordination in the natural speech of young children. *Journal of Child Language, 7,* 279-304.

Mackintosh, N. J. (1975). From classical conditioning to discrimination learning. In W. K. Estes (Ed.), *Handbook of learning and cognitive processes. Vol. 1. Introduction to concepts and issues.* Hillsdale, NJ: Lawrence Erlbaum Associates.

Macnamara, J. (1986). *A border dispute: The place of logic in psychology.* Cambridge, MA: MIT Press.

O'Brien, D. P. (1987). The development of conditional reasoning: An iffy proposition. In H. Reese (Ed.), *Advances in child behavior and development.* New York: Academic Press.

O'Brien, D. P., & Overton, W. F. (1982). Conditional reasoning and the competence-performance issue: A developmental analysis of a training task. *Journal of Experimental Child Psychology, 34,* 274-290.

Osherson, D. N. (1975). Models of logical thinking. In R. Falmagne (Ed.), *Reasoning: Representation and process in children and adults.* Hillsdale, NJ: Lawrence Erlbaum Associates.

Piaget, J. (1952). The origins of intelligence in children. New York: IUP.

Piaget, J. (1954). The construction of reality in the child. New York: Basic Books.

Rumain, B., Connell, J., & Braine, M. D. S. (1983). Conversational comprehension processes are responsible for reasoning fallacies in children as well as adults: *If* is not the biconditional. *Developmental Psychology, 19,* 471-481.

Smith, C. L. (1979). Children's understanding of natural language hierarchies. *Journal of Experimental Child Psychology, 27,* 457-458.

Wason, P. C. (1968). Reasoning about a rule. *Quarterly Journal of Experimental Psychology, 20,* 273-281.

# 8

## The Three Faces of If

Ellin Kofsky Scholnick
*University of Maryland*

## "IF" AND DEDUCTIVE THINKING

Thinking is not confined to the known facts of our daily existence. We plan, imagine, and make predictions. These hypotheses, suppositions, and predictions may, in turn, be the foundation for further conceptual extensions. In order to insure that the superstructure of reasoning does not collapse of its own weight, logicians have proposed a set of laws that define the permissible form of elementary assumptions and that govern legitimate extensions from them. Because those assumptions (or propositions) can vary widely in content, their form and the laws of extension or deduction must be relatively content free. It is irrelevant whether the assumptions involve physics, politics, biology, or religion, or even whether a hypothetical proposition is true. Logic provides methods for determining what legitimately follows from any assumption once it is made. The methods are derived from the opposition between affirmation and contradiction.

One form of proposition is an *if* statement, such as "If it snows, Eve will stay home." The *if* statement, or conditional, consists of two clauses: a subordinate clause that states an antecedent, and a main clause that states a consequent. In formal notation, the symbol for the antecedent clause is often *p*, and the consequent is called *q*. One interpretation of a conditional proposition is that when p occurs, only q follows and nothing else (i.e., not-q does not occur with p).

An initial proposition can be extended in four ways. Every conditional contains an antecedent and consequent clause. The next proposition can affirm or negate one of those two clauses. "If it snows, Eve stays home" can be followed by: (a) "It snows," (b) "Eve stays home," (c) "It does not snow," or (d) "Eve does not stay home." Forms of argument are labeled by the second statement that describes one clause of the conditional. The laws of logic deal with how one can legitimately derive or test a conclusion about the remaining conditional clause.

"If it snows, Eve will stay home. It is snowing." What can we conclude about Eve's location? In symbolic form, the argument is "If p, then q; p." Note that this argument (Affirm the Antecedent) resembles a sentence completion. The definition of *if* is that p goes with q and nothing else. Thus, to conclude the argument, the reasoner merely has to read the *if* clause and produce the missing main clause: Eve remains at home. That is why this argument is called *modus ponens*, because one builds on or affirms the definition of *if* directly to derive a conclusion. One can also invoke the logic of contradiction. An argument is valid if there is no way to interpret the premises that could lead to a denial of the conclusion. The premise implies that "Eve always stays at home when it snows" and precludes the opposite possibility that she goes out in a blizzard.

Suppose it does not snow. This second argument denies the content of the antecedent clause. "If p, then q; not p." Where is Eve? The initial premise says what happens when it snows; it does not say what happens in other weather. We can imagine Eve having a cold and staying home in sunny weather, or taking advantage of a sunny day to leave. Both conclusions are possible, and we cannot choose between them to make a valid inference.

The third argument also does not permit drawing a single valid conclusion. In this argument, the consequent clause is affirmed. "If it snows, Eve stays home. Eve stays home." What is the weather like? "If p, then q; q." We know that snow leads to Eve's confinement to her residence, because snow only has one consequence. But it is not clear that confinement to home has only one cause—bad weather. Perhaps, Eve is waiting for a repairman. Because two contradictory conclusions are possible, no single deduction is valid.

The fourth argument includes a second statement that denies the consequent clause: "If it snows, Eve stays home. Eve does not stay home. What is the weather?" "If p, then q; not q." This argument permits a valid conclusion and has a Latin label for that conclusion, *modus tollens*, where *tollens* refers to denial. We know that if it snows, Eve would have to stare at her four walls. She never goes out when it snows. She is outside, so it must not be snowing. No correct interpretation of the premises can lead us to conclude that Eve ventures outside in snow. There is no way the conclusion could be false and both preceding propositions true.

Conditional arguments play a central role in the study of deduction, because they mirror the conditions that define logical validity or invalidity (e.g., Niedorf, 1967). A valid argument is like "If p, then q," where p is the body of premises and q is the conclusion drawn from the premises. If the premises are accepted, only the conclusion should follow from them. You can prove an argument is invalid by using modus tollens. If the conclusion is false, so must one or more of the premises be (not p and not q).

The psychological study of deductive reasoning has been problematic, both because the laws of conditional logic have been the subject of debate,[1] and because there are a variety of ways to draw and test the correct conclusion. A correct evaluation of modus tollens arguments could be the result of a straightforward application of a learned formula: "When the consequent is denied, so is the antecedent." The reasoner could translate "If it is snowing, Eve stays home" into "In a snowstorm, Eve's only location is home." Only q is also p. Because Eve is not at home, it must also not be snowing. Another solution uses *reductio ad absurdum*. If it is snowing, Eve is home. Eve is not at home. When it snows, Eve is confined, but the statement says Eve is not confined. When it snows, Eve cannot be at home and not at home. That is absurd or contradictory. Therefore, it cannot be snowing; it must be some other weather (Wason & Johnson-Laird, 1972).

In addition to logical strategies, there are extralogical ploys. Logical formulas are abstract, but each sentence provides particular content and is uttered in a particular context. People construct explanatory models of human behavior. If we know Eve lives near Hudson Bay where icy winters block roads, we assume Eve is unlikely to go away when it snows, and she is likely to take advantage of a thaw to do some shopping. There are so many ways to arrive at a conclusion about Eve's location from knowledge of the weather, and determine the weather from examining Eve's behavior, that explaining how conclusions are drawn is problematic. Are deductions based on the laws of logic or the content of the clauses? This leads to ambiguities in our interpretation of the nature of deduction and the dilemma of the three faces of *if*.

## SOURCES OF DEDUCTION

The lady, *If*, who appears in deductive reasoning presents three faces, the features of which are controversial. A reader of papers on conditional logic has to decide which face the writer is contemplating and whether the writer believes there are multiple dissociated personalities, one fundamental face that two layers of makeup enhance, or facets of an integrated whole. An assessment of the author's viewpoint on the adult face provides the back-

---

[1]This chapter is written from the viewpoint that Evans (1982) labeled the rationalist perspective. It is assumed that people, however imperfectly, do employ reasoning strategies and that explanation of performance should focus on these strategies rather than errors on particular tasks that might reflect extralogical factors. If this assumption is not made, there is really little unique about deduction to address. The chapter is a selective survey of viewpoints that try to account for how people solve conditional problems as opposed to those that try to account for failures in solution due to response biases.

ground for evaluating why particular developmental periods or developmental processes might be especially revealing to observers of deductive thinking.

The face, however, is merely the outside appearance. Discussions of the nature and scope of deduction, and the nature and course of its development, reflect some assumptions about the anatomy of mental development (Overton, 1984). Conditional logic tasks tap how people decide whether a deduction is valid. Hence, descriptions of conditional logic rest on assumptions about the source of the criteria for validity: in logic alone, in knowledge of the world, in self-awareness of beliefs, or in some combination of these. In turn, the source of decision criteria dictates different developmental theories and even different definitions of deduction. There is no consensus about the implications of conditional statements and, therefore, the phenomenon to be accounted for. It is not always clear whether the *if* that we contemplate is some logical idealization or a natural face. Often, it is argued that deductive reasoning is a mien assumed by the writers of text books on logic who, in relaxation, slip back into a more natural expression. Thus, the choice of the face the individual researcher contemplates is based on views about the nature of conditionals and the origin of reasoning. This chapter examines the faces of *if* from several perspectives and evaluates whether it is possible to separate the diverse aspects from one another.

## PROPOSITIONS

The three faces of *if* are the propositional, the semantic, and the presuppositional. For many, the propositional face is basic, and all else is simply makeup. A propositional theory of reasoning claims people translate material into an abstract representation that has the form of a premise like "if p, then q." Some propositional theories (e.g., Inhelder & Piaget, 1958) also assume that the process of mapping statements onto formal representations is relatively uninfluenced by the content of the statement. The structure of "if p, then q," and the valid lines of argument derivable form it, are the same, regardless of the content of the proposition. Propositional theories often differ with respect to four issues:

1. Are conditional and other deductions isolated procedures or a coherent body of laws?
2. Is the nature of conditional reasoning based on a logical truth table or an inference schema or some other form of representation?
3. Do deductions originate in language or cognition?
4. Is the origin of logic innate or is logic learned or constructed from experience?

## The Empiricist Perspective

*A Typical Model.*   In Braine's (chap. 7 in this volume; Braine, Reiser, & Rumain, 1984; Braine & Rumain, 1983; Rumain, Connell, & Braine, 1983) propositional theory, the central component of reasoning is a set of abstract arguments. Young children use meaningful content and context to select the appropriate argument, but skilled adult reasoners can focus directly on the formal structure of arguments to determine what they say, rather than what they might mean in context. Braine assumes that the purpose of most deduction is to understand discourse and to integrate information from different sources. The tool for achieving this goal is ordinary, natural, or primary reasoning. Upon hearing a sentence, people try to map it onto an inference schema that stipulates what can follow from a set of sentences. An inference schema is a logical formula stating the initial and second premise of an argument, and the permissible conclusion. Failures in reasoning arise when the person does not understand a sentence, mismatches it with an inappropriate inference schema, or has problems in application, because the length of the chain of reasoning or the wordiness of the premises overwhelms the individual's processing capacity. Because these inference schemas are basic and automatic, and because the schemas merely conjoin information, the inference schemas that Braine postulates are simply interpretations of particular lexical logical particles such as *not*, *or*, and *if*. In each case, the meaning of the lexical element directly defines the conclusion to the argument. The only *if*-argument appearing among Braine's primary inference schemas is modus ponens: If p, then q; p; therefore, q. Because, logically, *if* means p can only appear with q; modus ponens is automatically available to someone who comprehends the meaning of *if*.

There is another valid *if*-argument. People can sometimes evaluate modus tollens correctly. Braine suggests that skill in analysis of such arguments and reasoning with them is the product of a literate and legalistic educational system that focuses on thorough analysis of written discourse.

There are four noteworthy assumptions of this view. First, reasoning is comprised of a set of procedures or formulas, and skill in application of these formulas is dependent on the information-processing demands of the task. Second, the application of these schemas, and possibly the schemas, themselves, are learned by induction from verbal input. Third, Braine reduces the meaning of *if*, because modus ponens, alone, is a primary inference schema. Finally, there is no structural connection between the learning of the conditional and other logical rules; each rule is part of a list.

The learning of the primary *if*-inference schema depends on learning the meaning of the lexical logical element the inference schema contains. A parent warns her child, "If you throw that ball against the screen door, the screen will break." The child throws the ball despite the warning, and the screen is ripped. The parent responds, "I warned you, but you still threw the ball at the door. The screen is broken, and I am taking away the ball." From multiple instances of *if*, the child eventually extracts its meaning, which consists of the inference: Whenever *if* connects two clauses, and the contents of the antecedent *if*-clause is affirmed, the contents of the main clause will also be true. Braine (this volume) is not sure whether the child is innately endowed with the inference schema and merely infers the sentences to which it applies, or whether the child actually infers from *if*-sentences both the meaning of the conjunction and the legitimate conclusions to modus ponens arguments.

The primary inferences schemas only incorporate modus ponens, although Braine does grant reasoners access to the *reductio ad absurdum* technique that enables solutions of modus tollens. In order to handle a wider range of conditional argument forms, people rely on factors such as meaning, context, and world knowledge to make inferences. Eventually, the individual may develop analytic reasoning skills that will enable inferring a schema for reasoning directly with modus tollens arguments but not with the other forms of *if*-arguments. Because Braine has drawn upon Falmagne's analysis (e.g., 1980, this volume) to explain the origin of primary schemas, perhaps acquisition of analytic reasoning schemas might proceed in a similar fashion. Given the same warning, "If you throw that ball against the screen door, the screen will break," the child is obedient. The harried parent sighs in relief, "I was worried about letting you play with the ball. The screen is not ripped, so you must not have thrown the ball against it." From statements of the form, "If p, then q; not q," the child learns that usually "not p" follows.

This secondary deductive schema is learned by induction and used in deduction, too. However, both the learning and the application process are difficult. Both knowledge of the rule and its application might improve during the course of development, probably as the result of an education that requires such deductions of students. During childhood, individuals become increasingly skilled in "analytic" comprehension, the ability to extract the logical form from sentences despite their content. Older children may also be better at retaining information so as to process it.

Adults' difficulty with syllogisms in which the antecedent is denied or the consequences affirmed has led Braine to assert that just two inference schemas are associated with *if*. He argues that logical models based on the full set of four arguments or truth-table cannot characterize mature though, because even adults are inexpert. I, also, suspect that it is too difficult to explain mastery of the full roster of *if*-arguments using a learning model. In order to differentiate valid from invalid arguments, the child would have to identify the clauses in the first premise, decide which clause appeared in the second premise, and whether it was negated. Then, the child would have to note whether each argument always had a single conclusion. Not only are these discriminations complicated, but the child would also need a sophisticated mechanism for selecting inference schemas appropriate to each argument.

The fourth important assumption is that skill with the two valid *if*-arguments is acquired separately. It is not just that modus ponens is a primary inference schema and modus tollens is not; each is a part of an assortment of rules for other arguments signalled by other logical connectives that the child assembles. One schema does not necessarily imply another.

*Critique.*    The claim that deductive logic can be induced from experience with language is problematic. An inference schema is an abstraction, and this raises an issue that Braine (this volume) recognizes. Can the child learn context-free schemas without an abstraction mechanism that is as powerful as the very inference rules the individual has to acquire? (See also Falmagne, 1980, chap. 6 in this volume.) A second problem is that it is unclear whether children could learn the conditional inference schema simply by extracting the lexical meaning of *if*. Logicians are very careful to distinguish the argument form of *if* from ordinary meanings, because *if* has many meanings in conversation (Cheng, Holyoak, Nisbett, & Oliver, 1986; Johnson-Laird, 1983). *If* expresses threats, promises, conditions, causes, associations, and speculations. *If* is often used to modulate the meaning of a sentence. Children hear statements like, "I will do it, if possible," or "You can visit, if you please," or "If he wins the race, I'll eat my hat." *If* appears in more than conditionals. Although the focus of reasoning with *if* is in natural discourse, the term functions heterogeneously in discourse! (See Scholnick & Wing, 1989, for an analysis of *if* use in conversation.) Only sentence meaning and pragmatics provide cues for determining when *if* signals a conditional argument. Hence, there must be an elaborate theory of semantics and pragmatics that determines when the inference schema is to be invoked, regardless of whether the schema is part of analytic or primary deduction. Braine (this volume) seems to be moving towards incorporating more pragmatic information into his theory. Perhaps, the child would have to possess, from the start, mature analysis skills and extensive pragmatic and semantic knowledge in order to sort out the appropriate conditionals before learning their meaning.

Yet a third problem is that Braine's theory combines several types of reasoning. How are explanations of each type consistent with one another, and how are the types of reasoning articulated with one another? The most interesting topic is analytic reasoning, because it goes beyond the information given; yet, this aspect of deduction is not elaborated very much.

There is also debate about the necessity of modifying the logician's analysis of the conditional to account for human performance. Overton (Overton, Byrnes, & O'Brien, 1985; Overton & Newman, 1982) suggested that normative logic may, indeed, an appropriate basis for understanding adult deduction, but some situations may not evoke those norms. Some people can think like logicians. Twelfth graders who are given counterexamples can operate with the full conditional. When they realize that people can stay at home because of weather conditions or the state of their health, they understand the ambiguity of arguments that affirm the consequent. Our models of scientific proof are based on deductive logic. Because logicians obviously derived their model from somewhere, the model that restricts *if* to a partial truth table neither explains the origin of formal logic nor the conditions under which it is evoked or neglected.

## Structuralism

*Piaget's Theory.* Piaget's analysis of reasoning contrasts sharply with Braine's account. To Inhelder and Piaget (1958), *if* is a face connected to a body or organic system of hypothetico-deductive logic. In Braine's procedural analysis, sentences are translated into a symbolic form associated with a specific inference schema that is used to derive or judge valid arguments. The theory of deduction is used to explain how people reason with syllogisms and comprehend discourse when it has an argument form that resembles syllogisms. Piaget asserts that logic pertains not merely to discourse, but to the organization of ideas about the nature of actions and events. For Piaget, logic is not procedural but structural. His aim was not to describe the mental processes that underlie deduction but to use a model of deduction to explain mental processes (see Inhelder & de Caprona, this volume). He claimed that possessors of logical competence will encode a proposition as an exemplar of a logical form such as "if p, then q" and will automatically embed that proposition in a network containing all logically possible relations. The network consists of truth values and the interrelations between p and q, p or q, etc. Reasoners know that there are four states of affairs; p and q, p but not q, q but not p, and neither p nor q. The relation, "if p, then q" stipulates that three of those states may be realized, excluding p with not q. "If p, then q" is actually a disjunction of q and not p. Thus, the person who completely understands "if p, then q" knows how it is different from "if q, then p"; knows which expressions are its logical equivalents; and understands what falsifies the relation. In summary, Piaget accepts the logical or truth-functional definition of *if* and has used it in his analysis of deduction. Reasoning reflects a structure that interconnects truth values. The network is inherently deductive. It is structured by logical necessity, and it consists of valid interconnections (see Piaget, 1987).

The structure of logic is built up in development through observing the exchange relations that occur during transformations such as pouring water from one glass to another of a different shape, and through appreciating the necessary relations between partitions and unions of sets. The child forms an understanding of necessity, and of the logic which searches for it, by reflecting on events (see Murray, chap. 9 in this volume). The child abstracts the conditions for necessity and discerns how propositions are interrelated. Thus, conditional logic cannot be divorced from other forms of logic, and the four conditional arguments (modus ponens, modus tollens, deny the antecedent, and affirm the consequent) cannot be divorced from one another. A particular deduction exists within a logical context of potential deductions.

*Critique.* Keating (chap. 13 in this volume) reviews some arguments against the Piagetian position. Piaget has used a model of deduction at several levels. Because propositional logic is used to describe the structuring of thought in the formal operational stage, the theory of deduction is open to attacks about the validity of stage theory that arise from the unevenness of people's reasoning. There are also attacks on the model as an explanation of performance on reasoning tasks, because people may not operate as if they worked with a coherent and interrelated truth table. There are attacks on the consistency and completeness of the logic of the INRC group of formal operations and its origins. For example, Piéraut-Le Bonniec (1980) claimed that Piaget has ignored modal logic in explaining the origin of concepts of necessity and possibility. She argued that the concepts of necessity and possibility arise in concrete operations and are derived from class inclusion relations.[2]

In her chapter in this volume, Piéraut-Le Bonniec turns to another controversial point that Piaget was just beginning to address at the end of his career (See Inhelder and de Caprona, this volume). Initially, Piaget argued that individuals had to abstract the fundamental form of propositional relations independent of their particular content in order to reason deductively. Formal reasoning evolved as an interrelated set of abstract constructions during the formal operational stage. However, as Piaget (1987) began to study procedures for generating solutions to problems, he realized that notions of necessity and possibility are voiced prior to formal operations: Yet, the ideas are related to specific contents, situations, and goals. The process of development involves abstraction of propositional forms from specific contents and interrelating the propositions into a set of necessary relations and necessary inferences. Thus, Piaget began to realize that logic is very much influenced by the content of events, that it is very situation-specific, and that the evolution of logic started early and was prolonged. There has been a growing body of evidence that even in adults, (e.g., Evans, 1982; Staudenmayer, 1975), skill in reasoning is affected by the semantics and pragmatics of the speech act in which the conditional is embedded.

---

[2]Piaget does not deny the origin of implication in class inclusion but claims the meaning is extended and transformed when the individual learns to generate all possible combinations so as to deal with classes of classes and their implications.

## Meaning as a Moderator of Propositional Analyses

*Theories.* Two recent propositional theories that are offshoots of the Piagetian approach attempt to deal with both semantic and cognitive input to reasoning and to account for inconsistencies in children's performance. People often fail to reason validly for reasons that have nothing to do with their logical skills. It is not always easy to sort out the antecedent from the consequent clause and remember their contents. Encoding and recall are easier when sentences are familiar and sensible. Given our limitations on processing, semantics aids encoding propositions, and, therefore, the application of deductive logic. Thus, semantics and logic operate in concert. However, which is more basic, the encoding of material or the inferential logic? Case (1985) implied that if you can remember a premise and have sufficient memory space to carry through the necessary inferential steps, you can handle deductive arguments. Expanded memory results from neurological maturation and from increasing familiarity with deductive problems, which makes them easier to encode. Actual deductive techniques may be taught and become well practiced. The expanded memory and representational capacities of adolescence permit propositional thought. However, even adults may falter due to momentary processing deficits arising from problems that are difficult to encode or an already overtaxed processing system.

Like Case, Overton (1985; Overton & Newman, 1982) has recognized that numerous stimulus and processing variables may impede reasoners in applying what they know. With minimal processing demands and familiar material, people perform optimally. Yet, there are severe constraints on these facilitators. They cannot have an effect unless the basic competence to perform deduction is there in the first place (e.g., Overton, Ward, Noveck, Black, & O'Brien, 1987). The emergence of formal thought in adolescence is a prerequisite for exploiting the meanings in propositions.

Meaning from either perspective is simply tacked on to propositions. Familiarity facilitates reasoning. Both theories mix structuralist and processing approaches in their explanations of development. Case used structuralism to analyze encoding and information processing to describe the deductions from coded information. Overton dealt with reasoning capacities from a structuralist perspective but claims environmental factors and world knowledge influence evocation and use of capacities.

*Critique.* Both Case and Overton move us beyond the pure propositional view to incorporate semantic factors in reasoning. For these theories to be complete, they must offer a thorough analysis of the nature of meaning and how it specifically helps in encoding information and selecting appropriate inductive strategies. As Overton and his collaborators noted (1987), we lack explicit criteria for defining familiarity. Sentences the experimenter thinks tap familiar knowledge do not always do so. The problem of meaning is also central to defining the unit to be processed in information-processing theory. The same item can be stored singly or as part of a chunk, depending on the meaning the processor gives the item. If items have different meanings for people, it will be hard to predict how much storage space or processing load they require. There is no standard metric for storage units. The review of propositional theories suggests that pure propositional theories often need to be embedded in a theory of linguistic processing, if they are to provide a complete view of deductive behavior.

## SEMANTICS

### Meaning in Language

The second face of *if* is semantic. A semantic theory presumes that reasoning is carried out through sentence interpretation. Arguments are represented as sentences, not abstract logical formulas, Interest in the role of semantics in deduction has been motivated by a concern with the soundness of an argument as well as its validity. Validity reflects adherence to the rules of argumentation regardless of argument content. Soundness refers to content and to the ability to find a referent for a premise in the real world. In a sound argument, the premises and conclusion are factually or definitionally true. Formal logic is propositional and *deductive*. It focuses on the precise meanings of connectives and quantifiers in premises, and the rules by which those logical elements can be interpreted and evaluated, to produce well-formed and valid arguments, regardless of the content of the premises. But reasoning about unsound or hypothetical statements might be considered an affectation of an educated elite. Reasoning is effortful, so why not concentrate on evaluation of true premises? Hence, semantic theories posit a natural logic that deals with semantic interpretation of ordinary language. The interpretive process takes into account what the sentence says and what the sentence refers to in the world. A reasoner evaluates the referents of sentences to determine whether they make sense, refer to one another, and are consistent with one another. Natural logic relies on background knowledge and linguistic facility to supplant deductive reasoning. It tends to be *inductive* and, hence, dependent on experiential input.

Johnson-Laird (e.g., 1983, p. 62) argued that "conditionals are not creatures of constant hue. . . . Their logical properties are in part determined by the nature of the propositions they interrelate." On hearing conditional statements (Stalnaker, 1981; Staudenmayer, 1975), we invoke a schematic picture of the world based on our experience, and, then, we evaluate whether a particular q really does follow from p, or whether there are counterexamples. Reasoning is nothing more than evaluation of reference. Semantics provides reference that is used to decide the plausibility of conclusions. In this view that converts deduction into interpretation of reference, adolescence is simply a time when we have a fuller or a different organization of world knowledge and better skills for evaluating evidence. Semantics is all, and propositional structure is a caricature of reasoning.

Among semantic theories, there are different claims about the nature of reference in reasoning. In the strong view (e.g., Griggs, 1983; Stalnaker, 1981), reasoners evaluate conditionals against their beliefs, experiences, and theories of what is possible. These beliefs or actual experiences of events are used in the search for counterexamples that could invalidate arguments. In a weaker view, more consistent with formal logic, we simply represent sentences (even manifestly false ones) and then evaluate their overlap to verify if they are consistent with one another.

*Mental Models.*    Johnson-Laird (1983) provided the most detailed example of this weaker approach. He claimed that for each premise we construct mental models that symbolize the content to which each premise refers. When the constituents of an argument refer to the same content, we examine whether the properties attributed to the entities in the premises are consistent with property descriptions in the conclusion. Inconsistency produces the judgment that the conclusion is false. Consistency prompts a further check. Because premises can have multiple interpretations or meanings, we examine whether any of them would be inconsistent with the conclusion. If so, we decide that the conclusion is possibly true. When there is no case where the premises could be true and the conclusion false, we decide that the conclusion is necessarily true. The search for counterexamples and for consistency is guided by our general knowledge of the world and of language. It is not influenced by logical formulas.

Children are fairly adept at constructing mental models, as long as they have the appropriate vocabulary. The child must know what *if* means before constructing a mental model of a sentence like, "If it is a square, it is black." Developmental differences are more apparent in skill in integrating premises and evaluating them. Conditionals may be expressed in diverse forms that need to be transformed into a common format, and children may err in making those transformations because of limitations in their understanding of grammar and in their transformational skills. In addition, memory limitations may force children to abandon prematurely the requisite search for alternative meanings. Thus, like Braine, Johnson-Laird has attributed advances in reasoning to expansion of the lexicon, the information-processing system, and knowledge. However, the nature of representation differs between the two theorists. Braine has claimed that reasoning involves a set of formulas. The reasoner listens to sentences and chooses which formula fits. Johnson-Laird has claimed that reasoning requires a semantic representation of each premise, combination of the models of premises, and scanning to see whether that integrated model is consistent only with the conclusion. Logic resides in the construction and evaluation of semantic representations, not invocation of cognitive inference schemas.

*Critique.*   Can a semantic theory of deduction bypass logic? Although Johnson-Laird (1983, p. 29) sought to eliminate explicit logical components in the mind, such as inference schemas, there are implicit logical components. Logic creeps in via the theory of reference, the procedures that evaluate and integrate sentences so as to draw conclusions from them, and the means by which sentences are deemed plausible. If we use world knowledge to evaluate links between sentences, what is the structure of that knowledge? Often, theories of semantics incorporate logical relations as primitives and describe events in terms of necessary or sufficient links (Falmagne, 1975). The claim that conditionals reside in the world, not in the mind that perceives them, is a strictly empiricist view.

Johnson-Laird (1983, pp. 143–144) suggested that human mental machinery has an inbuilt logic. The evaluation of the links between sentences for internal consistency is performed by an innate procedure that searches for counterexamples. People know inherently that to prove an argument, there should be no way in which the premises are true and the conclusion is false. Tests of validity require search for alternative meanings for the premises that might falsify the conclusion. Instead of possessing conditional logic, we possess a more powerful set of procedures that can derive any inference schema as well as generate meanings and test for compatibility. Those procedures enable us to learn and to make natural inferences. This logic is not learned or constructed as a separate entity. It is part of human information processing.

Logic also enters into the determination of reference. Evaluating the fit between a sentence and its representation requires verification procedures that incorporate some of the very principles of deduction that underlie conditional reasoning. In summary, Johnson-Laird (1983) reduced logic to reference, because either statements are matched against a logically structured world, or because the procedures for evaluating reference are inherently logical (pp. 399–442). As a consequence, it is difficult to concede that meaning is everything. Logic must enter in.

## Meaning and Concepts

*The Theory.*   Johnson-Laird's analysis of reasoning focuses on referential meaning whereas Piéraut-Le Bonniec (this volume) emphasizes the role of meaningful concepts in deduction by linking reasons (or explanations) to reasoning (See also, Matalon; Ricco, this volume). Knowing why p and q are related enables an understanding of why p must cooccur with q, but not with its opposite. If we understand why Eve hates snow, we also understand why she stays at home in a storm and does not go out. Thus, implication is grounded in the reasons that link p and q, not in the lexical connective between clauses. Semantic analysis does not just deal with the match between a statement and a real world event (plausibility) or other statement content, or with the match between statement content and past knowledge (familiarity), but with the reasons why p and q are in a conditional sentence (relevance).

Piéraut-Le Bonniec (chap. 4 in this volume) examines reasoning with two kinds of connections, categorical relations and permission schemes. Her research presents conditionals expressing categorical relations such as "If it is a square, its perimeter is a multiple of four." The sentences describe the overlap in the properties of the entity named in the *if* clause and the entity in the consequent clause. These sentences embody the logical definition of entailment (e.g. Ricco, chap. 3 in this volume; Matalon, chap. 5 in this volume; Strawson, 1952). Because a square has four equal sides, its perimeter must necessarily be a multiple of four.[3] To be consistent, espousal of nonviolence in one domain requires the same stance, elsewhere. She claims that people acquire an understanding of the structure of *if* as they redefine the relation between p and q. As contradictions in the meaning of square and length of the perimeter arise, the two terms are reworked until the definition of each term fits the category structure expressed by *if*. That structure is "All ps are part of the class of q" (see Piaget, 1987, p. 137). She has also discussed deontic or permission schemas (see Cheng & Holyoak, 1985) in which the action described in the antecedent clause is permitted only if some precondition in the main clause is met (p only if q). The statement, "If he is drinking beer, he must be over 21 years old," sets up a situation where beer drinking is allowable only for people who have reached the age of majority. The consequent clause provides the grounds for the circumstances described in the *if* clause. Each of these two examples, definitional entailment and permission rules, are inextricably linked to notions of necessity, possibility, and impossibility.

*The Role of Logic.*    Although Piéraut-Le Bonniec emphasizes the centrality of meaning in reasoning, her analysis of conditional reasoning reveals close interconnections among the cognitive and semantic faces of deduction. Let us examine how the child understands the entailment relation between the antecedent *if* clause and its consequent clause. In order to forge a relation between a square and its perimeter, the individual must be able to define "square" and "perimeter," and to select attributes that they share.

---

[3]In Piéraut-Le Bonniec's experiments, she imposes a restriction by using sticks. The perimeter of a figure must be a number that is a multiple of four whole units. In most situations, the sides of a square can contain fractional units.

Definitions are based on construction of a class in which all objects necessarily possess the same defining property (Inhelder & Piaget, 1964). All squares must have four equal sides. Hence, definitions require class logic. The definition of perimeter is given by the formula for computing it, which is the sum of the length of all sides. Both the terms, "square" and "perimeter," entail the notion of length of sides. In order to ascertain whether squares must have a perimeter, which when divided by four produces a whole number, and whether it is possible that other figures could also have perimeters that are divisible by four, the reasoner must draw upon knowledge of the taxonomy of quadrilaterals including squares (Piéraut-Le Bonniec, 1980). Some quadrilaterals are asymmetrical and have four unequal sides. The formula for the perimeter of any four-sided figure is: $side_1 + side_2 + side_3 + side_4$. Sometimes, the sum will be a number divisible by four. Thus, because squares are quadrilaterals, they could have, but need not have, a perimeter divisible by four. Squares also belong to the narrower class of symmetrical figures. The definition of symmetry reduces the formula to: $2 (side_2 + side_2)$. Symmetrical figures always have perimeters that are divisible by two. Some even numbers will also be divisible by four. Defining a square as a symmetrical quadrilateral increases the likelihood that its perimeter is divisible by four, but not all symmetrical quadrilaterals have perimeters of that length. Among the symmetrical figures, some have four equal sides, and these alone have perimeters that are always divisible by four, because the formula reduces to 4 (any side). Thus, the link between square and a perimeter with a multiple of four is necessary, but the link between rectangles and perimeters with multiples of four is only possible. It is impossible to draw a square with a perimeter that is not a multiple of four. The logic of class inclusion underlies definition of geometric figures and whole numbers. The relations between terms in a taxonomy also incorporate the logic of possible, necessary, and impossible connections. In her book on modal logic, Piéraut-Le Bonniec (1980) discussed how modal structures are built up from class inclusion situations. The necessary is a subset of the possible, just as squares are a subset of figures with perimeters that are multiples of four. Categorical logic is required for evaluating the validity of deductions. No wonder so many of her illustrations involve categorization.

Categories have a logical form and a semantic content. Therefore, Piéraut-Le Bonniec (chap. 4 in this volume) ties meaning to deduction. Unfamiliarity with the defining attributes of terms often prevents people from using class logic, and assessment of class logic is confounded by unwarranted assumptions about people's knowledge of terms (Klahr & Wallace, 1970). For example, in Piéraut-Le Bonniec's research, children may have performed poorly because of unfamiliarity with geometry, rather than because of poor reasoning. Class logic is extremely dependent on semantics. Conversely, semantics is also dependent on logic, if one assumes meanings to be classically defined by necessary intensions.

Categorical relations may underlie notions of necessity and possibility, but good categorizers are not necessarily expert in handling conditional syllogisms, because they must also learn that *if*, rather than *and* or *only if*, has a particular meaning that corresponds to inclusion relations. Although Briane (chap. 7 in this volume) and Johnson-Laird (1983) made the same point, Piéraut-Le Bonniec (1980) offered a different account of learning. She suggested that the child must first realize that some situations are doubtful. Sometimes an event has one outcome and sometimes another. This eventuality can be expressed by *if* sentences that signify the possible and the hypothetical. "If the perimeter is a multiple of four, it could be a square." Even when we know the length of a perimeter of a quadrilateral, the equality of its sides is uncertain or "iffy." Integration of the system of epistemic evaluation of uncertainty with notions of possibility permits self-consciousness of thought and evaluation of the truth of propositions. Those links begin to be forged in preadolescence.

*Critique.*    If we are to examine the role of meaning in deduction, then the theorist must define what meaning is. Piéraut-Le Bonniec is unclear. At one level, she argues that because we reason from premises with particular contents, researchers must examine the development of explanations that link those contents. We learn how people reason from geometric premises by studying geometry, not by studying syllogisms. Yet, she offers no theory of geometry or of any other content domain. Moreover, the approach has limitations because geometric reasoning may provide little insight into reasoning about physics. When one studies the development of specific contents without a general framework, there may be no general laws of deductive reasoning, only studies of the acquisition of specific knowledge (Overton, 1985). There is no special time for achieving competency in deduction, because timing will depend on the state of the person's knowledge within a given area. The only developmental constraint may be a grasp of necessity and possibility, because these are the prerequisites for defining terms and building a conceptual structure. Even the grasp of categorical logic would depend on the child's familiarity with particular concepts, because neither knowledge of necessity nor of classes could be abstract and content-free. Piéraut-Le Bonniec may advocate this approach, but her own research used age as an individual difference variable, not logical status or domain-specific knowledge. Thus, her claims about the role of knowledge and her own experimental research appear to be incompatible. Her research is structural, but her claims are nonstructuralist.

An alternative implication of her theory is that syllogistic reasoning rests on more general knowledge of the kinds of relations that connect antecedents with consequents. *If* can link definitions, cause and effect, and enabling conditions. *If*s appear in threats and conventional rules. Unlike her description of concepts, Piéraut-Le Bonniec (1980) has espoused an explicit theory of modal logic and the speech acts by which it is expressed. The child may first learn about possibility in the context of rules of permission, then rules of contingency, and then with respect to the rules governing the quantification of predicates. Perhaps, the order of development of understanding of different modalities predicts the difficulty of reasoning with different kinds of connections. A more elaborate theory of those relations and a way to integrate the theory with claims about input from knowledge of concept domains would be a real contribution. Cheng and Holyoak (1985; Cheng, Holyoak, Nisbett, & Oliver, 1986) have taken an interesting step in this direction. They suggest that people construct pragmatic schemes for obligation, contingency, and categorical statements. Some schemes happen to coincide with logicians' analyses and facilitate conditional reasoning, but others do not.

In addition to a more elaborate theory of meaning, Piéraut-Le Bonniec may also need a performance theory. At present, once a conceptual relation is established, she assumes that the process of deduction simply flows from it just as the nature of the facial musculature shapes emotional expression. However, people who link concepts do not always use those links to make deductions. Perhaps adolescence is a special time because of growth in the awareness of when these connections arise and growth in awareness of the implications of these connections (e.g., Moshman & Timmons, 1982; Moshman, chap. 10 in this volume).

## PRESUPPOSITION

### Its Role in Deduction

The third face of *if* is presupposition. Not all sentences have factual referents; some sentences comment about whether speakers believe, do not believe, or are uncertain about their utterances (Bates, 1976; Wing & Scholnick, 1981). This paragraph might open with: "*Because* presupposition is important, I will discuss it"; or "*If* presupposition is important, I will discuss it"; or "*If* presupposition were important, I would discuss it." *Because* implies the belief that presupposition matters. *If* with an indicative verb leave some room for doubt, whereas *if* coupled with a subjunctive verb denotes a belief that this section belies—presupposition is irrelevant to deduction. *If* can signal worlds with a truth status that is uncertain, hypothetical, or wholly imaginary. We use *if* to signal when we postulate conditions that are not or may not be true in order to analyze their consequences.

Presupposition plays a different role in deduction than either semantics or logical form. The meaning of a sentence, alone, may enable evaluation of the validity of an argument. The connective *if* refers to a logical relation that can provide sufficient information to make deductions, but a presupposition, in and of itself, does not specify the conclusions of arguments. The same deduction can be made whether or not the initial premise is counterfactual. Presupposition merely indicates speakers' awareness of the truth status of their statements (the soundness of a premise). Presupposition sets a pragmatic frame for syllogistic reasoning. Because *if* can signal that the speaker is unsure whether the initial premise is factually accurate, the second premise, confirming or denying one of the constituent clauses of the initial premise, continues the flow of discourse, which in turn prompts the concluding inference.

Both Piaget (Inhelder & Piaget, 1958) and Piéraut-Le Bonniec tied awareness of the presupposition of *if* to a deductive attitude. Logically, *if* refers to a situation in which p necessarily accompanies q but not vice versa. When p cooccurs with q, their relation cannot be specified before learning more about q. Thus, *if* expresses a logical relation that goes beyond the data of a particular instance to imply a set of possible event relations and a presupposition that goes beyond the literal meaning of a sentence. The logic of *if* implies possibility. as does the presuppositional content of *if*. Piaget (Inhelder & Piaget, 1958) also claimed that formal operations permit deductions from contrary-to-fact material, and, therefore, they enable the recognition and production of sentences that signal the expression of imaginary events. Piéraut-Le Bonniec (1980) described how recognition of uncertain outcomes leads to the search for the linguistic vehicle, *if*, to express possibility.

Aspects of presupposition are compatible with some aspects of Braine's theory. Recognition of presupposition taps a distinction between what people say and what they believe to be true, thus, grasp of presupposition may be an indicator of analytic comprehension in Braine's theory.

Presupposition poses most difficulty for theories that derive deductions and the learning of *if* from real world experiences (e.g., Griggs, 1983). When parental speech contains counterfactuals, children may not learn the meaning of *if* easily. Counterfactual conditionals are problematic if deductions are based on plausibility or familiarity, because the world to which the speaker refers is not real but imagined. Suppose people comprehend conditional sentences by constructing a schematic picture of the world and then checking for its correspondence with the real one. When there is no real world, one chooses the closest hypothetical one (Stalnaker, 1981). However, it is difficult to calculate the closest one, when there are so many dimensions on which imaginary worlds diverge from real ones. Moreover, if we check deductions by using counterexamples, what is the appropriate counterexample in an imaginary world? People would have to use different strategies for evaluating counterfactual, hypothetical, and true sentences. Counterfactuals are less problematic for weak theories of reference that simply require the person to accept sentences at face value without checking whether they are actually true.

## Research on Presupposition

Clara Wing and I have been interested in the development of understanding of the presuppositions implied in the development of understanding of the presuppositions implied by subordinating conjunctions such as *if*, and in the relationship of that understanding to deduction. In one study (Scholnick & Wing, 1983), adolescents and adults were given syllogisms with varied connectives. Some syllogisms began with premises like, "*If* it is April, the robins are returning." In others, the first premise was "*If* it were April, the robins would be returning"; in others, the first premise was "*Because* it is April, the robins are returning." If people evaluate arguments by searching for semantic referents, then counterfactual conditionals should be hardest, because they refer to an imaginary world. Alternatively, there might be an interaction between presupposition and the acceptance of conclusions based on linguistic form. Reasoning about arguments where it was uncertain what conclusion could be drawn (denying the antecedent or affirming the consequent) would be better when there was the ambiguous *if* + indicative. Modus tollens arguments might be easier for counterfactuals, because disbelief creates the set to negate. The modus ponens might be easier with *because* that also involves affirmations. These predictions were not confirmed. The connective had no impact. The link between presupposition and deduction was conceptual. People who understood the presupposition of *if* + indicative were more able to detect when *if* arguments produced uncertain conclusions.

Other research (Scholnick & Wing, 1982; Wing & Scholnick, 1981) demonstrates the links among deduction, presupposition, and semantics. As with deduction, judging the speaker's presupposition is easier when the sentence refers to familiar events. Often children use semantics to bypass attention to presupposition. When children believe something is true, they attribute the same stance to the speaker. Moreover, the same developmental trend appears in handling presupposition and syllogisms. In deductive reasoning tasks, children accurately judge when a conclusion is true or false much earlier than they can identify when a conclusion is sometimes true. When asked to identify presuppositions, until about age 10, children think speakers either believe or do not believe a statement. There is no uncertainty; thus, *if* is judged to be counterfactual only. In contrast, adults think *if* usually refers to uncertain events, and not to the counterfactual, perhaps under the assumption that things untrue now might later turn out to be true. Children and adults also define the sources of uncertainty differently (Wing & Scholnick, 1986). Preadolescents think uncertainty arises from a single hypothesis but that ambiguity arises about which data fit it. For example, you need to pick up a red-headed niece at the airport whom you have never met before. Unfortunately, two girls fitting the description disembark from the plane. Adolescents recognize that uncertainty also arises from several equally plausible mental alternatives that can account for the same data, such as that the red-headed girl might be your niece or someone else. Thus, notions of necessary and sufficient information also underlie presupposition. Our data support a link between the notions of necessity and possibility that are basic to deduction and to the understanding of the way subordinating conjunctions signal beliefs about the content of sentences.

## SUMMARY

*If* has three faces. Our definitions of them constrain our theories of deduction. Sometimes the faces overlap. Many researchers claim that their fortuitous overlap facilitates performance, yet the study of deduction really deals with only one facet, either semantic or propositional, that is best studied in isolation. Semantic theorists claim that deduction emerges early in familiar domains. French and Nelson (1985) noted that three-year-olds use conditionals and presumably reason with them in familiar scripts. As for propositional logic, Piaget argued that at adolescence, reasoners can analyze the structure of sentences, not their content, to determine the conclusions that can be deduced from them. The emergence of formal deduction is the culmination of experience with perceptual regularities, the evolution of a system to categorize and relate those regularities, and, then, a further systematization of different outcomes of classification. Braine and Rumain (1983) suggested that skill in pure deduction evolves in three steps. The child initially learns the meaning of sentences, and, then, by the early school years, abstracts the meaning of the connective, *if* that consists of the modus ponens inference schema. Finally, adults become facile in analytic comprehension where meaning is subjugated to formal analysis of sentences. Perhaps, analytic comprehension is produced by an education that rewards skill in text analysis.

However, the purist's case is often compromised. Logic slips in to semantics because the mapping of words onto referents is a logical process that requires rules for evidence to prove a mapping is adequate. Semantic analysis of some words includes logical components, and the referents in the real world may have a logical structure that permits inference. Similarly, although structuralists claim that mature reasoners are capable of using abstract rules, those rules and structures originate in a meaningful context.

In both content and developmental origin, propositions, semantics, and presuppositions overlap. The intersection is not fortuitous. *If*'s three faces are connected through the emerging concepts of necessity, possibility, and impossibility. These concepts are the foundation for each face. Necessity gives meaning to the constituents of *if* clauses, their entailment relations, and the speaker's belief about them. No matter which face is discussed or what theory of its representation is offered, absence of contradiction is fundamental. The premises cannot be true and the conclusion false. There can be no counterexamples. Avoidance of contradiction can be used to construct logical rules or to evaluate semantic representations against each other or against empirical observations. Thus, necessity is the skeletal structure for each face. Additionally, growth of the idea of necessity is influenced by growing linguistic and world knowledge (semantics), self-awareness (presupposition), and reasoning skills. Arguments about deduction are not ones about its common core, but its origins and the abstractness of its application.

Deduction is important in human functioning, because it allows us to transcend direct experience. It is so central that we probably have several routes to its development. Falmagne (this volume) characterizes the growth of deduction in terms of bootstrapping. Growth in one realm sparks advances in a second realm, which, in turn, mediate further development in the original realm. Any system in transition is very fragile. Children need multiple, redundant sources of input to support development and to serve as backups in case one source of input or one processing system fails. We need meaningful input to support logical processing. Similarly, we need logic to support meaning in order to detect failures of comprehension (e.g., Markman, 1977). Presuppositions may help the listener to detect the onset of a deductive argument, and background knowledge may facilitate the detection of presupposition. A person may eventually develop within a particular realm (e.g., logic) system-specific supports such as diagrams and charts or a set of automatic routines to help processing. Those methods may enable the person to deal with unique demands of a given realm and with the contrived cases where the material is divorced from other realms. However, pure situations remain the hardest to process. They are not the best tests of the ability to comprehend or reason.

The word, *if*, simultaneously conveys many interconnected meanings. We may possess the analytic ability to separate those meanings. As scientists, the experimental method dictates isolating variables or processes to ascertain their nature and contribution. However, if those meanings constitute an organic whole, it would seem wasteful to use only one facet of that whole to support deduction. Deduction may also have more than one source of origin: in learning, innate abilities, and reflections on activities. Those sources of development do not exist in isolation. Learning implies some innate receptive and evaluative capacities. Humans have the potential to reflect on and structure the outcomes of learning. The analytic approach to *if* is in the eye of the beholder, not in the face the beholder contemplates.

## ACKNOWLEDGMENTS

The author wishes to thank Clara S. Wing, who was my inspiration for and collaborator in research on presupposition.

# REFERENCES

Bates, E. (1976). *Language and context*. New York: Academic Press.

Braine, M. D. S.., Reiser, B. J., & Rumain, B. (1984). Some empirical justification for a theory of natural propositional logic. In G. H. Bower (Ed.), *The psychology of learning and motivation, 18* (pp. 313–371). New York: Academic Press.

Braine, M. D. S., & Rumain, B. (1983). Logical reasoning. In P. H. Mussen (Ed.), *Handbook of child psychology: Vol. III. Cognitive development* (pp. 266–340). (4th ed.). New York: Wiley.

Case, R. (1985). *Intellectual development: Birth to adulthood*. New York: Academic Press.

Cheng, P., & Holyoak, K. J. (1985). Pragmatic reasoning schemas. *Cognitive Psychology, 17,* 391–416.

Cheng, P., Holyoak, K. J., Nisbett, R. E., & Oliver, L. M. (1986). Pragmatic versus syntactic approaches to training deductive reasoning. *Cognitive Psychology, 18,* 293–328.

Evans, J. St. B. T. (1982). *The psychology of deductive reasoning*. London: Routledge & Kegan Paul.

Falmagne, R. J. (1975). Overview: reasoning, representation, process, and related issues. In R. J. Falmagne (Ed.), *Reasoning: Representation and process in children and adults* (pp. 247–264). Hillsdale, NJ: Lawrence Erlbaum Associates.

Falmagne, R. J. (1980). The development of logical competence: A psycholinguistic perspective. In R. Kluwe & H. Spada (Eds.), *Developmental models of thinking* (pp. 171–197). New York: Academic Press.

French, L. A., & Nelson, K. (1985). *Children's acquisition of relational terms: Some ifs, ors, and buts*. New York: Springer- Verlag.

Griggs, R. A. (1983). The role of problem content in selection and in the THOG problem. In J. St. B. T. Evans (Ed.), *Thinking and reasoning: Psychological approaches*. (pp. 16–43). London: Routledge & Kegan Paul.

Inhelder, B., & Piaget, J. (1958). *The growth of logical thinking from childhood to adolescence*. New York: Basic Books.

Inhelder, B., & Piaget, J. (1964). *The early growth of logic in the child: Classification and seriation*. London: Routledge & Kegan Paul.

Johnson-Laird, P. N. (1983). *Mental models: Towards a cognitive science of language, inference, and consciousness*. Cambridge, MA: Harvard University Press.

Klahr, D., & Wallace, J. G. (1970). An information processing analysis of some Piagetian experimental tasks. *Cognitive Psychology, 1,* 358–387.

Markman, E. M. (1977). Realizing that you don't understand: A preliminary investigation. *Child Development, 48,* 986–992.

Moshman, D., & Timmons, M. (1982). The construction of logical necessity. *Human Development, 25,* 309–323.

Neidorf, R. (1967). *Deductive forms: An elementary logic*. New York: Harper & Row.

Overton, W. F. (1984). World views and their influence on psychological theories and research; Kuhn-Lakatos-Laudan. In H. W. Reese (Ed.), *Advances in Child Development and Behavior, 18,* 194–226. New York: Academic Press.

Overton, W. F. (1985). Scientific methodologies and the competence–moderator–performance issue. In E. Neimark, R. DeLisi, & J. Newman (Eds.), *Moderators of competence* (pp. 15–41). Hillsdale, NJ: Lawrence Erlbaum Associates.

Overton, W. F., Byrnes, J. P., & O'Brien, D. P. (1985). Developmental and individual differences in conditional reasoning: The role of contradiction training and cognitive style. *Developmental Psychology, 21* 692–701.

Overton, W. F., & Newman, J. (1982). Cognitive development: A competence-activation/utilization approach. In T. Field, A. Houston, H. Quay, L. Troll, & G. Finley (Eds.), *Review of human development* (pp. 217–241). New York: Wiley.

Overton, W. F., Ward, S. L., Noveck, I. A., Black, J., & O'Brien, D. P. (1987). Form and content in the development of deductive reasoning. *Developmental Psychology, 23*, 22–30.

Piaget, J. (1987). *Possibility and necessity: Vol. 2. The role of necessity in cognitive development*. Minneapolis: University of Minnesota Press.

Piéraut-Le Bonniec, G. (1980). *The development of modal reasoning: Genesis of necessity and possibility notions*. New York: Academic Press.

Rumain, B., Connell, J., & Braine, M. D. S. (1983). Conversational comprehension processes are responsible for reasoning fallacies in children as well as adults: *If* is not the biconditional. *Developmental Psychology, 19*, 471–481.

Scholnick, E. K., & Wing, C. S. (1982). The pragmatics of subordinating conjunctions: A second look. *Journal of Child Language, 9*, 461–480.

Scholnick, E. K., & Wing, C. S. (1983). Evaluating presuppositions and propositions. *Journal of Child Language, 10*, 639–660.

Scholnick, E. K., & Wing, C. S. (1989, June). Speaking deductively: Preschool children's use of *if* in conversation. Paper delivered at the meeting of the Jean Piaget Society, Philadelphia.

Stalnaker, R. C. (1981). A theory of conditionals. In W. L. Harper, R. Stalnaker, & G. Pearce (Eds.), *Ifs: Conditionals, belief, decision, chance, and time*. Dordrecht: D. Reidel.

Staudenmayer, H. (1975). Understanding conditional reasoning with meaningful propositions. In R. J. Falmagne (Ed.), *Reasoning: Representation and process*. (pp. 55–79). Hillsdale, NJ: Lawrence Erlbaum Associates.

Strawson, P. F. (1952). *Introduction to logical theory*. London: Methuen.

Wason, P. C., & Johnson-Laird, P N. (1972). *Psychology of reasoning: Structure and content*. Cambridge, MA: Harvard University Press.

Wing, C. S., & Scholnick, E. K. (1981). Children's comprehension of pragmatic concepts expressed in *because, although, if,* and *unless*. *Journal of Child Language, 8*, 347–365.

Wing, C. S., & Scholnick, E. K. (1986). Understanding the language of reasoning: Cognitive, linguistic, and developmental influences. *Journal of Psycholinguistic Research, 15*, 383–401.

# 9

# The Conversion of Truth
# Into Necessity

Frank B. Murray
*University of Delaware*

The possibility of there being no necessity in the universe, let alone in our thinking, is such a disturbing thought that it led Albert Einstein to declare, in a letter to a friend in 1924, that if it were the case that the motion of an electron when exposed to a ray was not, of necessity, one path or another, he would rather be a cobbler or work in a gambling casino than be a physicist. As it turned out, he labored as a physicist for the remainder of his career to uncover an inconsistency in quantum mechanics that would guarantee an inherent necessity in the universe.

Nearly 200 years earlier, the possibility of there being no necessity, even in our lines of argument, was persuasively proposed by David Hume, who argued that our conviction about the necessity of cause in the universe was an illusion, one of the mind's tricks. There is nothing in our experience, he argued, that requires us to believe "*A* causes *B*" because no amount of careful observation can establish that *B* must follow *A*, or that it would always follow *A*. The fact that *A* comes before *B* regularly and reliably can be known, but that fact, no matter how clearly apprehended and closely studied, cannot in and of itself, justify our conclusion that *B* must follow *A*, that it would always follow *A*, or that *A* caused *B*.

Like Einstein, Kant labored to establish the existence of necessity, a necessity that did not depend on any experience we might have and that did not arise merely out of tautology or an analysis of the meaning of words. He concluded that necessity was guaranteed by the peculiar nature of the mind; by the working of the mind, itself (the categories or structures by which the mind knows). Kant's solution leaves unanswered several questions, one of which is the subject of this chapter—the origins of necessity. The question, more specifically, is about how our minds find necessity to be an attribute of some events we know, but not of others. It is about how some of our inferences, the deductive inferences, are connected by a chain of necessity, whereas other inferences, the inductive inferences, are not necessary despite the fact that they may be as true and useful as the inferences that are deduced. Both forms of inference, the deductive and inductive, of course, take us beyond what can be known by the most scrupulously conducted observation and measurement. The question is—to what can we attribute these differences in the way we go beyond what is empirically presented? Hume argued that the extension by necessity was a trick of the mind; Kant showed what the trick was, and Piaget and his colleagues have attempted to explain how it got there.

## THE PROBLEM

It is quite possible to know, for example, that the path between point A and point B is a straight line, without knowing that the path is, of necessity, a geodesic or the shortest possible path between the points. As we see in any number of examples, young children, and, even, adults, are slow to appreciate that some of the things they know to be true *must* be true as well.

How do we come to know that some portion of what we know to be true, a very small portion to be sure, has to be true? How does an idea that is true—like the idea that our parents are, in fact, older than we are—become converted into an idea that has to be true, that is always true, that cannot conceivably be otherwise? How does a "true" idea—like the idea that parents must be older than their children—become an idea that cannot be denied without the alteration of a very large number of other ideas that are at the foundation of our ability to reason correctly?

How, in other words, are synthetic *a posteriori* statements converted by us into synthetic *a priori* statements? For example, how does the countable fact that "seven and five things are twelve things" become not just that fact, true as it is, but the conviction that "7 + 5" *must* be 12 and could not be any other number? And, if it could somehow be some other number, then must not an entire system of reasoning need to be given up? Similarly, and equally important, how do we come to give up ideas we once held by self-evident necessity—such as the Euclidean fifth postulate: Through a point on a plane, not on a given line, only one line can be drawn parallel to the given line—and replace it, 2,000 years later, either with Lobachevski's notion that an infinite number of parallel lines can be drawn through the point or by Riemann's notion that no line can be drawn parallel to the given line? Ideas that have the attribute of necessity attached to them represent the highest levels our intellectual accomplishment and would be the sort of idea that could be beamed to outerspace to determine whether rational beings existed there.

The answer to these questions about the origins of our notions of necessity and the thesis of this chapter is that the Genevan theory of operations and the mechanism of equilibration provide a plausible account of the conversion of truth into necessity (see Inhelder & de Caprona, this volume). Even if the Piagetian account is ultimately found to be wanting, the theory is about these questions. An appreciation of this fact, alone, would eliminate much of the confusion in the speculation of the implications of Piagetian theory. For example, the notion that a stage represents a qualitatively different form of activity is clearer when one considers the shift that takes place when we apprehend that something we know to be true is not necessarily true; it is a fundamentally different way of knowing the thing. Similarly, this addition of necessity to what we otherwise know to be true is an emergent event, an event that is not predictable from what is empirically or contingently true. By this fact, alone, the event is qualitatively different from its empirically determined antecedent. As another example, it is clear why the Genevans are always, from the perspective of necessity, skeptical of the claims that reasoning at higher stages of logical reasoning has been trained on some reinforcement schedule or by some social interaction procedure. What can a teacher or peer possibly say or do that can give a pupil who has no notion of necessity the idea, for example, that if "A = B," and "B = C," then A not only equals C on a particular occasion, but has to equal C and will always, under these conditions, equal C. Obviously, it would not be enough for the teacher to show that "A = C," or for the pupil to demonstrate a command of the problem by merely responding that A equals C. The point of the problem is missed entirely if the focus of the teaching effort is solely on the fact that "A = C."

## Two Examples of Necessity

### Anno's Hat Tricks (Nozaki, 1985)

If we have a white hat and a red hat, and your friend puts on the red hat, and you put on the other hat, you and virtually all kindergarten pupils know that you are wearing the white hat, but only 20% of the kindergarten pupils in our samples know why they know this.

Even undergraduates in our samples hesitate in their response to the case of three hats, two red and one white, in which one hat is placed on the head of a friend and another is placed on our head. If our friend then says, without looking in a mirror, that he knows for sure he is wearing a red hat, we can know, with equal certainly and, also, without looking in a mirror, what color hat we are wearing. We know that we *must* be wearing the white hat, because that is the only way our friend can be sure he has on his head a red hat; each of the two remaining hats are known to be red. Because our friend looked only at the color of our hat and then made the statement about the

color of the one he is wearing, we each know—without the aid of a mirror—
the color of our respective hats. We know this by necessity

### The Bead Problem

In this problem, we are given two jars filled with 100 beads, one with 100
black beads and the other with 100 white beads. Ten white beads are taken
from their jar and mixed with the 100 black beads in the other jar, after
which ten beads, any ten beads, from the mixture, are returned to the jar of
white beads. The question is whether the number of white beads in one jar
equals the number of black beads in the other jar. To at least 80% of the
adults sampled (Murray & Armstrong, 1978), the answer was a surprise:
The number of white beads in one jar always equals the number of black
beads in the other jar, regardless of the proportion of white and black beads
that happened to be returned from one jar to the other. If two white beads
and eight black beads, for example, are returned, then we would have 92
white beads in one jar, 92 black beads in the other jar, and 8 black beads in
with the white beads and 8 white beads with the black ones. This, in other
words, is a number conservation problem under a spatial transformation
(shifting beads from one jar to another) that is a little more complicated
than expanding and contracting the length of rows of items in the traditional number conservation problem, but one that, nevertheless, preserves
the equivalence of the number of white and black beads in each jar. Although there are empirical ways to determine the color of the hat (look at it)
or the number of beads (count them), it is clear that at some point in their
development children and adolescents are able to employ a different approach to these problems, an approach that, in the end, allows them to
know with certainty and without empirical verification.

## NECESSITY AND OPERATIONAL THOUGHT

One test of the claim that the theory of operational thought is about the development of necessity concerns the criteria the Genevans use to decide
whether the child's responses indicate genuine operational thought or
*pseudo-operativity*; that is, whether the correct response is deduced from
the premises of the problem or whether it is empirically determined or based
on a rote algorithm. The classic operativity tasks are not about what the
child knows in the sense of how well-informed the child may be. In fact, to
the extent that school-learning contributes to the child's successful performance, the tasks will yield a false positive result, because the child may arrive
at the correct answer in a way that precludes her deducing it and seeing the
necessity in it. It is one thing to know that a flattened clay ball weighs the
same as the ball in its original unflattened state and that it can be rolled

back into the ball, but it is quite another thing to know that it *must* weigh the same.

In the assessment of concrete operational thought, it can be noted that when the child is misinformed about the effects of some action or transformation, a false negative diagnosis may also result when, for example, the child thinks flattening, or X-raying, or freezing the ball really makes it heavier (Murray, 1981). In this case, the child's operativity may be manifested in a nonconservation judgment should the child conclude that, for example, the flattened ball not only is heavier, but that it must be heavier, and so on. The nonconservation judgment, or an apparent lack of transitivity, or an apparently immature form of classification may be a proper deduction, nevertheless (e.g., in the case of transitivity, if "A = B," but "B > C," then A must be, of necessity, greater than C). Thus, correct performance on an operativity task may indicate necessity, and incorrect performance on the task may, also, indicate operativity, which is why the diagnosis of cognitive level is best embedded in a clinical setting that minimizes these false positive and false negative errors.

The tests of genuine operativity make sense only insofar as they are attempts to certify that the child's response was a deduction, that is, was a necessary conclusion. If these tests are not meant to be indicators of necessity, they are unreasonable tests, tests that, in fairness, would not be employed for the acquisition of any other kind of information. The usual tests for operational thought are these:

1. *Duration*. Operativity assessments are repeated at later time intervals, up to one or two months, on the assumption that ideas held by necessity are almost never given up, although those held on other grounds often fade.

2. *Resistance to countersuggestion*. On the assumption that necessary conclusions are not modifiable (e.g., the part cannot be modified to be greater than the whole), the child is presented with counterevidence, pressure, and argument in an effort to change the child's response. A response that is easily given up or modified cannot be based on necessity, because what can one say or do to have a person give up the idea that the whole is greater than any of its parts, for example.

3. *Specific transfer*. Operativity assessments are made with different materials and with tasks of the same specific form (viz., the various conservation tasks) on the assumption that the logical form of the tasks, which gives the tasks their necessity component, transcends any particular task features.

4. *Nonspecific transfer*. Operativity is assessed with a family of tasks in different domains (e.g., conservation, seriation, class inclusion, transitivity, horizontality, etc.), because they all have a common theoretical structure that manifests necessity. They are all, one way or another, about the same

thing. This overarching structure justifies the nonspecific transfer criterion, a criterion that is rarely justified in most other areas of assessment—with the notable exception of the assessment of a pervasive construct like "g." In Piagetian theory, the justification of the nonspecific transfer criterion is even threatened, to some degree, by the fact of the horizontal decalage, because operational responses are not found uniformly across a wide range of stage-specific tasks until the children have been in the stage a long time.

5. *Trainability*. This criterion is the converse of the countersuggestion criterion, because it assumes that a quick or abrupt change in response accuracy after feedback, hints, cues, argument, and so on indicates that the original response is not a valid indicator of nonoperativity. Because development is a relatively slow process and not amenable to fast change, we assume that a quickly trained response is not based on genuine preoperativity; rather, the child has really, at the outset, approached the problem in an operational way, and his initial "failure" is due to inattention or misinformation about some aspects of the task.

6. *Necessity*. Sometimes a direct attempt is made to assess the child's appreciation of the inherent necessity in the operativity task. The child may be asked whether the outcome has to be what it was, or can it be different from what it is, and so on. They can be asked, as well, whether the outcome will always be what it now is or just sometimes be the way it is. Although certainty and necessity are conceptually independent, some researchers (e.g., Miller, 1986) have attempted to assess necessity by determining how confident the children are in their judgments.

These more or less direct questions about necessary and indeterminate outcomes must be carefully worded, because it can be shown that children have preferred ways of expressing indeterminacy (Falmagne, this volume). If a box is filled only with squares, so that any object drawn from it *must* be a square, children will respond differently when asked to judge the truth of the following assertions about the contents of the box: "Can there be a circle in the box?" "Must there be a square in the box?" "There are nothing but squares in the box?" "There are only squares in the box?" "They are all squares in the box?" However, each assertion can be clearly evaluated if the child understands the necessity of a box containing only what is in it and nothing else.

7. *Good reasons*. The classic operativity reasons (viz. negation and reciprocity) are valid justifications only in cases where necessity is presupposed. Otherwise, they are poor reasons, even irrelevant and useless reasons; that the effect of flattening a ball into a pancake, in the conservation task, for example, can be negated by rolling the pancake back into a ball tells us nothing about whether its weight or anything else, except its shape, was changed when it was a pancake. The classic good reasons, in fact, beg the question, in each case, because they are not a cause of necessity but a conse-

quence of it. They hold as good reasons only when the child's solution is based on a preexisting structure of necessity.

The traditional conservation reasons are appropriate reasons only under the condition where nothing has changed; they *assume* that nothing—of necessity—does in fact change. They make no sense, for instance, in any case where there is genuine doubt. Suppose, in the case of weight conservation, for example, might there not be a quantitate change after a clay ball is bombarded with x-rays? Or, in the case of volume conservation, might there not be a quantitative change when temperature is raised or lowered?

Seriation, to continue the point, is about each stick's necessarily unique position in an array ordered by size; horizontality is about the necessary relationships that obtain from the grid of absolute space; classification is about the necessarily unique placement of class members in a classification scheme; and class inclusion is about the necessity of the whole being greater than any of its parts.

## THE EMPIRICAL LINKS BETWEEN
## OPERATIVITY AND NECESSITY

At each point of development there are documented empirical links between some plausible measure of necessity and operativity, including preoperativity (see Piaget, 1987; Inhelder & de Caprona, Chap. 2 in this volume; Ricco, Chap. 3 in this volume for discussion of necessity at each level of development).

### Formal Operations

The link between formal operational thought and the notion of necessity is virtually guaranteed by the characterization of formal operational thought as the adolescent's competence to make deductions from possible as well as actual events and circumstances. It is as if the adolescent is able to say, "If this were the case, which it is not, but if it were, then such and so would have to follow."

The difficulty in assessing the development of necessity is that the diagnostic problems used for this purpose are not solely logical reasoning problems. They invariably are a mixture of logic, information, and other nonlogical cues to the correct answer. If, for example, one sets the following problem for the child—"If a skyscraper is higher than a house, and a house is higher than a garage, is a skyscraper higher or shorter than a garage?"—one cannot be sure what the child's response indicates about his sensitivity to the necessary links in the problem. The child could avoid all considerations of logic and answer the problem correctly from his prior knowledge

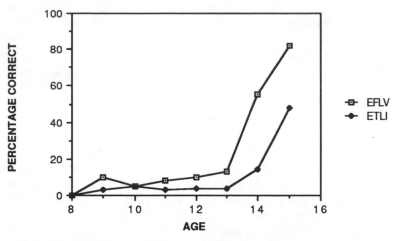

FIG. 9.1  Percentages of children, ages 8 through 15, who are correct on syllogisms whose validity and content are in conflict (EFLV are empirically false, but logically valid syllogisms; ETLI are empirically true, but logically invalid syllogisms). Fetzer & Murray, 1971.

of the relative heights of buildings. However, if the content of the problem is neutral or is actually in conflict with the logically valid conclusion (e.g., if the child has to conclude that a garage is *higher* than a skyscraper), then the course of the child's sensitivity to logical necessity can be more accurately and confidently determined.

Following this line of reasoning, Fetzer and Murray (1971) investigated children's performance on valid and invalid categorical and linear syllogisms whose premises and conclusions are either all empirically true, false, or neutral. A group of 206 children from the third through ninth grades solved four conservation problems, six linear syllogisms, 23 categorical syllogisms, and 2 formal operational tasks. As expected, children proved to be most successful (85%–95% correct) on the unambiguous problems where the empirical condition (true or false) is in agreement with the logical conditions (valid or invalid) because, presumably, their responses are determined largely, and in the case of the youngest children exclusively, by their knowledge of the content. Their performance on problems in which the empirical and logical conditions are in conflict (viz. true content-invalid syllogism, false content-valid syllogism) is presented in Fig. 9.1.

Before the age of 13 years, the children show virtually no sensitivity to necessity, but, thereafter, performance sharply increases, particularly in the cases where the children must reject the empirically false conclusions and accept them as valid. Overton and his colleagues (Overton, Ward, Noveck, Black, & O'Brien, 1987) confirmed the finding that a formal logical competence and a workable sensitivity to necessity become available during adolescence. Instead of varying the truth or falsity of the empirical content of a logical problem, Overton varied the familiarity of the content in a conditional reasoning problem in which the subjects had to establish the truth of the conditional rule, "if $p$, then $q$," by falsifying it under the $p$ and $-q$ condition.

The acceptance of the empirically true as logically invalid is more difficult for children at virtually all ages in the Fetzer and Murray study (1971). The child's difficulty in rejecting a conclusion as not necessary, as opposed to his accepting one as necessary, is a clear finding for all versions of the syllogisms—conflict between truth and validity, agreement between them, and empirically neutral content where the truth is unknown. The detection of the "not necessary" may implicitly require an awareness of the possibility of another conclusion (viz. the necessary one), although the detection of necessity may not require any such awareness but simply the recognition that the given conclusion is necessary.

The link to operativity in the children's performance on these tasks that require reasoning about necessity can be established in several ways. The tasks in the Fetzer & Murray study form an acceptable Guttman scale (92.3 reproducibility) that reveals strong associations with traditional operativity measures. The least difficult tasks are those in which truth and validity agree, followed by conservation of weight and the syllogisms that have neutral content, all of which are significantly more difficult than the "agreement" problems. These, in turn, arc followed by the next most difficult group of tasks—conservation of volume and the conflict syllogisms.

Apart from the association with volume conservation, performance on the conflict syllogisms show two other connections to formal operational thought. Older children (ages 12–15 years), children presumed to be in the formal operational stage, give significantly more correct and fewer incorrect responses than younger children (8–11 years) on the "conflict syllogisms" (i.e., on those syllogisms in which the child's appreciation of necessity overrides what is merely true about the statements the child is evaluating). In addition, there are significant positive associations between the conflict syllogisms and the formal operativity measures (viz. volume conservation, equal angles, and balance equilibrium), but not between these syllogisms and weight conservation.

When more direct attempts are made to assess necessity, the results confirm its link to formal operativity in several domains. For example, Murray and Armstrong (1978) examined the responses of 188 subjects (grades 2, 3, 5, 7, 11, and college) to a set of arithmetic problems—some with necessary outcomes and some with indeterminate outcomes. Subjects were asked whether the outcome of the problems and their response would always, sometimes, or never be what it is, should the problem be represented on other occasions. A factor analysis of the subjects' solutions shows two factors, one on which all the problems with necessary outcomes are loaded, and a second factor on which the problems with indeterminate outcomes are clustered. It is only by the seventh grade that the children exceed a 50% correct criterion for both sets of problems, but by the ninth grade there is a clear and consistent discrimination between what is necessarily true and what is not.

## Concrete Operations

Although it is not often done, the child's appreciation of the necessary connections in an operativity task can be probed directly. Cauley, Murray, and Smith (1983) gave 38 kindergarten and first-grade pupils four operativity tasks (mass conservation, seriation, transitivity, and class inclusion) and asked them whether the outcome they stated as their answers will always be what they just said or just sometimes, whether it has to be, and whether it can ever be some plausible alternative proposed by the experimenter. About 68% of the children responded that the outcome is always the same, has to be what it is, and cannot be different or be something else.

Similarly, Murray and Armstrong (1976, 1978) found that nearly all conservers give their judgments by necessity and give convincing evidence that they are aware of all the premises implicit in the conservation deduction. On the other hand, Cauley (1988) has been able to show that only about 30% of second- and third-graders who are flawless in their subtraction proficiency appreciate the logical knowledge that is embedded in the subtraction algorithm and that confers necessity on the outcome of the algorithm's application. Only 15% of the pupils they tested had integrated their knowledge of the algorithm, logical knowledge (e.g., that the minuend is conserved after borrowing), and conceptual knowledge about subtraction—its function and goals, how it is different from addition, and so on.

Using a more sensitive recognition measure, Russell (1982) showed that children in the concrete operational age range, once they are told that some statements can always be true while others are only sometimes true, can clearly discriminate this fact in a series of thirty pairs of contrasting necessary and contingent statements. For example, they know that statements, like "John's dad is a man," are a different kind of statement from statements like "John's dad is a farmer." However, the necessary-contingent distinction is not salient for children, because they were not able, on their own, to find a way to sort consistently the statements from each other.

## Preoperational Links

Although all the kindergarten and first grade children in the study by Cauley et al. (1983) knew that "2 + 1 = 3," only 60% knew that the sum would always be three and that it could not be any other number. In another sample of four- and five-year-olds, we found that, although nearly all children could add accurately single digit numbers below five and be confident that they had the right answer, about 70% believed the answer could be a different number, as well. When pressed they gave "justification at any price" responses for their beliefs that another number could also be a correct answer. In a year or so, these children, like those in the grades ahead, would be confident that only *one* number could be the right answer.

Substantial numbers of preoperational children appear to hold their incorrect judgments about operativity tasks by necessity as well as to appreciate the necessary and contingent attributes of other tasks and events. Fully 70% of six-year-olds in our samples know that sisters must always be girls, that fathers must be older than their children, that crayons do not have to be blue, that any jelly bean taken out of a jar of red beans has to be red, that two cookies plus one cookie are always three cookies, and so on.

About one-half the nonconservers in our samples have deduced their erroneous conclusions. Sixteen of 34 six-year-old nonconservers of number, amount, and weight gave evidence of necessity that was indistinguishable from that given by the conservers cited above; they, as well, knew all the implicit premises embedded in the conservation paradigm but were merely misinformed about the effects of the conservation transformation on number, amount, or weight. By any reasonable test, it appears that some "nonconservers" can support their conclusions with reasons that appear to have many of the features of genuine necessity.

Although the preoperational children in the Russell (1982) study showed some ability to discriminate necessary from contingent statements, their performance was much better with impossible statements (i.e., with necessarily false statements) of the sort, "the headmistress is a man," to be discriminated from contingent statements of the sort, "the headmistress is a singer." Convergent evidence for a sensitivity to necessity in three- to five-year-olds was also found by Fabricus, Sophian, and Wellman (in press) on tasks that required them to confirm that a certain object had to be the one described to them, because it contained the defining attributes.

Thus, it appears that in several domains necessity is embedded in the mental functioning of the child throughout the course of the child's intellectual development (e.g., Braine & Rumain, 1983; Haake & Somerville, 1985; Inhelder & de Caprona, chap. 2 in this volume; Moshman & Timmons, 1982; Piéraut-LeBonniec, 1980, and chap. 4 in this volume; Ricco, chap. 3 in this volume; Rumain, Connell, & Braine, 1981; Shultz, 1982).

However, the empirical connection of necessity to operativity raises all the old issues. Does, for example, our notion of necessity undergo qualitative changes over the lifespan or is necessity essentially the same notion throughout but applied at different rates and strengths to the several cognitive domains? Does knowing that "sisters have to be girls" or "things equal to same thing are equal to each other" require the same structural competence as knowing "any number necessarily entails a successor" or that an implication is falsified only through the negation of the consequent ($p. - q$), or that all events are caused, and so on.

## THE SOURCE OF NECESSITY: THE CASE OF CONSERVATION

### Nonconservers with Necessity

If it is the case that there are two kinds of nonconservers, those who hold their view by necessity and those who do not, the question naturally arises whether one of these two kinds is easier to train to conserve than the other. A plausible argument can be advanced that the position of the nonconserver who believes his response must be the way it is and cannot be different is more difficult to modify than the position of the nonconserver who feels his conclusion may be different on another occasion. On the other hand, if the operativity task is a measure of necessity, then those who possess a mental structure that confers necessity on events will have made substantially more developmental progress than those who cannot, or do not, support their conclusions with appeals to the necessity of the outcome. As a result, the nonconservers with necessity should profit more from any of the standard conservation training procedures than their counterparts who are without a trace of necessity in their reasoning.

Murray and Smith (1985) examined precisely this question by subjecting both kinds of nonconservers to a peer social interaction training procedure modeled after Ames and Murray (1982) and Doise, Mugny, and Perret-Clermont (1975, 1976). In this procedure, two nonconservers who hold contradictory views (e.g., one thinks the ball is heavier and the other that it is lighter) are told to come to a common agreed-upon answer to the conservation problem. Typically, nonconservers who are paired will come to a common answer (sometimes a conservation response) and will, when tested later on their own, show modest improvement in their performance on the task and on specific transfer tasks. If a nonconserver is paired with a conserver, there is far more improvement, so much so that, had Murray and Smith done so in their 1985 study, the magnitude of this improvement would have swamped the differential effect that was the object of the study.

Nonconservers without necessity (i.e., nonconservers who thought their response might be different on another occasion) showed no significant gains on the immediate posttest and one given four weeks later, both of which included the training task and transfer tasks. Of a possible score of 6, these nonconservers scored .25 on the pretest and .58 and .69 on the posttests, respectively. The nonconservers with necessity, on the other hand, had pretest scores of .72 and showed significant covaried posttest gains on both posttests with scores of 1.85 and 2.15 respectively, as well as significant superiority over the nonconservers without necessity on each posttest. These gains, although significant, are small, but they are in line with the results of other peer interaction studies in which neither participant in the dyad solves the problem correctly on the pretest.

We confirmed these results in a second study: 35 nonconservers of liquid amount, 16 of whom supported their judgments with an acknowledgment that the outcome will always be what it is and cannot be different from what it is, while the other 19 held the opposing view. Both groups of children, all from the first, second, and third grades, were presented a series of twelve episodes in which the reasoning of another child about the conservation of liquid amount was described. The children were asked whether they thought the other child was right or wrong in what he or she said. In the episodes, the "other" child gave classic operativity reasons for a decision about liquid amount (identity, negation, and compensation) as well as classic nonconservation reasons ("the tall glass has more, because it looks like there is more," "the liquid level is higher, so it has more," "pouring makes one have more," "there is more in the lower one, because it is wider," etc.). The nonconservers with necessity were more likely than the nonconservers without necessity to think the classic conservation arguments (viz. identity, negation, and compensation) were correct and that the nonconservation arguments were wrong. Conservers with necessity, incidentally, were essentially flawless in their ability to recognize the validity or invalidity of the "other" child's reasoning, whereas those conservers without necessity were not significantly different from those nonconservers with necessity. There were, of course, the usual age effects found in all conservation studies, with the older children showing superior knowledge of validity of conservation and the invalidity of nonconservation.

In sum, the nonconservers who can support their conclusions with the deductive force of necessity, even when they are wrong in their conclusion, appear to be more developmentally advanced than their colleagues who do not use necessity as part of the justification for their conclusion. Like conservers, nonconservers with necessity are aware of the truth of the classic operativity reasons, and they are, in adherence to the trainability criterion for operativity, relatively easy to train. There is still, of course, the question of the origin of the nonconserver's and the conserver's notion of necessity. A close examination of the conservation paradigm and the generic structure of the other operativity tasks will reveal the opportunities for the attachment of necessity to the child's judgment about the outcome of the operativity task the researcher typically sets for the child.

## Structure of Operativity Tasks

Operativity tasks consist of two or more factors: $x$, the concept in question (viz. conservation, seriation, class inclusion, etc.) and some other factors,

$y^1$, $y^2$, etc., which often mislead the child about the correct answer to the problem. An operational solution to the problem, as opposed to an otherwise correct solution, does not stem from the child's ignoring the $y$ factors, but rather from the integration of the $y$ factors with the $x$ factor into a coherent system in which the corrrect answer, along with other factors of the system, are direct implications of the system.

For example, in the seriation problem, the child is to find the correct location of a stick ($x$) in an array in which he must find the one place where the stick is both longer ($y^1$) and shorter ($y^2$)—longer than some of the sticks in the array and shorter than the remainder of them. In the conservation task, the child must decide whether the weight of the clay ball ($x$) has changed when the ball is made flatter, in other words, lower ($y^1$) and wider ($y^2$). In the transitivity task, the child must decide what the relationship is between $A$ and $C$ ($x$), given the relationships between $A$ and $B$ ($y^1$) and $A$ and $C$ ($y^2$). In the beam balance problem, the child must decide how the balance pan will move ($x$) when the weight is changed ($y^1$) and/or the weight's distance from the fulcrum ($y^2$) is changed. In each case, the proper solution to the problem requires the integration of the factors along the lines depicted in Table 9.1 for the conservation problem.

In the conservation situation, the child is presented with the following events (see Murray, 1981 for an elaboration of the paradigm factors):

1. Object $A$ = Object $B$ with respect to some quantitative attribute, $x$, and some other attributes, $y$, which are independent of $x$ and usually less abstract and not as easily quantified as the $x$ factors. The child acknowledges the $A$ and $B$ are the same with respect to $x$. The acknowledgment that "$A = B$" carries with it, according to Piaget (1986), the necessity of the equality relationship, which in turn is rooted in the necessity inherent in the implication that a thing implies itself atemporally. The relationship "$A = A$," for example, is not as much empirically given as much as it is derived from the implication "$A \supset A$" from one time to another; empirically, $A$ would differ from itself from one time to the next, thus eroding the equality relationship. Clearly, the entire conservation assessment depends on the child taking the equality relationship between $A$ and $B$ as a necessary one. In fact, experienced researchers in this field know that the child who has difficulty accepting the initial equality, or the child who requires that adjustments be made to $A$ and $B$ before he or she assents that the objects are equal with respect to $x$, will inevitably be a nonconserver of the quantity in question.

2. One of the objects, say $B$, is transformed into $B'$ with respect to $y$ and not $x$, and this, also, is acknowledged by the child. Although $x$ and $y$ are functionally independent, they are linked for the child in one of several ways. The link may be psychophysical insofar as changes in $y$ create the illusion of changes in $x$, or the salience of $y$ may preclude the evaluation of $x$

TABLE 9.1
Necessary Relationships Between Values of $y_1$, $y_2$ and $x$

| Condition | Transformations of y Attribute | | Changes in x from changes in $y_1$ and $y_2$[a] |
|---|---|---|---|
| | $y_1$ | $y_2$ | $x$ |
| 1. | $+ (y_1)$ | $+ (y_2)$ | x must be increased ($+$) |
| 2. | $- (y_1)$ | $- (y_2)$ | x must be decreased ($-$) |
| 3. | $+ (y_1)$ | $- (y_2)$ | x may be increased, decreased, or remain unchanged ($+$, $-$, 0) |
| 4. | $- (y_1)$ | $+ (y_2)$ | x may be increased, decreased, or remain unchanged ($+$, $-$, 0) |
| 5. | $0 (y_1)$ | $0 (y_2)$ | x must remain unchanged (0) |
| 6. | $+ (y_1)$ | $0 (y_2)$ | x must be increased ($+$) |
| 7. | $- (y_1)$ | $0 (y_2)$ | x must be decreased ($-$) |
| 8. | $0 (y_1)$ | $+ (y_2)$ | x must be increased ($+$) |
| 9. | $0 (y_1)$ | $- (y_2)$ | x must be decreased ($-$) |

[a]If $y_1$ and $y_2$ were increased, this could not be done without increasing x in line 1; or in line 6, if only $y_1$ were increased, x would need to be increased, etc. For conservation of liquid amount, changes in $y_1$ and $y_2$ might be changes in height and width; in conservation of number, changes in $y_1$ and $y_2$ could be changes in row length and density; in conservation of length, changes in $y_1$ and $y_2$ could be changes in right and left alignment with the standard, with $+ (y_1)$, for example, being a shift of the left end to the left, $- (y_1)$ a shift in it to the right, and with $y_2$ being a shift in the right end of the stick to the right ($+$) or left ($-$).

altogether. Or the link may be semantic insofar as the *y* factors are connotatively related to *x*, as in the case of weight, where it can be shown that the connotations of "heavy" provide a basis for seductive *y* factors. "Heavy" connotes "large," "strong," "rough," "hard," and so on, and transformations that have the effect of making the clay ball harder, larger, rougher and so forth, are effective *y* factors in weight conservation tasks; transformations based on attributes that do not have the connotative relationship with "heavy" (or "light") are relatively ineffective candidates for *y* factors.

The semantic root of the *x–y* confusion on the part of the nonconserving child is related, as well, to the notion of necessity, because it appears that the nonconserving child takes the *y* factor to be a necessary attribute of *x* insofar as the nonconservers tend to claim that heavy objects, for example, are *always* large, hard, rough, and so on; the conservers claim only that these attributes are sometimes true of heavy objects. The nonconserver accepts the connotation as a denotation, in other words. Moreover, the direction of the nonconservation error is predictable from whether the label for the conservation transformation is marked or unmarked; "heavy" is an unmarked adjective, and "light" is marked. Transformations labeled by unmarked adjectives are judged to make the ball heavier, whereas those that are marked, like "small," "soft," "smooth," have the opposite effect (see Murray, 1981 for a fuller account of these points). Thus, the link between $x$ and $y$ factors, although independent and inconsequential for the conserver, is taken by the nonconserver to be a necessary link.

3. The child is asked whether $A = B$ are equal with respect to $x$, when they are clearly unequal with respect to $y$. If the child knows that $B = B'$ with respect to $x$, he can deduce that $A = B'$ with respect of $x$ and be scored as a conserver. If, on the other hand, the child believes that $B$ does not equal $B'$ with respect to $x$, he can deduce that $A$ does not equal $B'$ with respect to $x$, and he will, as a result, be scored as a nonconserver—with necessity. What determines whether the child takes the transformed object, $B'$, as equal or unequal to $B$ with respect to $x$ and whether necessity manifests itself in a conservation or nonconservation response?

As Table 9.1 indicates, a number of possibilities are available to the child as he or she attempts to integrate the $x$ and $y$ factors in the operativity tasks. Consider the case of amount conservation as portrayed in Table 9.1. Lines three and four are the classic conservation situations, but these are ambiguous with respect to whether $x$ has changed. The other cases in Table 9.1 are unambiguous. Take, for example, the conservation of the amount of clay. The amount of clay will have to increase if both the height and the width of the clay ball increase, as they do in line 1. Under these conditions, the amount of clay will have to increase if either the height alone increases (line 6) or if the width alone increases (line 8). When confronting the conservation conditions (see lines 3 and 4), the child is, we find, under no obligation to conclude that the amount of clay has to be unchanged—unless the compensation of the increase in $y^1$ with the decrease in $y^2$ is integrated with knowledge that $x$ is, in fact, not increased or decreased. An increase in $y^1$ and a decrease in $y^2$, or vice versa, create only the possibility that the amount of clay is unchanged. How does this possibility become a necessity? How can the child, or anyone else for that matter, once having created the possibilities that $x$ is increased or decreased, eliminate them as possibilities and guarantee the necessity of the alternative that $x$ is unchanged?

## THE EQUILIBRATION SOLUTION

The plausibility of the Genevan proposal for the origins of necessity rests upon the weaknesses in other accounts. The arguments against the Genevan view are the historic arguments against the synthetic *a priori* as a route to new knowledge or cognitive advancement. These are that synthetic statements are either solely empirically determined or that the *a priori* statement is merely a linguistic convention, a tautological or analytic statement such that the subject of the statement contains the predicate in such a way that it can add no new information about the subject. Setting aside the possibility that, from a developmental perspective, analytic statements may have been synthetic at one time for the child, it is difficult to believe that any mind, upon first learning, for example, the initial Euclidean axioms, definitions and postulates would not have acquired something new when it came upon the Pythagorean relationship some 47 propositions later. Yet, the 48th proposition is contained in the axioms, definitions, and postulates in precisely the same way that 2 + 2 entails the idea, 4, or that the conclusion of the syllogism is contained in the premises.

To find the source of necessity in empirical regularities has the virtue of parsimony, but it would confer a necessity on the fact, for example, that rooms have four walls or that stop lights are red—a necessity that no one believes either have. Empirical regularity gives us the fact of the regularity, not the necessity of the regularity. In the end, the issue is not whether necessity is justified in nontautological areas, but how we come to attach the notion to some of the things we know, even if it turns out that the attachment is no more than the illusion Hume claimed it was, a mere sentiment of rationality, a feeling that is associated with ideals for which, to date, we have found no exceptions. The question is not whether "necessity" is out there as a property of the universe for us to acquire; the question concerns the very structure and contents of our minds and what conditions the nature of our minds places on our understanding that gives some of what we know an attribute of necessity—and a potential of necessity for the rest of what we know to be true (See Ricco, chap. 3 in this volume).

In the Genevan view, necessity resides in a system of reversible operations; the necessity is in the links between the elements of the system that give each element a fixed, and, therefore, necessary position in the system. To create the system, any system that has the attribute of necessity, the child must invent the opposite of something. In the operativity tasks, there are the $x$ and $y$ factors referred to above. The child must not only know that there is a *non-x* or a *non-y* but must find a way to determine exactly what the *non-x* or *non-y* is. Initially, these could be seen as independent factors that have no relationship to each other, thus, changes in $y^1$ have no consequence for $y^2$ or $x$; just as arithmetical addition can be learned and thought about independently of subtraction. By some mechanism, addition comes to be seen as the opposite of subtraction and vice versa, thus, one cannot be thought of apart from the other: The existence of one requires the existence of the other. Equilibration is put forth as that mechanism and is a hypothetical device for the invention of a common dimension that links the opposites together so that one is the reverse of the other with respect to that dimension, as addition is the reverse of subtraction. Thus, the opposite of $y^1$

TABLE 9.2

The Group Structure of the Necessary Relationships Between the
Increase ( + ), Decrease ( – ), and Constancy (0) Values of the
$y_1$, $y_2$, and $x$ Attributes of the Conservation Materials.

| $y_2$ Attribute | $y_1$ Attribute | | |
|---|---|---|---|
| | + ($y_1$) | – ($y_1$) | 0 ($y_1$) |
| + ($y_2$) | + (x) | 0 (x) | + (x) |
| – ($y_2$) | 0 (x) | – (x) | – (x) |
| 0 ($y_2$) | + (x) | – (x) | 0 (x) |

must be invented by the child before the child's solution to the operativity task can have the property of necessity. Early on, the opposite of $y^1$ will be found to be its negation ( – $y^1$); later $y^2$ will come to be seen as an opposite in the reciprocal sense: The effects of increasing $y^1$ can be undone by decreasing $y^1$ or $y^2$. The equilibrated system can take the form of a group structure, described in Table 9.2, that binds the $x$ and $y$ factors together so that the effects of increasing any one are correlated with the increases in some others and can be undone by decreases in others. Thus, an increase in the clay ball's height and width can be accomplished only by an increase in the mass of the ball (i.e., " + $y^1$ and + $y^2 \supset + x$"). The ambiguity in the ' + $y^1$' and ' – $y^2$' conservation case is resolved once those changes in $y$ are integrated with the fact that $x$ did not change (i.e., the changes in $y^1$ and $y^2$ become consistent with the fact that $x$ did not change). The only way $y^1$ or $y^2$ can increase with no increase in $x$ is if the increase in $y^1$ or $y^2$ is accompanied by a compensating decrease in the other one, as Table 9.2 indicates. The consistency in the group relationships between $x$, $y^1$, and $y^2$ and the conservation deduction hold when the child knows, as conservers do (Murray, 1981), that the causal links between the factors are unidirectional, with changes in $x$ causing changes in $y$ and not the other way around. Conservers, unlike nonconservers, know that the only way to change $x$ is to add or subtract from it. This knowledge of $x$ is integrated with $y$ by the group structure, and its consistency with the compensatory changes in $y^1$ and $y^2$ underwrites the conservation deduction. Moreover, this is why conservers who possess such an integrated structure for $x$ and $y$ can cite the full range of operativity justifications, each one speaking to a different aspect of the group structure of $x$, $y^1$, and $y^2$. The knowledge of $x$ is covered by the identity reason, namely, that nothing is added or subtracted, and the knowledge of the invention of the requisite opposites is covered by the reversibility reasons of negation and reciprocity. On these grounds, the Genevans distinguished genuine operativity from pseudo-operativity (or empirical reversibility) by requiring the citation of all three reasons—identity, negation, and reciprocity—as the most convincing way to tell true reversibility or genuine operational thought from empirical reversibility (Murray, 1982). These three reasons, each an aspect of the group, will be present when the structure represented in Table 9.2 is in place.

The same general analysis can be applied to any concept in which it will be seen that the mere identification of the factors, $x$ and $y$, is a considerable accomplishment in its own right for the child, let alone the task of inventing an opposite, especially a reciprocal, for each. In the beam-balance problem, for example, the child must figure out the principle or rule that determines under what conditions the balance pan will rise and fall ($x$). We know (e.g., Siegler, 1981) that the child early on discovers that the weight in the pan ($y^1$) is a contributing factor and appreciates that the effects of adding weight to the pan ($+ y^1$) can be undone by removing weight from it ($- y^1$). The invention of another way to undo the effects of adding or subtracting weight, namely, seeing that the distance from the fulcrum is the reciprocal, is slower in coming. At first, it is seen only under conditions where it can act independently, that is, when $y^1$ is held constant. The integration of the factors ($x$, $y^1$, and $y^2$) into the system described in Table 9.2 reveals that the pan will dip ($+ x$) when the weight is increased ($+ y^1$) and/or the distance is increased ($+ y^2$), and it will remain stationary when any increase in $y^1$ is compensated by a decrease in $y^2$, and so on. Thus, the child's competence to construct an opposite for each of the relevant factors in a problem and to find that effects of a factor can be undone by its inverse and reciprocal creates the condition for the attachment of necessity to the outcomes of thinking about the task. As Siegler (1981) and others have shown, the construction of the group structure for the beam balance is a slow accomplishment, taking several years, in which the several relevant factors are identified and fitted in with the previously known factors. These, in turn, are assimilated into more general principles that explain more of the working of the beam balance.

As Piaget argued (1986, 1987), equilibration gradually extends the range of necessary links so that the "necessities" established at one time become assimilated into more powerful structures that confer a deeper understanding of the concept in question (See also Inhelder & de Caprona chap. 2, Ricco, chap. 3 in this volume). Thus, the relationships between the beam-balance factors become extended to include other factors; for example, the factors associated with the left side of the balance become integrated with the factors on the right side of the balance, thus creating another set of reciprocals and negations and, thereby, a more intricate structure of reversible relationships. The group structure can be assimilated into a quantitative structure that permits more precise determinations (i.e., the magnitude of the dip of the pan [$x$] can be ascertained from a product relationship between $y^1$ and $y^2$). This product relationship, in turn, can be integrated into a more generic product moment structure, encompassing other physical phenomena, and this structure can be shown to fit with the structure of Newtonian mechanics, and so forth.

The root of the child's and adolescent's competence to invent these structures is, in the Genevan account, their capacity to invent opposites. This invention means that the necessity of something is defined by the impossibility of its opposite (Piaget, 1986). In addition, the group structure allows the child to see that the opposites are also similar and consistent with each other insofar as they are opposites of each other with respect to some attribute or dimension. The formation of opposites requires the differentiation of factors, the affirmative and its contradiction or opposite, from an undifferentiated whole or single entity. It, further, requires the integration or combination of the opposites into a structure in which each is seen as an aspect of the other—this differentiation and integration cycle is a product of the equilibration mechanism.

Whether the equilibration mechanism provides an advancement over traditional accounts of logical reasoning (see Scholnik, chap. 8; Brain, chap. 7; Falmagne, chap. 6 in this volume) remains, of course, an open question. The equilibration model has stature as an alternative to explanations that find the origins of necessity in social and linguistic conventions. The main difficulty with these accounts is that they provide very little in the way of indicating how the child comes to regard certain conventions as necessary and others as contingent. The virtue of the equilibration model is that it suggests a place to look for the origins of necessity and of the extension of necessity into areas in which truth is contingent. The difficulty of the extension can be imagined by our inability to conceive of a sensible opposite for most of what we know. The origins of necessity, according to the Genevan account, are to be had in precisely our ability to invent opposites and link them to other reversible systems of opposites.

## REFERENCES

Ames, G., & Murray F. (1982). When two wrongs make a right: Promoting cognitive change by social conflict. *Developmental Psychology, 18*, 894–897.

Braine, M., & Rumain, B. (1983). Logical reasoning. In J. Flavell & E. Markman (Eds.), *Handbook of Child Psychology: Vol. 3. Cognitive Development* (pp. 263–340). New York: Wiley.

Cauley, K. (1988). The construction of logical knowledge: A study of borrowing in subtraction. *Journal of Educational Psychology, 80*, 202–205.

Cauley, K., Murray, F., & Smith, D. (1983). Necessity in children's reasoning: Criteria for conservation and operativity. Paper presented at the Eastern Educational Research Association, Baltimore, Md.

Doise, W., Mugny, G., & Perret-Clermont, A. (1975). Social interaction and the development of cognitive operations. *European Journal of Social Psychology, 5*, 367–383.

Doise, W., Mugny, G., & Perret-Clermont, A. (1976). Social interaction and cognitive development: Further evidence. *European Journal of Social Psychology, 6*, 245–247.

Fabricus, W., Sophian, C., & Wellman, H. (in press). Young children's sensitivity to logical necessity in their inferential search behavior. *Child Development*.

Fetzer, M., & Murray F. (1971). The effect of empirical falsity on the development of syllogistic reasoning. Paper presented at the American Educational Research Association, New York.

Haake, R., & Somerville, S. (1985). Development of logical search skills in infancy. *Developmental Psychology, 21,* 176–186.

Miller, S. (1986). Certainty and necessity in the understanding of Piagetian concepts. *Developmental Psychology, 22,* 3–18.

Moshman, D., & Timmons, M. (1982). The construction of logical necessity. *Human Development, 25,* 309–323.

Murray, F. (1981). The conservation paradigm: Conservation of conservation research. In I. Sigel, D. Brodzinsky, & R. Golinkoff (Eds.), *New directions and applications of Piaget's theory.* (pp.143–175). Hillsdale, NJ: Lawrence Erlbaum Associates.

Murray, F. (1982). The pedagogical adequacy of children's conservation explanations. *Journal of Educational Psychology, 74,* 656–659.

Murray, F., & Armstrong, S. (1976). Necessity in conservation and nonconservation. *Developmental Psychology, 12,* 483–484.

Murray, F., & Armstrong, S. (1978). Adult nonconservation of numerical equivalence. *Merrill-Palmer Quarterly, 24,* 255–263.

Murray, F., & Smith, D. (1985). Pre-operative necessity in the acquisition of operativity. *Cahiers de Psychologie Cognitive, 5,* 314–315.

Nozaki, A. (1985). *Anno's Hat Tricks.* NY: Philomel Books.

Overton, W., Ward, S., Noveck, I., Black, J., & O'Brien, D. (1987). Form and content in the development of deductive reasoning. *Developmental Psychology, 23,* 22–30.

Piaget, J. (1986). Essay on necessity. *Human Development, 29,* 301–314.

Piaget, J. (1987). *Possibility and necessity,* (Vols. 1 & 2). Minneapolis: University of Minnesota Press.

Piéraut-Le Bonniec, G. (1980). *The development of model reasoning: Genesis of necessity and possibility notions.* NY: Academic Press.

Rumain, B, Connell, J., & Braine, M. (1981). Conversational comprehension processes are responsible for reasoning fallacies in children as well as adults: "If" is not the biconditional. *Developmental Psychology, 19,* 471–481.

Russell, J. (1982). The child's appreciation of the necessary truth and the necessary falseness of propositions. *The British Journal of Psychology, 73,* 253–266.

Shultz, T. (1982). Rules of causal attribution. *Monographs of the Society for Research in Child Development, 47,* No. 194.

Siegler, R. (1981). Developmental sequences within and between concepts. *Monographs of the Society for Research in Child Development, 46,* No. 189.

# 10

# The Development of Metalogical Understanding

David Moshman
*University of Nebraska—Lincoln*

Does logical reasoning develop? To answer this question, we must clarify precisely what we mean by logical reasoning and by development, and we must come to grips with a confusing morass of literature on logical reasoning in children and adults.

In the first section of this chapter, I will consider the concepts of logical reasoning and development and then apply the resulting definitions to the reasoning literature to conclude that logical reasoning does indeed develop, at least, through adolescence. My argument will rest on a critical distinction between *logic* (involving the application of unconscious inference schemata) and *metalogic* (involving metacognitive awareness of logic). I will argue that development beyond early childhood is primarily at the level of metalogic. Then, in the second section, I will distinguish two aspects of metalogic: *metalogical strategies* (involving relatively conscious coordination of inference schemata) and *metalogical understanding* (involving conceptions about the nature of logic).

The third section of the chapter will propose four stages in the development of metalogical understanding. Relevant evidence will be reviewed. The fourth section will, then, consider how the child moves through the proposed stages. A "knowing levels"approach (Campbell & Bickhard, 1986) will be highlighted and, then, placed in the context of a broader "dialectical constructivism."

## DOES LOGICAL REASONING DEVELOP?

### Logical Reasoning

Reasoning may be defined as a subset of thinking in which one's cognitive processes follow rules or principles so as to reach conclusions that, if not fully justified, are at least somewhat constrained. Although reasoning, thus, includes forms of thinking that may be less than fully rational, it does not encompass aspects of thinking such as free associating or daydreaming, where rationality is simply not relevant. The term, *logical reasoning*, will be used in this chapter to mean *deductive* reasoning—reasoning that, by following strict rules of deduction, reaches conclusions that are not merely plausible or likely but *logically necessary*. If, for example, sprognoids are known to be either animals or plants, and you find out they are not animals, you can conclude not merely that they are *probably* plants but that they *must* be plants. The conclusion is not merely a reasonable *in*duction but a necessary *de*duction.

## Development

Numerous studies find age differences in performance on a variety of logical reasoning tasks. Most developmentalists find it useful, however, to define development as referring only to age-related changes that are, in some sense, progressive—that is, those that tend toward greater differentiation and hierarchic integration, toward better adaptation and organization, toward higher levels of equilibrium, or, with respect to reasoning, toward increasing rationality. Thus, logical reasoning develops if it changes systematically with age in a way that shows increasing rationality.

### Rationality in Children and Adults

Using this definition of development, it is not immediately clear that logical reasoning develops. One basis for questioning the reality of development is the very impressive performance of preschool children on simple inference tasks—that is, tasks involving premises from which a conclusion can be immediately deduced. Young children presented with premises representing diverse logical domains (e.g., transitivity, class logic, propositional logic) commonly reach the same correct conclusions reached by adults (e.g., Hawkins, Pea, Glick, & Scribner, 1984; see reviews by Braine & Rumain, 1983; Thayer & Collyer, 1978). A case might be made that, if logical reasoning develops at all, its development is essentially complete by age five or six.

Another basis for questioning the view that logical reasoning develops is evidence of pervasive illogicality in the performance of adults on a wide variety of reasoning tasks (e.g., Cohen, 1981; Evans, 1982, 1983). Many researchers have concluded that human reasoning is essentially a collection of heuristics and response biases. If adult reasoning is as irrational as this literature suggests, there is little basis for asserting that logical reasoning develops with age.

Although the preschool rationality literature and the adult irrationality literature both cast doubt on the development of logical reasoning, they also appear to contradict each other. The two literatures, taken together, do not simply contradict the view that logical reasoning develops but suggest the highly counterintuitive conclusion that the pinnacle of rationality is reached by age five and reasoning goes rapidly downhill after that.

A closer look suggests that the source of the paradox is that the two literatures use quite different tasks. The preschool rationality research assesses the ability to make direct deductions from simple premises under favorable circumstances. The adult irrationality research, by contrast, tends to require subjects not simply to make an inference but to show substantial awareness and coordination of various ongoing and potential deductions, often under difficult and unfamiliar circumstances. We can make sense of both literatures by distinguishing logic, involving the use of basic inference schemata, from metalogic, involving a more explicit, metacognitive awareness of one's logical reasoning.

### Logic and Metalogic

Consider a child who is told that a hidden ball is either red or green and that it is not red. Even a preschooler is likely to conclude that the ball is green. It would be incautious, however, to propose that the preschooler understands the distinction between premises and conclusions, thinks about the process of deducing a conclusion from premises, or understands the logical necessity of deductions. A more conservative and justifiable conclusion is that the child has simply assimilated the given information to an unconscious schema that immediately transforms it into the conclusion. We might represent the schema, in this case, as *p or q*; *not p*; *therefore, q*. Braine and Rumain (1983) have proposed (See also Braine, chap. 7 this volume) what they consider the basic inference schemata used by human beings, and they conclude, from their review of the literature, that, with the exception of several indirect inference schemata, most of the major deductive schemata used by adults are used quite effectively by children by the time they are old enough to be meaningfully assessed. To a large extent, basic logic, involving competence with the basic human inference schemata, is established by age five or six.

The sorts of tasks commonly administered to older children and adults, however, require much more than a single, immediate inference. Intentionally or not, such tasks assess the ability to think about the nature and use of logic and to coordinate several inference schemata within a single problem. We may refer to this level of competence as metalogic. Research with a variety of complex reasoning tasks indicates that metalogical abilities continue to develop long after the establishment of basic logic. The adult irrationality literature notwithstanding, older children and adults do show metalogical competencies lacking in younger children (Braine & Rumain, 1983; Byrnes

& Overton, 1986; Moshman & Franks, 1986; O'Brien, 1987; O'Brien & Overton, 1980, 1982; Overton, Byrnes, & O'Brien, 1985; Overton, Ward, Noveck, Black, & O'Brien, 1987).

In other words, it appears that the preschool rationality literature has demonstrated genuine logical reasoning in preschool children, but this does not preclude further development of metalogical competencies. Similarly, the adult irrationality literature has indeed shown numerous instances of irrational *performance* by college students on a variety of tasks, but this does not disconfirm the existence of genuine metalogical *competencies* beyond anything observed in preschoolers. Although logical reasoning is neither absent in young children nor perfect in adults, it does appear to improve with age. Thus, logical reasoning does develop, not only in the weak sense of changing with age but in the stronger sense of progressing toward greater rationality (Moshman & Lukin, 1989).

## TWO ASPECTS OF METALOGIC

I have argued that the locus of development of logical reasoning beyond age five or six is at the level of metalogic. It is, thus, important to consider in more detail what metalogic consists of and how it develops. I will propose, in this section, that metalogic can be divided into two aspects: metalogical strategies and metalogical understanding.

### Metalogical Strategies

Metalogical strategies are strategies of reasoning that go beyond simply assimilating premises to unconscious inference schemata. They involve an explicit distinction between premises and conclusions and a purposeful use of inference to deduce the latter from the former. Such strategies are typically conscious, or at least accessible to consciousness. They include, for example, strategies for systematically generating multiple possibilities consistent with premises (Markovits, 1984), actively seeking counterexamples to potential conclusions (Johnson-Laird, 1983; Overton, Ward, Noveck, Black, & O'Brien, 1987), or coordinating several inference schemata to construct a line of argument (Johnson-Laird, 1975).

Johnson-Laird's (1983) "mental models" theory may be construed as proposing a general metalogical approach that he believes underlies all deductive reasoning. The theory suggests that children as well as adults typically solve syllogisms by imagining a state of affairs consistent with the premises, formulating a conclusion consistent with this state of affairs, and then searching for alternative possibilities consistent with the premises that would refute that conclusion (Johnson-Laird, Oakhill, & Bull, 1986; see also discussions by Braine, chap. 7; Scholnick, chap. 8 in this volume).

Unfortunately, for questionable reasons, this mode of solution is proposed as an alternative to the view that people use formal rules of deduction (i.e., inference schemata). It is probably better seen as a complementary view. On simple reasoning problems, such as determining the color of the hidden ball, above, there is no need to go through anything as complex as what Johnson-Laird has suggested. It is more likely that people simply apply basic inference schemata of the sort proposed by Braine and Rumain (1983). Johnson-Laird and his collaborators, however, have focused their research on complex syllogisms that cannot be solved by assimilation to simple inference schemata. On such problems, it is likely that older children and adults are capable of applying various metalogical strategies in increasingly conscious and systematic ways.

Another example of a metalogical strategy is the use of *reductio ad absurdum* arguments. In such arguments, one assumes the truth of what one is trying to disprove and, then, through deductions from that assumption, reaches a contradiction: This allows one to reject the assumed premise. Such a strategy is metalogical, in that it does not simply reach a conclusion by unconsciously assimilating presented information to an inference schema. Instead, it constructs a line of reasoning intended to reach a contradiction and, thus, to indirectly allow one to reach a conclusion that could not be reached directly.

Notice that, in the case of a strategy of this sort, the reasoning takes a noticeable amount of time, and the reasoner, if asked, could probably reconstruct some semblance of what she or he did, step by step, and why. Compare the individual who is told the hidden ball is red or blue and is not red. The conclusion that it is blue follows immediately. If asked to justify this, even an adult probably would say something like, "Well, you said it's red or blue, and it's not red, so it's blue." Notice that this really explains nothing—it simply restates the premises and conclusion. Inference schemas lend themselves to immediate unconscious inferences; metalogical strategies, by contrast, are more planful, temporally extended, and susceptible to introspection. Unlike simple inference schemata, metalogical strategies reflect genuine understanding about the nature of logic.

## Metalogical Understanding

Metalogical understanding consists of conceptions about the nature of logic. Such conceptions appear to be distinguishable from (although related to) strategies. For example, to consciously employ a strategy to generate a conclusion from premises requires a metalogical understanding of the distinction between premises and conclusions. To take a more specific illustration, the mental models strategy may require grasping the metalogical concept that a conclusion must be consistent with all possible states of affairs permitted by the premises. Similarly, understanding the role of contradiction in logic may be critical to effective use of the *reductio ad absurdum* strategy. The remainder of this chapter will attempt to describe and account for the development of metalogical understanding.

## STAGES IN THE DEVELOPMENT
## OF METALOGICAL UNDERSTANDING

The task of this section is to describe four stages of metalogical understanding and show that they are consistent with relevant empirical evidence. The following section will then attempt to explain the transition from stage to stage.

### Stage 1: Explicit Content-Implicit Inference

Consider the following argument:

1. Sprognoids are either animals or plants.
   Sprognoids are not animals.
   Therefore, sprognoids are plants.

A Stage 1 child, given the information that sprognoids are either animals or plants and that they are not animals, will conclude that they are plants. From an external point of view, we as psychologists can note that the child has deduced a conclusion from the premises and can infer the use of a disjunctive inference schema (X is $p$ or $q$; X is not $p$; therefore, X is $q$). The child herself, however, is not thinking about premises, conclusions, or the process of inference. She is thinking about sprognoids, animals, and plants. In other words, the object of her thinking, what she is explicitly aware of, is *content*. The process of inference, including a distinction between premises and conclusion, is implicit in her reasoning but is not itself an object of explicit awareness. The product of reasoning, then, is seen by the Stage 1 reasoner not as a conclusion (deduced from premises via a process of reasoning) but simply as a new fact.

Available evidence suggests that this picture of the Stage 1 child is an accurate account of most preschoolers. Although very young children can make correct inferences from a wide variety of premises, they do not expressly distinguish conclusions from premises or think about the process of reasoning (Sodian & Wimmer, 1987; Somerville, Hadkinson, & Greenberg, 1979). It appears that the preschool child *uses* inference to generate conclusions but does not think *about* inference or construe the conclusions *as* conclusions. Metalogical understanding is simply absent at this age.

## Stage 2: Explicit Inference-Implicit Logic

Consider now another argument:

2. Sprognoids are animals or plants or machines.
   Sprognoids are not animals.
   Therefore, sprognoids are plants.

Given the premises of this argument, a Stage 1 child may conclude that sprognoids are plants or may conclude that sprognoids are machines, perhaps depending on what the word sounds like. A Stage 2 child, in contrast, is likely to realize that there is a problem here. Depending on the situation, the child may withhold judgment, conclude you cannot tell exactly what sprognoids are, or request further information. His or her behavior shows awareness that conclusions are based on premises and are reached by a process of reasoning from those premises. The key difference between Stage 1 and Stage 2 children is not in basic logical reasoning but in metalogical understanding.

Again, as psychologists, we can examine Stage 2 behavior and see more than this. The Stage 2 child appears to respond differently to cases where a particular conclusion is logically necessary than to cases where certain conclusions are merely reasonable, plausible, probable, or conventional (Moshman & Timmons, 1982). We can infer that she or he is not simply applying inference schemas but is making quite sophisticated use of distinctions in logical form. The Stage 2 child apparently distinguishes cases such as Argument 1, in which the form is such that the conclusion is logically necessary ($X$ is $p$ or $q$; $X$ is not $p$; therefore, $X$ is $q$) from cases such as Argument 2, in which the form does not involve a relation of necessity ($X$ is $p$ or $q$ or $r$; $X$ is not $p$; therefore, $X$ is $q$). Thus, although there is no explicit awareness of logical form and the associated property of logical necessity, implicit intuitions of form and necessity do affect reasoning at this level.

Research suggests that implicit appreciation of logical necessity first appears about age six (Somerville et al., 1979) and, between then and age 10, becomes sufficiently consolidated and generalized to show on an increasingly wide variety of tasks (Bereiter, Hidi, & Dimitroff, 1979; Byrnes & Overton, 1986; Cormier & Dagenais, 1983; Fabricius, Sophian, & Wellman, 1987; Markman, 1978; Miller, 1986; Piéraut-Le Bonniec, 1980). The possibility of gaining knowledge via inference (as opposed to direct observation) also begins to be understood about age six (Sodian & Wimmer, 1987). Stage 2 reasoning is, thus, typical of elementary school-age children.

## Stage 3: Explicit Logic—Implicit Metalogic

Consider another argument:

3. Elephants are either animals or plants.
   Elephants are not animals.
   Therefore, elephants are plants.

Children at Stages 1 and 2 would reject this argument. Elephants, they would note, are *not* plants, so the argument is clearly illogical. A Stage 3 individual, on the other hand, would respond differently. Because she is explicitly aware of logical form and understands its distinction from empirical truth, she can appreciate that the form of Argument 3 is identical to the form of Argument 1, although the conclusion to Argument 3 is empirically false. She not only distinguishes logical form from empirical truth but understands their subtle interrelationship. Given the form of Arguments 1 and 3, the conclusion in each case necessarily follows from the premises. This does not guarantee that the conclusion *is* empirically true but shows that it *would be* true if the premises were true. The Stage 3 explicit understanding of the necessity of the relationship between premises and conclusion allows the individual to appreciate validity of argument form: An argument is valid if, regardless of the empirical truth of its premises and conclusions, it has a logical form such that, *if* the premises were true, the conclusion would have to be true as well.

Thus, sophisticated grasp of the interrelated concepts of logical form and necessity, and of their subtle relation to the concept of truth, is summed up in comprehension of the concept of inferential validity. Explicit awareness of the form of propositions and arguments allows the Stage 3 individual to systematically distinguish internal logical structure from the truth or falsity of content. The reasoning of the Stage 3 individual can be interpreted by a psychologist as showing an ability to work within a formal logical system as distinct from a natural language. Some degree of metalogical understanding is implicit in this distinction between logic and language, but metalogic is not itself the object of reflection.

Research by Moshman and Franks (1986) indicates that Stage 3 thinking begins to appear about age 11. They found that 9- and 10-year-olds had great difficulty with Argument 3 and others of this sort. On a variety of tasks involving several different forms of argument, children that age sorted and ranked arguments on the basis of the empirical truth or falsity of the content and appeared to ignore validity of argument form. Even after careful definition of validity, examples distinguishing validity from truth, explicit instructions to use the concept of validity to evaluate arguments, and up to 40 trials with systematic feedback, very few 9- and 10-year-olds seemed to grasp the concept of inferential validity as distinct from empirical truth. In sharp contrast, many 12- and 13-year-olds in the same series of studies spontaneously distinguished arguments on the basis of validity. With appropriate definition, examples, instructions, and/or feedback, most were quite consistent in evaluating arguments on the basis of validity rather than on the basis of empirical truth.

It appears that, although children between ages 6 and 10 have sufficient metalogical understanding to recognize when a conclusion is logically necessary, they are still strongly influenced by content. Only beginning about age 11 or 12 is there sufficient attention to the form of arguments to recognize that certain forms are inherently valid—their conclusions necessarily follow from their premises regardless of the content. Of course, the Stage 2 child's ability to distinguish necessary from merely plausible conclusions does show an implicit awareness of logical form and the associated quality of logical necessity. Only at Stage 3, however, is awareness of form and necessity sufficiently explicit to distinguish valid from invalid arguments independent of the empirical truth or falsity of their content (Moshman & Timmons, 1982).

Achievement of Stage 3 metalogical understanding has implications not only for deductive reasoning but, more broadly, for the development of natural epistemologies—that is, conceptions about the nature of knowledge. An explicit grasp of necessity allows one to distinguish logical from empirical domains. Logical knowledge includes propositions that are necessarily true (tautologies) or necessarily false (self-contradictions), whereas the truth or falsity of empirical propositions can only be determined on the basis of evidence external to those propositions.

Osherson and Markman (1975) investigated reactions to a variety of propositions, including tautologies (e.g., *either the chip in my hand is not red or it is red*), self-contradictions (e.g., *the chip in my hand is white and it is not white*), and empirical statements (e.g., *the chip in my hand is yellow*). Subjects were asked whether they could decide the truth or falsity of the statements without seeing the chip. Children ranging in age from 6 through 11 years typically saw a need for empirical information in all cases, whereas most adults distinguished logical propositions (which were necessarily true or false) from empirical propositions (which could not be evaluated without seeing the chip). Cummins (1978), replicating the study with some methodological refinements, found that sixth graders did significantly better than third graders, but most still had great difficulty with nonempirical propositions.

Komatsu and Galotti (1986) used a different methodology in which children (ages 6, 8, and 10) were asked about various social conventions (e.g., the school year begins in September), empirical regularities (e.g., banging on a pot makes a loud noise), and logical necessities (e.g., there cannot be more apples than fruit). The questions focused on whether each of the various truths could be changed by consensus or could fail to hold in a different culture or on a different planet. They found distinctions between social conventions and other phenomena even in the youngest participants and increasing grasp of these distinctions with age. Children at all three ages, however, had trouble with the distinction between empirical regularities (which cannot be changed by consensus but might fail to hold on another planet) and logical necessities (which must hold in any conceivable world). A comparison group of college students appeared to grasp the distinction between empirical and logical knowledge.

Evidence from diverse sources, thus, suggests that Stage 3 understanding is not seen in children before the age of about 11 but is fairly common in adolescents and adults.

## Stage 4: Explicit Metalogic

The Stage 3 individual can reason about the logical form of arguments and propositions from the metalogical perspective of a formal logical system. Only the Stage 4 individual, however, can think *about* such a system—that is, take it as an object of understanding. She or he can think about the system *as a system*, and grasp its interrelationships with other formal systems and with natural language.

The work of logicians in formalizing systems of logic, exploring their interrelationships with each other and with natural languages, and devising metalanguages for the purposes of such research is clearly at least at this level. It seems likely that the great difficulty of some abstract reasoning tasks typically administered to college students (Cohen, 1981; Evans, 1982, 1983) is due to the very challenging conflicts (for the Stage 3 thinker) between logical and linguistic systems (Politzer, 1986). The minority of undergraduates who succeed on such tasks may be those who have made progress toward Stage 4.

Consider, for example, the well-known "selection task" (Evans, 1982, 1983; Overton et al., 1987). It may be postulated that a Stage 3 grasp of formal logical relationships is adequate for easier versions of the task. Spontaneous success on the more abstract versions, however, may require a Stage 4 explicit understanding of the relationship between material implication (a formal logical relationship embedded in the structure of the task) and the conditional "if . . . then" (a linguistic connective central to the expression of the problem). This would explain why most college students and many younger adolescents do well in easier versions but only a minority of college students spontaneously solve the more difficult versions. The fact that even the most difficult versions are accessible to some undergraduates, however, suggests that progress toward Stage 4 is not limited to professional logicians.

It is worth noting a theoretically interesting ambiguity in determining at what stage an individual achieves metalogical understanding. Consistent with my earlier suggestion that most development beyond age five or six is at the level of metalogic, one could reasonably argue that even the Stage 2 child is reflecting on logic and, thus, has achieved some degree of metalogi-

cal understanding. The inferential processes such a child reflects on, however, have to do with logic only from the external viewpoint of the
psychologist who understands the nature of logic and the course of later development. The Stage 2 subject's own point of view does not yet include explicit knowledge of the central logical concepts of form and necessity. Thus,
a case can be made that genuine metalogic, in the sense of thinking about
the nature of logic, does not appear until Stage 3. However, at Stage 3,
metalogical understanding merely provides the framework of reasoning
rather than being itself the object of explicit attention. Using a still stronger
criterion, then, genuine understanding (as opposed to use) of metalogic is
not present until Stage 4 and is probably never achieved by most people.
From a developmental perspective, the key point here is not to decide the
"correct" criterion for metalogic in order to determine at what age, if ever,
metalogic is achieved. On the contrary, the key point is that development
moves progressively through increasingly powerful levels of metalogical
understanding.

Is Stage 4 the highest level? It may be postulated that the explicit metalogic of Stage 4 is understood only from the perspective of an implicit "metametalogic". Stage 5 may be defined as a reflective differentiation and
reconstruction of that metametalogic.

## Summary

Available evidence supports a four-stage model of the development of metalogical understanding (see Table 10.1). Preschool children often make correct inferences but think about content rather than about the deduction of
conclusions from premises. Beginning about age six, children show better
understanding of the purpose of inference and the nature of conclusions as
new propositions derived from and, thus, justifiable on the basis of premises. This can be seen, for example, in the ability to distinguish necessary
from merely plausible conclusions. Beginning about age 11, there appears
to be a more explicit grasp of logical form and the associated property of
logical necessity. This is revealed in the ability to grasp the concept of inferential validity and distinguish logical from empirical propositions. Finally,
some adults construct Stage 4 conceptions of logical systems and their relationship to natural languages.

## THE CONSTRUCTION OF METALOGICAL
## UNDERSTANDING

Having described four stages of metalogical understanding, the remaining
task is to explain the transitions. Nearly all modern developmentalists are
constructivist in their view of developmental change. Extreme empiricism,

TABLE 10.1
Development of Metalogical Understanding

| Stage | Explicit Object of Understanding | Knowledge Implicit in Reasoning (Subject) |
|---|---|---|
| Stage 1 Explicit Content Implicit Inference | *Content* | *Inference:* Conclusion deduced and, thus, distinct from premises |
| Stage 2 Explicit Inference Implicit Logic | *Inference:* Conclusion deduced from and, thus, related to premises | *Logic:* Form of argument distinct from empirical truth of premises and conclusions (necessity) |
| Stage 3 Explicit Logic Implicit Metalogic | *Logic:* Relation of argument form and empirical truth of premises and conclusions (validity) | *Metalogic:* Formal logical system distinct from natural language |
| Stage 4 Explicit Metalogic | *Metalogic:* Interrelations of logical systems and natural languages | |

in which an active environment impresses itself upon a blank and passive mind, is now commonly referred to as "naive empiricism" and seen as just that—naive. Extreme nativism, in which mature knowledge is seen as encoded directly in the inherited genotype, is commonly called "preformationism" and seen by most biologists and psychologists as an equally untenable position (Moshman & Lukin, 1989). Mature knowledge is generally construed as actively constructed by the developing mind.

There are, however, a wide variety of constructivist views, which can be usefully divided into three general categories: exogenous constructivism, endogenous constructivism, and dialectical constructivism (Moshman, 1982). *Exogenous constructivism* includes a range of views derived from or related to the empiricist perspective. Although knowledge is constructed by an active mind, the course of development is primarily directed by the environment with which that mind interacts. This position includes modern social learning theory and most information processing theories. *Endogenous constructivism* includes a variety of views derived from or related to either nativism or Piagetian theory. Nativist variants suggest that development is an epigenetic construction involving continuing interaction between the genotype and the environment. Although the endpoint is not preformed in the genotype, the process is, nevertheless, strongly guided by heredity. Piagetian variants stress determination of development by the active mind rather than by the genes but remain endogenous in emphasizing internal guidance of the constructive process and, thus, relatively predictable stages. Finally, *dialectical constructivism* proposes a more balanced interaction of internal and external factors in determining the direction of development. The three parts of this section will propose, respectively, exogenous, endogenous, and dialectical constructivist accounts of the development of metalogical understanding.

## An Exogenous Constructivist Account

Theorists in this tradition would probably be disinclined to see metalogical understanding as a distinct domain. An exogenous constructivist might propose that the development of logical reasoning includes the learning of basic inference schemata and, later, of various metalogical strategies. The inference schemata are implicit in language (e.g., in the meanings of logical connectives such as *and, or*, and *if . . . then*) and are, thus, learned as part of the general process of learning language. Metalogical strategies are learned primarily in academic contexts. Some, such as how to use a *reductio ad absurdum* argument, may be explicitly taught (e.g., in a math or logic class). Others may be constructed by the child in the course of general schooling. Learning to write, for example, may orient the child toward combining inferences into extended arguments.

The exogenous theorist would propose that most metalogical concepts are reducible to learned strategies. The concept of inferential validity, for example, consists of one or more strategies (e.g., hypothetico-deductive reasoning) that are used to solve validity tasks. These strategies are learned, primarily in academic contexts, although such learning may involve active information processing rather than passive incorporation.

Language learning and later academic experience are indeed critical to the development of logical reasoning and specific theorics within the exogenous framework may be useful in explaining the relevant processes. It is unlikely, however, that metalogical understanding is merely a collection of learned strategies (Moshman & Lukin, 1989). In particular, exogenous constructivist theories have great difficulty explaining why, if all knowledge is learned from the environment, the child comes to see certain knowledge as logically necessary (Moshman, 1979; Moshman & Timmons, 1982).

## An Endogenous Constructivist Account

In contrast to exogenous accounts, endogenous accounts typically emphasize the sorts of cognitions I have labeled metalogical understandings. They are likely to see specific strategies as less fundamental in that they are either spontaneous outgrowths of one's level of understanding or are learned techniques sharply constrained by one's level of understanding. Constructing an explicit concept of logical necessity, for example, might make it possible to engage in hypothetico-deductive reasoning, but it is the former that is more basic. Similarly, purposeful search for counterexamples—which, according to Johnson-Laird's (1983) mental models theory, is central to solving complex (two- and three-model) syllogisms—requires a metalogical understanding of the role of counterexamples in logic. Strategies learned before the requisite level of metalogical understanding is attained would be superficial techniques or empirical generalizations without a firmly grasped logical basis.

In accounting for the development of metalogical understanding, I will draw most heavily on a specific variant of endogenous constructivism that can be seen in Campbell and Bickhard's (1986) theory of knowing levels, Kegan's (1982) theory of personality development, and Piaget's (1985) concept of reflective abstraction. In this view, knowing can always be divided (from an external perspective) into subject and object. The object is what the subject is explicitly aware of. It is never, of course, reality itself, but rather a constructed object of consciousness. The subject consists of implicit knowledge that is used to know the object but that is not itself explicitly known (except to the psychologist studying the process).

Development, from this perspective, consists of the construction of new, higher levels of subjectivity. In each transition, the previously implicit knowledge of the subject now becomes an explicit object of understanding. But the construction of the new subject, of course, entails a new level of implicit knowledge. Development, thus, never escapes subjectivity but, nevertheless, moves toward increasing objectivity.

Reflective abstraction may be thought of as involving two closely interrelated and mutually facilitative processes: (a) the construction of a new subject at a higher level of abstraction and (b) reconstruction of the old subject as an object of understanding. The construction of the new subject involves abstraction of elements of the old subject and the production of new implicit differentiations. The reconstruction of the old subject involves a reflection on previously implicit differentiations to refine them and ultimately coordinate them at a higher level of integration. The result is that the old subject now becomes an object known from the perspective of the new subject. The knowledge implicit in the old subject is now explicitly known by the new subject, which includes an implicit knowledge that is itself knowable only from the next higher level. At higher levels, the constructive process includes anticipatory construction of possibilities such that reflective abstraction (unlike empirical abstraction, which relies on inductive generalizations) leads to a sense of logical necessity (Piaget, 1986).

This theoretical perspective greatly clarifies the development of metalogical understanding (see Table 10.1). At Stage 1, *Explicit Content—Implicit Inference*, the child thinks about content. The fact that the child can reach appropriate conclusions from various sorts of premises leads the psychologist to suggest that the child is using a variety of inference schemata. Implicit in the use of such schemata is the concept of inference, involving the generation of a conclusion based on but distinct from a set of premises.

Reflection on the process of inference involves refinement of the distinction between conclusions and premises. As this differentiation becomes increasingly explicit, it becomes possible to coordinate conclusions and premises at a higher level, involving realization that the conclusion is derived from the premises by a systematic process of inference. The inference process is itself understood from the perspective of newly constructed logical systems (classification, seriation, arithmetic, and so forth) based on the form (as opposed to the content) of inferences. These systems themselves, however, are not known by the subject. On the contrary, they *are* the Stage 2 subject, the perspective from which inference is understood. Because of their formal nature, they include a sense of logical necessity. If, for example, one has completed the structure of elementary arithmetic, $4 + 2$ *must* $= 6$, or the entire structure (including $6 - 4 = 2$, $6 - 2 = 4$, etc.) becomes incoherent. The child does not think *about* necessity, but can think about inferences from the perspective of their necessity.

Stage 2 appreciation of the necessity of a conclusion relative to certain premises requires knowledge of the logical necessity of the formal relation between premises and conclusion. The psychologist can, thus, infer an understanding of logical form and necessity. This understanding, however, is only implicit in the child's behavior. The child *uses* a structured logic, including the necessity of certain logical forms, to recognize that certain conclusions are logically necessary, but is not explicitly aware of logical structure or of the associated necessity of the relations between premises and conclusions. In other words, explicit awareness of inference at Stage 2 is associated with implicit concepts of logical form and necessity embedded in the use of logical structures.

As equilibrium is reached between the Stage 2 subject (logic) and object (inference), further reflective abstractions become possible. By taking the necessary relations between accepted premises and their required conclusions as objects of further metacognitive reflection, the child increasingly grasps the distinction between these formal relations and the empirical truth or falsity of the premises and conclusions. As awareness of logical form becomes increasingly explicit, however, it becomes possible to reintegrate the concept of form with the concept of empirical truth from which it has now been sharply differentiated. It is understood that some logical forms are better than others in that they guarantee the empirical truth of the conclusions provided the premises are empirically true. Thus, explicit reflection on necessary formal relations between premises and conclusions (the Stage 2 subject) gives rise to the concept of inferential validity (the Stage 3 object). (For detailed presentation of a protocol illustrating this transition in a 13-year-old, see Moshman & Lukin, 1989.) As Stage 3 achieves consolidation, the Stage 2 concept of a necessary conclusion (based on an implicit awareness of the form of the premise–conclusion relationship) becomes a special case of the Stage 3 concept of validity of inference (based on an explicit awareness of necessary form as distinct from, but subtly related to, truth or falsity of content). It now becomes possible to distinguish the domain of logic, in which truth is based on logical form, from the domain of empirical reality, in which truth is an inductive generalization and can never attain logical necessity.

Implicit in Stage 3 conceptions is a distinction between a formal logical system and a natural language. Further reflective abstraction can, of course, refine this differentiation and lead to Stage 4 coordinations, as the complex interrelations of logical systems and natural languages become objects of explicit reflection. There is no limit, in principle, to the number of stages that can be generated by the process of reflective abstraction, although there may be pragmatic constraints on the speed of the process and the highest stage attained due to biological limitations of the human information processing system.

## A Dialectical Constructivist Account

The endogenous account suggests that the environment, by stimulating or discouraging reflection, may facilitate or hinder development, but that it has no impact on the direction of development (i.e., the stages through which one passes). With respect to the proposed stages of metalogical understanding, this is a plausible claim. In fact, it is difficult to see how else one can account for the emergence of a sense of logical necessity that goes beyond recognition of empirical regularities and social conventions.

It is much less likely, however, that the environment has such minor and indirect impact on the emergence of specific metalogical strategies. Such a conclusion can only be defended by asserting that metalogical strategies are relatively superficial extensions of metalogical understanding that either emerge spontaneously as metalogical understanding develops or are learned in a manner determined more by developmental constraints than by environmental influences. Evidence in many areas of cognitive development suggests that specific strategies and exogenous learning are far more influential than the endogenous perspective suggests (Flavell, 1985).

It appears that the exogenous and endogenous accounts have complementary strengths and weaknesses. Exogenous constructivism better accounts for the learning of strategies than for the developing grasp of their logical nature, whereas endogenous constructivism better accounts for the emerging grasp of logical necessity but trivializes the learning of strategies as a superficial extension of this.

A dialectical view suggests a substantive role for both exogenous and endogenous factors, and stresses the continuing interplay between the two. Exogenous construction may be predominant in the acquisition of metalogical strategies, whereas endogenous construction may be predominant in the emergence of metalogical understanding. Moreover, strategies and understanding are seen as equally fundamental and as continually enriching each other. Endogenous construction of understanding may enrich one's grasp of the logic behind the reasoning strategies one has learned and facilitate refinement and coordination of these strategies, as well as the learning of additional strategies. Correspondingly, exogenous construction of strategies may sometimes constitute the leading edge of metalogical development, as the process of endogenous construction endeavors to coordinate and reconstruct learned strategies at a deeper level of understanding (Moshman & Timmons, 1982). The disequilibrium inherent in these complex interactions may provide much of the motivation for further exogenous and endogenous constructions (Piaget, 1985).

Consider, for example, the relation of the concept of validity and the strategy of hypothetico-deductive reasoning. An exogenous view might suggest that students learn hypothetico-deductive reasoning (e.g., in a math class), and this leads to a conception of what valid arguments are. An endogenous approach might suggest that the concept of validity is constructed out of Stage 2 precursors and then makes it possible to produce or learn hypothetico-deductive reasoning. The dialectical approach suggests that either the relatively endogenous construction of the concept of validity or the relatively exogenous construction of hypothetico-deductive reasoning may precede the other, but whichever comes first is likely to facilitate the other. A continuing pattern of mutual facilitation in which neither strategy nor understanding gets very far ahead is the typical pattern of development.

The dialectical account cannot replace the exogenous and endogenous accounts. Metalogical strategies are learned primarily through exogenous mechanisms, whereas metalogical understanding is more endogenously constructed. The dialectical perspective reminds us, however, that there is a complex interplay between these two facets of development—their separation as distinct aspects is less a reality of cognition than a useful theoretical fiction. Metalogic may be construed as a strategy/understanding continuum ranging from (a) specific, discrete logical techniques; through (b) more general, structured sorts of strategies; through (c) more abstract metalogical concepts, such as tautology and validity; through (d) core conceptions of logical necessity. Toward the strategy end of the continuum, exogenous forces tend to predominate—at the extreme, specific techniques may be learned by rote and applied with minimal conceptual understanding. Toward the understanding end, endogenous forces tend to predominate—at the extreme, general conceptions of necessity develop in a sequence virtually impervious to environmental variations. But most of metalogical development falls between the extremes, and it involves varying proportions and complex interactions of external and internal factors. Thus, accounts of the exogenous construction of strategies and the endogenous construction of understanding, although providing genuine insight, are each partial and approximate stories abstracted from a larger and more complicated picture.

## CONCLUSIONS

At the 1981 meeting of the Society for Research in Child Development, as discussant for a symposium on logical necessity, I concluded the session with the following limerick:

> The child thinks you only can know
> What the evidence happens to show
> Till she cries out, "FORSOOTH!
> There are logical truths
> That *are* necessarily so!"

Although my general perspective has not changed since I penned those immortal lines, I can be a bit more specific in concluding this chapter.

To make sense of the literature on the development of logical reasoning, it is critical to distinguish basic logic (involving the ability to reach correct conclusions) from metalogic (involving metacognitive awareness of logic). It appears that basic logical competence is quite impressive even in preschool children, whereas metalogic develops at least through adolescence. Metalogic includes metalogical strategies (relatively conscious and systematic coordination of inference schemata) and metalogical understanding (conceptions about the nature of logic, including the concept of logical necessity).

The development of metalogical understanding can be divided into four stages:

Stage 1.  A stage of implicit inference about content.
Stage 2.  A stage of explicit inference based on an implicit logic.
Stage 3.  A stage in which logical necessity is explicitly understood on the basis of implicit metalogical awareness.
Stage 4.  A stage involving explicit reflection on metalogic

Progress through these stages may be accounted for in terms of reflective abstraction, an internally-driven constructive process in which knowledge implicit at any given stage becomes an explicit object of understanding at the succeeding stage. This endogenous process cannot be fully understood, however, without considering its continuing dialectical interaction with the more externally driven process of learning metalogical strategies.

Therefore, we ask: Does logical reasoning develop? If logic consisted only of basic inference schemata, we might conclude that its development is largely complete by age five or six. Considering, in addition, a variety of exogenously learned metalogical strategies, we might make a case for substantial change through adolescence. Because the specific strategies one learns are a function of one's environment, however, this would not be development in the stronger sense of systematically progressive change. In fact, given that one can learn incorrect strategies as well as correct ones, reasoning might even become more and more irrational.

Fortunately, there is more to logical reasoning than inference schemata and metalogical strategies. There also appear to be endogenously constructed metalogical conceptions, or, more broadly, an internally directed metalogical understanding. This understanding moves systematically through a sequence of differentiations and reintegrations toward increasingly explicit logical and metalogical conceptualization of inference. Exogenously learned strategies are endogenously coordinated and reconstructed along the way, ensuring that they too will show increasing coherence. Thus, the individual becomes increasingly able to reach defensible conclusions and generate sophisticated justifications. Although the specific nature of mature reasoning depends in part on the particular strategies one has learned, the endogenous construction of metalogical understanding ensures that logical reasoning will develop, not only in the sense of changing with age, but in the theoretically more meaningful sense of moving systematically toward an increasingly self-reflective rationality.

## REFERENCES

Bereiter, C., Hidi, S., & Dimitroff, G. (1979). Qualitative changes in verbal reasoning during middle and late childhood. *Child Development, 50*, 142–151.

Braine, M. D. S., & Rumain, B. (1983). Logical reasoning. In J. H. Flavell & E. M. Markman (Eds.), *Handbook of child psychology: Vol. 3, Cognitive development* (pp. 263–340). New York: Wiley.

Byrnes, J. P., & Overton, W. F. (1986). Reasoning about certainty and uncertainty in concrete, causal, and propositional contexts. *Developmental Psychology, 22*, 793–799.

Campbell, R. L., & Bickhard, M. H. (1986). *Knowing levels and developmental stages*. Basel: Karger.

Cohen, L. J. (1981). Can human irrationality be experimentally demonstrated? *The Behavioral and Brain Sciences, 4*, 317–370.

Cormier, P., & Dagenais, Y. (1983). Class-inclusion developmental levels and logical necessity. *International Journal of Behavioral Development, 6*, 1–14.

Cummins, J. (1978). Language and children's ability to evaluate contradictions and tautologies: A critique of Osherson and Markman's findings. *Child Development, 49*, 895–897.

Evans, J. St. B. T. (1982). *The psychology of deductive reasoning*. London: Routledge & Kegan Paul.

Evans, J. St. B. T. (Ed.). (1983). *Thinking and reasoning: Psychological approaches*. London: Routledge & Kegan Paul.

Fabricius, W. V., Sophian, C., & Wellman, H. M. (1987). Young children's sensitivity to logical necessity in their inferential search behavior. *Child Development, 58*, 409–423.

Flavell, J. H. (1985). *Cognitive development* (2nd ed.). Englewood Cliffs, NJ: Prentice-Hall.

Hawkins, J., Pea, R. D., Glick, J., & Scribner, S. (1984). "Merds that laugh don't like mushrooms": Evidence for deductive reasoning by preschoolers. *Developmental Psychology, 20*, 584–594.

Johnson-Laird, P. N. (1975). Models of deduction. In R. J. Falmagne (Ed.), *Reasoning: Representation and process in children and adults* (pp. 7–54). Hillsdale, NJ: Lawrence Erlbaum Associates.

Johnson-Laird, P. N. (1983). *Mental models.* Cambridge, MA: Harvard University Press.

Johnson-Laird, P. N., Oakhill, J., & Bull, D. (1986). Children's syllogistic reasoning. *Quarterly Journal of Experimental Psychology, 38A*, 35–58.

Kegan, R. (1982). *The evolving self: Problem and process in human development.* Cambridge, MA: Harvard University Press.

Komatsu, L. K., & Galotti, K. M. (1986). Children's reasoning about social, physical, and logical regularities: A look at two worlds. *Child Development, 57*, 413–420.

Markman, E. M. (1978). Empirical vs. logical solutions to part–whole comparison problems concerning classes and collections. *Child Development, 49*, 168–177.

Markovits, H. (1984). Awareness of the "possible" as a mediator of formal thinking in conditional reasoning problems. *British Journal of Psychology, 75*, 367–376.

Miller, S. A. (1986). Certainty and necessity in the understanding of Piagetian concepts. *Developmental Psychology, 22*, 3–18.

Moshman, D. (1979). To *really* get ahead, get a metatheory. In D. Kuhn (Ed.), *Intellectual development beyond childhood* (pp. 59–68). San Francisco: Jossey-Bass.

Moshman, D. (1982). Exogenous, endogenous, and dialectical contructivism. *Developmental Review, 2*, 371–384.

Moshman, D., & Franks, B. A. (1986). Development of the concept of inferential validity. *Child Development, 57*, 153–165.

Moshman, D., & Lukin, L. E. (1989). The creative construction of rationality: A paradox? In J. A. Glover, R. R. Ronning, and C. R. Reynolds (Eds.), *Handbook of creativity*. New York: Plenum.

Moshman, D., & Timmons, M. (1982). The construction of logical necessity. *Human Development, 25*, 309–323.

O'Brien, D. (1987). The development of conditional reasoning: An iffy proposition. In H. W. Reese (Ed.), *Advances in child development and behavior* (Vol. 20). Orlando, FL: Academic Press.

O'Brien, D., & Overton, W. F. (1980). Conditional reasoning following contradictory evidence: A developmental analysis. *Journal of Experimental Child Psychology, 30*, 44–60.

O'Brien, D., & Overton, W. F. (1982). Conditional reasoning and the competence–performance issue: A developmental analysis of a training task. *Journal of Experimental Child Psychology, 34*, 274–290.

Osherson, D. N., & Markman, E. (1975). Language and the ability to evaluate contradictions and tautologies. *Cognition, 3*, 213–226.

Overton, W. F., Byrnes, J. P., & O'Brien, D. P. (1985). Developmental and individual differences in conditional reasoning: The role of contradiction training and cognitive style. *Developmental Psychology, 21*, 692–701.

Overton, W. F., Ward, S. L., Noveck, I. A., Black, J., & O'Brien, D. P. (1987). Form and content in the development of deductive reasoning. *Developmental Psychology, 23*, 22–30.

Piaget, J. (1985). *The equilibration of cognitive structures: The central problem of intellectual development.* Chicago: University of Chicago Press.

Piaget, J. (1986). Essay on necessity. *Human Development, 29*, 301–314.

Piéraut-Le Bonniec, G. (1980). *The development of modal reasoning: Genesis of necessity and possibility notions.* New York: Academic Press.

Politzer, G. (1986). Laws of language use and formal logic. *Journal of Psycholinguistic Research, 15*, 47–92.

Sodian, B., & Wimmer, H. (1987). Children's understanding of inference as a source of knowledge. *Child Development, 58*, 424–433.

Somerville, S. C., Hadkinson, B. A., & Greenberg, C. (1979). Two levels of inferential behavior in young children. *Child Development, 50*, 119–131.

Thayer, E. S., & Collyer, C. E. (1978). The development of transitive inference. *Psychological Bulletin, 85*, 1327–1343.

# 11

# Formal Operational Thought

William M. Gray
*Center for Applied Cognitive Science, The University of Toledo*

In 1975, Suzanne Martorano presented a paper at the biennial meeting of the Society for Research in Child Development entitled *Formal Operations Thinking: Now You See It, Now You Don't*. In that paper, she reported data from three small studies of various aspects of formal operations. More important than the data she reported was her ambivalence (which was clearly captured in the title) regarding the manifestations of formal operations. In the years since her presentation, numerous studies have focused on formal operations (see Neimark, 1975, 1982; Keating, 1980; Lawson, 1985, for extensive reviews) and more is now known about them. Yet, her title is still appropriate, as formal operations are still only manifested some of the time by some of the people. Furthermore, crucial aspects of the theory describing formal operations have not been addressed, or they have been sporadically addressed, and the reasons suggested for their "now you see it, now you don't nature" have come more from an Americanized, mechanistic orientation to development rather than one that incorporates or extends Piaget's own constructive organismic orientation (Overton, 1985). In Piaget's terminology, there has been a dominance of the concrete observables (i.e., confusing detail of "factual" data) and traditional environmental-based interpretations of the data without the construction of necessary negations (i.e., theoretically appropriate integration of the data).

The present chapter is a step toward providing these necessary integrations: First, formal operations are described, and, second, why their construction is so tenuous is discussed. Within the present chapter, formal operations are considered as a combination of inductive or "hypothetical reasoning based on a logic of all possible combinations" (Parsons, 1958, p. xiii; see also Piaget, 1953/1957, p. 18) and deductive reasoning based on propositional logic where the combination of inductive reasoning and de-

227

ductive reasoning *is necessarily psychologically adaptive for individuals with(in) their acknowledged existing environment*, which is not restricted to what has traditionally been considered *the* environment. Although Piaget combined inductive reasoning and deductive reasoning in the theoretical description of formal operations, the present chapter focuses on ideas that directly derive from Piaget's theorizing and/or Inhelder's tasks. Other chapters more directly address the development of deductive reasoning, as does related work on approaching formal operations from the perspective of deductive reasoning (e.g., Overton, Ward, Noveck, Black, & O'Brien, 1987). Psychological adaptation is emphasized, because, at its heart, Piaget's description of formal operations and other forms of thought is a description based on the construction of necessary biological/psychological adaptations.

## WHAT ARE FORMAL OPERATIONS?

### Historical Contexts

Before formal operations are described, it is necessary to clarify some continuing confusion that surrounds them. First, contrary to the citations and contexts of many researchers and reviewers of formal operations, they are not something that were created with the 1958 publication of the English translation of *The Growth of Logical Thinking* (Inhelder & Piaget, 1955/ 1958), although this is the work most frequently cited when formal operations are discussed. Formal operations are mentioned as early as 1924 in *Judgment and Reasoning* (Piaget, 1924/1964) as well as in a series of 1942 lectures at the Sorbonne (Piaget, 1947/1966). Second, *The Growth of Logical Thinking* is not the only source of a theoretical description of formal operations (see Piaget, 1947/1966, 1949, 1952, 1953/1957) nor is it the only source of data on the behavioral manifestations of formal operations (see Piaget 1946/1970; Piaget & Inhelder, 1941/1974, 1951/1975; and even Piaget, 1924/1964). Third, formal operations are not necessarily a theory of adolescent thinking and reasoning, although the majority of subjects who were described as manifesting formal operations on Inhelder's simple inductive physics problems (Inhelder & Piaget, 1955/1958, pp. xxi, xxii; Piaget, 1953/1957, pp. 19, 38) were adolescents. Finally, the essence of formal operations is not the logical models of reasoning that have been variously criticized (Braine & Rumain, 1983; Brainerd, 1976–77; Ennis, 1975, 1976, 1978; Leiser 1982; Parsons, 1960). Formal operations are one type of psychological adaptation, and the logical models represent the structure of those adaptations with all the logical imperfections inherent in the adaptations. The models are not the adaptations themselves.

## Theoretical Contexts

Piagetian theory is a biological theory of adaptation extended to the psychological. Like biological adaptation, psychological adaptation is oriented toward survival and enhancement of the individual with(in) an existing environment. Adaptation involves physically or mentally transforming something considered "real" in the environment and incorporating the transformed entity into one's biological or psychological structures through assimilation and accommodation. Adaptations do not occur in a vacuum. Rather, they *require* an environment that is acknowledged by the adapting person as existing at any one moment in time. This acknowledged environment is created through adaptations with(in) an "existing" environment, and it provides the context with(in) which adaptations are created and sustained.

A person's actions with(in) an environment are continuous, and these actions become organized as an equilibrium between the person and the acknowledged environment is constructed. This equilibrium is manifested in stable characteristics that describe, define, and "direct" the organized actions (adaptations); adaptations are commonly known as cognitive structures. Major types of adaptations are the classic stages of cognitive development, each of which has its own set of defining characteristics. The adaptations of concrete operations and formal operations are defined as mental operations. "Psychologically, operations are actions which are internalizable, reversible, and coordinated into systems characterized by laws which apply to the system as a whole" (Piaget, 1953/1957, p. 8). Operations are "means for transforming data about the 'real' world so that they can be organized and used selectively in the solution of problems" (Parsons, 1958, p. xiii), and "reversibility is defined as the permanent possibility of returning to the starting point of the operation in question" (Inhelder & Piaget, 1955/1958, p. 272). As a set of actions becomes organized and defined through activity, its defining qualities, as evidenced through observable behaviors, determine what "exists" or is "real." That is, what is considered the environment or what is considered "real" within an environment is constructed by a person's actions as the actions become adaptive with(in) the existing acknowledged environment. Furth (1981) described the process in two ways: First, "just as in development the internal structure of intelligence is built up, so also meaningful aspects of the physical environment are constructed by this growing intelligence" (p. 180). And, second:

> Whereas in sensorimotor assimilation and accommodation a form (of knowledge) modifies material content (e.g., an infant pushes open a door), on the plane of representation the form modifies mental content (the child imagines the opening of a door). In the first case the child is doing something externally, and knowledge regulates the external action so that it is organized and purposeful. In the second case there is an internal doing and knowledge is not

merely an inferred capacity related to an observable event; it now also constructs the reality in which the doing takes place. It is the realm of knowledge, or psychological reality. (p. 264)

The construction of "reality" is a pivotal part of Piaget's theory and is necessary because a structure can only adapt to, and consequently be in equilibrium with(in), an environment that "exists"; and an environment "exists" only when it is acknowledged via organized actions—adaptations. A person's physical or mental actions and the qualities of the actions define the adaptations and the specific qualities of what is "real." With regard to the major types of adaptations, sensorimotor adaptations define "reality" as motor actions on sensory impressions; preoperational adaptations define "reality" as representations of motor actions on sensory impressions; concrete operational adaptations define "reality" as concrete, physically, real "facts" whose properties are classifiable and relatable; and formal operational adaptations define "reality" as abstract possibilities that may or may not physically exist where the abstract possibilities are represented and mentally manipulated as hypotheses.

When Piaget's descriptions of behaviors that illustrate the different types of adaptations are read, it is easy to conclude that when more sophisticated adaptations become sufficiently organized, the less sophisticated, earlier constructed adaptations are eliminated or discarded. However, this is an incorrect conclusion. When more complex, sophisticated adaptations are constructed, the previously constructed, less complex, less sophisticated adaptations and their accompanying "definitions" of reality do not disappear but, instead, are retained intact as well as being transformed and incorporated into the more complex sophisticated structures. For example, Inhelder and Piaget (1955/1958) wrote:

With the appearance of concrete thought, the system of regulations, though maintained in an unstable state until this point, attains an elementary form of stable equilibrium. As it reaches the level of complete reversibility, the concrete operations issued from the earlier regulations are coordinated into definite structures (classifications, serial orders, correspondences, etc.) *which will be conserved for the remainder of the life span. Of course this is no bar to the organization of higher systems; but even when higher systems emerge, the present system remains active in the limited area of the organization of immediately given data* [emphasis added]. (p. 248)

In addition, "once an operational system is established it may remain unchanged for the remainder of a person's life" (Inhelder & Piaget, 1955/1958, p. 256). Although approaching the issue from a more environmentally based perspective than Piaget, Neimark (1975) came to a similar conclusion:

Although the abstract logical thought of formal operations constitutes an a priori optimal state of final equilibrium, it is clear that this final state may not be attained in practice. The prior stages of development are, in effect, forced upon every normal human being by virtue of the structure of the physical world and the conditions of human existence. The final stage, on the other hand, may be a refinement of advanced civilization rather than a necessary condition of survival. (p. 556)

## Transition from Concrete Operations

For concrete operations, what are adaptationally "real" or elements of thought are relations among physical entities (e.g., differences in height) or properties of physical entities (e.g., eye color, hair color). If an element is a relation then individual examples of the relation can be combined (i.e., logically added) to produce a description of the relations among a set of physical entities (e.g., entities are seriated by the differences among their heights). In addition, individual examples of two relations (e.g., height and width) can be coordinated (i.e., logically multiplied) to produce a description of the relations among a set of physical entities where the entities are simultaneously described by both relations (e.g., glass A is taller and thinner than glass B). There are two logical models of combination and two logical models of coordination that describe the organization of concrete operational relation adaptations. Relations, their combination, and their coordination are induced from adaptational experience. (Because of the complexity in symbolically representing the complete logical models of concrete operational relation adaptations and because a full description of the models is outside the purview of this chapter, the reader is referred to Flavell, 1963, and Gray, 1970, for detailed descriptions.)

If an element is a property (e.g., hair color), then individual examples of the property (e.g., redheads and nonredheads) can be combined (logical addition symbolized by " $+$ ") to produce the property (e.g., redheads + nonredheads = all hair color). Symbolically, if R = the class of all people who are redheads, R $'$ = the class of all people who are nonredheads, and H = all people who have hair, then R + R $'$ = H. If two properties (e.g., hair color and eye color) are coordinated (logical multiplication symbolized by " $\times$ "), then the resulting product is a description of a set of physical entities each simultaneously described by one subproperty from each property. Using the previous symbols (R & R $'$) and defining G = the class of all people who are green eyed, G $'$ = the class of all people who are not green eyed, and E = all people with eye color, the coordination of H and E (i.e., H $\times$ E = HE) can be defined as RG + RG $'$ + R $'$G + R $'$G $'$, where RG = all redheads who are green eyed, RG $'$ = all redheads who are not green eyed, R $'$G = all nonredheads who are green eyed, and R $'$G $'$ = all nonredheads who are not green eyed. Concrete operations can generate and understand such a set of associations based on the coordination of two properties and their respective subproperties, but they can not determine whether there is any *necessary* relation between the properties or subproperties. Concrete operations can only focus on the associations, or lack thereof, between properties or subproperties as they exist in empirically "real" objects. They can not use the results of their own functioning as elements for further thought. Inhelder and Piaget (1955/1958) describe this aspect of concrete operations as follows:

> Our observations show that at the level of concrete operations the subject tries to structure reality as completely as possible but that he remains close to reality in its raw form—*i.e.,* as it appears without isolation of variables. When the subject classifies, orders, formulates correspondences, etc., he registers the facts directly without adopting a critical attitude toward the empirical world or adopting systematic methodological precautions. This is due to the fact that as concrete operations develop . . . their function is to structure reality factor-by-factor. (282–283)

The combination of subproperties to form a property and the coordination of properties including their respective subproperties illustrate the two types of concrete operations. Each of the operations has its own specific necessary reversible operation (e.g., $H - R' = R$ and $HE \div E = H$, logical subtraction and logical division, respectively). These simple algebraic representations of the two operations and their respective reversible operations briefly summarize two of the four logical models that describe the organization of concrete operational property adaptations. There are two logical models of combination and two logical models of coordination that describe the organization of concrete operational property adaptations. Like relations, properties, their combination, and their coordination are induced from adaptational experience. (Because of the complexity in symbolically representing the complete logical models of concrete operational property adaptations and because a full description of the models is outside the purview of this chapter, the reader is referred to Flavell, 1963, and Gray, 1970, for detailed descriptions).

Concrete operations are adult-like adaptations with a focus on the empirically real, both in what has been traditionally considered the "real" aspects of the acknowledged "physical" environment and the "real" aspects of the acknowledged social or interpersonal environment. This orientation to "real" characteristics of the acknowledged environment(s) produces an emphasis on "the real facts" and nothing but the facts. Whatever is being reasoned about must be real, even if what is being reasoned about is abstract. Nonreal abstract possibilities and nonexperientially based aspects of physical reality are transformed into, and treated as if they were, an extension of one's own experientially based adaptations. Thus, for concrete operations, reality is assumed to be physically real, classifiable, relational, and quantifiable (Elkind, 1967, 1978, pp. 85–128).

Concrete operational adaptations with(in) the acknowledged environment are successful as long as they do not acknowledge too many properties and/or relations to be classified, serially ordered, etc. at any one time, or they do not acknowledge too many irregularities in the properties and/or relations. If concrete operational adaptations acknowledge too many properties and/or relations, or if they acknowledge too many irregularities in the properties and/or relations, then concrete operational adaptations overwhelm themselves with too many "facts" (i.e., properties, relations, and/or irregularities). In Piaget's terms, through their own functioning, concrete operations create a lack of equilibrium between themselves as viable adaptations and their acknowledged environment. Simply stated, the functioning adaptations create a situation in which they are no longer adaptive.

When concrete operations are no longer psychologically adaptive with(in) their acknowledged existing environment and/or when the results of the classification and relational operations are taken more and more as facts, concrete operational adaptations take these *factual results* of previous concrete operational adaptations as elements of thought (Inhelder & Piaget, 1955/1958, pp. xxiii, 56) and operate on them as a means of simplifying and clarifying the increasing number of elements and/or acknowledged irregularities with(in) the elements themselves (Inhelder & Piaget, 1955/1958, pp. 283–293; Neimark, 1975, p. 555). In terms of the example using the properties of hair color and eye color, not only are the four associations of their subproperties generated (i.e., RG, RG ', R 'G, R 'G '), the four associations are used as elements (as were the four subproperties R, R ', G, G ' used as elements for concrete operational adaptations) for the construction of all possible associations (i.e., classifications) of the four base associations (e.g., RG + RG ', RG + R 'G, RG + RG ' + R 'G, etc.). This extension of the concrete operation of classification to the four base associations produces six doublets (e.g., RG + R 'G '), four triplets (e.g., RG + R 'G + R 'G '), one quadruplet (i.e., RG + RG ' + R 'G + R 'G '), and one null set that with the original four associations yields a total of sixteen possible empirical associations (combinations). These combinations are represented as propositions (hypotheses). By convention, when propositions are used, (a) the operations are "different" as logical addition becomes the operation of "v" ("or"), logical multiplication or coordination becomes the operation of "•" ("and"), the complement or negation of a class becomes "–" ("not"); (b) classes become propositions, and are represented differently as R becomes p, R ' becomes $\bar{p}$ (not p), G becomes q, and G ' becomes $\bar{q}$ (not q); and (c) combinations of propositions are also represented differently (for example, p•q for RG, $\bar{p}$•q for R 'G, p•q v p•$\bar{q}$ for RG + RG ', and p•q v p•$\bar{q}$ v $\bar{p}$•q for RG + RG ' + R 'G). Table 11.1 provides a list of the sixteen formal operations generated from all possible combinations of the original base combinations of propositions, including the names assigned to each operation by Piaget, the symbol of each operation, the combination representing each

TABLE 11.1
Formal Operations Combinations

| Name | Symbol | Combination | Complement[a] | Symbol | Combination |
|---|---|---|---|---|---|
| Conjunction | p•q | p•q | Incompatibility | p/q | p•q̄.qvp̄.q̄ |
| Affirmation of q | q[p] | p•q v p̄.q | Negation of q | q̄[p] | p•q̄.q̄ |
| Affirmation of p | p[q] | p•q v p•q̄ | Negation of p | p̄[q] | p̄.q v p̄.q̄ |
| Equivalence | p = q or p↔q | p•q v p̄.q̄ | Reciprocal Exclusion | pvq | p̄•q v p•q̄ |
| Disjunction | pvq | p•q v p•q̄ v p̄•q̄ | Conjunctive Negation | p̄•q̄ | p̄.q̄ |
| Implication | p→q | p•q v p̄.q v p̄.q̄ | Nonimplication | p•q̄ | p•q̄ |
| Reciprocal Implication | q→p | p•q v p•q̄ v p̄.q̄ | Negation of Reciprocal Implication | p̄•q | p̄•q |
| Complete Affirmation | p*q | p•q.qv p̄q̄.q̄ | Negation | | |

[a]Each operation's complement is the operation whose union (v) with the original operation will yield all four of the original base combinations (i.e., complete affirmation). Thus, the disjunction of the combination in the third column with the combination in the sixth column will produce all four of the original base combinations of propositions: for example, p•qvp̄.q = p*q and p→qvp•q̄ = p*q.

operation, and the complement of each operation. Table 11.1 is organized around the operation of p•q (conjunction) as each of the eight operations in the first column includes the operation of p•q and the complements of those operations in the fourth column do not include p•q. Table 11.1 could just as easily be organized around one of the other three base combinations: p̄•q̄, p•q̄, or p̄•q. For example, if the table were organized around p̄•q̄ (conjunctive negation), then p v q would be listed as the complement for p̄•q̄ and p/q, q̄[p], and p̄[q] would be switched with p•q, q[p], and p[q], respectively. These sixteen different combinations are treated as propositions of possibility that can be systematically tested for their truth value.

In contrast to misunderstandings of Piaget's conception of formal operations (e.g., Ennis, 1975, 1976, 1978) that suggest that Piaget believed that propositions are adaptationally real only to formal operations, Inhelder and Piaget (1955/1958) clearly stated that propositions are "real" for preoperational, concrete operational, and formal operational adaptations. The difference among the types of adaptations is what aspect of the propositions is real. Inhelder and Piaget (1955/1958) wrote:

> The combinatorial composition deals with *propositions*. Even during the concrete stage (and moreover, in preoperational thinking), reasoning is obviously based on propositions, with or without perceptual presence of the objects described. But the concrete operation consists in *de*composing and *re*composing the content of the propositions—*i.e.,* classes and relations as constituents of the proposition. Thus, at the concrete level a proposition is still linked to another not by virtue of its being a proposition but exclusively on account of its logical content, consisting of structures of classes and relations corresponding to actual objects. On the other hand, as soon as the proposition states simple possibilities and its composition consists of bringing together or separating out these possibilities as such, this composition deals no longer with objects but rather with the truth values of the combinations. (p. 292).

In her translators' introduction to *The Growth of Logical Thinking*, Parsons (1958) provided a complementary perspective:

> The formal operations enable him to combine these propositions mentally and to isolate those which confirm his hypotheses . . . . The *combinatorial system* is the structural mechanism which enables him to make these combinations of facts.
>
> In other words, formal operations are ways of transforming propositions about reality so that the relevant variables can be isolated and relations between them deduced. The operations described . . . are *different kinds of combination*, any one of which may be appropriate depending on the particular situation observed. The frequently recurring term "association" refers to an observed conjunction of facts . . . . The kind of relationship formulated depends on the particular association of facts observed. (p. xviii)

Implication, conjunction, disjunction, etc. are some examples. The sixteen possible combinations and the relations among them (INRC transformations) are the logical models of formal operational adaptations in the same way as there are eight logical models of concrete operational adaptations. Like individuals who use concrete operations and are unaware that their thought can be described by the eight logical models, individuals who use formal operations are unaware of the logical models that can describe their thought. Inhelder and Piaget (1955/1958) wrote:

> We have never encountered a stage III [formal operational] subject or an adult (logicians excluded) who has successfully calculated these 16 possible combinations or who has even become aware of the existence of such a combinatorial system in any explicit form. The deliberate and reasoned use of these combinations is as foreign to the subject who begins to reason formally as are the laws of harmony to the child or to the popular signer who retains a melody or whistles an improvised tune. (p. 310)

## Formal Operations

Aside from the classically listed characteristics of formal operational adaptations (e.g., conceiving of possibilities, hypothetical-deductive thought, interpropositional reasoning, combinatorial thought, contrary-to-fact reasoning, proportional reasoning, etc.; see Inhelder & Piaget, 1955/1958), the major characteristic of formal operations is their integrated nature. Where the individual classes and subclasses that are constructed by concrete operations are dependent or defined based on their complement relative to their immediate superordinate class (e.g., $H - R' = R$ and $H - R = R'$), each of the sixteen logically possible propositional operations are not necessarily dependent on the other operations, yet, they are all related to—integrated with(in)—each other. This integration has been described as a "structured wholeness" of the thought processes and has generated much controversy because of the difficult of statistically producing appropriate relationships among the propositional operations.

Traditionally, researchers have looked at the concept of integration/structured wholeness as meaning that subjects should use the same level of operations on various formal operational problems. This has meant using some relational statistic (e.g., correlations, factor analyses, joint frequency table analyses, etc.) as a measure of the integration. Obviously, if subjects' performance on formal operational problems is not consistent across problems, and it is typically not consistent across problems, then typical relational statistics will indicate that the operations measured by the problems will not be related (i.e., integrated). Flavell's (1971) discussion of developmental sequences and Pinard and Laurendeau's (1969) discussion of stages illuminate the potential hazards of using such a psychometrically-driven approach to measure the integration of cognitive operations. In addition, in their psychometrically-oriented evaluation of Ford's (1979) analyses of the data on egocentrism, Waters and Tinsley (1985) clearly indicated that only focusing on the psychometric aspects of cognitive development can leave the data theoretically barren: For example, partialing out the effect of age from correlations among various measures of cognitive development in samples that include a variety of ages will underestimate the true correlations, because such a procedure eliminates some of the variance generated by the expected normal development of cognition with increasing age. Although such considerations are necessary for reliable and valid measurement of cognitive development in general, and formal operations in particular (Neimark, 1975; Keating, 1980; W. A. Farmer & M. A. Farrell, personal communication, June, 1983), Piaget did not discuss integration from a psychometric perspective. Rather, he looked at it from the view of how the various formal operations are related to each other and what these relations implied for the integrated reasoning of individuals who demonstrate formal operational adaptations. There are at least three ways in which formal operational adaptations are integrated with each other. Those ways may be labeled as inclusion, interpretation, and the INRC group.

### Inclusion

Integration of formal operations as inclusion is the most direct translation of the concrete operations of classification. Any one of the four base associations that can be produced by coordinating each of the subproperties (e.g., R & R') from one property (e.g., H) with each of the subproperties (e.g., G & G') from a second property (e.g., E) is included in seven of the remaining fifteen operations, along with being a separate operation itself. Table 11.1 is structured to illustrate integration as inclusion for p•q and, as previously noted, the table could be structured to illustrate integration as inclusion for any of the other three base associations. Integration as inclusion means that whenever one of the base associations of subproperties is recognized as part of a problem, there is the understanding that any one of seven other possible combinations that include the recognized base association may be true, and the reality of each of the eight combinatorial possibilities can be systematically explored to determine which is true by looking for the falsehood of each operation's logically complementary operation within the framework of the sixteen binary propositional operations (Inhelder & Piaget, 1955/1958, p. 304). Unfortunately, the inclusion approach to integration has not been investigated as part of any known research on formal operations (see Neimark, 1975, 1982; Keating, 1980; Lawson, 1985, for extensive reviews).

### Interpretation

A second type of integration involves various interpretations of the different formal operations. Two examples of integration as interpretation will be presented, one focusing on the operation of disjunction and the other focusing on the operation of implication. The operation of disjunction, $p \vee q$, may be represented as $(p \bullet q) \vee (p \bullet \bar{q}) \vee (\bar{p} \bullet q)$, and it may be interpreted in seven different ways: Each of the combinations may be individually true (three interpretations), two of them together may be true (three interpretations), or all three together may be true. This is equivalent to saying that the operation, $p \vee q$, represents seven possibilities. Inhelder & Piaget (1955/1958) suggested that interpreting disjunction in seven possible ways "is certainly what the integration of the possible associations means to the subject" (p. 292).

A second example of integration as interpretation involves implication or conditional propositions: $p \rightarrow q = (p \bullet q) \vee (\bar{p} \bullet q) \vee (\bar{p} \bullet \bar{q})$. Inhelder and Piaget (1955/1958) wrote:

> It is important to remember that even at stage III [formal operations] the subject begins by classifying the data, by relating them, etc.; in other words, one must keep in mind that a concrete structuring of the data is an indispensable prerequisite of the propositional structure. Thus, we must ask: what are the most spontaneous forms of implication and what are their relations to the corresponding concrete linkages?
>
>     . . . Implication can be expressed in at least three equivalent ways: $p \rightarrow q$; $\bar{p} \vee q$ and $p = p \bullet q$, expressions which can be transformed to give the same product $p \bullet q \vee \bar{p} \bullet q \vee \bar{p} \bullet \bar{q}$. For example, if $p$ expresses the fact that a rod is thin and $q$ the fact that it is flexible, it does not matter whether the proposition is stated: "If it is thin, then it is flexible" $(p \rightarrow q)$; "Either it is not thin, or it is flexible" $(\bar{p} \vee q)$; or "To say that it is thin is equivalent to saying it is both thin and flexible" $(p = p \bullet q)$. It should also be noted that, according to a well-known law of lattices, given $p = p \bullet q$, it follows that $q = p \vee q$, an equivalence which is itself equal to $p \rightarrow q$ (for its transformation also gives $p \bullet q \vee \bar{p} \bullet q \vee \bar{p} \bullet \bar{q}$). This said, it seems clear that the simplest psychological form of implication must be $p = p \bullet q$. For, before he can maintain "If this rod is thin, then it is flexible," the subject must assure himself that thin always means thin and flexible. Moreover, $p = p \bullet q$ and $q = p \vee q$ are the most direct translations of the product $A \times B = A$ and the sum $A + B = B$, foundations of the inclusion $A < B$. (pp. 298–299)

If Inhelder and Piaget are correct that the interpretation of $p \rightarrow q$ as $p = p \bullet q$ is the simplest psychological form of implication, it may explain the common error of interpreting a conditional as a biconditional. (See O'Brien & Overton, 1982 and Overton, Byrnes, & O'Brien, 1985 for discussions of this error.) Continuing with Inhelder and Piaget's example of the flexibility and size of the diameter of a rod, interpreting a conditional as a biconditional would mean that when a rod is thin, it is thin and flexible $(p = p \bullet q)$, and when it is not thin, it is not thin and not flexible $(\bar{p} = \bar{q} \bullet \bar{q})$. Within Piagetian theory that describes formal operations, how can this reasoning occur? Recall that concrete operations have two operations (logical addition and logical multiplication), their respective reverse (negation) operations (logical subtraction and logical division, respectively), and each property and its complement are always defined within the context of the next higher order class. In addition, when these concrete operations are "transformed" into beginning formal operations, the available operations are "v," "•," and "-." Theoretically, when these transformed consolidated concrete operations take the results of previous concrete operations as elements of thought, the focus will be on observable positive/affirming cases such as the rod is thin and flexible ($p \bullet q$). Empirically, this appears to occur, as O'Brien and Overton (1980, 1982) found a tendency in adolescents to emphasize $p \bullet q$ as providing proof of the truth of conditional statements and Moshman (1979) found an increasing tendency with age to consider conditional relations as inductive relations. Because beginning formal operations are an extension of concrete operations, and concrete operations only negate a property (variable), to study the effect of the negation on the variable negated and not for the purpose of studying other variables (Inhelder & Piaget, 1955/1958, pp. 284–285), the following is inevitable: Beginning formal operations will also acknowledge that when the rod is not thin, it is not flexible ($\bar{p} \bullet \bar{q}$), and they will conclude that when a rod is not thin, it is not thin and not flexible ($\bar{p} = \bar{p} \bullet \bar{q}$). $\bar{p} = \bar{p} \bullet \bar{q}$ is equivalent to $q \rightarrow p$, the reciprocal of $p \rightarrow q$. Given $p \rightarrow q$ and $q \rightarrow p$, an emphasis of focusing on observable positive/affirming cases, and the operations of "v" and "•," beginning formal operations have three possible alternatives for trying to understand/process/interpret a conditional problem.

The first alternative is what may be termed the classical logical approach, which requires testing for the negations (nonaffirming cases) of $p \rightarrow q$ and $q \rightarrow p$ ($p \bullet \bar{q}$ and $\bar{p} \bullet q$, respectively). Because this approach amounts to testing for the existence of $p \bullet \bar{q}$ or $\bar{p} \bullet q$ and then interpreting the existence of either as a negation of $p \rightarrow q$ or $q \rightarrow p$, respectively, and negations are always difficult to construct (Gallagher & Reid, 1981), this is a theoretically unlikely alternative, especially for formal operations in creation. Empirically, it infrequently occurs, as evidenced by difficulties in solving the infamous four card problem, which, although not a traditional test of formal operations, requires the formal operation of implication for success.

A second alternative is to use the "v" operation to investigate the relation between $p \rightarrow q$ and $q \rightarrow p$. That is, what is the result of $(p \rightarrow q) \vee (q \rightarrow p)$? The result is $p*q$, a complete affirmation of every combination of p and q that includes the negations of $p \rightarrow q$ and $q \rightarrow p$, $p \bullet \bar{q}$ and $\bar{p} \bullet q$, respectively. This alternative will have a low probability of occurring, because it produces the conclusion of no relation between p and q, but formal operations in creation as transformed concrete operational adaptations are still oriented toward establishing some positive relation between two physical variables in the empirical world. Thus, there is a conflict between what can be produced in thought (no relation) and adaptational experience (i.e., there is, and there *must be,* some relation between characteristics of the physical world); consequently, the conclusion of no relation between p and q will be rejected.

The third alternative is to use the "•" operation to investigate the relation between p → q and q → p. That is, what is the result of (p → q)•(q → p)? The result is p = q, what Piaget (Inhelder & Piaget, 1955/1958, p. 300) labeled as equivalence and what may also be labeled as the biconditional. This alternative will have a high probability of occurring because (a) its result produces the conclusion of a "positive" relation between p and q—whenever p occurs q occurs and whenever p̄ occurs q̄ occurs; (b) when concrete operations adapt to the empirical world, they inevitably focus on what "positively" exists, a conjunctive relation (p•q) and a conjunctive negation (p̄•q̄) between two variables; and (c) beginning formal operations are just a generalization or "transformation" of concrete operations. In essence, there is an emphasis on the "positive," or what exists, and what exists is induction from adaptational experiences without the construction of the necessary complementary operation of deduction. Thus, what has been traditionally considered an error in solving formal operational-type conditional reasoning problems may be an indication of beginning formal operations, and not an error in reasoning. That is, the common error of interpreting a conditional as a biconditional may be a necessary first step in the development of the formal operation of implication (conditional) and not necessarily an error in reasoning, as would be the case when the classical logical approach (the first alternative discussed) is used to explain subjects' general lack of success on conditional reasoning problems such as the four card problem.

However, it may be that the error of interpreting a conditional as a biconditional is a genuine logical error (according to the classical logical approach), and not a sign of emerging formal operations, or it may be a sign of concrete operational logical addition and/or logical multiplication of classes, which also may be considered an error. How can the alternatives be tested to determine which is the most accurate description of what is occurring? Inhelder and Piaget (1955/1958) provided some guidelines:

> The difference between a true implication and a many–one correspondence can be recognized psychologically by the progression of the totality of the subject's reasoning. As long as he proceeds by inclusions [logical addition of classes] or correspondences [logical multiplication of classes] . . . , the subject is limited to classifying and ordering serially the raw experimental data, whereas the discovery of implication as such consists of differentiating it from the other possible combinations ($p \lor q, p = q$, etc.). Moreover, this discovery is distinguished by the fact that the subject begins to separate out the potential factors; his goal is to verify exactly which combinations occur among the possible combinations compatible with the given situation. (p. 298)

Thus, Inhelder and Piaget suggested that to evaluate integrated reasoning as interpretation, the steps subjects used to solve the problem, and not just the answer they gave to the problem, must be considered. Unfortunately, the literature on formal operations is void of any study that directly addresses this issue from the perspective of integration as interpretation.

### INRC group

A third form of integration involves the general transformations known as the INRC group (Identity, Negation, Reciprocal, Correlative). These are logical rules that describe how one formal operation may be transformed into another formal operation (or, to say it in a different way, how each formal operation may be derived from another formal operation or combination of operations) and, thus, they are also rules for describing how each formal operation is related to each of the other formal operations. (See Gray, 1970, pp. 113–136; Mays, 1953/1957, pp. xii–xiv; or Piaget, 1953/1957, pp. 32–37 for a detailed description of the transformations.) They are a necessary part of formal operations, because formal thought is more than propositional logic (Inhelder & Piaget, 1955/1958, p. xxii). In a sense, the INRC transformations are the glues of formal operations, because they provide a theoretical means for binding each formal operation with each of the other formal operations within a single relational system. This is in contrast to concrete operations that are described by eight models of operational adaptation, with no theoretical means of moving from one operation to another. Each concrete operation has no relation with any other concrete operation other than that four operations involve properties of physical reality as elements of thought, four operations involve relations among aspects of physical reality as elements of thought, four operations involve logical addition, and four operations involve logical multiplication. Empirically, this means that the dominant/positive/affirming/observable characteristic(s)/property(ies) of an acknowledged reality determine(s) the concrete operation invoked (physical properties require classification operations, and relations among physical entities require relational operations), including the concrete operational characteristic of just noting what positively occurs rather than invoking an entire system of possible operations that can systematically test for relations among the observables. Once the "facts" of the reality are established, that is, once it is acknowledged that the reality is classifiable or relational, it is extremely difficult to adapt with an operation that is incongruent with the acknowledged reality or to systematically test for something that appears to contradict (negate) "the facts." This is especially true for concrete operations that are well established, consolidated, and beginning to be transformed into formal operations. Elkind (1967, 1978) labeled this phenomenon as *assumptive reality*. Everything, abstract or otherwise, is assumed to be real. Further, if everything is assumed to be real, then reality-based adaptations (concrete operations) are necessary.

The INRC transformations are manifested most clearly in the classic Inhelder problems designed to measure the operational schemata of proportions (equilibrium in the balance, hauling weight on an inclined plane, projections of shadows, centrifugal force), coordination of two systems of reference and the relativity of motion (snail on a plank) or acceleration (bicyclists passing a doll), mechanical equilibrium (communicating vessels, equilibrium in the hydraulic press, equilibrium in the balance, hauling weight on an inclined plane), and multiplicative compensations (equilibrium in the balance, hauling weight on an inclined plane, projections of shadows, centrifugal force)—concepts that require formal operations for understanding. Operational schemata are considered as actualized structures of the diverse possibilities inherent in the structured wholeness of the equilibrium of the propositional operations (Piaget, 1953/1957, pp. 40–42). Most of the problems that involve the operational schemata are among the most difficult and complicated of the formal operational problems (Martorano, 1977; Neimark, 1975). In fact, some are so complicated that it is very difficult to adequately construct the problems so they are reasonably valid measures of the concepts they are designed to measure (Farrell & Farmer, 1983; W. A. Farmer & M. A. Farrell, personal communication, June, 1983). The INRC-based task most frequently used has been the equilibrium in the balance task (Neimark, 1975, 1982; Keating, 1980; Lawson, 1985). Although many studies have used the balance problem, none of them have focused on the INRC group as a form of integration (see Neimark, 1975, 1982; Keating, 1980; Lawson, 1985).

It is clear that many studies have used the classic formal operational tasks, or some variation of them, with a variety of subjects, but no known study has investigated integration, whether as inclusion, interpretation, or the INRC group. However, the Butch and Slim logical game (Ward, 1972), or its subsequent modifications, appears to be appropriate for investigating each of the three types of integration. The reason why this lack of investigation exists is not clear, but Neimark's (1982) opening comments about the veneration of Inhelder's tasks and investigators approaching the study of formal operations in a very concrete operational way is a possible explanation. However, what is more important than the adaptations used by investigators in their research on formal operations is: Why are formal operational adaptations not manifested with the frequency and/or consistency that appear to be expected by theorists and researchers?

## WHY ARE THE MANIFESTATIONS OF FORMAL OPERATIONS SO TENUOUS?

Explaining why formal operations are not manifested with as much frequency or consistency as expected is very difficult. One possible fact-based answer is that the subjects constituting the samples simply have not developed formal operational adaptations and that, given a few more years, they will develop the adaptations. Although this may be a possible explanation for subjects in their early teenage years, it is not necessarily acceptable for late teenagers, early adults, or older adults as these latter subjects are clearly beyond the years when they theoretically should have begun developing formal operations. What, then, are other possible explanations for this phenomenon? Within the Piagetian theoretical framework, there are two possible orientations toward explaining the phenomenon; one emphasizes exogenous knowledge, and the other emphasizes endogenous construction of knowledge.

### Exogenous Knowledge

The exogenous knowledge orientation considers the lack of manifestation of formal operations to be a function of something(s) outside the constructed adaptations of the individual. Two approaches to this orientation are noteworthy, one because it is derived from a classic, Americanized, mechanistic, environmental orientation to experimental psychology; one because it is relatively new and attempts to integrate numerous mitigating factors into a comprehensive approach to the tenuousness of formal operations.

The classic, mechanistic approach places the problem of the lack of manifestation of formal operations in the environment, specifically with the tasks (physical or otherwise) that are used to test for formal operations. The argument is something like the following: Almost all of the traditional tasks for eliciting formal operations are based on the mechanical aspects of physics (Broughton, 1977). Most subjects will not have had much experience with physics, thus, their performance on the tasks will be restricted, because they will not have had the opportunities to develop the formal operational concepts that are represented in the physics-based tasks. If different tasks are presented that are more appropriate to subjects' lives, then their performance should be better on the tasks. This is the reasoning underlying Sinnott's (1975), Kuhn's (1986; Kuhn & Angelev, 1976; Kuhn & Brannock, 1977), and other's (e.g., Danner & Day, 1977) attempts at simplifying the classic formal operational tasks or using tasks that are "more appropriate" (more familiar?) for the subjects being tested.

Kuhn's (1986) approach of using semi-everyday problems is instructive for what it suggests. Her subjects (sixth graders, ninth graders, average/nonacademic adults, and advanced PhD candidates in philosophy) were presented with a list of foods and asked what they thought regarding the relation between each of the foods and "catching" lots of colds. After obtaining subjects' ideas on the relationship between each food and "catching a cold," four foods are selected by "each subject, two which the subject believes are related to colds and two which the subject believes are not. At a second session, the subject is asked to evaluate evidence bearing on the relation of these four foods to colds" (Kuhn 1986, p. 6). For *each* subject, two foods (one which the subject previously indicated has a relationship with "catching" colds and one which the subject previously indicated has no relationship with "catching" colds) are presented as having a relationship to colds and two foods (one which the subject previously indicated has a relationship with "catching" colds and one which the subject previously indicated has no relationship with "catching" colds) are presented as having no relationship to colds. (Note that in the second session, the foods presented are totally based on each subject's expressed beliefs/experience as determined in the first session; except for the sixth graders, all subjects were beyond the age theoretically considered as the end of concrete operations and the beginning of formal operations; the older subjects would have had much experience with similar types of real world problems, including the relationship of foods to colds.) Kuhn's (1986) results were as follows:

> All but the philosophers frequently failed to make exclusion inferences though the evidence was present to support them and did make inclusion inferences though the evidence was not present to support them. Only two of 20 adults and four of the five philosophers resisted succumbing to false inclusion of one of the two covarying variables—in other words, claiming that one of the two "makes a difference" in whether children get lots of colds or not, when of course their common covariation with outcome makes it impossible to conclude that either of them plays a causal role. About half the adults and just a few younger subjects recognized the indeterminacy at some point, but they then succumbed to false inclusion as the covariation evidence mounted. Only about half the sixth graders and two-thirds of the ninth graders and adults concluded that the two noncovarying variables did not make a difference. No subject attempted a controlled comparison, by looking for two tables where all foods but one were identical. (p. 7)

Thus, it is very clear that even with familiar (simpler), real word objects and/or experiences, formal operations were not manifested by a substantial number of the subjects. Such data support the argument that simplifying formal operational tasks (e.g., Danner & Day, 1977) and/or making them more congruent with previous real world experiences does not necessarily make it easier for individuals to manifest formal operations in solving the problems. However, assuming that the simplification approach is successful in helping individuals manifest formal operations in solving the problems, Lawson's (1985) trenchant comments still must be considered.

> Even if we assume that . . . familiar formal tasks were valid measures of formal reasoning, the finding that performance was slightly better on them does not constitute convincing evidence that familiarity enhances formal reasoning. If one is very familiar with a situation, reasoning may not even be re-

quired. Such a view would suggest that the only way to really test one's reasoning ability is with contexts sufficiently novel to insure that reasoning (not memory) is the route to successful performance. (p. 585)

Lawson's reasoning is analogous to Piaget's (1941/1965) reasoning for using a set of sticks in the classic seriation problem where the adjacent sticks only differed by .4 cm. By using sticks that differed so little, subjects' reasoning, not a "perceptual reading" of the sticks, is required for the task to be successfully completed. If the differences in lengths of the adjacent seriated sticks are too great or if the formal operational tasks are too simplified, then the question of what are the necessary adaptations for successfully solving the problems can be raised.

A particularly compelling version of the exogenous knowledge orientation to the tenuousness of formal operations is the competence-moderator-performance perspective (Overton, 1985; Overton & Newman, 1982). This approach suggests that an individual's performance is a *joint* function of competence (e.g., operational adaptations) and a set of moderator variables including various psychological processes, states, and styles (e.g., selective attention, attentional or mental capacity, memory, ability to comprehend verbal instructions and produce verbal explanations, motivation and emotional states, variation in information processing approaches associated with cultural factors, and cognitive style) and/or situational and task factors (e.g., complexity of task instructions, figurative task features, stimulus salience and complexity, and task familiarity, Overton & Newman, 1982, p. 226). This approach is compelling, because it provides an intuitively reasonable explanation for many types of results involving the lack of manifestation of formal operations (see Overton & Newman, 1982, for a review, or Overton, et al., 1985, Overton, et al., 1987, for specific applications of the approach), and it is constructed on a powerful philosophy of science (Overton, 1985). However, Overton's (1985, p. 36) statement about the construction of concepts and his indication that the epistemology of organismic theories is constructivist because the "knower actively constructs the known" (Overton, 1985, p. 28), notwithstanding, the competence-moderator-performance approach is not Piagetian and not necessarily constructivist.

The major reason why the competence-moderator-performance approach is clearly not Piagetian and not necessarily constructivist is its emphasis on the separate preexistence of competence and moderator variables (internal or external to the individual) that interact to produce a performance. For Piaget, competence (i.e., adaptations) does not exist without a complementary, constructed environment (e.g., internal and external moderator variables). It is the active functioning of existing adaptations with(in) the acknowledged environment that constructs the reality of various aspects of the tasks (e.g., complexity of task instructions, figurative task features, stimulus salience and complexity, and task familiarity), the moderating psychological processes, and so forth (e.g., selective attention, attentional or mental capacity, memory, ability to comprehend verbal instructions and produce verbal explanations, motivation and emotional states, variation in information processing approaches associated with cultural factors, and cognitive style), as well as competence itself; the tasks, psychological processes, and so on, cannot exist prior to the functioning competence that creates their existence.

Both the classic mechanistic and competence–moderator–performance approaches suffer from problems discussed by Taylor (1987) in her reflections on the use of Piaget's ideas to investigate the thinking and reasoning of adults. She suggested that much of the research on adult functioning has transformed Piaget's orientation into a psychometric approach emphasizing whether certain skills are manifested or not manifested and has ignored the continuing process of adaptation that is the foundation of Piaget's ideas about relatively enduring forms of adaptation (i.e., the "stages" of cognitive development). This transformed Piagetian orientation is found in the language used by many who knowingly emphasize an exogenous knowledge approach and in the language of many who are basically Piagetian in orientation but unknowingly emphasize an exogenous knowledge approach. The language of this approach refers to responses, performance, eliciting, for example, terms that are not reflective of a constructivist position. Lawson's previously cited comments as well as those emphasizing the competence–moderator–performance approach (Overton, 1985; Overton & Newman, 1982; Overton, et al., 1987) are especially telling, as the spirit of their arguments is clearly Piagetian, but the language is clearly from an exogenous perspective. For example, in their study of the effects of form and content on subjects' solutions to the Wason selection task, Overton, et al. (1987) wrote:

> From the perspective of the present research it is assumed that semantic facilitation [a moderator variable] *operates on* [emphasis added] an underlying logical competence. It is therefore expected that both the nature of the logical competence and the nature of the semantic content affect task solution. (p. 23)

In addition, an emphasis on difficulties with the classic Inhelder tasks (e.g., see Neimark, 1975, for a list of such difficulties) and not on how adaptations to the tasks are constructed is clearly a psychometric approach. The emphasis is on the subjects' performances (responses, answers, etc.) and the tasks themselves (which are part of *the* environment), not on the necessary relations among subjects' existing adaptations and *what the adaptations define/determine the tasks to be.*

## Endogenous Construction of Knowledge

The endogenous construction approach to explaining the tenuousness of formal operations considers how adaptations are constructed in general, and, specifically, how formal operations are constructed. Recall that any cognitive structure is an adaptation, whether that structure is called an operation or not, and formal operations, like any other adaptations, are constructed when they are *necessarily psychologically adaptive with(in) the acknowledged environment*. This means that the formal operational combination of inductive or "hypothetical reasoning based on a logic of all possible combinations" (Parsons, 1958, p. xiii; see also Piaget, 1953/1957, p. 18) and deductive reasoning based on propositional logic will be constructed when the combination enhances the biological or psychological functioning of the individual with(in) the existing acknowledged environment. If formal operational adaptations are not necessary for the existence and/or enhancement of the person with(in) the acknowledged environment, then they will probably not be constructed. It is clear that the acknowledged environment of most individuals, including school for those in school, work places for those who work, and the general environmental milieu, does not require formal operations for successful psychological functioning (Blasi & Hoeffel, 1974; Keating, 1980). There are three possible explanations for the acknowledged environment not requiring formal operational adaptations, one focusing on concrete operations, one focusing on formal operations, and one which integrates adaptations with pseudo-necessity.

First, with regard to concrete operations, it is clear that the sophistication of consolidated concrete operations has been seriously underestimated because of the centration of research on beginning concrete operations, especially the incredible amount of research on conservation. Although that centration has provided help in understanding beginning concrete operations, indirectly it has led to the assumption that concrete operations, in general, are not as appropriate or necessary as formal operations theoretically are for adapting to the everyday world (Blasi & Hoeffel, 1974). Our reasoning seems to have been as follows: (a) Piaget suggested that formal operations are different and better adaptations than concrete operations; (b) formal operations are constructed from/after concrete operations; (c) adolescents and adults are older than (occur after) children; (d) it is clear that children demonstrate concrete operations; (e) therefore, because adolescents and adults are older than children, and children construct concrete operations, then adolescents and adults should construct formal operations. It is very clear that this line of reasoning, manifested by many who are interested in formal operations, is more suggestive of transduction than induction or deduction, concrete or formal.

Second, with regard to formal operations, it is clear that the essence and sophistication of formal operational adaptations has been underestimated.

According to Inhelder and Piaget (1955/1958), the four major characteristics of formal operations are conceptions of possibilities, hypothetical-deductive reasoning, interpropositional reasoning, and combinatorial or systematic thinking. Although each characteristic is equal to each of the other characteristics in its power to describe formal operational adaptations, like the pigs in Orwell's *Animal Farm*, one characteristic is more equal than the other characteristics. That characteristic is conceiving of possibilities, where the possibilities do not have to be actualized. By their very nature, formal operational adaptations must require a considerable amount of energy, effort, and possibly "knowledge," because they are adaptations to possibilities, not just relations or properties of the acknowledged "physical" or social environment. They will not necessarily be constructed if less sophisticated and easier adaptations are successful. Thus, if concrete operational adaptations are successful for individuals, although they may not be considered so by a researcher or theorist, and if formal operational adaptations are difficult to produce and are not necessary for biological/psychological survival and/or enhancement with(in) an acknowledged environment, why should individuals go to all the work to adapt to possibilities? Under these conditions, which are typical adaptational conditions for most adolescents and adults (Lawson, 1985), they will not adapt in a formal operational way. They *will* necessarily adapt in the most appropriate way: concrete operational, preoperational, or sensorimotor.

A third explanation, which integrates the previous discussion of the underestimation of concrete operations and formal operations, involves the interpenetrating relations among adaptations and their acknowledged environment on the one hand, and the idea of pseudo-necessity on the other hand. Interpenetration of adaptations and an acknowledged environment means that present adaptations are dependent on an acknowledged environment and previous adaptations, and an acknowledged environment is dependent on a previously acknowledged environment and previous adaptations, and so forth. Thus, adaptations and their acknowledged environment provide for the construction of each other.

Construction occurs when an experience is acknowledged as contradictory to what is expected by the habitual functioning of an adaptational structure, and the disturbance produced by the contradiction is understood by the adaptations in their continuing functioning (Furth, 1981, pp. 263–277). Unfortunately, a possible contradictory experience as the producer of a disturbance may not be acknowledged by the adaptational structure if the element that could produce the contradictory experience, and/or the contradictory experience itself, is considered an impossibility by the adaptations. This adaptationally created impossibility is called pseudo-necessity (Furth, 1981; Piaget & Voyat, 1979) and it is the resistance of existing adaptational structures to adaptation. Piaget and Voyat (1979) wrote about pseudo-necessity:

I[/]t may be described simply as an overestimation of current reality, or of given factual states of affairs, either in the sense that the particular, and hence limited, characteristics of this reality can only be perceived as general and necessary (whence 'pseudo-necessity') or else in the more simple sense that current reality is treated as the only possible one, thus inhibiting any opening up of new possibilities. (pp. 78–79)

With regard to the will-o'-the-wisp nature of the construction of formal operations and the integrated nature of formal operations, what does pseudo-necessity mean?

The obvious answer is that the errors made by many subjects on formal operational type reasoning problems, whether the problems are based on Inhelder's tasks or are various versions of conditional reasoning problems, are the result of pseudo-necessity. For example, the earlier discussion of the third alternative of why many subjects interpret a conditional as a biconditional (see previous discussion on pp. 240–241) clearly suggests what Furth (1981) wrote is occurring: "the familiar overestimation of the positive experience [of the "facts" of the problem] ('what happens must happen,' 'what does not happen cannot happen') resulting in a faulty mental coordination" (Furth, 1981, pp. 266–267). (Note that both parts of the first statement—what happens must happen—are positive, roughly corresponding to $p \bullet q$ of a biconditional, and both parts of the second statement—what does not happen cannot happen—are negative, roughly corresponding to $\bar{p} \bullet \bar{q}$ of a biconditional.) On the classic Inhelder tasks and their various mutations (e.g., Kuhn's plant problem), more real world tasks (Kuhn, 1986; Sinnott, 1975), or conditional reasoning problems, the positive acknowledged "facts" of the problems become pseudo-necessities that can not be easily negated. This adaptational resistance to negating "known facts" occurs, because the "known facts" are created from adaptations that are the constructed relations among the acknowledged environment and the acting person, and negating the "known facts" would negate these relations, which, in turn, would alter (possibly negate) what the individual is. This alteration of what a person is would occur because a person is psychologically defined by his/her adaptations (knowledge), and the adaptations are manifested in what a person does. Furth (1981) wrote that "as Piaget puts it, knowledge is not something that I know (as a conscious object); it is something that I (as an agent) know how to do" (p. 271); it is something that *I do*, something that *I am*. Kegan (1979, 1982) explained that individuals who demonstrate concrete operations *are* the operations and their classifiable, relational, quantifiable facts. Individuals who demonstrate formal operations *are* the operations, systematic possibilities, and their hypotheses. Thus, if formal operational adaptations are to be constructed, existing concrete operations must be transformed (negated) *and* conserved with(in) an acknowledged environment that "requires" formal operational adaptations but also supports their tentative, halting, difficult construction. Neimark (1982) wrote:

To the extent that each stage has its own distinctive properties, conditions which enhance those properties should be favorable for the development of that stage but not necessarily of the next stage. Thus freedom for exploration in an environment rich with potential for discovery should promote rapid sensorimotor development. The same environment, however, may be much less conducive, and perhaps even inimical, to fostering of formal operations if exploration is conducted at a purely manipulative level. Formal operational thought involves exploration at a symbolic level; therefore, conditions which foster reflection and discourage immediate direct response probably become increasingly more conducive to its development—an implication which does not seem to be evident to many educators attempting to apply Piagetian theory to curriculum development. (p. 498)

Intuitively, such a supportive encouraging environment should have the characteristics of an authoritative-reciprocal parenting style (Maccoby & Martin, 1983), but that is an hypothesis that needs to be tested.

As stated in the introduction, the present chapter is a first step toward providing a "Piagetian" integration of the theory of formal operations and the data on formal operations. As a first step, it was not designed to be comprehensive nor was it designed to formally evaluate the literature on the development of deductive thought as one perspective on formal operations. Rather, the ideas are presented to produce disturbances in the reader's constructions regarding formal operations. As an acting being, it is for the reader to decide whether the intended disturbances will produce alpha, beta, or gamma compensations.

## ACKNOWLEDGMENTS

Preparation of this chapter was supported in part by a State of Ohio Excellence Grant to The University of Toledo, educational psychology faculty, and by funds from The University of Toledo.

I am indebted to previous reviewers of formal operations, but especially to Edith Neimark, whose 1975 description of formal operations is still the most lucid description of the structural transition from concrete operations to formal operations presently available. Bill Overton clarified some issues for me and also allowed me time to resolve some conceptual issues in my own way and time—he was a superb editor.

## REFERENCES

Blasi, A., & Hoeffel, E. C. (1974). Adolescence and formal operations. *Human Development,* *17,* 344–363.
Braine, M. D. S., & Rumain, B. (1983). Logical reasoning. In J. H. Flavell & E. M. Markham

(Eds.), *Handbook of child psychology: Vol. 3. Cognitive development* (pp. 263–340). New York: Wiley.

Brainerd, C. J. (1976–77). On the validity of propositional logic as a model for adolescent thought. *Interchange, 7*, 40–45.

Broughton, J. (1977). "Beyond formal operations": Theoretical thought in adolescence and early adulthood. *Teachers College Record, 79*, 87–97.

Danner, F. W., & Day, M. C. (1977). Eliciting formal operations. *Child Development, 48*, 1600–1606.

Elkind, D. (1967). Egocentrism in adolescence. *Child Development, 38*, 1025–1034.

Elkind, D. (1978). *The child's reality: Three developmental themes.* Hillsdale, NJ: Lawrence Erlbaum Associates.

Ennis, R. H. (1975). Children's ability to handle Piaget's propositional logic. *Review of Educational Research, 45*, 1–41.

Ennis, R. H. (1976). An alternative to Piaget's conceptualization of logical competence. *Child Development, 47*, 903–919.

Ennis, R. H. (1978). Conceptualization of children's logical competence: Piaget's propositional logic and an alternative proposal. In L. S. Siegel & C. J. Brainerd (Eds.), *Alternatives to Piaget: Critical essays on the theory.* New York: Academic Press.

Farrell, M. A., & Farmer, W. A. (1983). *An in-depth analysis of the projection of shadows task.* Paper presented at the Thirteenth Annual Symposium of The Jean Piaget Society, Philadelphia. (ERIC Document Reproduction Service No. ED 230 409)

Flavell, J. H. (1963). *The developmental psychology of Jean Piaget.* Princeton, NJ: D. Van Nostrand.

Flavell, J. H. (1971). Stage-related properties of cognitive development. *Cognitive Psychology, 2*, 421–453.

Ford, M. E. (1979). The construct validity of egocentrism. *Psychological Bulletin, 87*, 1169–1188.

Furth, H. G. (1981). *Piaget and knowledge: Theoretical foundations* (2nd ed.). Chicago: University of Chicago Press.

Gallagher, J. McC., & Reid, D. K. (1981). *The learning theory of Piaget and Inhelder.* Monterey, CA: Brooks/Cole.

Gray, W. M. (1970). *Children's performance on logically equivalent Piagetian tasks and written tasks.* Dayton: University of Dayton. (Doctoral dissertation, State University of New York at Albany, 1970). *Dissertation Abstracts International, 31*, 2736A. (University Microfilms No. 70-25,450)

Inhelder, B., & Piaget, J. (1958). *The growth of logical thinking from childhood to adolescence: An essay on the construction of formal operational structures* (A. Parsons & S. Milgram, Trans.). New York: Basic Books. (Original work published 1955)

Keating, D. P. (1980). Thinking processes in adolescence. In J. Adelson (Ed.), *Handbook of adolescent psychology* (pp. 211–246). New York: Wiley.

Kegan, R. G. (1979). The evolving self: A process conception for ego psychology. *The Counseling Psychologist, 8*(2), 5–34.

Kegan, R. (1982). *The evolving self: Problem and process in human development.* Cambridge, MA: Harvard University Press.

Kuhn, D. (1986, May). *Coordinating theory and evidence in reasoning.* Invited address presented at the Sixteenth Annual Symposium of The Jean Piaget Society, Philadelphia.

Kuhn, D., & Angelev, J. (1976). An experimental study of the development of formal operational thought. *Child Development, 47*, 697–706.

Kuhn, D., & Brannock, J. (1977). Development of the isolation of variables scheme in experimental and "natural experiment" contexts. *Developmental Psychology, 13*, 9–14.

Lawson, A. E. (1985). A review of research on formal reasoning and science teaching. *Journal of Research in Science Teaching, 22*, 569–617.

Leiser, D. (1982). Piaget's logical formalism for formal operations: An interpretation in context. *Developmental Review, 2*, 87–99.

Maccoby, E. E., & Martin, J. A. (1983). Socialization in the context of the family: Parent-child interaction. In E. M. Hetherington (Ed.), *Handbook of child psychology: Vol. 4. Socialization, personality, and social development* (pp. 1–101). New York: Wiley.

Martorano, S. (1975, April). *Formal operations thinking: Now you see it, now you don't.* Paper presented at the meeting of the Society for Research in Child Development, Denver.

Martorano, S. C. (1977). A developmental analysis of performance on Piaget's formal operations tasks. *Developmental Psychology, 13*, 666–672.

Mays, W. (1957). An elementary introduction to Piaget's logic. In J. Piaget, *Logic and psychology* (W. Mays & F. Whitehead, Trans.). (pp. ix–xvi). New York: Basic Books. (Original work published 1953)

Moshman, D. (1979). Development of formal hypothesis testing ability. *Developmental Psychology, 15*, 104–112.

Neimark, E. D. (1975). Intellectual development during adolescence. In F. D. Horowitz (Ed.), *Review of child development research* (Vol. 4, pp. 541–594). Chicago: University of Chicago Press.

Neimark, E. D. (1982). Adolescent thought: Transition to formal operations. In B. Wolman (Ed.), *Handbook of developmental psychology* (pp. 486–502). Englewood Cliffs, NJ: Prentice-Hall.

O'Brien, D. P., & Overton, W. F. (1980). Conditional reasoning following contradictory evidence: A developmental analysis. *Journal of Experimental Child Psychology, 30*, 44–60.

O'Brien, D. P., & Overton, W. F. (1982). Conditional reasoning and the competence-performance issue: A developmental analysis of a training task. *Journal of Experimental Child Psychology, 34*, 274–290.

Overton, W. F. (1985). Scientific methodologies and the competence–moderator–performance issue. In E. D. Neimark, R. De Lisi, & J. L. Newman (Eds.), *Moderators of competence* (pp. 15–41). Hillsdale, NJ: Lawrence Erlbaum Associates.

Overton, W. F., Byrnes, J. P., & O'Brien, D. P. (1985). Developmental and individual differences in conditional reasoning: The role of contradiction training and cognitive style. *Developmental Psychology, 21*, 692–701.

Overton, W. F., & Newman, J. L. (1982). Cognitive development: A competence–activation/utilization approach. In T. M. Field, A. Huston, H. C. Quay, L. Troll, & G. E. Finley (Eds.), *Review of human development* (pp. 217–241). New York: Wiley.

Overton, W. F., Ward, S. L., Noveck, I. A., Black, J., & O'Brien, D. P. (1987). Form and content in the development of deductive reasoning. *Developmental Psychology, 23*, 22–30.

Parsons, A. (1958). Translators' introduction: A guide for psychologists. In B. Inhelder & J. Piaget, *The growth of logical thinking from childhood to adolescence: An essay on the construction of formal operational structures* (A. Parsons & S. Milgram, Trans., pp. vii–xxiv). New York: Basic Books. (Original work published 1955)

Parsons, C. (1960). Inhelder and Piaget's *The growth of logical thinking* II. A logician's viewpoint. *British Journal of Psychology, 51*, 75–84.

Piaget, J. (1949). *Traité de logique.* Paris, Colin.

Piaget, J. (1952). *Essai sur les transformations des operations logiques.* Paris: Presses Universitaires de France.

Piaget, J. (1957). *Logic and psychology* (W. Mays & F. Whitehead, Trans.). New York: Basic Books. (Original work published 1953)

Piaget, J. (1964). *Judgment and reasoning in the child* (M. Warden, Trans.). Paterson, NJ: Littlefield, Adams. (Original work published 1924)

Piaget, J. (1965). *The child's conception of number* (C. Gattegno & F. M. Hodgson, Trans.). New York: Norton Library. (Original work published 1941)

Piaget, J. (1966). *The psychology of intelligence* (M. Piercy & D. E. Berlyne, Trans.). Totowa, NJ: Littlefield, Adams. (Original work published 1947)

Piaget, J. (1970). *The child's conception of movement and speed* (G. E. T. Holloway & M. J. MacKenzie, Trans.). New York: Basic Books. (Original work published 1946)

Piaget, J., & Inhelder, B. (1974). *The child's construction of quantities: Conservation and atomism* (A. J. Pomerans, Trans.). London: Routledge & Kegan Paul. (Original work published 1941)

Piaget, J., & Inhelder, B. (1975). *The origin of the idea of chance in children* (L. Leake, Jr., P. Burrell, & H. D. Fishbein, Trans.). New York: W. W. Norton. (Original work published, 1951)

Piaget, J., & Voyat, G. (1979). The possible, the impossible, and the necessary (D. N. Smith, Trans.). In F. B. Murray (Ed.), *The impact of Piagetian theory: On psychiatry, and psychology* (pp. 65–85). Baltimore: University Park Press.

Pinard, A., & Laurendeau, M. (1969). "Stage" in Piaget's cognitive-developmental theory: Exegesis of a concept. In D. Elkind & J. H Flavell (Eds.), *Studies in cognitive development: Essays in honor of Jean Piaget* (pp. 121–170). New York: Oxford University Press.

Sinnott, J. D. (1975). Everyday thinking and Piagetian operativity in adults. *Human Development, 18*, 430–443.

Taylor, C. A. (1987, May). *Equilibration theory: Piaget's legacy to students of adult development*. Paper presented at the Seventeenth Annual Symposium of The Jean Piaget Society, Philadelphia.

Ward, J. (1972). The saga of Butch and Slim. *British Journal of Educational Psychology, 42*, 267–289.

Waters, H. S., & Tinsley, V. S. (1985). Evaluating the discriminant and convergent validity of developmental constructs: Another look at the concept of egocentrism. *Psychological Bulletin, 97*, 483–496.

# 12

# Reasoning, Logic, and Thought Disorder: Deductive Reasoning and Developmental Psychopathology

Jeffrey S. Black
Willis F. Overton
*Temple University*

The literature on thought disorders is extensive. Since Bleuler's (1911) emphasis on "loosened associations in thought" as the core feature of schizophrenia, the field has been flooded with case reports, empirical studies, and theoretical formulations designed to explain various physiological, interpersonal, and psychological dimensions of disordered thinking. The purpose of this review is to question and examine the place of reasoning and logic in that form of pathology referred to as "thought disorder." This examination will be framed by a Piagetian model of deductive reasoning development. Related theories of thought pathology, along with the extant research literature, will be explored from this perspective.

The focus of this review leads to the exclusion of several topics related to the issue of thought disorders. The extensive genetic and neuropsychological literatures that have accumulated on the topic of psychopathology are not considered. Interpersonal theories of schizophrenia and depression as they relate to thought disorder (Bateson, Jackson, Haley & Weakland, 1956; Lidz, Fleck & Cornelison, 1965; Singer & Wynne, 1965) are also omitted. Linguistic and speech disorder analyses of thought disorders are not examined, except to point out that the major argument presented by linguists is that disordered thought is really disordered speech (Grove & Andreasen, 1985; Chaika, 1982; Chaika & Lamb, 1985). Finally, the review does not examine every cognitive model offered in the thought disorder literature. Excluded from consideration, for example, are various learning models (Broen, 1966; Broen & Storms, 1966; Mednick, 1958), and a full examination of the voluminous information processing literature. (For a comprehensive review on information processing models of schizophrenic thought disorder, the reader is directed to Callaway & Naghdi, 1982; Garmezy, 1977; Gjerde, 1983; Hemsley, 1975; Nuechterlein & Dawson, 1984).

Excluding various components of cognitive processing (attention span, memory, etc.) from a discussion of reasoning pathology seems arbitrary, because many of these components have a major impact on overall thought performance. In the history of the research literature, however, reasoning has been treated as a distinct cognitive activity and has been viewed as a separate area of inquiry. Beyond that, there has been, within the literature on thought disorders, a strong, sometimes, implicit, interest in *deductive* reasoning (versus other reasoning forms) and its development. As a consequence, this review will be exclusively concerned with deductive logic and thought pathology.

A second preliminary consideration concerns the relation between schizophrenia and thought disorder. Traditionally, researchers and clinicians have regarded formal thought disorder as a necessary, but not sufficient, condition in the diagnosis of schizophrenia. In fact, a patient can be diagnosed as schizophrenic without a formal thought disorder provided that they report delusions or hallucinations (DSM III-R, 1987). One might get the impression when reading this literature, however, that all thought disordered patients are schizophrenic, and all schizophrenics are continually thought disordered. Both of these assumptions are false. Thought disorder has been examined in other forms of psychopatholgoy (Andreasen, Tsuang, & Canter, 1974; Andreasen & Powers, 1974; George & Neufeld, 1985). The variability in diagnostic criteria indicates the heterogeneity of schizophrenia and is the source of a thorny methodological problem. Subjects included in experimental groups in thought disorder research, because they meet the diagnostic criteria for schizophrenia, might not be formally thought disordered at all.

An analysis of deductive reasoning in schizophrenics from a Piagetian viewpoint, bringing traditional cognitive-developmental theory into contact with the clinical sciences, is one more example of the recent emergence of developmental psychopathology as a distinct subdiscipline of developmental psychology (Cicchetti, 1984). The underlying assumption common to various models of developmental psychopathology is that we can best understand abnormal functioning by understanding the organism's normal developmental paths, and, in like manner, we can acquire important information about normal functioning by studying pathology. In view of the historic research interest in deductive reasoning in developmental psychology, and the increased interest in developmental psychopathology, this paper will explore whether the literature concerned with reasoning and thought disorder supports the logic and reasoning hypotheses that appeared early in the literature, and, more specifically, whether a Piagetian structural model of logical competence can provide a viable heuristic for explaining the aberrant reasoning process often present in diagnosed schizophrenics and other forms of psychopathology.

## DEDUCTIVE REASONING AND MODELS RELATING THOUGHT AND LOGIC

### Deduction

When people make statements, they may or may not offer evidence to support them. A statement that is supported by evidence is the conclusion of an argument. The proper construction of arguments, for example, the *formal* connection between the conclusion and the statements offered as evidence (premises), and the certainty of arguments is what the study of logic is about. Logicians classify arguments as "inductive" or "deductive" depending on whether the construction of the argument calls for a conclusion that is merely probable or one that is necessary and certain. In a properly constructed (formally valid) deductive argument, a conclusion *must* be true if the premises offered as evidence for the conclusion are true. This ability to guarantee the preservation of truth when moving from premises to conclusion is what distinguishes deductive arguments from inductive arguments. The truth-preserving character of deduction results from an analytic relationship between the factual content of the conclusion of an argument and the information provided by the premises. In deductive arguments, factual information presented in the conclusion is completely contained, at least implicitly, in the premises. The conclusion of an argument is a reformulation or recombination of information given by the premises, but does not provide new information not already contained in the premises. The ability to reason deductively entails a grasp of the concept of *necessity* attributed to conclusions on the basis of argument form, alone. The deductive reasoner is able to successfully grasp that the organization of sentences within an argument or a particular use of certain logical connectives fully justifies the truth of a conclusion.

### Models Relating Logic and Thought

Logic is concerned with the validity of argument forms. It exists as a formal philosophical discipline and stands apart from the content domains or issues that people reason about, much in the way that mathematics as a formal system stands apart from the "things" that are counted. In practice, however, logic is closely linked with the psychological processes that operate in reasoning and has often been defined as the science of reasoning (Copi, 1968). The exact nature of the relationship between formal logic and reasoning has been debated by philosophers and psychologists since the publication of *An Investigation of the Laws of Thought* by Boole (1854; Piaget, 1957). Boole's concern with the application of algebraic methods to logic led him to view the operations of logic, in particular the logic of classes, and the operations of ordinary algebra as emerging from a common higher-order logic. These higher-order rules of logic were thought to be a formalization of the laws of thought. Cognitive psychologists have continued to debate about the relationship between logic and thought, and logic and language (Braine & Rumain, 1983; Evans, 1982; 1983; Falmagne, 1975; Wason & Johnson-Laird, 1972). Controversy centers on whether logical relations should be understood as constructions that correspond with cognitive structures that organize experience, as empirical contingencies, or as analytic relations within natural language. Piaget identified four views on the nature of the relationship between logical relations and knowledge structures that correspond to these three categories: platonism, conventionalism, logical structures as well formed language, and operationalism (Piaget, 1957).

According to the Platonist view—a perspective adopted by Russell and Whitehead—logical principles correspond to universal, supra-empirical nonpsychological truths. In traditional Platonism, the mind acquires copies of these supra-empirical realities and applies them in understanding the empirical world. Traditional Platonists do not tell us how the mind acquires its copy of logic; Russell and Whitehead were similarly unconcerned with the acquisition of logic. In fact, Russell was especially concerned to exclude all psychological considerations from the operation of logic (Russell, 1956). Traditional Platonic notions skirt around the psychological–epistemological problem of accounting for the development of logic by placing a fully defined logic both in the knower and outside of the knower simultaneously. This view, however, is not represented in any current model of reasoning in the cognitive psychology literature.

Conventionalism and models of logic as well-formed language regard the rules of logic as either empirical conventions (the product of S–R pairings, for example) or convenient, subjective principles of organization. Conventionalism, as has Piaget described it, is closely related to logical positivist views of logic and knowledge, and corresponds with a mechanistic understanding of the development of reasoning (Evans, 1982; Griggs, 1983; Mandler, 1983). Logical positivists operate from a realist epistemology, separating empirical truths from the syntactical relations or structures used to express empirical truths.

Piaget has criticized the conventionalist and well-formed language notion on several grounds. The principal criticism of conventionalism, similar to Braine & Rumain's (1983), is that explanations of reasoning that rely entirely on empirical contingencies have difficulty accounting for the high degree of uniformity and consistency among deductive reasoners. Piaget criticized well-formed language models on the lack of psychological validity in separating the experiential and structural components of knowledge. He has pointed out that empirical truths apart from logical relations are impossible. Experience, Piaget stated, "cannot be interpreted in abstraction from the conceptual and logical apparatus which makes such an interpretation possible" (Piaget, 1957, p. 4). A second difficulty with the view that logic (in thought) represents well formed language is that this view does not account for the development of logical knowledge. Syntactical relations appear to be *superimposed* onto the individual's empirical reality without a clear sense that these relations emerge from the organism or are an intrinsic part of the developing cognitive processes.

The Boolean tradition has been passed on in post-Kantian forms of rationalism, especially in Piaget's work on cognitive development. The fourth model relating psychological and logical processes following his own focus on psychological operations and borrowing, in part, from Bridgman's "operationalism" Piaget calls an operatory logic. Piaget (1957) stated, "operations play an indispensable role in logic, since logic is based on an abstract algebra and made up of symbolic manipulations. On the other hand, operations are actual psychological activities." (p. 7). Cognitive operations represent the nexus of logic and thought in the Piagetian system. A cognitive "operation" functions according to the structural features that define it. The structural features of the concrete and formal operational thought correspond to a logical algebra that gives rise to a formal deductive logic. The logico-methematical properties begin to describe the organizational features of the child's thought, when the child's cognitive activity begins to center on classifying and ordering objects in a formal fashion (Piaget, 1957; Inhelder & Piaget, 1958).

Theoretical models concerned with the development of deductive reasoning and the relationship between logic and thought can also be classified as representing either a mechanistic or an organismic research tradition (Overton, 1984). As we indicated earlier, conventionalist and logic as language formulas subscribe to a mechanistic research program; the operationalism of Piaget is organismic. In the reasoning literature, the basic question that distinguishes mechanistic (conventionalism) and organismic (operationalism) explanations concerns the way in which logical knowledge is acquired and how logical knowledge articulates with the other components of the person's knowledge structure, especially experience. Specifically, what is the nature of the interplay between the individual's mechanisms for acquiring and constructing logical knowledge and the contribution of empirical experience to this knowledge?

Mechanistic, empiricistic models explain the development of logical reasoning by referring to environmental variables, reinforcement contingencies, or associations. According to these models, the individual presents few, if any, biological or transformational constraints. Thus, the mature individual behaves "logically" (reasons) not because of the acquisition of a system of transformations characterized as logic, but because the proper past experience is present (Evans, 1977, 1982; Griggs, 1983; Cox & Griggs, 1982; Mandler, 1983; Revlis, 1975). We have already noted the major criticism directed at this form of explanation.

Rationalism is the epistemological corollary of organismic models. The organism actively constructs knowledge according to biological and transformational constrains that represent the individual's cognitive structures. In the psychology of reasoning, constructivist models are called models of logical competence. From a logical competence point of view, the individual possesses structures that correspond in some way to formal logical principles that organize experience (Falmagne, 1975). As both Falmagne (1975) and Braine & Rumain (1983) note, however, competence models that furnish the individual organism with the capacity to reason must then explain why the competent reasoner often fails to reason validly. Explanations for reasoning failures by logical competence theorists are referred to as "moderator variables" (Overton & Newman, 1982; Overton, 1985; Overton, Ward, Black, Noveck, & O'Brien, 1987). Much of the psychology of reasoning literature is devoted to discovering the effects of moderator variables on logical competence (Geis & Zwicky, 1971; O'Brien & Overton, 1980; Overton, Byrnes & O'Brien, 1985; Overton et al. 1987; Wason & Johnson-Laird, 1972; Wason, 1983; Wilkins, 1928). Research on moderator variables (Byrnes & Overton, 1986; Henle, 1962; O'Brien & Overton, 1980, 1982; Overton, Byrnes & O'Brien, 1985) for example, indicates that errors in reasoning may result from task interpretation, cognitive style, and semantic content rather than a lack of logical competence. These or other moderator variables may also help to account for reasoning failures in psychopathological individuals with otherwise intact logical competencies.

The earliest and most influential competence model of logical reasoning is Piaget's own model. Cognitive development consists in a series of transformations in the patterns (structures) of person–environment interactions. These transformations are controlled by certain biological constraints (adaptation and organization) that operate in concert with a general explanatory principle Piaget has called "the equilibration princple." The assimilation and accommodation of the organism's cognitive structures represents the organism's movement towards increasingly higher states of equilibrium. Similar to Werner's (1957) orthogenetic principle, the equilibration principle states that cognitive development progresses towards more complex and stable levels of organization. More highly equilibrated structures are those organizational patterns that are most differentiated, most mobile, and have the greatest explanatory power. According to Piaget, intellectual structures go through a series of stages until the organism develops its most highly equilibrated set of operational structures. These changes in organizational forms have been described by Fodor (1980) as a succession of increasingly powerful logical systems. The structure of thought can be represented as first an approximation of deduction (preoperational thought), less mature forms of deduction (logic of classes and relations), and, finally, a logic of propositions. Propositional or sentential logic, according to Piaget, represents the organism's highest form of cognitive equilibrium.

## Stage Development of Logical Structures

The sensorimotor period extends from birth to around the second year of life. In Piaget's view, the growth of formal logical structures and the ability to reason deductively are rooted in sensorimotor activity (Langer, 1986). The precursors of abstract intellectual operations like the reversibility involved in class inclusion are found in the practical "action" intelligence of the infant. Piaget points out that even in the child's sensorimotor activity, there is a "tendency toward reversibility" and the construction of invariants. In discussing object permanence, Piaget (1957) stated:

> The object's permanent character results from the organization of the spatial field, which is brought about by the coordination of the child's movements. These coordinations presuppose that the child is able to return to his starting-point (reversibility), and to change the direction of his movements (associativity), and hence they tend to take on the form of a "group." Thus, even at the sensorimotor stage, one observes the tendency of intelligence towards reversibility and conservation. (p. 10)

In the early portion of the sensorimotor period, the infant's cognitive development involves the development, elaboration, and coordination of reflexive schemas. Primitive, action-based causality that emerges near the end of the sensorimotor period serves as a precursor to adult forms of reasoning. Class inclusion, for example, is prefigured in the infant's ability to hierarchically differentiate subschemes in causal relations. (According to Piaget, a baby's knowledge that there are various means to a single goal is analogous to a child's successful differentiation of wooden and colored wooden beads.) At the end of the sensorimotor period, intentional acts that had, at the beginning of the period, emerged out of the action-oriented sensorimotor milieu now become represented in consciousness. The emergence of representation and the internalization of means-end relationships marks the beginning of deduction. Intentional acts, controlled by empirical intelligence (sensorimotor stages 3–5), that is as Piaget (1952) wrote, actions "controlled by things themselves and not deduction alone" are supplanted by acts of reflective intelligence (stage 6). Referring to stage 6, Piaget (1952) said, acts are controlled "from within by the consciousness of relationships [and so mark] the beginning of deduction" (p. 331).

The preoperational period represents the beginning of a transition in the child from action-oriented intelligence to formal logical structures. Sensorimotor schemes now become internalized as symbolic representations. The reversibility of overt behaviors also becomes internalized. In addition to the development of symbolic representations, the child also begins to develop a series of signs [language] labeling both actions and objects. Classification, which in its later operational form will organize logico-mathematical thinking in general, develops, as the child now actively coordinates internalized sensorimotor operations with linguistic forms (Piaget, 1957, 1962).

Operational thought begins to supplant preoperational thought at about age seven. Operational thought reaches its fully equilibrated form as a propositional logic sometime during adolescence. The transitional logic of the concrete operational period results from the development of a set of reversible and coordinated logical action systems called "groupings." Grouping operations describe the child's developing competence in solving class and transitive relations problems. The structures that define classes and relations and govern concrete operations are limited, however, to contiguous class inclusions, and do not integrate both mechanisms (inversion for classes and reciprocity for transitive relations) of reversibility into an integrated whole (Inhelder & Piaget, 1958). For this reason, Piaget does not view the concrete operational logical structures as the structural endpoint of the reasoning process. As these groupings become more highly differentiated, integrated, and abstract, they serve as the framework for a two-value propositional logic that Piaget believed best depicts the formal dimensions of mature adolescent and post-adolescent reasoning.

The cognitive operations of the concrete and formal operational periods are clearly defined by Piaget in terms of logico-mathematical structures. Having stated something about logical algebra and structures and operations, we can further state how logic and thought interface in Piaget's system. According to Piaget, certain formal logical structures constitute the organization and process of reasoning. When Piaget had stated that a concrete operational child develops or possesses classification schemes, he had meant for us to understand that the concrete operational child's thought organization with respect to classification can best be represented by certain formal properties, like reversibility, similar to the properties that define or apply to class logic. Logical structures, then, are to be taken as the theoretical pattern for actual cognition.

The development of the propositional logic of the formal operational period is rooted in the eight logical-operational groupings of concrete operational thought. These structures result from a synthesis of the logical properties of the group and the lattice. The "group," a concept borrowed from logical algebra, is any abstract structure or system that possesses the properties of "composition," "associativity," "identity," and "reversibility." The "lattice," also a structure, is a set of elements and a rule defining those elements as having a "least upper bound" and a "greatest lower bound." Of these eight logical-operational groupings, four describe the cognitive-logical structures necessary for a class logic, and four describe the logical structures required to make transitive inferences. Piaget had summarized the difference between the logical-operational structures of the concrete operational period and the formal operational period, first in terms of the breadth of the combinatorial system created by the groupings, and, second, in terms of the nature of the propositional operators (class inclusion vs. implication) that are based on the combinatorial system.

Inhelder and Piaget (1958) wrote:

In sum, the elementary "groupings" which constitute the only integrated structures accessible at the concrete operational level can be distinguished from formal structures on these two counts:

1. The groupings are systems of simple or multiple class inclusion or linkage, but they do not include a combinatorial system linking the various given elements *n-by-n*. As a result, they do not reach the level of a fully developed lattice structure, which would imply such a combinatorial system ("structured whole"); instead, they remain in a state of semi-lattices.

2. The mechanism of reversibility consists either of inversion (for classes) or reciprocity (for relations), but the two are not integrated into a single system.

Consequently, they do not coincide with the group structure of inversion and reciprocities (the INRC group) and remain in the state of incomplete groups. (p. 275)

In formal operations, the intrapropositional class logic gives way to a two-value propositional logic. From two variables (e.g., "p" and "q") and their negations, and the application of cross multiplication (concrete operational grouping III), Piaget had constructed an exhaustive set of conjunctions (p•q, -p•q, p•-q, -p•-q). Each of these pairs, taken one at a time, two at a time, three at a time, and four at a time, yields a set of 16 binary operations (based on concrete operational groupings I & II). These operations yield a combinatorial system forming a lattice in which the 16 combinations form the elements, and the operations of conjunction and alternation the greatest lower bound and least upper bound for each pair (Inhelder & Piaget, 1958).

The binary operations also serve as elements for a series of transformations defined as follows: (a) *Identity*: an operation, which, when performed on any proposition, leaves the proposition unchanged; (b) *Inversion*: an operation in which both the truth value of the variables and the logical operation is transformed (i.e., an alternation becomes a conjunction, and a conjunction becomes an alternation); *Reciprocal*: an operation in which only the truth values of the variables is changed; *Correlative:* an operation in which the logical operation is transformed These four transformations themselves form the elements of a group, when combined. Piaget had indicated that every deduction in a propositional or sentential logic represents some transformation of the sixteen binary operators and, consequently, can be reduced to a combination constructed from these four fundamental conjunctions.

| Sensorimotor & Preoperational<br>Stage | Concrete Operational<br>Stage | Formal Operational<br>Stage |
|---|---|---|

| Pre-logical Structures | Logical Structures of<br>Classification and<br>Seriation | Logical Structures<br>Corresponding to a<br>Two-value<br>propositional logic |
|---|---|---|

|  | 1) Transitive inferences<br>2) Proper use of<br>categorical propositions<br><br>formation of<br>logical classes<br><br>competence in<br>syllogistic logic | Competence in solving<br>reasoning problems<br>using conditionals,<br>bi-conditionals, etc. |
|---|---|---|

FIG. 12.1   Relation between logical structures stages of development and forms of logical reasoning.

## THE RELATION BETWEEN LOGICAL STRUCTURES
## AND DEDUCTIVE LOGIC:
## APPLICATIONS TO REASONING PATHOLOGY

The progression of deductive systems as themselves a series of equilibrated formal structures does not directly correspond to Piaget's analysis of the progression of cognitive structures. Distinguishing between Piaget's representation of logical-cognitive structures and formal systems of deductive logic will prove helpful in outlining the current state of deductive reasoning in the thought disorder literature. Figs. 12.1 and 12.2 portray the relation-

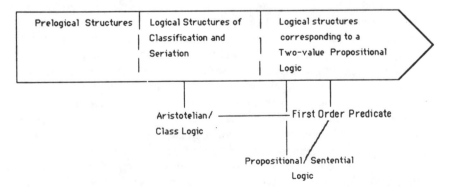

FIG. 12.2   Relation between logical structures and formal systems of deductive logic.

ship between the progression of cognitive structures of thought as forms of logical reasoning, and the systemic progression or "equilibration" of formal systems of deductive logic. As Figs. 12.1 and 12.2 indicate the logical structures in Piaget's system do not precisely correspond with the various forms of deductive logic as known to the logician. Knowledge structures beginning with sensorimotor schemes and preoperations are prelogical. True logical knowledge structures only begin to emerge when the child reaches the period of concrete operations.

## Concrete Operations and Class Logic

The difference between Piaget's use of the terms, "classification" and "class logic," and traditional class logic is illustrated in the differences between Piagetian analyses of class logic competence among thought disordered populations (e.g., Trunnel, 1964, 1965) and the analysis of class logic competence by early thought disorder reasearchers (Von Domarus, 1944). This distinction is crucial in understanding how thought disorder researchers use the terms "reasoning," "logical" or "illogical," "rational," and so forth.

In certain respects, the different emphases reflected in these two lines of empirical research parallel the distinction between the understanding and correct use of categorical propositions, and, the application of syllogistic argument forms to categorical propositions. It is this latter application of syllogisms to category sentences that has traditionally been identified as "class logic" by logicians. It is also this form of class logic that has been the focus of research by early, non-Piagetian thought disorder researchers (Von Domarus, 1944; Arieti, 1955). This approach consists of giving schizophrenic and normal subjects various forms of categorical syllogisms and requiring them to identify valid conclusions. Poor performance by schizophrenics on syllogism problems is interpreted as indicating reasoning pathology.

Piagetian researchers, on the other hand, understand class logic as the individual's ability to understand classification hierarchies; knowledge of the relationship between intension and extension; or from a structural standpoint, the competent utlization of the concrete operational operations entailed in classification (Groupings I-IV). In traditional Aristotelian logic, these abilities are presupposed, and, in traditional texts on formal logic, fall under the domain of the proper use of categorical propositions. Even here, however, the competence to actually form a "class," or to understand the meaning of the concept of "class," is also presupposed.

Two different sets of empirical investigations of thought pathology regarding classification have been conducted. These include research on the Vygotsky–Goldstein loss of abstraction hypothesis and the Cameron overinclusion hypothesis, and a small number of empirical studies utilizing Piagetian classification tasks. The use of logical terminology in this research is somewhat misleading. "Reasoning," "logical," "rational," and "abstract" in these hypotheses refer to the proper construction of classes. Classifications can be considered "logical" in the sense that we recognize invalid classifications based on the principles of contradiction and excluded middle. Classifications may also be considered logical from a Piagetian point of view, if the construction of classes is dependent on logical (versus pre-logical) knowledge structures. Classification or concept formation, however, is not a logic concerned with deductive inferences, or the relation between premises and conclusions.

## Formal Operations and Propositional Logic

The logical properties of formal operational reasoning correspond to traditional sentential or propositional logic (see Figs. 12.1 and 12.2). Sentential logic represents a macro-level analysis of the properties of formal arguents. As its name implies, this form of logical analysis is concerned with the logical validity of sentences or propositions. In a propositional logic, validity is determined entirely by the logical properties of the four logical connectives that make up the "operators" of the logical language. These are conjunction (&), alternation (v), implication ( → ), and logical equivalence ( ←→ ). These connectives, along with the negation operator ( − ), define all of the operations in a propositional logic. Validity may be determined by examining the ways in which these logical connectives or operators are used to form complex or molecular sentences.

One difficulty with a propositional logic, however, is that many deductive arguments cannot be reduced to an analysis of logical connectives.

An example is the following:

All men are mortal.
Socrates was a man.
Therefore, Socrates was mortal.

From the viewpoint of a propositional logic, this deduction is made up of three distinct atomic sentences, occurring in the form:

p.
q.
Therefore, r.

The conditional that corresponds to this argument form is (p & q) → r. This argument can be made to appear invalid by assigning "T" to both "p" and "q" and "F" to "r." In an instance where the antecedent is true and the consequent is false, a conditional is considered false. Yet, the argument itself, of course, is perfectly valid. The point here is that, in this case, validity is not determined solely by the ways in which atomic sentences are combined, but by the internal structure of these sentences—for example, the recurrence of the same terms in different parts of the argument and the role of the logical quantifiers (all, some).

The inability of propositional logic to solve a class logic problem points to an interesting dilemma that is reflected in Figs. 12.1 and 12.2. Propositional logic had been viewed by Piaget as representing the highest order of equilibrated logical-operational structures. It would appear that these structures cannot fully assimilate all logic tasks, and that some more comprehensive, more integrated set of structures is required. This task is performed in formal logic by first order predicate logic. Predicate logic represents a microlevel of analysis of formal arguments. The fundamentals of a macrolevel analysis includes sentence structures, but expands to also include an account of simple sentence forms as well as their connectives. It is called a first order predicate logic, because in it the notion of "some" and "all" are applied only to individuals and not classes. Thus, predicate logic assimilates both a propositional and a class logic (Braine & Rumain, 1983).

Given this distinction, one might expect a research literature devoted to examining and comparing thought disordered subjects and normals on tasks that require formal operational competence, as it is reflected in the ability to solve problems in a propositional logic (e.g., Wason & Johnson-Laird, 1972) or in a first order predicate logic. At present, however, no such literature exists.

## Thought Pathology and Reasoning

A number of important preliminary questions face the thought disorder researcher concerned with reasoning pathology. The first, of course, is whether diagnosed schizophrenics demonstrate an impairment in their ability to reason deductively. A second question concerns the type of deduction impairment being measured. Is the subject being assessed on tasks requiring a class logic solution or a propositional logical solution? Piaget, of course, had argued that these implicate two different levels of logical structure, and that the logical structures involved in classification and seriation precede those required to reason using a propositional logic. A third question that will not be addressed here is whether the logical structures of classification can also account for the proper use of categorical syllogisms? A number of theories of syllogistic reasoning have been proposed that attempt to outline the sequence of steps used to solve categorical syllogisms (e.g., Braine, 1978; Johnson-Laird & Steedman, 1978; Revlis, 1975), but no empirical research on this topic has been found that is specifically concerned with reasoning disorders.

A second series of related questions concerns the sort of research program utilized to provide the best explanation of the reasoning deficit. We have argued that organismic explanations that emphasize the development of logical structures provide the best explanation for the development of reasoning. Explanations and predictions concerning reasoning pathology based on a logical competence model take two forms. The first is that reasoning pathology represents a form of cognitive stage arrest or regression (Inhelder, 1971; Rosen, 1985). Schizophrenics utilize prelogical structures when attempting to solve classification problems or make deductive inferences. An alternative hypothesis is that schizophrenics have not lost their logical competence, but performance has been impaired, resulting from disease-specific moderator variables (Siomopoulos, 1983). Each hypothesis is considered briefly.

## SYLLOGISTIC LOGIC
## AND THOUGHT DISORDERED POPULATIONS

Much that schizophrenics say appears irrational. Not surprisingly, then, it has been suggested that the schizophrenic's odd verbalizations and poor performance on tests measuring reasoning can be best understood as a failure to correctly apply the rules of logic. This view, offered first by Von Domarus (1944) and later modified by Arieti (1955), assumes, in the Boolean tradition, that the laws of logic are the laws of reasoning. Arieti (1955) stated, for example, that the normal individual "automatically applies the Aristotelian laws of logic without even knowing them (p. 27)." Researchers interested in testing Von Domarus' and Arieti's formulations have interpreted the "laws of logic/reasoning" as referring to traditional or Aristotelian class logic (Copi, 1968).

According to the Von Domarus/Arieti view, thought disorders occur when the schizophrenic systematically applies an alternate set of logical rules. The hypothesis holds great interest, in part, because it was the first to propose a *specific* cognitive mechanism explaining thought disordered behavior. Von Domarus argued that schizophrenic thought (verbalizations) could be explained as a violation of logical principles represented in traditional syllogistic forms. Specifically, the schizophrenic regressed to a previous level of cognitive functioning, reasoning on the basis of the identity of predicates rather than the identity of subjects (Von Domarus, 1944, pp. 111). Von Domarus gave the following syllogism as an illustration of reasoning on the basis of identical predicates:

Certain Indians are swift.

Stags are swift.

Therefore: Certain Indians are stags.

Arieti expanded the Von Domarus principle, fitting it into a general theory of schizophrenia. According to Arieti, the schizophrenic regresses to less mature levels of personality integration and cognitive functioning during periods of stress. The rules of regressed reasoner correspond to prelogical principles reflected in the reasoning of children and primitive cultures (Levin, 1938; Siomopoulos, 1983). Arieti interpreted many aspects of the child's reasoning process as exemplars of the Von Domarus principle. According to Arieti, the child who mistakes all male figures for "Daddy," or mistakes a picture of car for the real object is organizing reality in essentially the same way a schizophrenic does who talks to pictures or who deludes himself into the belief that he is Jesus, because he is wearing white. In both instances, subjects are reasoning on the basis of a duplication of predicates. Arieti offered a similar explanation for Freudian symbolism. Arieti states that objects or events that become represented symbolically in dreams might be analyzed syllogistically. A woman, for example, who dreams that she stumbles and falls acts out her belief that she has succumbed to sexual desire. To Arieti, the syllogism might read like the following:

A prostitute is a fallen woman.

When I stumble, I am a fallen woman.

Therefore: When I stumble, I am a prostitute.

### Empirical Investigations on Syllogistic Logic and Thought Disorder

Attempts to empirically validate the Von Domarus principle have been entirely unsuccessful. Nims (1959) compared 25 adult male schizophrenics with 25 normal controls and found no significant difference on reasoning ability when subjects were required to determine the validity of syllogisms. An important consideration in the Nims study was his interpretation of the Von Domarus error as the reasoner's failure to detect undistributed middle terms in the syllogism. As Williams (1964) noted, however, emphasis on the fallacy of the undistributed middle term detracts from the emphasis placed on identity of predicates by Von Domarus and Arieti. The fallacy of the undistributed middle term may occur in any of the four traditional syllogistic figures (see Appendix A). It is only in the second figure, however, that the terms of the syllogism are arranged where predicates of both the major and minor premise are the same and where the Von Domarus error is likely to occur. Nims' interpretation of the fallacy, therefore, seems unwarranted. Studies reported by Wyatt (1965) and Jacobs (1969) using Figure II forms of categorical syllogism have also failed to find significant differences between schizophrenics and normals on measures of syllogistic reasoning.

In a study reported by Gottesman and Chapman (1960), 30 schizophrenic subjects and 30 adult normals were asked to solve 40 syllogistic problems similar to the syllogisms used by Nims, but all four of the traditional syllogistic figures were used. The procedure was a modified version of the Chapman and Chapman (1959) syllogism task. Each item contained two premises, the word "therefore," and five alternative conclusions. A typical

test item appears below. The correct response is item three, (none of the conclusions is proved):

All of Tom's ties are red.
Some of the things Ada is holding are red.
Therefore:
1. At least some of the things Ada is holding are Tom's ties.
2. At least some of the things Ada is holding are not Tom's Ties.
3. None of these conclusions is proved.
4. None of the things Ada is holding are Tom's ties.
5. All of the things Ada is holding are Tom's ties.

Each response set contains one example of each of the four kinds of categorical propositions (A, I, E, O), and a fifth alternative that states that
none of the four are correct.

Gottesman and Chapman reasoned that although subjects were presented with all four syllogistic figures, by logially converting one or both affirmative premises in Figures I, III, and IV they could logically derive a
Figure II syllogism and, therefore, create a Von Domarus identity on the basis of predicates syllogism. For example, consider a syllogism of the form:

All A's are B's.
Some B's are C's.

This could be converted to the form:

All A's are B's.
Some C's are B's
Therefore, Some C's are A's.

Thus, the presupposition that the premise, "Some B's are C's," is logically
equivalent to the premise, "Some C's are B's."

Gottesman and Chapman also suggested that the Von Domarus effect
would be obtained best by syllogisms designed to maximize performance by
normal subjects. For this reason, syllogisms were constructed in which the
subjects in both categorical propositions were very specific and the middle
term in the syllogism was known to apply to a large number of objects.

Of the 40 items, 28 served as measures of the Von Domarus error. The
proper solution on the multiple-choice format to each of these items was always that none of the sample conclusions were valid. In addition, eight of these
items were designed specifically to elicit the Von Domarus identity on the basis
of similar predicates response. Gottesman and Chapman also included 12 syllogisms in which one of the conclusions offered could be validly inferred from

the premises. These items were included to guard against a response set. It is not clear, however, how many of the 156 possible distinct syllogistic forms involving both figure and mood were used by Gottesman and Chapman.

Gottesman and Chapman report a significant difference between schizophrenics and normals on total errors made (40 items) and significantly more errors on the experimental items (28 items), but the two groups did not differ on the percentage of errors that coincided with the Von Domarus error. The findings suggest that schizophrenic thinking may be characterized by reasoning problems of various sorts, but not the reasoning problem hypothesized by Von Domarus and Arieti. It is also important to note that the average IQ score of schizophrenics in Gottesman and Chapman's study was 18 points lower than the study's controls, and it is possible that the schizophrenic's poor performance reflected general intellectual decline or inability rather than a specific reasoning deficit.

A more carefully designed study by Williams (1964) also failed to support the Von Domarus/Arieti hypothesis. Williams attempted to test four hypotheses relevant to Arieti's elaboration of the Von Domarus prediction. According to hypothesis 1, schizophrenics should perform more poorly than normal adults on syllogistic reasoning tasks. In view of the schizophrenic's reported insufficiencies in thinking with abstract content, Williams' second hypothesis predicted that schizophrenics should have greater difficulty with syllogistic problems involving abstract content than those involving concrete content. Williams' third hypothesis attempted to determine the role of personal content in the schizophrenic's performance with syllogisms corresponding to Arieti's theorizing and clinical data that schizophrenic's regression to developmentally less-sophisticated forms of reasoning results from the stress of emotionally charged issues. Therefore, he predicted that if Arieti was correct, schizophrenics would commit more errors on syllogism problems involving personal content than on problems not involving personal content. The final hypothesis examined differences in performance on figure II versus figures I or III of the traditional syllogistic forms. Williams reports no significant differences on any hypothesis tested.

Subjects in this study consisted of 50 adult schizophrenics and 50 adult controls. All subjects in this study were male, and were matched for level of education and verbal intelligence. Subjects in both groups were administered test items in small groups. Each subject received the Gallup–Thorndike Vocabulary Test (Thorndike & Gallup, 1944) first, followed by 96 syllogism problems presented in a multiple choice format. Each problem was designed in a manner similar to the five-choice format employed by Gottesman and Chapman (1960), but varied in several important ways. First, test items were varied according to content type. Syllogisms were classified as "abstract," "concrete," "personal," and "nonpersonal" based on the use of letters, names of common inanimate objects, the use of personal pronouns related to individual thoughts or feelings, and the use of names of nonhuman animate objects. Syllogisms were presented in forms corresponding to either figures I, II, or III. Each content category consisted of 12 positive and 12 negative items. In one half (12) of each content category, subjects were provided with a valid response alternative. In the other 12 items, a correct response entailed the selection of a variant on the statement, "No valid conclusion is given here." Items were also matched for word length. 96 problems were presented in two parts to subjects. Assignment to parts ("A" or "B") was done randomly, and done for the purpose of counterbalancing fatigue and practice effects. The only finding of significance in this study was a difference between schizophrenics and normals on negative syllogisms. Schizophrenics performed more poorly on these items.

Recently Watson and Wold (1981) compared frequencies of the major types of syllogistic reasoning errors in schizophrenics, brain damaged, and control subjects both before and after subjects were matched for the effects of age, education, IQ, length of hospitalization, and the effects of medication. Watson and Wold also correlated performance of schizophrenics on their logic measures with relevant diagnostic subcategories (process/reactive; paranoid/nonparanoid; anhedonic/nonadhedonic; length of illness; and, length of hospitalization) in order to determine whether logical errors might be more prominent in one or more subclasses of the disorder. Test items given to Watson and Wold's subjects were presented in standard syllogistic form with a multiple-choice response format. Following each syllogism, subjects could choose between a logically valid conclusion or an invalid conclusion. Invalid conclusions were of two types. 25 invalid items were designated "overexpansive" errors. Overexpansive errors were defined as conclusions that reached beyond the information given in the premises. For example:

Jimmy is overweight.
Jimmy's mother is overweight.
Therefore:
1. Jimmy eats too many sweets.
2. Valid conclusion.

25 syllogisms were constructed to test the Von Domarus notion that similarity implies identity. The authors do not comment on nature of figure or mood in each test item. Moreoever, it is unclear from Watson and Wold's description of the Von Domarus type test items the kinds of correct conclusions subjects are offered. In a traditional figure II format in which both premises are universal affirmative propositions, the only valid response could be a "no conclusion is possible" response or a response that merely reaffirms one of the syllogism's premises.

Watson and Wold presented two sets of analyses: comparison of between-group errors before matching for education and IQ, and error comparisons after matching for education and IQ. Prior to matching differences in the number of overexpansive errors made by schizophrenic subjects, subjects with organic impairment, and controls differences between schizophrenics, organics, and controls was significant, although differences in Von Domarus errors was insignificant. After matching, both the overexpansive and the Von Domarus error differences fell to nonsignificant levels. Watson and Wold also report no significant relationships between schizophrenic subtypes and the presence of logical errors. They concluded that there is no empirical support for the Von Domarus hypothesis.

## Summary

Empirical research on faulty syllogistic reasoning has not supported the contention of Von Domarus and Arieti. Schizophrenic performance is not appreciably poorer than adult normals or nonthought-disordered psychiatric controls. The relationship between this form of class logic, and the logical structures involved in classification or the correct reasoning with categorical propositions, has not been carefully defined. The fact that categorical syllogisms can be correctly solved using Venn Diagrams, which are pictorial representations of class inclusion relations, suggests that there is some overlapping competence. At present, no research has been done to compare performance on logical classification and syllogistic reasoning in order to determine how these two competencies might be related. One possibility is that the logical competence required to correctly solve problems involving categorical propositions is all that is required to also solve categorical syllogisms. Another possibility is that additional competence in understanding certain characteristics of logical quantifiers is acquired prior to the acquisition of propositional logic, but is independent of the logical structures involves in classification. This notion is in line with the previous observation that propositional logic is not able to subsume the role of quantifiers without the aid of a predicate logic. Further research is needed here, especially if schizophrenics do demonstrate an impairment in the use of logical structures involved in classification.

## ABSTRACTION AND CLASSIFICATION
## IN THOUGHT DISORDERED POPULATIONS:
## THEORETICAL MODELS
## AND EMPIRICAL INVESTIGATIONS

## Theoretical Models

In this section we will review the theoretical models explaining thought disorders as an abstraction impairment. Traditional abstraction impairment hypotheses, measured especially by class formation tasks, are compared with Piaget's logical structures model of classification.

The tendency of schizophrenics to make greater numbers of errors on abstraction or concept formation tasks and to produce overly concrete verbalizations was examined extensively early in the psychological deficit literature (Bolles & Goldstein, 1938; Elmore & Gorham, 1957; Goldstein, 1939, 1944; Goldstein & Scheerer, 1941; Gorham, 1956; Hanfmann & Kasanin, 1937; 1942; Kasanin, 1944). Two basic theoretical explanations have been offered to explain these behaviors. The first, called the loss of abstraction hypothesis, was developed by Vygotsky and Goldstein. First, Vygotsky, and, later, Goldstein argued that the schizophrenic's bizarre behavior reflected a loss of their ability to think and develop concepts abstractly. Wright (1975) and Shimkunas (1972) argued that the notion of a "loss" of abstraction does not accurately describe Goldstein's hypothesis, emphasizing instead a nonspecific impairment in the schizophrenic's ability to generalize. Wright emphasized a logical structures definition of abstraction, stating that Goldstein's definition is synonymous with Olver and Hornsby's (1966) notion of "supraordinate grouping." The second general hyothesis, proposed by Norman Cameron (1938, 1939) as a repudiation of Goldstein's hypothesis, suggested that schizophrenics had not lost their ability to form abstract concepts but had lost their ability to control their concept formation strategies. This resulted in the inappropriate inclusion of non-essential attributes in the formation of concepts, most often tested by class formation tasks.

## Vygotsky

Vygotsky (1934) published the first theoretical proposal concerned with an abstraction deficit in schizophrenics, and was the first to offer a cognitive regression hypothesis to explain schizophrenic verbalizations. Vygotsky's hypotheses about thought disorder emerged from his analysis of developmental changes in the thinking of children. He proposed that as children enter adolescence, they pass from a "complex," nonabstract form of thought and concept formation to a "conceptual" form of thought, characterized by the ability to form abstract concepts. Complex classes are regarded as prelogical, based on paired associations or other nonlogical criteria. Conceptual classes, on the other hand, are formed on the basis of logical rules. A prelogical use of the term, "chair," as a class refers to only those objects that are part of the child's experience (Hanfmann & Kasanin, 1937). In contrast, the conceptual thinker knows that "chair" refers to any object whose primary function is to provide a place to sit. This formulation is rule governed and not limited to experience.

## Goldstein

Based on comparisons of brain-damaged and schizophrenic patients on object sorting and color sorting tasks, Goldstein (Bolles & Goldstein, 1938; Goldstein, 1939, 1944; Goldstein & Scheerer, 1941), like Vygotsky, concluded that schizophrenics had lost their capacity to function abstractly. Goldstein, however, did not describe the schizophrenic's impairment as a specifically *cognitive* deficit. "Concrete" and "abstract" represented global personality dimensions. Goldstein described the concrete attitude as realistic, automatic, and limited or bound by sensory information. Eight behavioral forms defined the abstract attitude (Goldstein & Scheerer, 1941). These included the detachment of the ego from the limits of sensory or empirical experience, and the abilities to assume a mental set consciously; to reflect verbally on experience; to shift reflectively from one aspect of a situation to another; to consider several aspects of a situation simultaneously; to grasp part-whole relationships; to abstract common properties and form hierarchic concepts; and to plan ahead ideationally. Goldstein greatly emphasized the volitional character of each of the attributes as its principal distinguishing feature.

A major criticism of Goldstein's hypothesis centers on the generality of his descriptions and the lack of precision in operationalizing "abstraction." This is largely the result of his insistence on emphasizing volition and consciousness. Subjects bound to the concrete attitude were assumed to be compelled to respond unreflectively to any stimulation. As a consequence, in an experimental situation, a schizophrenic subject might be either overly distracted or rigidly transfixed by the same stimulus. This lack of specificity made prediction impossible and the general explanation untestable. Goldstein, himself conceded that he could not predict which type of deviant response might result when a concrete-bound patient was stimulated (Goldstein & Scheerer, 1941, pp. 74).

As a result of this lack of definitional clarity, most investigators have ignored Goldstein's descriptions of volition and focused on abstract reasoning. The schizophrenic's inability to "abstract out" essential attributes, that is, the competence required to coordinate intension and extension, appears to represent the heart of Goldstein's description of cognitive impairment (Goldstein & Scheerer, 1941, pp. 8). This notion parallels Piaget's observations about less mature forms of reasoning. The concrete and abstract attitudes appear to develop in sequence, resulting from different maturational paths within the central nervous system. The child appears to progress from a concrete level of functioning to the abstract attitude during middle childhood. Other properties also resemble aspects of Piaget's description of the development of reasoning. The capacity to shift reflectively from one aspect of a situation to another, to reflect on several features simultaneously, and the ability to grasp part-whole relationships are featured in Piaget's description of class inclusion (Inhelder & Piaget, 1969, pp. 103.). Goldstein also underscored the centrality of supraordinate categories in class formation; the property, according to Piaget, that distinguishes logical classification from less mature forms of class formation (graphic and nongraphic collections).

A fundamental difference between Piaget and Goldstein centers on what represents the most sophisticated level of reasoning. Goldstein (Goldstein & Scheerer, 1941) stated:

> For instance, the highest degree of abstract behavior is required for the conscious and volitional act of forming generalized and hierarchic concepts or of thinking in terms of a principle and its subordinate cases and to verbalize these acts. (p. 8)

Piaget, of course, viewed the logical structures required for classification as not fully equilibrated. These structures eventually give way to a propositional logic. Goldstein's position, however, helps to explain why the early focus on reasoning and logic in the thought disorder literature is restricted to classification and syllogistic logic.

## Cameron

Normal Cameron (Cameron, 1938, 1939, 1944, 1947; Cameron & Magaret, 1951) developed a different view of schizophrenic thought disorder from his examination of subject performance on concept formation-classification tasks and sentence completion tasks. In his initial formulations, he described thought disorder in terms of several overlapping categories. These include cluster thinking, metonymic distortion, scatter by amplification, incongruity of acts and words, interpenetration of themes, defects in generalization, and altering the condition of the problem. Most of these categories, like Goldstein's, have been ignored by empirical investigators. Cameron believed, however, that schizophrenics' poor performance on object classification or sorting tests, like the Goldstein–Scheerer, resulted from a problem of "overinclusion," not a loss of abstraction. In overinclusive thinking, boundaries of concepts became overextensive. Associated ideas, tangents, and even distantly related concepts were inappropriately incorporated into a concept, making them broad, vague, and imprecise.

## Piaget

During the period of concrete operations, the child acquires logical structures that enable him to form and manipulate logical classes. Cognitive operations during the concrete operational period consist of the eight groupings; groupings 1–4 specifically apply to the formation of classes. Piaget also defined classes in terms of their logical properties (deductive inferences made from the rules of identity, contradiction, and excluded middle), the coordination of extension and intension, and the proper use of the logical quantifiers, "all" and "some." His description of the logical properties of classes is especially helpful in distinguishing between logical classes from nonclass and pseudoclass collections. Inhelder and Piaget (1969) summarized these properties as follows:

> 1. There are no isolated elements (i..e. elements not belonging to a class). All elements must be classified. Any singular element must give rise to its own specific (but singular) class.
> 2. There are no isolated classes, for example, every specific class $A$ (characterized by the property $a$, implies its compliment $A'$ (characterized by not-$a$).
> 3. Classes are defined by the presence of specific attributes, and includes only members with that attribute.
> 4. A complimentary class is a class of the same rank not possessing $a$.
> 5. A class $A$ (or $A'$) is included in every higher ranking class, which contains all its elements, starting with the closest, $B$: $A = B - A'$ (or $A' = B - A$) and $A \times B = A$, which amounts to saying that "all" $A$ are "some" $B$. (p. 48)

This set of criteria, along with a series of classification tasks, discriminate developmental levels of classification competence starting with preoperations and ending with concrete operations. Piaget identified three states: graphic collections (I), nongraphic collections (II), and class inclusion (III). The stage I child forms collections on the basis of the spatial arrangement of the elements being classified (Inhelder & Piaget, 1969, p. 18). He is unable to divorce the abstract properties of the elements (similarities) from the graphic arrangements that develop during classification (the infralogical whole). Thus, the child who begins separating geometrical figures according to similar shapes may, midway through the process, place a square under a triangle, because it reminds him of a house. The description of the graphic collection is similar to Goldstein's description of concrete collections based on "sensory cohesion" and Vygotsky's associative complex. In each instance, the child has not developed a complete understanding of the logical necessity entailed in the coordination of intension and extension. The child may refuse to classify all the elements in the stimulus set or may introduce nonmembers into the collection. The child who forms collections in nongraphic terms (age five to seven or eight) continues to lack class inclusion, but is able to verbalize notions of similarity. The stage III child has the capacity to pose a class ($A$) and its complement ($A'$), locate both as subclasses in a supraordinate category ($B$), and dissolve the supraordinate category by inversion (Inhelder & Piaget, 1969; Piaget, 1928).

Class logic competence was determined by three experimental situations.

The first involved a free-form classification procedure similar to the Gold-stein–Scheerer Object Sorting Test. The logical-structural features of classi-fication, however, are more effectively demonstrated by two other procedures measuring class inclusion competence. The first involves the child's ability to handle the class quantification concepts, "some" asnd "all." Here, the child is presented with a series of objects that can be parti-tioned into a series of classes and subclasses. The child is presented with a series of blue squares, red squares, and blue circles. The objects may be clas-sified on the basis of color—blue objects (B) with subclasses blue circles (A) and blue squares (A')—red objects (B') being the complement of the supra-ordinate category—or the objects can be classified according to shape—class of squares (B) with subclasses (A) blue squares and (A') red squares, dircles (B') being the supraordinate complement. The child is then asked a series of questions designed to indicate his understanding of logical quanti-fication. The questions posed are of two forms. Are all the Bs A (or A')? (Are all the blue ones circles?) Second, Are all the As (or A's) B? (Are all the circles blue?) Piaget suggested that the child who has not fully grasped the logical meaning of "all" and "some" will interpret both questions as $A = B$ and $B = A$, and, as a result he/she will answer one question correctly. He may correctly conclude that not all Bs are A (not all blue objects are squares, because there are also blue circles) but will incorrectly conclude that all As are B is false (not all circles are blue), pointing to the blue squares as evidence for his conclusion.

The second procedure is designed to demonstrate the presence or absence of class inclusion. Here, the child himself constructs a class hierarchy from a set of objects or pictures of objects provided by the examiner. After the child has constructed the hierarchy, the examiner asks a series of questions to determine whether or not the child can quantify his inclusions. Thus, in the case where a child had constructed class hierarchy consisting of flowers (B) and nonflowers (B'); under the heading flowers, sublcasses of primulas and other flowers; and a further subclass of yellow and other-colored pri-mulas; the child might be asked: "Which would make a bigger bunch: One of all the primulas or one of all the yellow primulas." (Inhelder & Piaget, 1969; p. 109) A correct response, "primulas," indicates an adequate grasp of the logical relations that obtain between classes and subclasses $(A = B - A'$.

There is general agreement among loss of abstraction theorists, overin-clusion theorists, and Piagetian theorists that the formation of classes in-volves some form of logical competence, and that the competence involved in class formation is marked by developmental changes (Markman & Seibert, 1976; Rosch, Mervis, Gray, Johnson, & Boyes-Braem, 1976; Wil-kinson, 1976). As a result, the abstraction impairment literature reflects two basic themes. The first is an attempt to demonstrate an impairment in the logical structures of schizophrenic's organization of his experience; the second is an attempt to compare this disorganization with developmental changes that reflect the movement from childhood forms of reasoning to adult forms of reasoning.

The ability to form a logical class entails the identification of higher-order similarities. Higher-order similarities or generalizations result when a person distinguishes between essential and nonessential features that define objects. Abstraction impairment theorists often identify the process of identifying similarities as the logical meaning of a class. This, however, is not an entirely appropriate application of the term, "logic," because it confuses the process of concept formation and the logical relations that define concepts. Conceptual classes are collections of nonidentical stimuli that are treated as if they were identical. Only some operations on these collections, however, reveal the subject's understanding of logical relations. The logical meaning of abstraction is summarized in putting together and taking apart collections in ways that reflect a consistent use of the logical principles of identity, contradiction, and excluded middle. Piaget had defined these principles operationally by relating them to the construction of hierarchies and the use of logical quantifiers. Abstraction tasks that fail to clarify logical relations fail as measures of reasoning. Most abstraction and overinculsion measures fail as measures of logical reasoning.

**Empirical Investigations: Introduction**

The theoretical positions of Vygotsky, Goldstein, and Cameron have framed the empirical research on reasoning and thought pathology. These authors have viewed the failure of schizophrenics to generate "logical" sortings in class formation tasks as one indication of a reasoning deficit. A review of the empirical literature raises issues concerning construct validity, in particular whether these various abstraction impairment notions actually focuses on deductive logic as the authors imply, and, whether the tasks measuring abstraction deficits are also measures of deductive reasoning. Historically, the major criticisms of the reasoning impairment hypotheses of Goldstein and Cameron have focused on the difficulties operationalizing these constructs. The inferential fashion by which Goldstein and Cameron linked a wide variety of behaviors to reasoning disturbances has made emirical evaluations of these constructs difficult. Goldstein, for example, included subject's failures to respond to a question as an indication of concreteness. Cameron included interpenetration of themes in his definition of overinclusion. The inclusion of so many different clinical phenomena under a single construct gives that construct an infallible status. No experimental procedure can be simultaneously concerned with every aspect believed to reflect thought disorder. As a consequence, any specific experimental measure that isolates one aspect of the clinical description is open to the criticism that it has not focused on the most appropriate feature of the hypothesized variable.

The primary solution to the measurement problem has been to ignore the more esoteric features of the definition and focus on those with the greatest degree of face validity. As a result, most of the follow-up research has examined *cognitive* dimensions of abstractions and overinclusion. Both constructs have been measured by three different procedures: conceptual (object) sorting tasks, proverb meaning tests, and the analysis of performance on the Similarities subtest of the WAIS. In addition, overinclusion has been evaluated by tests measuring verbal expansiveness. Of the measures used to evaluate cognitive abnormalities, object sorting tasks are most closely linked with logical reasoning. Proverb interpretation (the ability to distinguish between literal and metaphorical (abstract meanings) and the analysis of similarities and analogies (generalizations as forms of abstractions) measure qualitative changes in concepts formation but not changes in logical reasoning.

A second solution to the measurement problem involved the use of multi-dependent measures to evaluate the abstraction or overinclusion construct. In the absence of an agreed upon definition, a minimum requirement using a multi-measure design is that measures of the hypothesized construct reflect both convergent and divergent validity. That is, various measures of abstraction must be more highly correlated with one another than they are with other measures, such as socio-economic status or intelligence. A few studies have used this multiple measure procedure in evaluating the overinclusion construct and will be reviewed.

Related to the construct validity issue is the question of whether object sorting tests can, in fact, detect logical classification competence. Goldstein and Cameron (Goldstein & Scheerer, 1941; Cameron, 1938) have argued that the capacity to form and manipulate abstract concepts is demonstrated by a subject's ability to sort objects or pictures of objects into categories. Early versions of object sorting tests were criticized for their lack of standardization and quantification, and scoring and administration was later modified. There is, however, a more fundamental inadequacy in the free-form classification task (See Inhelder & Piaget, 1969, pp. 100). Subjects are able to form collections that only *appear* to be true logical classes (nongraphic collections). The presence of logical structures are reflected, however, when the child is able to construct class hierarchies. Any measure of logical classification, therefore, that involves only free-form classification cannot detect differences between class inclusion and nongraphic collections.

## Empirical Investigations

The first construct reviewed is the loss of abstraction hypothesis of Vygotsky and Goldstein. Hanfmann and Kasanin (1937, 1942) were the first to empirically evaluate this form of the abstraction impairment hypothesis. Their procedures were adopted from Vygotsky and involved sorting blocks of various shapes, sizes, and colors on the basis of several predetermined categories. Simple solutions based on classifying the blocks according to a single attribute were incorrect. The required solutions to the sorting problem entailed conjunctive concepts such as "flat and tall." Subjects were told that there were four kinds of blocks, and each block has a name. The examiner began by picking up one of the blocks showing the subject, the block's name (nonsense words printed on the bottom of one of the blocks designating a particular conjunctive concept), and asking the subject to select all of the blocks that belonged with it. The subject was required to formulate solutions until the solution was discovered. Performance was scored in terms of the time spent in solving the problem and how many experimenter "helps" were received. The performance of 50 schizophrenic subjects, evenly divided for sex, and matched for age and educational level were compared with 45 nonpsychiatric normals. Hanfmann and Kasanin reported that the average score of the schizophrenic subjects exceeded the scores of normals by nearly one-half. They concluded that schizophrenics were impaired in their ability to generate conceptual categories. The results have been viewed as inconclusive, however, because the scoring procedure confounds abstraction with slow performance, an attribute of schizophrenics demonstrated by other investigators (Payne & Hewlett, 1960).

Goldstein and Scheerer (Bolles & Goldstein, 1938; Goldstein & Scheerer, 1941), using the Gelb–Goldstein–Weigl–Scheerer Object Sorting Test, cited relatively poor performance by schizophrenics to argue that schizophrenics were deficient in abstraction. Testing involves three phases. In phase one, the subject groups objects with an object he selects himself. In the second phase the subject groups all objects he believes belong together. After this initial sorting, the subject again sorts (phase three), but according to a different set of criteria. If he fails to comply, he is presented with a new sorting created by the examiner and asked to explain why those items might belong together. Sortings are evaluated according to a predetermined set of criteria, augmented by the subject's rationale for particular sortings. The Goldstein procedure has been criticized for this lack of standardization, the highly subjective nature of the scoring criteria, and a lack of control groups (Buss & Lang, 1965; Reed, 1970).

Later investigations using more adequate control groups and quantitative methods did not find that schizophrenics were abnormally concrete (Chapman & Taylor, 1957; Fey, 1951; Lothrup, 1960; McGaughran, 1957; McGaughran & Moran, 1956, 1957; Rashkis, 1947). Chapman and Taylor (1957) employed a card sorting task to investigate two schizophrenic and one normal group of male subjects. Names of objects belonging to either a designated category (e.g., fruits), a similar category (e.g., vegetables), or a markedly dissimilar category (e.g., birds) were printed on cards. Subjects were given a prototype card from the designated category and instructed to place the remaining cards with the category represented by the prototype. As predicated, schizophrenics made more similarity versus dissimilarity errors than normals. Chapman and Taylor interpreted these results as indicating a problem of overinclusion, rather than loss of abstraction. That is, schizophrenics tended to overgeneralize rather than categorize in an excessively concrete manner.

Fey (1951) reported significant differences in sorting times and errors made by schizophrenic versus normals. Fey administered the Wisconsin Sorting Test, which required subjects to complete six different card sortins. Results indicated that 16 of the 22 schizophrenics, but only 8 of the 47 controls failed to complete all six sortings. Fey indicated that schizophrenic rationales, however, did not differ from those of normals.

McGaughran and Moran (1956, 1957) reported a series of studies in which they scored sorting responses to Rapaort's (Rapaport, Gill, & Schafer, 1945) version of the Goldstein–Scheerer object sorting test along two dimensions. Performance was measured both in terms of conceptual level (open–closed), representing the subject's ability to abstract common attributes, and conceptual areas (private–public), reflecting the degree of social communicability of a concept sorting. McGaughran and Moran tested two groups: chronic and paranoid schizophrenics, comparing them with hospitalized nonpsychiatric controls. They reported two areas of significant differences in conceptual level responses. First, schizophrenics produced fewer failures than controls. This finding is opposite of Goldstein's prediction, because Goldstein considered failures as instances of concreteness. Secondly, schizophrenics produced more responses that were so overly generalized that no clear sorting was possible, but nevertheless were abstract in nature. McGaughran and Moran's analysis of conceptual level indicated that schizophrenics were capable of making abstractions, but their abstractions were frequently unusual or vague.

Several studies testing the abstraction impairment hypothesis have employed multi-test, multi-measure designs. As mentioned earlier, this procedure is designed to combine several aspects of abstraction. These studies have also compared the loss of abstraction construct with the overinclusion construct. Payne, Mattussek, and George (1959) compared acute schizophrenics with neurotics on the Goldstein–Scheerer Object Sorting test and the Benjamin Proverbs test. Schizophrenics were found to be significantly more concrete on the object sorting measure, but were not significantly different on the proverbs measure. In a follow-up study, Payne (1962) compared depressives, acute schizophrenics, neurotics, and normals on the same measures and found significant differences on both object sorting and proverbs measures. Schizophrenics were considered the most concrete. Herron (1962) reported significantly more concreteness from process versus reactive schizophrenic subjects compared on five measures of abstraction.

Research findings have generally not supported the loss of abstraction hypothesis. The object sorting findings do not consistently support the view that schizophrenics cannot generate logical or abstract sortings. Although early studies have claimed to demonstrate a logical deficit, most later investigations have failed to distinguish between schizophrenic and nonschizophrenics. In addition, free-form object sorting measures do not accurately discriminate between pseudological and logical sortings. The results of proverb interpretation and similarities are similarly inconsistent. The relation between these procedures and logical reasoning is also dubious.

The next empirical literature examined concerns the overinclusion hypothesis. Nine variations of object classification tests, all modifications of the original Goldstein–Scheerer Object Sorting Test, have been used in the evaluation of overinclusion. The Payne Classification Test (1962) is generally regarded as the best of the object sorting evaluations of overinclusion. The test consists of presenting subjects with 12 objects varying in weight, thickness, and so forth, and asking subjects to form as many collections as possible. Payne identifies 10 correct classification strategies. He reasoned that schizophrenics would generate more than 10 classes (overinclude) by forming classes based on nonrelevant stimulus dimensions.

One problem with the overinclusion versions of object sorting tasks that is relevant to the issue of reasoning, is that it is not automatically the case that *irrelevant* sortings are illogical, although they may be psychopathological. The logicality of sortings or abstractions are not measured by their relevance but whether they violate rules of identity, contradiction, and excluded middle. Sortings based on obscure sorting strategies can be overly concrete, bizarre, and nonadaptive but logically valid. Problems in the relevancy or obscurity of sorting criteria more closely resembles McGaughran and Moran's (1956, 1957) view that schizophrenics' sortings are idiosyncratic. Consequently, overinclusive sorting may not be very meaningful, but they may, nevertheless, be logically valid.

The empirical literature on overinclusion can be divided into three overlapping areas. The first, representing the early studies, is concerned with validating the overinclusion hypothesis itself (Cameron, 1939, 1944, 1947; Cameron & Magaret, 1951; Chapman, 1961; Epstein, 1953; Goldstein & Salzman, 1965; Craig, 1965; Foulds, Hope, McPherson & Mayo, 1967; Lothrup, 1960; Moran, 1953; Payne, 1962; Payne, Caird, & Laverty, 1964; Payne & Hewlett, 1960; Payne, Mattussek, & George, 1959; Phillips, Jacobson, & Turner, 1965; Watson, 1967; Zaslow, 1949). A second set area focuses on the relationship among various overinclusion measures, especially regarding their performance as diagnostic or prognostic indicators of schizophrenia (Andreasen & Powers, 1974; Bromet & Harrow, 1973; Craig, 1965; Craig & Verinis, 1979; Datson, King, & Armitage, 1953; Foulds, Hope, McPherson, & Mayo, 1967; Hammer & Johnson, 1965; Hawks, 1964; Hawks & Payne, 1971; Payne, Hawks, Friedlander, & Hart, 1972; Payne &

Friedlander, 1962; Watson, 1967). A third category of studies assumes the presence of overinclusion and is concerned instead with evaluating specific explanatory hypotheses for overinclusion (Al-Issa, 1972; Davis & Blaney, 1976; Harrow, Himmelhoch, Tucker, Hersch, & Quinlan, 1972; Johnson & Bieliauskas, 1971; Knight, Sherer, & Shapiro, 1977; Knight, Sims-Knight, & Petchers-Cassell, 1977; Payne & Caird, 1967; Payne, Hochberg, & Hawks, 1970). These investigations emphasize attention deficits and are not concerned with overinclusion as a problem of reasoning: Therefore, these will not be reviewed further. With respect to this third category, Harrow et al. (1972) identified three isomorphic categories of overinclusion (behavioral, conceptual, and perceptual) and attribute different causal mechanisms to each. These authors identify the concerns of reasoning with conceptual overinclusion, but they attribute this overinclusion to perceptual disorganization.

The first category of overinclusion research consists of early anecdotal reports by Cameron (1938, 1939, 1944, 1947; Cameron & Magaret, 1951). Subsequent investigations on overinclusion have generally supported Cameron's hypothesis but suffer from a similar conceptual flaw seen in the Goldstein loss of abstraction hypothesis. A difficulty with the overinclusion construct is that a large number of relatively dissimilar experimental procedures have been accepted as valid measures of overinclusion. These measures include number of words produced in a proverb interpretation, (Payne & Friedlander, 1962), number of objects classified (Payne, 1962) number of incorrect guesses in a multiple-choice auditory recognition test (Payne & Caird, 1967), underlining of conceptually related words (Epstein, 1953), and tasks requiring judgments of circularity and triangularity (Zaslow, 1949). In many cases, the defining operational characteristics of these tasks are only distantly related.

Epstein (1953), for example, presented subjects with a stimulus word and number of response words. Subjects were required to underline response words they felt were an essential part of the concept denoted by the stimulus. Epstein reported that schizophrenics underlined significantly more response words than 45 normals matched for age and vocabulary level: He concluded that schizophrenics formed overincluded categories. Moran (1953) and Datson, King, and Armitage (1953) reported similar examples of overinclusion. Moran (1953) and Datson, King, and Armitage (1953) have been criticized, however, because of confounding effects of vocabulary and intelligence (Gathercole, 1965). Gathercole's criticism is especially relevant, because overinclusion is purported to be a reasoning deficit. He criticized object classification, proverb interpretation, and verbal expansiveness measures by pointing out that high scores on each measure can be obtained by excessive responding, without reference to particular, qualitative conceptual (logical) aberration. Hawks and Payne (1971) reported data that support Gathercole's interpretation. Hawks and Payne found significant correlations (.39–.59) between measures of overinclusion and talkativeness.

Zaslow (1949) developed a simple test of overinclusion consisting of a series of 14 cards, each containing a drawing that gradually progressed from an equilateral triangle to a perfect circle. In the study, cards were placed in order, and subjects were required to identify cards fitting into either the circle or the triangle category. As predicted, schizophrenic subjects included significantly more cards in each category. Zaslow interpreted this as indicating that schizophrenics's categories tended to be overly broad or overinclusive. This task, however, is more closely related to concept formation (definition of triangle and circle) rather than a problem in reasoning, and it may also be interpreted as an example of excessive responding rather than the ability to form mutually exclusive (logical) categories.

The second area of research is concerned with the relationship between overinclusion measures. Payne and Hewlett (1960) tested 20 normals, 20 neurotics, 20 depressives, and 20 schizophrenics matched for age, sex, occupational level, and vocabulary performance on a large number of measures, including three measures of overinclusion (Payne OCT, a modification of the Benjamin Proverbs Test, and a modified version of the Goldstein–Sheerer Object Sorting Test). A factor analytic evaluation of subject group performances of the 68 measures obtained revealed no differences between neurotic and normal subjects. Three measures were obtained that Payne and Hewlett called overinclusion, psychoticism, and retardation. the two remaining groups were combined and shown to differe significantly from the combined normals and neurotics. The schizophrenics scored higher on overinclusion, and the depressives scored significantly higher on retardation. Utilizing data collected in two previous studies (Payne, Mattussek, & George, 1959; Payne & Hewlett, 1960) and new data, Payne (1962) evaluated the performance of 120 normals and 34 neurotics, 20 depressives, 35 acute schizophrenics, and 37 chronic schizophrenics on object classification. Payne reported that only acute and chronic schizophrenics produced significantly fewer appropriate sortings than normals sortings. These findings were followed up by a multi-measure investigation (Payne, Caird, & Laverty, 1964) that evaluated 15 paranoid schizophrenics, 15 nondelusional schizophrenics, and 15 controls on the Benjamin Proverbs Test, the Mill Hill Vocabulary Scale, and three of Babcock's Psychomotor Speed Tests. Based on average number of words used in explaining proberbs, it was concluded that there was a significant positive relationship between the presence of delusions and overinclusive thinking. This data has been subject to criticism, however, from investigators who were unable to reproduce these results (Goldstein & Salzman, 1965; Hawks, 1964; Hawks & Payne, 1971). Number of words used in proverbs is also subject to the previously cited problem (Gathercole, 1965) that overinclusion is excessive responding rather than an abstraction impairment. Overinclusion has been related to paranoid delusions and ideas of reference, because both represent types of unwarranted generalizations.

Watson (1967), evaluating the relations between overinclusion measures, found verbal expansiveness unrelated to proverb interpretation and object sorting measures. Phillips, Jacobsen, and Turner (1965) and Desai (1960) found verbal responsiveness measures unrelated to the Payne Object Classification Test. Investigators of overinclusion (Hawks, 1964; Payne, Hawks, Friedlander, & Hart, 1972; Phillips, Jacobson, & Turner, 1965; Watson, 1967) have criticized the validity of summing batteries of overinclusion measures, citing weak and inconsistent correlations between measures, and inconsistent findings when comparing acute and chronic schizophrenics.

Overinclusion has been regarded as a distinctive cognitive deficit in which schizophrenics generate illogical sortings, because they fail to exclude irrelevant or unrelated elements in their collections. Many different procedures have been devised to demonstrate that schizophrenics do not generate clear categories. The underlying rationale in these studies is that schizophrenics do not possess concepts that are governed by the logical principles of identity, contradiction, and excluded middle. Similar to investigations of loss of abstraction, the logical features of class formation are best revealed by object classification tasks. The object classification tests used to measure overinclusion, however, suffer from the same difficulty previously discussed. These measures do not clearly discriminate between logical and illogical sortings. These findings do, however, support the idea that schizophrenics are able to generalize, refuting Goldstein's notion that schizophrenics are excessively concrete. Other measures that have been employed to measure overinclusion are less closely connected to the logical kernel of the overinclusion construct and are frequently confounded with other variables such as level of verbal responsiveness.

We now turn to empirical investigations concerned with abstractions and classification from a Piagetian point of view. Despite the theoretical interest in class formation in psychopathological populations, and its relation to the development of logic structures during concrete operations, very few empirical studies have explicitly explored this area from a Piagetian viewpoint. Approaches to thought disorder by Piagetians concerned with class logic competence reflect the assumption that disordered thinking represents a form of cognitive regression (Inhelder, 1968, 1971; Bosen, 1985; Strauss, 1967). This regression assumption accounts for the general design of studies in which schizophrenic performance on various tasks of logical competence is contrasted explicitly with cognitively developmentally normal children.

Trunnel (1964, 1965) reported data from two studies in which it was hypothesized that adult schizophrenics and cognitively normal children would perform similarly on concrete operational tasks. Trunnel (1964) was especially concerned to compare adult schizophrenics and children on classification and seriation tasks. In the first study, a battery of four tests (similarities, color form sorting test, a puzzle tests involving conjunctive class formation and seriation, and a test of logical multiplication) was administered to 10 normal children, 10 adult controls, and 10 hospitalized schizophrenics. The schizophrenic subjects were predominantly acute/reactive schizophrenics. Three, however, had been diagnosed as process or chronic schizophrenics, based on long periods of hospitalization. The most interesting tasks employed were traditional Piagetian tasks measuring concept formation and seriation. In the puzzles series, subjects were given four puzzles: two puzzles involved classification (e.g., If this animal has long ears, it is a mule or a donkey; If it has a thick tail, it is a mule or a horse. This animal has long ears and a thick tail, what is it?). Two other puzzles involved transitivity (e.g., Edith is fairer than Suzanne, who is darker than Lili; Who is the darkest, Edith, Suzanne, or Lili?). Trunnel hypothesized that schizophrenics would perform similarly to preoperational children, who are unable to simultaneously consider information in both premises, and would fixate on part aspects or single predications and form incorrect conclusions (Piaget, 1928; pp. 88, 161). Both children and schizophrenics in this condition lacking a grasp or part-whole relations would have fewer correct solutions to the problems, request more information in attempting to solve the problems, and would be less able to offer logically valid explanations for their answers (even if making the correct choice).

The results generally confirmed Trunnel's hypotheses. Performance was measured both in terms of subtest scores and reasons given for the performance. Both measures were collapsed into a single-rank ordering. Adult normal controls performed mroe logically on all four measures. Significant differences were found between adult controls and schizophrenics, and adult controls and the children, but not between the adult schizophrenics and children. It was concluded that schizophrenics and normal children did reason and perform similarly on cognitive tasks designed to assess class formation and seriation. Adult schizophrenics appeared to be less able than normal adults to classify and declassify conjunctive concepts. In addition, Trunnel has contended that adult schizophrenics, like their child counterparts, are less able to form accurate judgments about relationships involving multiple simultaneous variables.

In a follow-up study, Trunnel (1965) included a larger sample (24 subjects in each cell) and several new measures of class formation. In this study, the color form sorting and the chemical multiplication task were eliminated and replaced with Vygotsky's Object Sorting Test and a different version of a combinatorial analysis task (subjects were asked to see how many combinations of two colors they can form with colored poker chips). Care was also taken to control for scoring bias (single blind procedure), enhance intertester reliability, match subject variables (sex, age, and education), and weight both the experimental and control groups with high levels of educational advancement. Subjects had successfully completed an average 2.5 years of undergraduate study. In addition, none of the subjects were actively psychotic at the time of testing. The child control group ranged from 6 years to 11 years of age, with most falling into the lower end of the age range. Trunnel also decreased the likelihood of low IQ measures confounding the results by including only schizophrenic subjects with some college education. Similarities between child controls and adult schizophrenics would not result from similar educational level or a global intellectual deficit.

In the original study, Trunnel hypothesized that on all measures of class logic (similarities, puzzles involving multiplication of classes and seriation, the object sorting, and the combinatorial task) schizophrenics and normal children would perform more poorly than normal adults. In the puzzles task, schizophrenics and normal children were expected to have fewer correct solutions and fewer complete logical explanations, giving answers based on one attribute or one relationship. Similarly, in the Vygotsky object sorting task, schizophrenic subjects and children were expected to have difficulty forming as many groups as normals. Moreover, it was predicted that schizophrenic and normal children would form complexes or groups based on criteria other than simple class membership. In the combinatorial task, Trunnel argued, experimental subjects would form fewer combinations than controls.

Generally speaking, the hypotheses were confirmed. There were differences in performance between schizophrenics and adults, and adults and children, on all four measures. There were significant differences, however, between schizophrenics and the children controls on the similarities task and the puzzles task. Comparisons of children and schizophrenic subjects on object sorting and formation of combinations were insignificant. Comparisons of children and schizophrenics on the puzzles test and the similarities test was significant. Schizophrenics performed more competently on these measures. Trunnel treated the significant differences between schizophrenics and child subjects as indicating that the breakdown of cognitive processing characteristic of a thought-disordered patient is not a matter of simple regression. Superior performance by schizophrenics (vs. the children controls) on tasks heavily dependent on verbal ability indicates that performance deficits on reasoning related and are not a reflection of a simple and more global intellectual regression to "childlike" intelligence. The "no difference" results on measures on more logically complex tasks (object sorting task and then combination problem) support the reasoning regression hypothesis.


## FORMAL OPERATIONS
## AND REASONING PATHOLOGY
## IN THOUGHT-DISORDERED POPULATIONS:
## EMPIRICAL INVESTIGATIONS

No research specifically concerned with deductive inferences appears in the thought disorder literature. One study on the correct formation of analogs is reported here. A study presented by Kilburg and Siegel (1973) compares the performance of process and reactive schizophrenics on the Lunzer Analogies Test. They predicted that both process and reactive schizophrenics should perform more poorly on formal oerational tasks, and that process schizophrenics, because of the effects of chronicity, should perform even more poorly than reactive schizophrenics. One difficulty, however, appears in the procedure for subject selection. Although process and reactive subtypes were distinguished by both the Phillips (1953) Prognostic Rating Scale and Ullmann and Giovannoni's (1964) Self-Report Inventory, there was a very small difference between subgroups on length of hospitalization, a significant criteria in subtyping schizophrenics. Because length of hospitalization is one of the dimensions that distinguishes process and reactive schizophrenics, and, as the authors note, other investigators might classify these reactives schizophrenics as process schizophrenics, the design is potentially left with only one experimental group rather than two. Kilburg and Siegel themselves noted this problem but suggested that inclusion of "long term reactives" in the reactive schizophrenic subgroup provides the opportunity to make a more conservative test of the hypothesis.

Both experimental subjects and control subjects were administered the Lunzer Analogies Test, a Self-Report Inventory, and the WAIS vocabulary subtest. Experimental subjects completed all of the measures during one testing period (although they were given as much time as they needed). By contrast, control subjects were provided with "take-home" packets of the same test measures. No comment is made on the possible confounding effects of this variation in procedure, except to note that control subjects were encouraged to do the work on their own and return the packets quickly.

The Lunzer Analogies Test consists of four subtests (Analogies I, Analogies II, Number Relations, Number Series) designed to capture an individual's ability to reason with second order relations (relations between relations). A significant main effect for groups was reported. Normal subjects performed better than both process and reactive schizophrenics, and reactive schizophrenics performed more competently than process schizophrenics. In addition, the same linear trend was reported for each Lunzer Analogies subtest. These results remained consistent when the covariation of verbal intelligence (WAIS scores) was statistically controlled for.

These results, however, do not necessarily reflect a reasoning deficit, because the Lunzer Analogies Test appears to more closely resembles concept formation and does not measure the validity of deductive inferences.

## CONCLUSION: REASONING PATHOLOGY AND THOUGHT DISORDER

This chapter has reviewed a series of research findings concerned with the problems of logical reasoning and thought pathology. The obvious conclusion is that despite various clinical interpretations and theoretical approaches, there is currently little empirical research currently available that speaks directly to the relationship between deductive reasoning and thought pathology. Much of the research that purports to evaluate reasoning in the schizophrenic does not evaluate reasoning at all. A small amount of literature that isolates the logical structures required for classification and class logic indicates that schizophrenics are deficient in their ability to form true logical classes or understand class logic relations. The larger portion of this research, however, does not effectively isolate the logical requirements of classification. Empirical research on syllogistic inferences does not support the notion that schizophrenics are logically deficient or have regressed to less mature forms of reasoning. Virtually no research has been done on more advanced forms of deductive inferences, associated in a Piagetian model, with formal operations. Research is needed addressing the question of whether schizophrenics reason in a faulty fashion in tasks assessing propositional or predicate logic, and whether performance deficits in logics requiring formal operational structures are related to other logical-structural deficits in the schizophrenic.

The second concern of this review was to evaluate available empirical evidence to determine whether, within the logical competence framework, cognitive regression or moderator variables explanations were empirically supported. Currently, no empirical research has specially addressed which of these hypotheses is correct. Inhelder (1971) has suggested that psychotic children do possess a partial competence, but perform poorly on problems involving inductions, suggesting the presence of decalage or developmental delay (Rosen, 1985). Siomopoulos (1983) argued with Arieti (1955) that intact reasoning becomes impaired when affective themes interfere with the reasoning process. Whether a reasoning deficit is described as the result of a stage regression or moderator variables appears to depend on how long the impairment manifests itself and whether it appears in a few or many decisions made by the individual. Further empirical comparisons of these models are needed.

The field of psychopathology has been framed, for many years, by the notion that schizophrenics and other clinical populations manifesting thought disorders suffer from "reasoning" impairments. Schizophrenics have frequently been labeled as irrational, illogical, or faulty reasoners. In light of the present review, there is not sufficient evidence to warrant this conclusion. In fact, many empirical investigators have abandoned the reasoning construct altogether in their analysis of thought disorder, turning to other cognitive constructs, especially information processing constructs. This review suggests, however, that it is possible that the principal problem with reasoning research to date is not that schizophrenics might not have a reasoning competence deficit, but that many of the procedures used to examine reasoning and deduction are fundamentally inadequate. Procedures that highlight logical structures represent a promising alternative to traditional reasoning measures.

## ACKNOWLEDGMENTS

We would like to express our gratitude to Nora Newcombe, Ron Taylor, Diana Woodruff-Pak, Hugh Rosen, and Terry Brown for their helpful comments on this chapter.

## REFERENCES

Al-Issa, I. (1972). Stimulus generalization and overinclusion in normal and schizophrenic subjects. *Journal of Consulting and Clinical Psychology, 39*(2), 182–186.

American Psychiatric Association, (1987). *Diagnostic and Statistical Neudl, Third Education—Revised.* Washington D.: American Psychiatric Assoc.

Andreason, N., & Powers, P. (1974). Overinclusion thinking in mania and schizophrenia. *British Journal of Psychiatry, 125,* 452–456.

Andreason, N., Tsuang, M., & Canter, A. (1974) The significance of thought disorder in diagnostic evaluations. *Comprehensive Psychiatry, 15*(1), 27–34.

Arieti, S. (1955). *Interpretation of Schizophrenia.* New York: Brunner.

Bateson, G., Jackson, D., Haley, J., & Weakland, J. (1956). Toward a theory of schizophrenia. *Behavioral Science, 1,* 251–264.

Bleuler, E. (1911). *Dementia praecox or the group of schizophrenias.* New York: International Universities Press.

Bolles, M., & Goldstein, K. (1938). A study of the impairment of "abstract behavior" in schizophrenic patients. *Psychiatric Quarterly, 12,* 42–65.

Boole, G. (1854). *An investigation of the laws of thought.* London: Walton & Maberly.

Braine, M. D. S. (1978). On the relation between the natural logic of reasoning and standard logic. *Psychological Review, 85,* 1–21.

Braine, M. D. S., & Rumain, B. (1983). Logical reasoning. In J. H. Flavell & E. M. Markman (Eds.), *Handbook of child psychology. Vol. 3. Cognitive development* (pp. 263–340). New York: Wiley.

Broen, W. (1966). Response disorganization and breadth of observation in schizoprenia. *Psychological Review, 73*(6), 579–585.

Broen, W., & Storms, L. (1966). Lawful disorganization: The process underlying a schizophrenic syndrome. *Psychological Review, 73*(4), 265–279.

Bromet, E., & Harrow, M. (1973). Behavioral overinclusion as a prognostic index of schizophrenic disorders. *Journal of Abnormal Psychology, 82*(2), 345–349.

Buss, A. H., & Lang, P. J. (1965). Psychological deficit in schizophrenia: I. Affect, reinforcement, and concept attainment. *Journal of Abnormal Psychology, 70*(1), 2–24.

Byrnes, J. P., & Overton, W. F. (1986). Reasoning about certainty and uncertainty in concrete, causal, and propositional contexts. *Developmental Psychology, 22,* 793–799.

Callaway, E., & Naghdi, S. (1982). An information processing model for schizophrenia. *Archives of General Psychiatry, 39,* 339–347.

Cameron, N. (1938). Reasoning, regression and communication in schizophrenics. *Psychological Monographs, 50,* No. 221, 1–33.

Cameron, N. (1939). Deterioration and regression in schizophrenic thinking. *Journal of Abnormal and Social Psychology, 34,* 265–270.

Cameron, N. (1944). Experimental analysis of schizophrenic thinking. In J. Kasanin (Ed.), *Language and thought in schizophrenia.* New York: Norton.

Cameron, N. (1947). *The psychology of behavior disorders.* Boston: Houghton Mifflin.

Cameron, N., & Magaret, A. (1951). *Behavior Pathology.* Boston: Houghton Mifflin.

Chaika, E. (1982). Thought disorder or speech disorder in schizophrenia? *Schizophrenia Bulletin, 8*(4), 587–590.

Chaika, E., & Lamb, R. (1985). The locus of dysfunction in schizophrenic speech. *Schizophrenia Bulletin, 11*(1), 8–14.

Chapman, L. J. (1961). A reinterpretation of some pathological disturbances in conceptual breadth. *Journal of Abnormal and Social Psychology, 62*, 514–519.

Chapman, L. J., & Chapman, J. P. (1959). Atmosphere effect re-examined. *Journal of Experimental Psychology, 58*, 220–226.

Chapman, L. J., & Taylor, J. (1957). Breadth of deviate concepts used by schizophrenics. *Journal of Abnormal and Social Psychology, 54*, 118–124.

Cicchetti, D. (1984). The emergence of developmental psychopathology. *Child Development, 55*(1), 1–7.

Copi, I. M. (1968). *Introduction to logic.* New York: Macmillan.

Cox, J. R., & Griggs, R. A. (1982). The effects of experience on performance in Wason's selection task. *Memory and Cognition, 10*, 496–502.

Craig, W. J. (1965). Objective measures of thinking integrated with psychiatric symptoms. *Psychological Reports, 16*, 539–546.

Craig, R., & Verinis, J. S. (1979). Evidence for organicity in concrete vs. overinclusive thought-disordered schizophrenics. *Journal of Clinical Psychology, 35*(4), 696–703.

Datson, P. G., King, G. F., & Armitage, S. G. (1953). Distortion in paranoid schizophrenia. *Journal of Consulting Psychology, 17*, 50–53.

Davis, K., & Blaney, P. (1976). Overinclusion and self-editing in schizophrenia. *Journal of Abnormal Psychology, 85*(1), 51–60.

Desai, M. M. (1960). Intelligence and verbal knowledge in Epstein's overinclusion test. *Journal of Clinical Psychology, 16*, 417–419.

Elmore, C. M., & Gorham, D. (1957). Measuring the impairment of the abstracting function with the proverb test. *Journal of Clinical Psychology, 13*, 263–266.

Epstein, S. (1953). Overinclusive thinking in a schizophrenic and control group. *Journal of Consulting Psychology, 17*(5), 384–388.

Evans, J. St. B. T. (1977). Toward a statistical theory of reasoning. *Quarterly Journal of Experimental Psychology, 29*, 621–635.

Evans, J. St. B. T. (1982). *The psychology of deductive reasoning.* London: Routledge & Kegan Paul.

Evans, J. St. B. T. (1983). Selective processes in erasoning. In J. St. B. T. Evans (Ed.), *Thinking and reasoning: Psychological approaches* (pp. 135–163). London: Routledge & Kegan Paul.

Falmagne, R. J. (1975). *Reasoning: Representation and process in children and adults.* Hillsdale, NJ: Lawrence Erlbaum Associates.

Fey, E. (1951). The performance of young schizophrenics and young normals on the Wisconsin card sorting test. *Journal of Consulting Psychology, 15*, 311–319.

Fodor, J. A. (1980). On the impossibility of acquiring "more powerful" structures. In M. Piattelli-Palmarini (Ed.), *Language and learning: The debate between Jean Piaget and Noam Chomsky* (pp. 142–162). Cambridge, MA: Harvard University Press.

Foulds, G., Hope, K., McPherson, F. M., & Mayo, P. R. (1967). Cognitive disorder among the schizophrenias, I. The validity of some tests of thought-process disorder. *British Journal of Psychiatry, 113*, 1361–1368.

Garmezy, N. (1977). The psychology and psychopathology of attention. *Schizophrenia Bulletin, 3*(3), 360–369.

Gathercole, C. E. (1965). A note on some tests of "overinclusive thinking." *British Journal of Medical Psychology, 38*, 59–62.

Geis, M., & Zwicky, A. M. (1971). On invited inference. *Linguistic Inquiry, 2*, 561–566.

George, L. & Neufeld, R. (1985). Cognition and symptomatology in schizophrenia. *Schizophrenia Bulletin, 11*(2), 264–285.

Gjerde, P. (1983). Attentional capacity dysfunction and arousal in schizophrenia. *Psychological Bulletin, 93*(1), 57–72.

Goldstein, K. (1939). Special mental tests in Schizophrenia. *Journal of Abnormal and Social Psychology, 74*, 575–587.

Goldstein, K. (1944). Methodological approach to the study of schizophrenic thought disorder. In J. Kasanin (Eds.), *Language and Thought in Schizophrenia*. New York: Norton.

Goldstein, R., & Salzman, L. (1965). Proverb word counts as a measure of overinclusiveness in delusional schizophrenics. *Journal of Abnormal Psychology, 70*(4), 244–245.

Goldstein, K., & Scheerer, M. (1941). Abstract and concrete behavior: An experimental study with special tests. *Psychological Monographs, 53*(2, Whole No. 239).

Gorham, D. (1956). Use of the proverbs test for differentiating schizophrenics from normals. *Journal of Consulting Psychology, 20*(6), 435–440.

Gottesman, L., & Chapman, L. J. (1960). Syllogistic reasoning errors in schizophrenia. *Journal of Consulting Psychology, 24*, 250–255.

Griggs, R. A. (1983). The role of problem content in the selection task and in the THOG problem. In J. St. B. T. Evans (Ed.), *Thinking and Reasoning: Psychological approaches* (pp. 16–43). London: Routledge & Kegan Paul.

Grove, W., & Andreasen, N. (1985). Language ad thinking in psychosis: Is there an input abnormality. *Archives of General Psychiatry, 42*, 26–32.

Hammer, A. G., & Johnson, L. (1965). Overinclusiveness in schizophrenia and organic psychosis. *British Journal of Social and Clinical Psychology, 4*, 47–51.

Hanfmann, E., & Kasanin, J. (1937). A method for the study of concept formation. *Journal of Psychology, 3*, 521–540.

Hanfmann, E., Kasanin, J. (1942). Conceptual thinking in schizophrenia. *Nervous and Mental Disease Monographs, No. 67*.

Harrow, M., Himmelhoch, J., Tucker, G., Hersch, J., & Quinlan, D. (1972). Overinclusive thinking in acute schizophrenic patients. *Journal of Abnormal Psychology, 79*(2), 161–168.

Hawks, D. (1964). The clinical usefulness of some tests of over-inclusive thinking in psychiatric patients. *British Journal of Social and Clinical Psychology, 3*, 186–195.

Hawks, D., & Payne, R. (1971). Overinclusive thought disorder and symptomatology. *British Journal of Psychiatry, 118*, 663–670.

Hemsley, D. R. (1975). A two-stage model of attention in schizophrenia research. *British Journal of Social and Clinical Psychology, 14*, 81–89.

Henle, M. (1962). On the relation between logic and thinking. *Psychological Review, 69*, 366–378.

Herron, W. G. (1962). Abstract ability in the process-reactive classification of schizophrenia. *Journal of General Psychology, 67*, 147–154.

Inhelder, B. (1968). *The diagnosis of reasoning in the mentally retarded*. New York: Day.

Inhelder, B. (1971). Developmental theory and diagnostic procedures. In D. R. Green, M. P. Ford, & G. B. Flamer (Eds.), *Measurement and Piaget*. (pp. 148–171). New York: McGraw-Hill.

Inhelder, B., & Piaget, J. (1958). *The growth of logical thinking from childhood to adolescence*. New York: Basic Books.

Inhelder, B., & Piaget, J. (1969). *The early growth of logic in the child*. New York: Norton.

Jacobs, M. R. (1969). *The effect of interpersonal content on the logical performance of schizophrenics*. Unpublished doctoral dissertation, Case Western University.

Johnson, J., & Bieliauskas, L. (1971). Two measures of overinclusive thinking in schizophrenia. *Journal of Abnormal Psychology, 77*(2), 149–154.

Johnson-Laird, P. N., & Steedman, M. (1978). The psychology of syllogisms. *Cognitive Psychology, 10*, 64–98.

Kasanin, J. S. (1944). The disturbance of conceptual thinking in schizophrenia. In J. S. Kasanin (Ed.), *Language and thought in schizophrenia* (pp. 41–49). New York: Norton.

Kasanin, J., & Hanfmann, E. (1937). An experimental study of concept formation in schizophrenia. *American Journal of Psychiatry, 95*, 3552.

Kilburg, R., & Siegel, A. (1973). Formal operations in reactive and process schizophrenics. *Journal of Consulting and Clinical Psychology, 40*, 371–376.

Knight, R. A., Sherer, M., & Shapiro, J. (1977). Iconic imagery in overinclusive and nonoverinclusive schizophrenics. *Journal of Abnormal Psychology, 86*(3), 242–255.

Knight, R. A., Sims-Knight, J., & Petchers-Cassell M. (1977). Overinclusion, broad scanning, and picture recognition in schizophrenics. *Journal of Clinical Psychology, 33*(3), 635–642.

Langer, J. (1986). *The Origins of logic: One to two years*. Orlando FL: Academic Press.

Levin, M. (1938). Misunderstanding the pathogenesis of schizophrenia, arising from the concept of "splitting." *American Journal of Psychiatry, 94*, 877–889.

Lidz, T., Fleck, S., & Cornelison, A. (1965). *Schizophrenia and the family*. New York: International Universities Press.

Lothrop, W. (1960). Psychological test covariates of conceptual deficit in schizophrenia. *Journal of Consulting Psychology, 24*(6), 496–499.

Mandler, J. M. (1983). Structural invariants in development. In L. S. Liben (Ed.), *Piaget and the foundation of knowledge* (pp. 97–124). Hillsdale: NJ: Lawrence Erlbaum Associates.

Markman, E. M., & Seibert, J. (1976). Classes and collections: Internal organization and resulting holistic properties. *Cognitive Psychology, 8*, 561–577.

McGaughran, L. S. (1957). Differences between schizophrenic and brain damaged groups in conceptual aspects of object sorting. *Journal of Abnormal and Social Psychology, 54*, 44–49.

McGaughran, L., & Moran, L. (1956). "Conceptual level" vs. "conceptual area" analysis of object sorting behavior of schizophrenic and non-psychiatric groups. *Journal of Abnormal and Social Psychology, 52*, 43–50.

McGaughran, L., & Moran, L. (1957). Differences between schizophrenic and brain damaged groups in conceptual aspects of object sorting. *Journal of Abnormal and Social Psychology, 54*, 44–49.

Mednick, S. (1958). A learning theory approach to research in schizophrenia. *Psychological Bulletin, 55*(5), 316–327.

Moran, L. J. (1953). Vocabulary knowledge and usage among normal and schizophrenic subjects. *Psychological Monographs, 67*, No. 20 (whole No. 370).

Nims, J. P. (1959). *Logical reasoning in schizophrenia: The Von Domarus principle*. Unpublished doctoral dissertation, University of California.

Nuechterlein, K., & Dawson, M. (1984). Information processing and attentional functioning in the developmental course of schizophrenic disorders. *Schizophrenia Bulletin, 10*(2), 160–203.

O'Brien, D., & Overton, W. F. (1980). Conditional reasoning following contradictory evidence: A developmental analysis of a training task. *Journal of experimental child psychology, 30*, 44–60.

O'Brien, D., & Overton, W. F. (1982). Conditional reasoning and the competence–performance issue: A developmental analysis of a training task. *Journal of Experimental Child Psychology, 34*, 274–290.

Olver, R. R., & Hornsby, J. R. (1966). On equivalence. In J. S. Bruner, R. R. Olver, and P. M. Greenfield (Eds.), *Studies in Cognitive Growth*. New York: Wiley.

Overton, W. F. (1984). World views and their influence on psychological theory and research: Kuhn—Lakatos—Laudan. In H. W. Reese (Eds.), *Advances in child development and behavior. Vol 18*. (pp. 191–226). New York: Academic Press.

Overton, W. F. (1985). Scientific methodologies and the competence–moderator–performance issue. In E. Neimark, R. DeLisi, & J. Newman (Eds.), *Moderators of competence* (pp. 15–41). Hillsdale NJ: Lawrence Erlbaum Associates.

Overton, W. F., Byrnes, J. P., & O'Brien, D. (1985). Developmental and individual differences in conditional reasoning: The role of contradiction training and cognitive style. *Developmental Psychology, 21*, 692–701.

Overton, W. F., & Newman, J. (1982). Cognitive development: A competence-activation/utilization approach. In T. Field, A. Houston, H. Quay, L. Troll, & G. Finley (Eds.), *Review of human development* (pp. 217–241). New York: Wiley.

Overton, W. F., Ward, S. L., Black, J. S., Noveck, I. A., & O'Brien, D. (1987). Form and content in the development of deductive reasoning. *Developmental Psychology, 23*(1), 22–30.

Payne, R. (1962). An object classification test as a measure of overinclusive thinking in schizophrenic patients. *British Journal of Social and Clinical Psychology, 1*, 213–231.

Payne, R., & Caird, W. (1967). Reaction time, distractibility and overinclusive thinking in psychotics. *Journal of Abnormal Psychology, 72*(2), 112–121.

Payne, R., Caird, W., & Laverty, S. (1964). Overinclusive thinking and delusions in schizophrenic patients. *Journal of Abnormal and Social Psychology, 68*(5), 562–566.

Payne, R., & Friedlander, D. (1962). A short battery of simple tests for measuring overinclusive thinking. *Journal of Mental Science, 198*, 362–367.

Payne, R., Hawks, D., Friedlander, D., & Hart, D. (1972). The diagnostic significance of overinclusive thinking in an unselected psychiatric populatio. *British Journal of Psychiatry, 120*, 173–182.

Payne, R., & Hewlett, J. H. G. (1960). Thought disorder in psychotic patients. In H. J. Eyseneck (Ed.), *Experiments in personality, Vol. II Psychodiagnostics and psychodynamics* (pp. 3–104). London: Routledge & Kegan Paul.

Payne, R., Hochberg, A., & Hawks, D. (1970). Dichotic stimulation as a method of assessing disorder of attention in overinclusive schizophrenic patients. *Journal of Abnormal Psychology, 76*(2), 185–193.

Payne, R., Mattussek, P., & George, E. I. (1959). An experimental study of schizophrenic thought disorder. *Journal of Mental Science, 105*, 627–652.

Phillips, L. (1953). Case history data and prognosis in schizophrenia. *Journal of Nervous and Mental Disorders, 117*, 515–525.

Phillips, J., Jacobson, N., & Turner, W. (1965). Conceptual thinking in schizophrenics and their relatives. *British Journal of Psychiatry, 111*, 823–839.

Piaget, J. (1928). *Judgment and reasoning in the child*. London: Routledge and Kegan Paul.

Piaget, J. (1952). *The origins of intelligence in the child*. New York: International Universities Press.

Piaget, J. (1957). *Logic and psychology*. New York: Basic Books.

Piaget, J. (1962). *Play, dreams and imitation in childhood*. New York: Norton.

Rapaport, D., Gill, M., & Schafer, R. (1945). *Diagnostic psychological testing. Vol. 1*. Chicago: Year Book Publishers.

Rashkis, H. (1947). Three types of thinking disorder. *Journal of Nervous and Mental Disease, 106*, 650–670.

Reed, J. L. (1970). Schizophrenic thought disorder: A review and hypothesis. *Comprehensive Psychiatry, 11*(5), 403–431.

Revlis, R. (1975). Syllogistic reasoning: Logical decisions from a complex data base. In R. Falmagne (Ed.), *Reasoning: Representation and process in children and adults*. New York: Wiley.

Rosch, W., Mervis, C. B., Gray, W. D., Johnson, D. M., & Boyes-Braem, P. (1976). Basic objects in natural categories. *Cognitive Psychology, 8*, 382–439.

Rosen, H. (1985). *Piagetian diensions of clinical relevance*. New York: Columbia University Press.

Russell, B. (1956). *Logic and knowledge*. Boston: Allen and Unwin.

Shimkunas, A. (1972). Conceptual deficit in schizophrenia: A reappraisal. *British Journal of Medical Psychology, 45*, 149–157.

Singer, M. T., & Wynne, L. C. (1965). Thought disorder and family relations of schizophrenics. IV. Results and implications. *Archives of General Psychiatry, 12*, 201–212.

Siomopoulos, V. (1983). *The structure of psychopathological experience*. New York: Brunner Mazel.

Strauss, J. (1967). The classification of schizophrenic concreteness. *Psychiatry, 30*, 294–301.

Thorndike, R. L., & Gallup, G. H. (1944). Verbal intelligence of the American adult. *Journal of General Psychology, 30*, 75–85

Trunnell, T. L. (1964). Thought disturbance in schizophrenia. *Archives of General Psychiatry, 11*, 126–136.

Trunnell, T. L. (1965). Thought disturbance is schizophrenia. *Archives of General Psychiatry, 13*, 9–18.

Ullmann, L. P., & Giovannoni, J. (1964). The development of a self-report measure of the process-reactive continuum. *Journal of Nervous and Mental Disorders, 138*, 38–42.

Vygotsky, L. (1934). Thought in schizophrenia. *Archives of Neurology and Psychiatry, 31*, 1063–1077.

Vygotsky, L. (1962). *Thought and language*. Cambridge MA: MIT Press.

Von Domarus, E. (1944). The specific laws of logic in schizophrenia. In J. S. Kasanin (Ed.), *Language and thought in schizophrenia* (pp. 104–114). Berkeley: University of California Press.

Wason, P. C., & Johnson-Laird, P. N. (1972). *Psychology of reasoning: Structure and content*. Cambridge, MA: Harvard University Press.

Wason, P. C. (1983). Realism and rationality in the selection task. In J. St. B. T. Evans (Ed.), *Thinking and reasoning: Psychological approaches* (pp. 44–75). London: Routledge & Kegan Paul.

Watson, C. (1967). Interrelationships of six overinclusion measures. *Journal of Consulting Psychology, 31*(5), 517–520.

Watson, C. G., & Wold, J. (1981). Logical reasoning deficits in schizophrenia and brain damage. *Journal of Clinical Psychology, 37*(3), 466–471.

Werner, H. (1957). The concept of development from a comparative and organismic point of view. In D. B. Harris (Ed.), *The concept of development: An issue in the study of huma behavior* (pp. 125–147). Minneapolis: University of Minnesota Press.

Wilkins, M. C. (1928). The effect of changed material on the ability to do formal syllogistic reasoning. *Archives of Psychology*, no. 102, New York.

Wilkinson, A. (1976). Counting strategies and semantic analysis as applied to class inclusion. *Cognitive Psychology, 8*, 64–88.

Williams, E. B. (1964). Deductive reasoning in schizophrenia. *Journal of Abnormal and Social Psychology, 69*(1), 47–61.

Wright, D. (1975). Impairment in abstract conceptualization in schizophrenia. *Psychological Bulletin, 82*(1), 120–127.

Wyatt, L. D. (1965). *The significance of emotional content in the logical reasoning ability of schizophrenics*. Unpublished doctoral dissertation, Purdue University.

Zaslow, R. (1949). A new approach to the problem of conceptual thinking in schizophrenia. *Journal of Consulting Psychology, 14*, 335–339.

# APPENDIX A

Traditional or Aristotelian logic centers on the analysis of categorical propositions (Copi, 1968). Categorical propositions are statements about classes, affirming or denying class inclusion, either in part or in whole. Categorical propositions appear in four forms, depending on the quantity (all, some) of the subject, and the quality (denial, affirmation) of the predicate. The four traditional forms are: (a) All "p" are "q." (universal affirmative); (b) Some "p" are "q." (particular affirmative); (c) No "p" are "q." (universal negative); (d) Some "p" are not "q." (particular negative).

Distribution of the terms in a proposition refers to whether or not a particular term (either the subject or the predicate) refers to all members of the class or only some. A term is said to be distributed in a proposition if it applies to every member of the class. The four traditional statement forms differ systematically in the distribution of their subject and predicate terms. In universal propositions, subject terms are always distributed. In negative propositions, predicate terms are always distributed. In the particular affirmative statement, neither subject nor predicate term is distributed. The value of distribution of terms is relfected in solving categorical syllogisms, because in a valid categorical syllogism the middle term can only be distributed once.

A syllogism is a particular argument form consisting of exactly two premises and a conclusion. In a categorical syllogism, both premises and conclusion are statements asserting one of the four traditional class inclusion propositions. Labels are given to denote various components within the syllogism: major term, minor, term, and middle term. These terms correspond to the position and/or role terms play as subjects and predicates. The predicate term of the conclusion is the major term of the syllogism. The subject term of the conclusion is the minor term. The third term of the syllogism, which does not appear in the conclusion, is called the middle term.

Categorical syllogisms are classified according to "figure" and "mood." Figure refers to the positions taken by the various terms (major, minor, and middle). Four different figures correspond to the four possible arrangements of the terms. These are:

| First Figure | Second Figure | Third Figure | Fourth Figure |
|---|---|---|---|
| M–P | P–M | M–P | P–M |
| S–M | S–M | M–S | M–S |
| ∴ S–P | ∴ S–P | ∴ S–P | ∴ S–P |

Mood refers to the arrangement of each of the propositions according to the quantity and quality of each proposition. A syllogism might consist of the first premise as a universal affirmative proposition, the second premise as a universal affirmative proposition, and the conclusion as a universal affirmative proposition. These three propositions, in turn, might appear in the first figure. Combining all possible moods and figures, there are 256 possible varieties of categorical syllogisms.

# 13

# Structuralism, Deconstruction, Reconstruction: The Limits of Reasoning

Daniel P. Keating
*Ontario Institute for Studies in Education*

In the more than a quarter-century that has elapsed since the appearance of Inhelder and Piaget's (1958) seminal work on *The Growth of Logical Thinking from Childhood to Adolescence*, there has been a striking resurgence of interest in the nature of logical thinking, especially its development. Elsewhere (Keating, 1984; Keating & MacLean, 1987), I have characterized several phases of the reaction of North American scientists to that line of research, which is by now quite large.

We might call the first phase "liberation" of scientifically guided "thinking about thinking." The appearance of the Genevan work on "mature" logic coincided with the resurgence of interest, within American experimental psychology, in "mental" explanations of performance on a range of experimental tasks. This cognitive psychology "revolution," as Gardner (1985) has recently termed it, freed our thinking from the constraints of SR and verbal learning models. Within the Piaget-inspired wing of that revolution, the second phase is perhaps best termed "replication research." During this period, many researchers explored the characteristics of performance on the tasks introduced by Inhelder & Piaget (1958). At this time, there was less interest in expanding the theoretical formulations, and more in discovering the properties of the formal operations tasks.

The third phase, which I have termed "revisionist," collected together in a systematic way many of the emerging empirical difficulties with both concrete and formal operations performance theories, and often viewed these as revealing fundamental flaws with these theories—at least as theories of cognitive performance. For example, in an earlier review of the formal operations literature (Keating, 1980), I sought to systematize the core performance theory, as it had been used in empirical research, and in so doing identified a number of serious validity concerns that had not been successfully addressed. These and other similar critiques (e.g., Brainerd, 1978; Feldman, 1980; Gelman, 1978) have served to focus attention on mechanisms that might underlie stage-like shifts. The attempt to explain cognitive performance and its development in terms of elemental mechanisms has clearly gained influence, even when the target of explanation is performance on Piagetian tasks.

The tenor of this current phase, which could be termed "dissolution," is reflected in the variety of diverse, and sometimes incompatible, models that allude to Piaget's work as their inspiration: postformal operations, or fifth-stage models, which run the gamut from highly mechanistic (Commons, Richards, and Armon, 1984) to explicitly dialectical (e.g., Riegel, 1973); essentially associationist models (e.g., Siegler, 1985); stage models that are explicitly *not* general, but rather are domain-specific (e.g., Feldman, 1980; Fischer, 1980; Fisher, Hand, & Russell, 1984); and revisions of stage models that introduce a separate processing account (e.g., "utilization," Overton, 1985) to explain undesirable performance variability on theoretically key tasks. These only sample the available options on the table at the moment—I mean no offense to any favorites that were omitted—in order to give a flavor of the diversity that one might seek to reintegrate, if a unified and coherent theory is a goal. Indeed, in the current state of affairs, Piaget-inspired research seems to have no more theoretical coherence, at least on this side of the Atlantic, than the overtly eclectic "information-processing" theory.

The purpose of this brief, and undoubtedly simplistic, historical review is to provide some perspective. It is helpful to indicate at the beginning where this argument leads. I contend that the structuralist approach to logic, as advanced by Inhelder & Piaget (1958), and as incorporated into empirical research on logical performance, "deconstructs" itself both empirically and theoretically. Later, I describe what this means in a practical fashion: For the moment, let me specify what I do *not* mean. I do not mean "destruction" of Piagetian or other structuralist approaches to understanding logical thinking. Instead, I argue that there are fundamental limitations to the Piagetian—or to any structuralist—theory of mature logical thought. Further, I argue that these limitations, although often commented on individually, have not been recognized neither as a unified set, nor as *fundamental* limitations. Finally, I argue that is precisely the recognition of these limitations that permit us to "reconstruct" some of the key insights in the Piagetian approach by incorporating them into a more general approach (Keating & MacLean, 1988).

In order to make this somewhat abstruse argument as clear as possible, it is useful for me to make a distinction in Piagetian theory between a core performance theory of the development of logico-mathematical thinking versus an epistemological metatheory. The former—the performance theory—has dominated the American research agenda; the metatheoretical language that surrounds the core theory has been of only passing interest, at least if one judges by the relative quantities of research within each. Very few—including Piaget—have studied in any detailed way the actual "constructions" of a concrete or formal operations system, with the same intensity as Piaget (1954) described the emergence of symbolic thinking during the sensorimotor period of infancy. In contrast, there is a vast literature on children's and adults' performance on nominally concrete or formal operational *tasks*.

This distinction is useful in two ways for my argument. First, I review briefly these literatures separately, as much as is feasible. The literature on the success of the core performance theory is principally the empirical research; within that, I focus on the theory of formal operations. On the other hand, the relevant critiques of the metatheory are principally epistemological. In addition, the elements that I hope to save for a future reconstruction of cognitive development are somewhat different in each case. Following each review, I briefly specify what I see as the crucial elements for reconstruction and offer a bare outline of that reconstructive perspective (cf. Keating & MacLean, 1988, for a more complete description).

## FORMAL OPERATIONS:
## THE PERFORMANCE THEORY

In this section of the chapter, I briefly review the major validity issues that are problematic for the core performance theory on the development of formal operational thinking. In an earlier review of this question (Keating, 1980), I examined many of the same issues, and, thus, I merely summarize and describe the nature of these key validity concerns.

Before turning to the review, it is helpful to clarify the nature of the claims a performance theory of formal operations does make. These claims can be rather straightforwardly summarized. First, it is argued that the logical operations that underlie thinking change, in a structurally coordinated fashion, from a logic of classes to propositional logic (that is, concrete to formal operations). Second, it is presumed that these changes in logic are generalized, both within and across individuals. The internal generalization is across domains of knowledge or thinking: The fundamental form of logic is what changes, and, thus, we should expect those logical shifts to be evident across different domains of content knowledge. The external generalizability is usually referred to as universality; that is, there is an assumption that the structure of these changes emerges from the individual's interaction with the world, and the notion of logical necessity requires that similar changes be observed across individuals and across cultures—although the developmental timing of these changes is of course unspecified in the theory. Fourth, these logical shifts are demonstrable in the context of performance on experimental tasks designed to tap formal operational thinking

(Inhelder & Piaget, 1958). It is assumed that task performance, again within limits and with appropriate clinical insight, can be used diagnostically to assess the status of the individual's logical structure. These four interrelated claims—structurally coordinated emergence, internal generalizability (that is, across-domain expression of the logical shifts), external generalizability (that is, universality of the logical shifts), and the use of task performance to infer logical structure status—strike me as the core of the performance theory of formal operations. Without doubt, they are the claims that have in fact been primarily investigated empirically (Keating, 1980). It is the validity of these claims that I briefly review in this section.

Before doing so, one other disclaimer should be noted. If one were to return to Inhelder and Piaget's (1958) seminal work, or to other subsequent sources (e.g., Piaget, 1972), one would *not* find this set of claims explicitly laid out. How, then, can I justify the summary? On two grounds. First, I would argue that literary criticism, or quasi-Biblical exegesis of the central texts, although interesting, is not the best way to proceed. In fact, in a modest attempt at such exegesis in the review I have cited (Keating, 1980), I was persuaded that Inhelder and Piaget (1958) did not specify how the theory's validity was to be tested. To be sure, there are any number of tasks described, and the performance of children and adolescents on these tasks, but it is not clear that task performance is to be used in any formal, theory-testing sense. Rather, they are portrayed as illustrations or demonstrations.

Second, whatever the *explicit* validity claims in Inhelder & Piaget (1958), the practical *interpretation* of the theory, at least the American interpretation as seen in the research that emerged from it, is largely as I have characterized it earlier. Thus, we can only criticize the validity of the performance theory as it has revealed itself in practice. If some *different* set of validity claims is to be advanced—and some of these are reviewed below—then the appropriate empirical tests of those claims require similar analytic attention (Keating, 1988). On the other hand, I would not attribute the centrality of this reading of the Genevan claims about formal operations *only* to an American reading (or misreading). In fact, I argue below that this core theory represents one polarity in a theoretical tension that exists throughout Piaget's writings. I believe this tension—between closed structures and open systems—is central not only to understanding Piaget's work historically, but also for the reconstructive project to which I've previously alluded (Keating & MacLean, 1988). Let us turn, then, to a brief overview of the empirical literature with regard to the core validity claims as outlined above.

## Competence versus Performance

The majority of the empirical effort in the study of formal operations has focused in one way or another on diagnosing the presence or absence of formal operational structures. In some cases, this has been a goal in itself, but more often it has been to relate it to some other variable. For example, formal operations task performance has been related to chronological age, in order to specify developmental patterns; to performance on other tasks such as academic aptitude or achievement in order to examine its relationship to more traditionally assessed psychometric ability (e.g., Keating, 1975; Keating & Schaefer, 1975); or on some occasions, merely to performance on other formal operations tasks in order to look for consistency of the underlying logical structures. From the rather extensive empirical literature, answers to each of these questions are robust and not surprising (Keating, 1980): Older children and adolescents do better than younger children; high ability individuals do better than lower ability individuals; and, within limits, there is reasonable reliability across formal operations tasks, especially if the assessment battery is restricted to the set of tasks described originally by Inhelder and Piaget (1958). None of these findings are contrary to the core performance theory, and for some time were regarded as reasonable confirmation of its general outlines.

A more disquieting perspective arises when we take one step further back in considering how well this evidence actually confirms the validity claims. In each case, the confirmatory nature of the evidence *presumes* that the formal operations tasks are rather pure measures of logical competence. That is, if it is the case that the performance variance on formal operations tasks is tapping differences between subjects that do *not* originate in logical structure differences, then the value of the observed performance patterns for validating the theory is compromised or lost. As but one example, we know from nearly a century of systematic research, older children are better than younger children on virtually any task that has a cognitive component. Thus, the fact that older children outperform younger children on formal operations tasks is hardly surprising—and can not very well be used to validate the developmental claims of the core performance theory.

Given this recognition, it was not long before researchers began to decompose the logic tasks, to present them in different ways or with different content, in order to see how the performance patterns were affected. A notable early example was the work of Trabasso (1975) and his colleagues on transitive inference in which they reported that a memory component accounted for a significant amount of the age-related variance on this task. They reported that if young children who did not make the appropriate inference were tested on recall of the premises, they could not do so accurately. It is reasonable to assume that, if young subject can not recall the premises of the syllogism, then their failure to make the correct inference can not unambiguously be attributed to their poor logic. Further, Trabasso (1975) reported that if young children reviewed the premises until they *could* recall them accurately, then their performance on the inference questions improved dramatically—from near zero performance to over 80% correct in several instances.

Following this work, there sprang up what I have elsewhere (Keating, 1984) described as a "cottage industry" of revisionist research. By altering the procedures, materials, or sequencing of many standard logical tasks, researchers were able to show that the apparent consistency of the empirical evidence was in fact quite patchy. Especially, younger children's performance on logical reasoning tasks from both the concrete and formal operational periods has been shown to be higher than expected when nonlogical components of the task (e.g., memory demands, attention, familiarity of content, and so on) are altered (Gelman, 1978; Siegler, 1976).

There is at least one obvious defense against the findings from this research. It is to argue that the alterations to the task that were thought *not* to lessen the logical demands *did* inadvertently do so. For example, one might argue that by arranging for the younger children to overlearn the premises of the transitive inference task, one has subtly altered the logical characteristics of the original version. Specifically, it might be argued that the overlearning of the premises allowed, or even compelled, the children to establish a spatial analog to the comparisons. At test, then, they did not have to actually infer anything: All they need do is read off from this analog.

The above is a short-lived defense. If the altered task is no longer valid as an indicator of underlying logic, because there is a short-cut to get around the logic, how can we be certain that adults did not spontaneously use the short-cut, thus, bypassing the logical requirements of the original, unaltered task? Indeed, in some research at about the same time as the transitive inference studies, we found suggestive evidence that a spatial analog strategy is used by many subjects on transitive inference tasks (Keating & Caramazza, 1975). The more general point is also clear: If one wishes to argue that some versions of tasks *are* validly diagnostic of formal operations reasoning but other versions are not, then it is necessary to specify precisely what differentiates them. These rules, of course, must be both unambiguous and nonarbitrary, as is the case for any validity claims (Keating & MacLean, 1987).

A second difficulty encountered in the application of the formal operations tasks has been the unexpectedly poor performance of late adolescents and adults, including college students (Keating, 1980; Martorano, 1977). Typically, only about half, give or take 10%, of the adult population is able to perform successfully on the Inhelder & Piaget (1958) tasks. For a development that is presumed to arise as a logical necessity from one's encounters with the world, this is disappointing.

It was disappointing enough for Piaget (1972) to have advanced the following explanations. First, one might suggest that the original formal operations tasks are not adequate to detect formal reasoning in everyone, because differential content familiarity might limit performance. That is, for adults who have little experience with physical, chemical, or mathematical content knowledge, the content of the standard formal operations tasks might be limiting. We might expect some adults to be able to reason more effectively with different content, such as that involving social or interpersonal relationships. Second, formal reasoning might be regarded as a potential for development, which may not always be expressed if the environmental pressure or opportunity is not adequate.

Although both of these arguments are quite plausible, they do little to support the competence features of the theory. If we argue that some adults do not perform well on these tasks due to the absence of relevant content knowledge, then it is not possible, on the basis of *identical* performance failures by children, to assert that the young subjects lack hypothesized logical structures. In any case, empirically it is not clear that older adolescents who do not perform well on the standard tasks do any better on tests of interpersonal reasoning.

In one study (Keating & Clark, 1980), we showed that the proportion of 17-year-olds classified as formal operational on the standard tasks was the typical 60% or so; including those individuals who scored formal operations on *either* the standard or a set of interpersonal tasks increased the proportion only slightly, to about 70%. Similarly, the argument for structures as potentials is hard to deal with empirically. How can we assess a potential? Although we might think initially of training studies—using as a criterion of potential, the more rapid improvement in performance by adults as compared to children, for example—these are likely to be of little help, unless we can specify that in training we are *not* simultaneously bringing to bear the generally greater content knowledge that we know adults possess.

### Generalizability

It seems clear from these arguments that performance on designated tasks of concrete or formal operations can not be used directly to diagnose the underlying logical structures. Even so, it might be possible to establish the validity of these structures by looking at *patterns* of performance across a range of plausible tasks. Specifically, two kinds of generalizability have been advanced: within-individuals across domains, and across individuals who differ culturally, historically, or otherwise.

The evidence on both counts is weak or inconclusive. Although there is reasonable intra-individual consistency on formal operations task performance, in the sense of test reliability (Keating, 1980), the basis of this consistency is not clear. The logical problem is that the consistency can be attributed to a wide range of subject factors, not just the status of their logico-mathematical structures. Factor analytic evidence that shows separation of logical structures versus general ability factors, which might be more convincing evidence, has often been based on erroneous assumptions—such as using age-partialled ability tests, but age-sensitive formal operations tasks (Keating, 1980). The resulting factor separation, which shows chrono-logical age loading heavily on the "Operational" (or Piagetian) factor, is al-most certainly artifactual. Lacking such clarifying evidence, the claim that the within-individual consistency of task performance supports the struc-tural interpretation is no more than the original claim that the formal oper-ations tasks are directly diagnostic—a claim that, as we have seen, can not be rigorously established.

In addition, there is accumulating evidence of less consistency within in-dividuals across domains when additional knowledge domains are investi-gated. Thus, task or domain specificity seems the more likely outcome as we expand our empirical investigation more widely (Feldman, 1980). This is not surprising, because exactly the same phenomenon is observed when we seek to generalize any of a number of hypothesized cognitive processes in the information-processing literature (Keating & MacLean, 1987).

Finally, the difficulties of cross-cultural generalization have been well documented (Cole & Means, 1981). The observation that successful per-formance on formal operations and other tests of logic varies across cul-tural and subcultural groups, and that the best-educated members of Western societies are the best performers on such tasks, should give us pause to reflect. One might argue that the mature, sophisticated logical structures are in fact universal, but that, for some reason, different cultural environ-ments fail to elicit them. In addition to the many opportunities for inferen-tial pitfalls in this argument (Cole & Means, 1981), it should be clear that the practical implications of such an argument for less powerful social groups are not entirely benign. It is a short jump from asserting difference to inferring deficit. The belief in deficiencies—whether cultural or innate—serves a powerful ideological role, and the use of observations about poorer logical performance to infer differential competence is in fact ideological, if we can not validate the task measures as pure indicators of logical structures.

## Coordinated Emergence

If the tasks that have been used diagnostically to detect the presence and ab-sence of certain logical structures are not in themselves capable of making these distinctions, then it is apparent that emergence of that performance within individuals at about the same time is not strong evidence for the un-derlying structures. Various confounding factors—other cognitive pro-cesses, effects of schooling, and so on—might as easily be responsible for these developments as the presumed shifts in underlying logical structures. One type of evidence that would be more persuasive is a highly regular, and robustly replicated, sequence of emergence of performance. That is, even if a single task or set of closely related tasks were not adequate to detect the underlying structure, it would be strong evidence for the performance theory if success on tasks tapping differing aspects of the structure always emerged in a particular order, that is, as a coordinated sequence.

Such arguments encounter two substantial, but not necessarily insurmountable, difficulties. First, the criteria for coordination needs to be both clear and plausible. Some such attempts in the past have somewhat subjectively counted "hits" and "misses" in the predicted patterns, sometimes ignoring measurement error in the former and relying heavily on it to explain away the latter (Keating, 1980). More rigorous approaches to this issue are methodologically possible, and replications of coordinated patterns of emergence would be critical to the theory. Second, it is advisable to have a range of converging measures to assess whether a particular logical concept has truly emerged. A student of mine and I (Keating & Crane, 1990) presented research that illustrates the difficulties in assessing conceptual understanding. We wished to investigate how broadly college students were able to extend a presumably well-entrenched concept. The domain we examined was proportionality, one of several formal operations subdomains (Inhelder & Piaget, 1958). We selected college students, of about average age (21 years), who possessed an understanding of mathematical proportion. All subjects were students in precalculus or calculus courses in college, for which they had been required to pass specific entrance criteria. Additionally, we gave each of them a written pretest of proportions, both as arithmetical problems and as word problems. Only subjects demonstrating mastery on this pretest of mathematical proportion were included. Following this, each subject was then given a series of comparisons on a quite simple test of real-world proportionality. We presented to them paris of wooden objects of varying shapes (circles and squares) and sizes (small and large), each of which had been cut into geometrically regular fractions (halves, thirds, sixths, or eighths). In each trial we posed a straightforward questions: After removing one or more of the fractional pieces from each object in the pair, we asked which object had lost more of its own total area. In the series of trials, we had embedded key trials, in which a simple visual comparison would likely be misleading, but in which the proportional reasoning was quite simple (one-third versus three-eighths, for example). Nearly half of this selected sample—45%—made two or more errors on these eight key "conflict" trials, whereas virtually no errors were made by any subject on the simple visual comparison trials. Thus, it would seem that, in addition to nongeneralizability of logic *across* domains of content knowledge, we may need to consider *within-domain* failures to generalize simple logical rules. For claims of coordinated emergence of logical performance, the implication is clear: Converging assesments of each predicted concept, rather than a single task, is necessary. With these two constraints—nonarbitrary criteria for how much coordination a particular empirical pattern reveals, and converging measures of each predicted subdomain—it might be possible to establish such claims. The limitations discussed in the earlier sections, however, might temper our expectations for discovering such sequences.

## FORMAL OPERATIONS: "NEW" PERFORMANCE THEORIES

Many of these empirical limitations of a performance-based model of logical competence have been argued previously, and attempts to bolster the competence model have been undertaken. Space considerations prohibit a comprehensive review of these efforts, but a brief overview of them is in order. I summarize these attempts, and related validity concerns, under three headings: attempts to rigorize, attempts to build domain-specific models, and attempts to separate competence more clearly from performance variables.

### Rigorizing

In response to the critique that the judgments of underlying logical competence based on performance on formal operations tasks is too global and/or subjective to be validly diagnostic, one avenue to pursue is to define more rigorous and objective methods of scoring performance on the tasks. The most prominent of such approaches is that described by Siegler (1976, 1981, 1986; Siegler & Richards, 1979). In this rule assessment approach, an individual's performance is characterized as following one of several logical rules, on the basis of the specific error patterns that emerge as she/he confronts the task. These rules are hierarchically organized to allow greater complexity to be taken into account.

Such an approach has a number of advantages, among them the ability to specify rather precisely the performance on particular problem types, for example, the unexpectedly poorer performance of transitional children compared to younger children on certain conflict problems on the balance beam task (Siegler, 1976): The younger children do not know enough to get confused, and by using a simple but erroneous rule are able to solve this particular problem type quite accurately. The transitional children know just enough to make errors—they know that both weight and distance from the fulcrum are important, but they do not yet know how to integrate this knowledge.

Elsewhere (Keating, 1984), I have described some of the difficulties such an approach must contend with. Basically, they are three:

1. Is there within-individual consistency of rule use across different, closely related tasks? If not, then the rule assessment process is perhaps more accurately viewed as a sensitive index of domain knowledge than as a

more objective index of underlying logical structure than global, clinical assessment. Existing evidence within Siegler's paradigm (e.g., Siegler, 1981) argues against such consistency, even on highly similar tasks.

2. Can a wide range of logical tasks be described using the rule-assessment approach? More specifically, does such assessment accurately describe the performance of individuals on a diversity of tasks? Here again, the evidence is mostly negative (Siegler & Richards, 1979). If tasks with less discrete, quantified variables (such as weight and distance) such as time are used, the proportion of individuals *not* classified as using specified logical rules increases substantially. If one moved to even more distant tasks, the likelihood is that this would emerge as an even more crucial problem.

3. Is the proposed logical analysis of the rules the only plausible one to account for the performance patterns? Wilkening and Anderson (1982) have proposed a different rule model for information integration on the balance beam task, and have argued that it accounts for the error patterns in Siegler's data as well as does Siegler's (1976) original model. If this is so, then the models are, therefore, ambiguous and not of immediate use for theoretical clarification. Additional research, sensitive to these concerns, would represent progress, but it is of course an empirical question whether these difficulties can be resolved.

Another approach is to attempt to specify underlying components of the logical performance and then to relate these components to each other in a variety of proposed mathematical models. Because the empirical evidence for these mathematical models of underlying mechanisms is in a rather primitive state (Keating, 1985), I reserve judgment on their ultimate utility. I do, however, suggest some reservations. There has been substantial interest among researchers studying psychometric intelligence in componential models for explaining cognitive ability variance (see reviews by Keating, 1984; Keating & MacLean, 1987). They have encountered substantial validity problems on their own, most particularly in relating measures of information processing nonarbitrarily to specific abilities, and in interpreting the measures of processing unambiguously. It is likely that componential models of logical structure will confront some of the same problems.

## Domain-Specific Models

Another approach to the difficulties that theories of logical structure have encountered is to accept provisionally the reality of domain specificity (e.g., Feldman, 1980; Fischer, 1980). In doing so, one of the most problematic claims of such performance theories is eliminated, the claim to universality or generalizability. Instead, what one seeks to describe is the development of the logical components of performance within specified domains of knowledge. This seems a more accessible goal. By contrasting the performance of experts and novices, by identifying the specific misunderstandings that novices are subject to, and by describing the transition from novice to expert (e.g., Chi, Glaser, & Rees, 1983), it is reasonable that the acquisition of both content knowledge and procedural knowledge (including logical operations) might be adequately accounted for.

If this were the final goal of such approaches, the validity claims are quite modest, and although likely to encounter difficulties, these difficulties are also more modest. The magnitude of the validity problems is likely to be correlated highly with the inclusiveness of the theory. Some may wish to view these domain-specific models as a back-door entrance to more universal theories at some later time. Such efforts are welcome, of course, but it is helpful to understand what problems are and are not solved by such an approach. As one specific example, it may not be possible to assume that models of "expertise" in one domain can be easily transferred to other domains. That is, components of expert performance may *not* be content-free (Keating, in press). Arguments by analogy in these cases do not suffice; some independent criteria of similarity need to be argued.

## Moderators of Competence

Yet another approach is to remain at the more unified theoretical level, but to try directly to partial out the variance in performance on key logical tasks into two components: The variance that indicates the differences in underlying logical competence and the variance that serves as "moderators" of that competence in actually doing the task (Overton, 1985). By systematically varying those aspects of the task that are putatively "non-logical" and observing the effects of this variation on a third variable, such as age, it might be possible to partial out the obtained performance data. Byrnes and Overton (1986) have reported one such empirical attempt, in which first, third, and fifth graders were presented with a series of logical tasks. Some of the tasks had concrete content and some did not; some children received "contramands"—designed to call their attention to the erroneous inferences—and some did not. On the basis of these children's performance, Byrnes and Overton (1986) argued for an interpretation that there are in fact multiple competencies—specifically, concrete and propositional reasoning—that emerge developmentally (or, at least, related to the age of the subject).

This is a reasonable approach, and it will be interesting to see where it leads. On the basis of the empirical data presented by Byrnes and Overton (1986), however, I harbor some nontrivial doubts that multiple competencies, rather than knowledge differences, have been demonstrated. On the modus tollens syllogisms, to which the correct propositional response is that the conclusion is wrong, older children increasingly say "Can't tell" (4% in first grade, 20% in third grade, and 39% in fifth grade—see Table 2 in Byrnes & Overton, 1986). This seems crucial, because it is a similar increase in the "Can't tell" response for Denied Antecedents and for Affirmed Consequents, when such a response is the *correct* one (averaging across these two, the "Can't tell" responses increase from 5%, to 22%, to 50%) that is taken as evidence for the emergence of a new competence in propositional reasoning. What is stikingly similar, to me, is the pattern for modus tollens and for these two types of syllogisms. Fifth graders, especially, seem to be wildly overgeneralizing the "Can't tell" response, which in modus tollens syllogisms is far from logical (in the propositional sense). I suspect that they have learned a general rule or convention: Do not trust the logic of content-empty syllogisms, and when you are not sure of the answer, it is ok to guess "Can't tell." It may prove difficult to obtain a clear separation, either conceptually or empirically, between the aspects of performance that indicate competence and those that indicate moderators of that competence. As I argue more directly below, it seems likely that knowledge differences are implicated in both sets of performance indicators.

It is worth noting, at this point, that the pursuit of this approach has led Byrnes (1988) to suggest a rather drastic revision of the formal operations construct. He proposes that some elements that have been regarded as crucial to the theory are in fact not essential, and that structural organization can be found, if we delete those nonessential features. One of the deletable features is the requirement for cross-domain generalizability. Byrnes (1988) argues that as long as the changes in structural organization occur with regularity *within* any domain, then the (revised) theory is supported. His critique raises two key concerns. First, the establishment of formal similarity across domains for the purposes of evaluating structural organization is formidable. The definition of "operations on operations," for example, in interpersonal reasoning is not easily determined (Keating & Clark, 1980). Notably, almost all the research reviewed by Byrnes (1988) concerns only the solution of problems with specifically logical content (e.g., syllogisms). Second, if levels of structural organization progress within domains of knowledge only insofar as content knowledge progresses, then the conflating of formal and content knowledge is completed. It seems possible that the deletion of nonessential aspects of the theory, once begun, will be difficult to contain.

## EPISTEMOLOGY AND DECONSTRUCTION

To this point, I have focused on what I have termed the core performance theory of formal operations, and of a logico-mathematical structuralism more generally. As some observers have pointed out (Byrnes, 1988; Keating, 1980), this perspective may represent, to some extent, a distortion of Piaget's initial agenda. While leaving that question for future intellectual historians—although I anticipate that such analyses will reveal that the heavy focus on the performance theory is not *entirely* a distortion of Piaget's work—it is clear that this aspect of the theory has some significant, or perhaps even fundamental, problems in validly establishing its key claims. If we concentrate briefly, however, on the epistemological claims of a structuralism addressed to logic, we encounter similar difficulties.

As is often the case with significant and prolific theorists, Piaget is difficult to critique fairly. The number of important issues he addressed, the breadth with which he treated them, the extensive development of the theory over time, and, for the English-language audience, the unavailability of some important work in translation: Each contribute to this difficulty. Critical work on Piaget's theory is destined for a long life, and, here, I present a sparse outline to address several key epistemological issues.

I argue that a productive reading of Piaget is to be found principally *not* in the performance accounts, as I have outlined above, but rather in the theoretical tensions that are inherent within Piaget's conscious attempts toward structuralism. This reading of Piaget aims to preserve the desirable features of open systems thinking, and to undermine the excessive and premature order advanced by the logico-mathematical structural model—particularly the order imposed by those aspects that are universalist and, in fact, *a priori*.

## Open Systems and Closed Structures

Let me draw this crucial distinction a bit more clearly. The late philosopher Michel Foucault described three major epistemological "moves" to try to establish a firmer grounding for our knowledge of the world (Dreyfus & Rabinow, 1982; Foucault, 1982). These epistemological moves were necessitated by the fact of the modern (that is, post-Kantian) recognition that the means by which we speak about truth in a philosophical sense are not validated by the language we use to describe these claims. Instead, the total confounding of that which represents (that is, thought and language) with that which is represented (that is, assertions about the nature of the world or humanity) undermines such truth claims. Dreyfus and Rabinow (1982) wrote: "Only when classical discourse no longer appears as a perfectible medium whose natural elements represent the natural elements in the world, only then does the representing relation itself become a problem (p. 27)." One solution is to ground the understanding of the world in the subjective qualities of the knower; a second is to give no special status to the knower, but to view the truth as discoverable in the objective world; and the third is to admit of no division between the subjective and objective, but to view them as immanently suited to each other—that is, our capacity to know and the structure of the objective reality are co-extant. The current versions of these three perspectives are, respectively: theories of the subject's organization of knowledge, or internal structuralisms, of which Piaget's is the most explicit (other examples are psychometric ability theories and information-processing models of cognitive activity); hermeneutic approaches, in which the "correct" reading of the actual forces in the objective world that determine knowledge are believed possible (as in many "Marxist" theories of consciousness, excluding, I think, Marx himself); and phenomenological approaches, which view the subjective knower and the objective reality as intimately attuned (e.g., Merleau-Ponty, 1962; or, more empirically, J. J. Gibson, 1979).

The endpoint of this long epistemological search for a firm basis for certain answers to the question, "How do we know that what we know is so?" is cogently summarized by Dreyfus and Rabinow (1982) using Foucault's work as a touchstone. It is that *none* of these approaches can yield positive, that is certain, "truth." The argument is too complex to review here; in essence, it is that each of these perspectives—the structure of the knower, the objective reality, and their inseparability—is prescientific assumption. Within their own set of assumptions, they are unassailable, but each is undermined by recognizing even the possible validity of either of the remaining two options. *This* epistemological dilemma, which we might usefully term postmodern, is one that will require different mindsets as well as different methods of investigation.

### Piaget's Genetic Epistemology

Returning from this brief but necessary epistemological excursion, we might well ask how this impinges on our understanding of structural models of deductive logic. Recall that one of Piaget's original goals (e.g., 1950) was precisely to replace these circular epistemological arguments with something more substantive, specifically a genetic (that is, developmental) epistemology. His metatheoretical assertions represent an openess to these interactive influences. Piaget (1968) characterized cognitive activity as constructivist, interactive, historically evolved and evolving, always tending toward the forging of a unified structure, and dialectical: "Structuralism has always been linked with a constructivism from which the epithet 'dialectical' can hardly be withheld." In practice, however, we encounter discrepant claims: the notion of logical necessity, the universality of logical structures, and the likely and hoped for neuronal basis of logical structures—the Bourbaki structures of the brain, as it were.

Different commentators have identified each of these clusters as the correct reading of Piaget. Sameroff (1983), for example, a strong open systems proponent, views Piaget as a shining example of an open systems model of cognitive development. Earlier, I characterized the performance theory as much more of a closed structure. Gruber and Vonèche (1977) contend that Piaget attempted to push a structuralist agenda as far as possible *against* a systems account. "It is fair to describe Piaget as a structuralist rather than a systems theorist (p. xxiii)."

Why such confusion? It is important to realize that the confusion is not mere misunderstanding. Instead, it reflects the essential tension at the heart and beginning of the structuralist project. On the one hand, there is the "open systems" beginning, in which arbitrary differences become significant by virtue of the network in which they participate. Saussure's (1974) distinctions between diacritical and synchronic functions of language are prototypical examples. Most structural models (Chomsky's grammars, Levi-Strauss's myths, Piaget's logical models) have tended, in practice, toward the capture of the meaning-giving networks, or the synchronies.

This tension is inherent in Piaget's work and has been a creative tension. The outcome of the tendency toward closure, however, is the establishment of a *particular* way of knowing the world—in this case, of propositional logic that is more compatible with idealist versions of logical positivism than with dialectical approaches—as possessing *general* validity. Below, I consider two specific problems that this engenders: a commitment to content-free logical necessity and the inappropriate extension of such logical models to other domains of human experience.

## Deconstruction

Before considering these specific examples, let me note the way in which I am employing the controversial method of deconstruction (Leitch, 1984; Norris, 1982, 1984). Deconstructive criticism advances the notion that all claims to truth sow their own self-critical seeds. Thus, a close literary reading of many philosophical texts reveals that it is precisely on the crucial points of the claims that key, and unfounded, assumptions are to be found. As both a formal epistemology and as an experimental epistemology, Piaget's work is subject to deconstruction in two ways: by following the history of the epistemological claims directly and by examining the empirical work that has been produced. Although not a thorough "deconstruction" of Piaget's epistemological claims, my analysis suggests that such a critique might be productive. As one example for the formal epistemology, a crucial but never-answered question concerns the ontological status of the logical structures—that is, are they in the mind of the performer or the eye of the beholder? If the former, then a fully closed structure is claimed. If the latter, then the structures are hermeneutic—that is, *my* interpretation of *your* thinking—and are not intended to be relevant to a performance account.

This tension between open systems and closed structures is as central to structuralism in general as it is generative within Piaget's work. Deconstructive criticism has concentrated on this tension to undermine the "closing" tendencies of a structuralist project. Norris (1982) wrote:

Structuralism lives on what (Derrida, 1978) calls "the difference between its promise and it practice." The practice has mostly given way to those enticing metaphors, derived from structural linguistics, which elevate "form" at the expense of "force," or structure to the detriment of what goes on *within* and *beyond* structure. The "promise" survives in that other, self-critical strain of structuralist thought which implicitly questions its own methodical grounding. There is always, according to Derrida (1978, p. 160), an "opening" which baffles and frustrates the structuralist project. "What I can never understand, in a structure, is that by means of which it is not closed." (p. 54)

## THE LIMITS OF REASONING

Which of these—"open" or "closed"—is the more accurate reading of Piaget? Neither—and both. A generative reading of Piaget must recognize the tensions between these polarities as the central and productive struggle within Piaget's work. A reconstruction of human development (Keating and MacLean, 1988) requires a conception of structure, but it can not make do with a closed structure. Such models always work to establish a privileged epistemology and, thus, to foreclose the criticism of alternative epistemologies—that is, different ways of viewing the world—by ruling them literally off limits or outside the structure.

The rejection of privileged epistemological standpoints is crucially important, but hard to say in words. Clearly, a socially necessary goal of human socialization is to create a deeply embedded epistemology about how the world works. That is, in order for any society to function, it seems necessary that it share a substantial common core of understanding. This is, of course, most clearly embedded in its language. Given the existence of this standard for looking at the world, speaking in another epistemology seems so unnatural as to be literal "non-sense." Uncomfortable though it may be, it is a "re-cognition" that is unavoidable because of the inherent instability of any privileged epistemological standpoint.

### Logical Necessity and Different Voices

To make the significance of these arguments more concrete, I briefly examine two related examples. One of the most cherished aspects of the Piagetian tradition is the confidence that we can examine the human condition scientifically. Piaget's subject—the structure of logic—plays a central role in this approach. Indeed, one of the many labels used to describe formal operational reasoning is scientific reasoning. The import of this belief system is that there *is* a scientific method, and the best description of that method is framed in terms of an internally consistent propositional logic.

Unfortunately, that comforting belief is not supported by historical investigation into either science or mathematics. Feyerabend (1975, 1978) has argued, with considerable acumen, that scientific understanding has historically advanced, when individuals have refused to be constrained by formal rules of method. This does not mean that method is unimportant, but rather that correct method is no guarantee of scientific success—and may be antithetical to scientific progress. Less iconoclastically, Kline's (1984) recent review of the history of mathematics makes the same point. There is no unified logic that underlies modern mathematics. In fact, as he points out, it is incorrect to speak of mathematics; there are, in fact, many mathematics, none of which is valid in any inherent sense. Thus, the eager search of Western culture for certainty—a content-free set of logical methods, which, when assiduously and carefully applied, could yield confident assertions about many aspects of reality—is a chimera. Not in epistemology, not in logic, not in mathematics, and not in science can such a solution be found. Thus, there is no basis on which we can argue for the "logical" necessity of any conclusion about the world.

Let me hasten to add that we are not totally bereft of meaning as a result of this recognition. Of course, we know, in every sense of the term, more about our world than the ancients or than our more immediate predecessors. But what has shaped that knowledge is not the identification of correct method or of logical necessity.

One can make a sound argument that the criterion is entirely practical (Feyerabend, 1975; Habermas, 1975; Kline, 1984; Keating & MacLean, 1988). We know the mathematics works, when the bridge stands instead of falling. We know the science is correct, when the plane flies instead of crashing. The criterion of truth is *practical success*, not correct method. Certainly it is the case that some methods have a better track record and should have pre-eminence on that basis. But it does not mean that the validity inheres in the method or form of thinking.

This takes on central importance in the critique of social or interpersonal reasoning. Jürgen Habermas (1971, 1975) has made an important distinction between two types of practical success. The first involves those examples just described; the physical world can be controlled and exploited, and we have developed rather sophisticated methods to aid in that kind of understanding.

But what is the equivalent criterion for the human sciences? There is no direct analog to the self-evident criterion of success in controlling the physical world. Each such question in the human sciences has a criterion defined not in self-evident physical terms, but rather a criterion arrived at by a process of social consensus about what success means—that is, what we desire or value. Is a particular child-rearing practice or educational innovation successful or not? Such questions can not be answered without reference to a hidden question: What constitutes success in this instance? We may, for example, easily chart the decrease in classroom disruptions as a result of behavior modification applications. Is that, then, successful? Is that, in fact, a desired outcome? To answer that, we need to know more: Desired by whom? What other effects do the practices have? Are those effects desired? Again, by whom?

Given this distinction, the risk is that we will ignore it and assume that the kind of logic that has worked for success in controlling the physical world will work equally well in the human sciences. This seems not only a risk but a present reality (Gilligan, 1982). I have argued elsewhere (Keating, 1978; Keating & Clark, 1980) that the models we have used of social intelligence and of interpersonal reasoning are inappropriate, because they fail to take into account the differences between these two kinds of reasoning. In doing so, the different voices of which Gilligan (1982), Chodorow (1978), Hartsock (1984) and others have written are unheard or viewed as illegitimate. When we fail to recognize the limits of reasoning, we open ourselves to the unthoughtful and possibly dangerous application of the only methods we *do* know, whether they lead to outcomes we desire or to something else.

## Reconstruction

A major goal of the reconstructive project that has been outlined elsewhere (Keating & MacLean, 1988) is precisely to open up the field for alternative models of thinking and acting. Specifically, the integration of hermeneutic—or social critical—methodologies with structural or schema accounts, is a goal. As well, the recognition that our phylogenetic histories have equipped us with some important phenomenological priors, such as perception of objects and motion, is central to understanding the common core of experience that we all share. Interpretations of the world are constructed, but some aspects of reality are directly perceived (Gibson, 1979).

A reconstruction of human development will need to take each of these perspectives into account. In doing so, the intellectual debt to Piaget is enormous. The value of his perspective is, I think, yet to be entirely realized. And paradoxically, the means to realize its value is to first understand fully its limitations.

## REFERENCES

Brainerd, C. J. (1978). *Piaget's theory of intelligence*. Englewood Cliffs, NJ: Prentice-Hall.

Byrnes, J. P. (1988). Formal operations: A systematic reformulation. *Developmental Review, 8*, 1–22.

Byrnes, J. P., & Overton, W. F. (1986). Reasoning about certainty and uncertainty in concrete, causal and propositional contexts. *Developmental Psychology, 22*, 793–799.

Chi, M. T. H., Glaser, R., & Rees, E. (1982). Expertise in problem solving. In R. J. Sternberg (Ed.), *Advances in the psychology of human intelligence*, (Vol. 1, pp. 7–75). Hillsdale, NJ: Lawrence Erlbaum Associates.

Chodorow, N. (1978). *The reproduction of mothering*. Berkeley, CA: University of California Press.

Cole, M., & Means, B. (1981). *Comparative studies of how people think*. Cambridge, MA: Harvard University Press.

Commons, M., Richards, F. A., & Armon, C. (Eds.). (1984). *Beyond formal operations: Late adolescent and adult cognitive development*. New York: Praeger.

Derrida, J. (1978). *Writing and difference*. (Alan Bass, Trans.). London: Routledge & Kegan Paul.

Dreyfus, H. L., & Rabinow, P. (1982). *Michel Foucault: Beyond structuralism and hermeneutics*. Chicago: University of Chicago Press.

Feldman, D. (1980). *Beyond universals in cognitive development*. Norwood, NJ: Ablex.

Feyerabend, P. (1975). *Against method*. London: NLB.

Feyerabend, P. (1978). *Science in a free society*. London: NLB.

Fischer, K. W. (1980). A theory of cognitive development: The control and construction of hierarchies of skills. *Psychological Review, 87*, 477–531.

Fischer, K. W., Hand, H. H., & Russell, S. (1984). The development of abstractions to adolescence and adulthood. In Commons, M., Richards, F. A., & Armon, D. (Eds.), *Beyond formal operations: Late adolescent and adult cognitive development* (pp. 43–73). New York: Praeger.

Foucault, M. (1982). Afterword: The subject and power. In H. L. Dreyfus & P. Rabinow (Eds.), *Michel Foucault: Beyond Structuralism and hermenentics*. Chicago: University of Chicago Press.

Gardner, H. (1985). *The mind's new science*. New York: Basic.

Gelman, R. (1978). Cognitive development. *Annual Review of Psychology, 29*, 297–332.

Gibson, J. J. (1966). *The senses considered as perceptual systems*. Boston: Houghton-Mifflin.

Gibson, J. J. (1979). *The perception of the visual world*. Boston: Houghton-Mifflin.

Gilligan, C. (1982). *In a different voice*. Cambridge, MA: Harvard University Press.

Gruber, H. E., & Voneche, J. J. (1977). *The essential Piaget*. New York: Basic Books.

Haberman, J. (1971). *Communication and the evolution of society*. (T. McCarthy, Trans.). Boston: Beacon Press.

Habermas, J. (1975). *Legitimation crisis*. (T. McCarthy, Trans.). Boston: Beacon Press.

Hartsock, N. (1983). *Money, sex and power*. New York: Longman.

Inhelder, B., & Piaget, J. (1958). *The growth of logical thinking from childhood to adolescence*. New York: Basic Books.

Keating, D. P. (1975). Precocious cognitive development at the level of formal operations. *Child Development, 46*, 476–480.

Keating, D. P. (1978). A search for social intelligence. *Journal of Educational Psychology, 70*, 218–223.

Keating, D. P. (1980). Thinking processes in adolescence. In J. Adelson (Ed.), *Handbook of adolescent psychology* (pp. 211–246). New York: Wiley.

Keating, D. P. (1984). The emperor's new clothes: The "new look" in intelligence research. In R. J. Sternberg (Ed.), *Advances in the psychology of human intelligence* (Vol. 2, pp. 1–43). Hillsdale, NJ: Lawrence Erlbaum Associates.

Keating, D. P. (1985). Beyond Piaget: The evolving debate [Review of *Beyond formal operations*, edited by M. Commons, F. Richards, & C. Armon]. *Contemporary Psychology, 30*, 449–450.

Keating, D. P. (1988). Byrnes' reformulation of Piaget's formal operations: Is what's left what's right? *Developmental Review, 8*, 376–384.

Keating, D. P. (in press). Adolescent thinking. In S. Feldman & G. Elliott (Eds.), *At the threshold: The developing adolescent*. Cambridge, MA: Harvard University Press.

Keating, D. P., & Caramazza, A. (1975). Effect of age and ability on syllogistic reasoning in early adolescence. *Developmental Psychology, 11*, 837–842.

Keating, D. P., & Clark. L. V. (1980). Development of physical and social reasoning in adolescence. *Developmental Psychology, 16*, 23–30.

Keating, D. P., & Crane, L. L. (1990). Domain general and domain specific processes in proportional reasonging. *Merrill-Palmer Quarterly, 36*(3).

Keating, D. P., & MacLean, D. J. (1987). Cognitive processing, cognitive ability, and development: A reconsideration. In P. A. Vernon (Ed.), *Speed of information-processing and intelligence* (pp. 239–270). Norwood, NJ: Ablex.

Keating, D. P., & MacLean, D. J. (1988). Reconstruction in cognitive development: A poststructuralist agenda. In P. B. Baltes, D. L. Featherman, & R. M. Lerner (Eds.), *Life-span development and behavior* (Vol. 8, pp. 283–317). Hillsdale, NJ: Lawrence Erlbaum Associates.

Keating, D. P., & Schaefer, R. A. (1975). Ability and sex differences in the acquisition of formal operations. *Developmental Psychology, 11*, 531–532.

Kline, M. (1984). *Mathematics: The loss of certainty*. New York: Oxford University Press.

Leitch, V. B. (1984). *Deconstructive criticism*. New York: Columbia University Press.

Martorano, S. C. (1977). A developmental analysis of performance on Piaget's formal operations tasks. *Developmental Psychology, 13*, 666–672.

Merleau-Ponty, M. (1962). *The phenomenology of perception*. London: Routledge & Kegan Paul.

Norris, C. (1982). *Deconstruction: Theory and practice*. London: Methuen.

Norris, C. (1984). *The deconstructive turn*. London: Methuen.

Overton, W. F. (1985). Scientific methodologies and the competence–moderator performance issue. In E. Neimark, R. DeLisi, & J. Newman (Eds.), *Moderators of competence* (pp. 15–41). Hillsdale, NJ: Lawrence Erlbaum Associates.

Piaget, J. (1950). *The psychology of intelligence*. London: Routledge & Kegan Paul.

Piaget, J. (1972). Intellectual evolution from adolescence to adulthood. *Human Development, 15*, 1–12.

Riegel, K. (1973). Dialectic operations: The final period of cognitive development. *Human Development, 16*, 346–370.

Sameroff, A. (1983). Developmental systems: Contexts and evolution. In P. Mussen (Ed.), *Handbook of child psychology* (Vol. 1, pp. 237–294). New York: Wiley.

Saussure, F. (1974). *Course in general linguistics*. (Wade Baskin, Trans.). London: Fontana.

Siegler, R. S. (1976). Three aspects of cognitive development. *Cognitive Psychology, 8*, 481–520.

Siegler, R. S. (1981). Developmental sequences within and between concepts. *Monographs of the Society for Research in Child Development. 46*, Serial No. 189.

Siegler, R. S., & Richards, D. (1979). Development of time, speed, and distance concepts. *Developmental Psychology, 15*, 288–298.

Trabasso, T. (1975). Representation, memory, and reasoning: How do we make transitive inferences? In A. Pick (Ed.), *Minnesota Symposium on Child Psychology* (Vol. 9, pp. 135–172). Minneapolis, MN: University of Minnesota Press.

Wilkening, F., & Anderson, N. H. (1982). Comparison of two rule-assessment methodologies for studying cognitive development and knowledge structure. *Psychological Bulletin, 92*, 215–237.

# Author Index

# Subject Index